ALSO EDITED BY
ARNOLD KRUPAT AND BRIAN SWANN

*I Tell You Now: Autobiographical Essays
by Native American Writers*

HERE FIRST

HERE FIRST

Autobiographical Essays by

Native American Writers

EDITED BY

ARNOLD KRUPAT AND

BRIAN SWANN

THE MODERN LIBRARY

NEW YORK

MODERN LIBRARY and colophon are registered trademarks of
Random House, Inc.

"Rituals—Yours and Mine" by Kimberly Blaeser was originally published in
Trailing You, published by Greenfield Review Press.
"The Road to Chitina" by John E. Smelcer was originally published in *The Kenyon
Review—New Series,* winter 1996, vol. XVIII, no. 1.
"Hahshi mi Mail" by LeAnne Howe was originally published in *Gatherings: The
En'owkin Journal of First North American Peoples,* vol. IV, 1993.

Owing to limitations of space, permission acknowledgments
can be found on page 421.

LIBRARY OF CONGRESS CATALOGING-IN-PUBLICATION DATA

Here first: autobiographical essays by Native American writers/edited by
Arnold Krupat and Brian Swann.
p.   cm.
ISBN 0-375-75138-6
1. Indians of North America—Biography.   2. Autobiography—Indian authors.
3.   American literature—Indian authors. I. Krupat, Arnold. II. Swann, Brian.
E89.5.E84   2000   810.9'897—dc21   98-9843
[B]

Modern Library website address: www.modernlibrary.com

2 4 6 8 9 7 5 3

First Edition

THIS BOOK IS DEDICATED TO
THE MEMORY OF
CARROLL ARNETT (GOGISGI)
(1927–1997)

AND

VICKIE SEARS
(1941–1999)

INTRODUCTION

This book is a follow-up volume to *I Tell You Now: Autobiographical Essays by Native American Writers*, published by the University of Nebraska Press in 1987. We began putting the collection together more than ten years ago, in 1985, BCQ—Before the Columbian Quincentennial—and also, therefore, before *Dances With Wolves*, *Blackrobe*, various "Geronimos," and the Tony Hillerman explosion. The appetite of the American public for things Indian has expanded, as happens from time to time. This has resulted, on the one hand, in an increase in the production of what might be called "cultural fast food" (and New Age "plastic shamanism"—for example, the egregious decision by Marvel Comics to publish an issue involving Hopi kachinas)—but also, on the other, has opened a very real, if still small, space for Native American writers, painters, and scholars to present some spiritually and intellectually nourishing fare.

Our concern in *Here First*, as it was in the earlier volume, is with Native American writers and with aspects of autobiography.[1] For a brief history of Native American autobiography, the reader might wish to turn to the Introduction to *I Tell You Now*, and there are also a number of fine studies of the genre currently available.[2] In the preparation of this volume we set out in much the same way we did then: we attempted to contact as many contemporary Native American writers as we knew of for contributions, and we asked them to speak of their lives and their relation to their art. Inevitably, there are some people we missed, and we can only apologize for that; any Native writer who is *not* represented in this volume was in no way intentionally excluded. Some who do not appear told us they were simply too busy to produce essays in time for our deadline; others felt that they had spoken about themselves sufficiently—in essays, interviews, and, indeed, earlier autobiographical texts—not to wish to undertake the task again. In one instance, however, a Native writer chose to exclude himself because many of the Native writers we had published in *I Tell You Now* were unenrolled, or, as he wrote, "self-nominated Indians," and he did not wish to appear in any follow-up volume that might include other, to him, at least, questionable Natives.

This matter of identity—Who is an Indian?—has become a very hotly debated issue of late, and it would be irresponsible of us not to say just a brief word about it. There are, to speak broadly, three positions on this matter; they can be designated the nationalist, the indigenist, and the cosmopolitan positions. Nationalists *generally* define Indian identity as a matter of tribal enrollment regardless of what a particular tribal nation's criteria for enrollment may be—and "among federally recognized tribes in the United States, blood quantum . . . is the most common criterion of membership." (Strong and Van Winkle, 555)[3] Indigenists find this position unacceptably "Eurocentric," and, instead, look to an ecologically based philosophy or system of indigenous *values* that define a global "Fourth World." In the United States, adherence to these values should be constitutive of an indigenous identity regardless of "blood," although indigenists seem somewhat ambivalent about whether just anyone can be Indian.[4] The cosmopolitan position, represented foremost by the Chippewa (Anishinaabe) writer Gerald Vizenor, seems fairly clear on this matter, however. In several of the essays in his *Manifest Manners: Postindian Warriors of Survivance* (1994), and in his novel, *The Heirs of Columbus* (1992), Vizenor is critical (as are the indigenists) of "the racist arithmetic measures of tribal blood," and he has Stone Columbus, one of the "heirs" of Columbus, affirm that he would accept as "tribal" anyone committed to the values of healing rather than stealing tribal cultures, "no blood attached or scratched." (*Heirs*, 162)

For all of this, as non-Native scholars, we find the position articulated by Brian Swann some years back in his Introduction to Duane Niatum's *Harper's Anthology of 20th Century Native American Poetry* the most useful to adopt in practice: "Native Americans are Native Americans if they say they are, if other Native Americans say they are and accept them, and (possibly) if the values that are held close and acted upon are values upheld by the various native peoples who live in the Americas." (Niatum, xx). So far as we know, all those represented in this book have legitimate, if on occasion complex claims to Native American identity.

Native American writers, as we knew from our experience editing *I Tell You Now*—in this they are rather different from most Euro-American writers—are sometimes reluctant to talk about themselves, to dwell on "merely personal" matters. Although all of those who appear here have, in the end, committed themselves to writing autobiographically, a substantial number of them told us, often more than once, how very difficult they found the process. Indeed, one poet who had been unwilling to contribute to *I Tell You Now*, with the passage of time, decided she might, now, offer an essay; as formerly to do so seemed inappropriate, presently she felt it would be a *good* thing to try.

The regret we feel about those who are not represented in this volume should not obscure our great satisfaction at how many fine writers are represented, twenty-six in all. The reader will decide, of course, what to make of this volume as a whole, but we want to offer here some observations of our own. Structurally, as will be immediately apparent, we have chosen to present the authors in alphabetical order. The arrangement of *I Tell You Now* was chronological, the elder contributors appearing first, so that anyone reading the volume from beginning to end would begin with Mary Tallmountain, born in 1918, going on then to Ralph Salisbury and Maurice Kenny, born in the twenties, to Elizabeth Cook-Lynn, born 1930, and concluding with our youngest essayist, Joy Harjo, born 1951. This arrangement, we thought, would enable the reader to have a sense of continuity and change in the life experience of Native writers. Although the present volume is pleased to include some older Native American writers, the bulk of what appears is from writers born in the forties and after, a fact that seemed to dilute the potential usefulness of a chronological presentation: thus the decision to organize the book alphabetically.

Reading and rereading these essays, what has emerged for us most powerfully is, on the one hand, how many different ways there are today to be Indian, and, on the other—no surprise, given that our contributors are creative writers—how many different ways there are to *write about* being Indian. Thus there are Native writers whose first language was not English and whose first memories are of kin and clan relations of a quite traditional sort. Others are urban or rural mixed-bloods whose relation to their Native heritage was sometimes belated, often hard-won, occasionally conflicted. While no one of our writers comes from what is in Western terms an affluent background, any material poverty he or she may have experienced is not easily reduced to sociological cliché. To be sure, some are conscious of being poor but loved, and some are conscious of having been poor and abused; but others, the traditionally raised people most of all, had no notion whatever that they might be considered "poor" until their encounter with the dominant culture so classified them. Educational experiences also differ: no single generalization about Indians in American schools will suffice to explain what our contributors gained or lost there—except perhaps that all were moved by some of the European and American writers they discovered so as eventually to feel their own way to authorship. In much the same way, these essays warn us against generalizing about contemporary Native Americans and religious experience: all of the writers represented have a strong feeling for the spiritual and sacred dimensions of their Native heritage. Yet Western religion, Catholicism in particular, has also played an important role in the formation of some. Meanwhile, as will be apparent, others mention religion little or not at all.

So far as these writers' approaches to their essays are concerned, it is once more variety rather than sameness or consistency that is to be noted. We have a self-interview (Geiogamah), an account of a Catholic education (Hill), a meditation on traditional prayerfulness (Jim), and many pieces focusing on the importance of language (Bell, Owens, Zepeda, et al.). Clifford Trafzer, professionally a historian, offers a quite *historical* account of his life; urban mixed-bloods like Hilden and Penn, along with Louis Owens, whose mixed-blood background was thoroughly rural, choose not to develop issues of particular tribal affiliation, while Tapahonso and Walters respectively (yet in quite different ways) focus on the specifics of being Navajo and Pawnee. The late Carroll Arnett (to whom, along with Vickie Sears, this volume is dedicated) learned from Ezra Pound, from the Marine Corps, and from a number of inspiring college teachers—yet it was in a dream that he got his name from his Cherokee grandmother.

The testimony of this book, as we see it, is to the extraordinary flowering of some wonderful writing by Native American people. We offer these autobiographical reflections most of all for their power as literature. We hope as well that for any who have already encountered these writers' work, these essays will add to the reader's comprehension. Finally, for those who do not as yet know these writers' work, we hope the essays presented here will whet their appetite for more.

In this regard, let us note that we have not attempted to provide a comprehensive listing of the small presses that have published some of our contributors' work as we did in *I Tell You Now*. The reader who has trouble finding some of our authors' work will do best to consult *The International Directory of Little Magazines and Small Presses,* published annually by Dustbooks, P.O. Box 100, Paradise, CA 95969.

It remains only for us to thank some of the people who have helped us in compiling this volume, in particular, Joseph Bruchac, Alfred Bush, Duane Champagne, and the late Michael Dorris.

NOTES

1. Recent collections of interviews with Native American writers include Joseph Bruchac's *Survival This Way: Interviews with Native American Poets* (University of Arizona Press, 1987) and Laura Coltelli's *Winged Words: American Indian Writers Speak* (University of Nebraska Press, 1990). Patricia Riley's *Growing Up Native American* (Morrow, 1993) is an uneven collection of autobiographical material about the childhoods of various Native people from Black Elk to Louise Erdrich. Volumes focusing on individual Native writers include Charles L. Woodard's *Ancestral Voice* (University of Nebraska Press, 1989), a collection of conversations with N. Scott Momaday, and Ron McFarland's *James Welch: Interviews and Essays on His Work* (Confluence Press, 1986). In addition to such fairly well-known autobiographical texts as Momaday's *The Way to Rainy Mountain* (Ballantine Books, 1973 [1969]) and *The Names* (Harper & Row, 1976), and Leslie Marmon Silko's *Storyteller* (Seaver Books, 1981), we

would also note Gerald Vizenor's *Interior Landscapes: Autobiographical Myths and Metaphors* (University of Minnesota Press, 1990), and Anna Lee Walters's *Talking Indian: Reflections on Survival and Writing* (Firebrand Books, 1992). Recently published in the Smithsonian Series of Studies in Native American Literatures is Patricia Penn Hilden's *When Nickels Were Indians* (Smithsonian Institution Press, 1995). Other accounts by Native people appear in W. S. Penn, ed., *As We Are Now: Mixblood Essays on Race and Identity* (University of Nebraska Press, 1998). For the autobiographical statements of Native American painters and visual artists, see Lawrence Abbott, ed., *I Stand in the Center of the Good* (University of Nebraska Press, 1994). For Native American autobiography in general, the indispensable sourcebook is H. David Brumble, Jr.'s *Annotated Bibliography of American Indian and Eskimo Autobiographies* (University of Nebraska Press, 1981) and its supplement, in Brumble's *American Indian Autobiography* (University of California Press, 1988). For a comprehensive anthology of Native American autobiographies, see Arnold Krupat's *Native American Autobiography: An Anthology* (University of Wisconsin Press, 1994).

2. See, for example, Gretchen M. Battaille and Kathleen Mullen Sands's *American Indian Women: Telling Their Lives* (University of Nebraska Press, 1984), Arnold Krupat's *For Those Who Come After: A Study of Native American Autobiography* (University of California Press, 1985), H. David Brumble, Jr.'s *American Indian Autobiography* (University of California Press, 1988), and Hertha Wong's *Sending My Heart Back Across the Years: Tradition and Innovation in Native American Autobiography* (Oxford University Press, 1992). A fine, brief overview of Native life history and autobiography exists in A. Lavonne Brown Ruoff's *American Indian Literatures: An Introduction, Bibliographic Review, and Selected Bibliography* (The Modern Language Association of America, 1990).

3. The foremost proponent of a nationalist position is the Lakota novelist, poet, and scholar Elizabeth Cook-Lynn. See her recent collection of essays (most of them formerly appearing in *The Wicazo Sa Review*, edited by Cook-Lynn), *Why I Can't Read Wallace Stegner* (University of Wisconsin Press, 1996).

4. Ward Churchill's "I am Indigenist: Notes on the Ideology of the Fourth World" (in Churchill, *Struggle for the Land: Indigenous Resistance to Genocide, Ecocide and Expropriation in Contemporary North America*, Common Courage Press, 1993) is probably the strongest statement of the indigenist position, along with M. Annette Jaimes's "Native American Identity and Survival: Indigenism and Environmental Ethics" (in Michael Green, ed., *Issues in Native American Identity*, Peter Lang, 1994). Arif Dirlik attempts to resolve the many confusions in both these writers' presentations in "The Past as Legacy and Project: Postcolonial Criticism in the Perspective of Indigenous Historicism" (*American Indian Culture and Research Journal* 20 (1996): 1–31). Pauline Turner Strong and Barrik Van Winkle's " 'Indian Blood': Reflections on the Reckoning and Refig-

uring of Native North American Identity" (*Cultural Anthropology* 1(1996): 547–576), although quite critical of Krupat's comments on the use of "blood" imagery in the work of N. Scott Momaday, is a fair and balanced presentation of a variety of positions. Krupat's *The Turn to the Native* (University of Nebraska Press, 1996) offers further commentary on issues of identity.

HERE FIRST

The Unauthorized
Autobiography of Me

SHERMAN ALEXIE

The Spokane/Coeur d'Alene writer Sherman Alexie was born in 1966 on the Spokane Indian Reservation in Wellpinit, Washington. He has published poetry and fiction in many journals, and his first book of poems, The Business of Fancy Dancing, *was published by Hanging Loose Press in 1992. He is the author of four other poetry collections (*I Would Steal Horses, *1992,* Old Shirts & New Skins, *1993,* First Indian on the Moon, *1993, and* The Summer of Black Widows, *1996). His first collection of stories,* The Lone Ranger and Tonto Fist Fight in Heaven, *was published by Atlantic Monthly Press in 1993, and received a citation for the 1994 PEN/Hemingway Award for Best Short Fiction. Atlantic Monthly Press published his first novel,* Reservation Blues, *in 1995, and published his second,* Indian Killer, *in 1997. He has won a NEA fellowship for poetry and a Lila Wallace/Reader's Digest Award. He wrote the screenplay for and coproduced* Smoke Signals, *a feature film that won the Audience Award and Filmmakers Trophy at the 1998 Sundance Film Festival.*

Late summer night on the Spokane Indian Reservation. Ten Indians are playing basketball on a court barely illuminated by the streetlight above them. They will play until the brown, leather ball is invisible in the dark. They will play until an errant pass jams a finger, knocks a pair of glasses off a face, smashes a nose and draws blood. They will play until the ball bounces off the court and disappears into the shadows.

Sometimes, I think this is all you need to know about Native American literature.

Thesis: I have never met a Native American. Thesis reiterated: I have met thousands of Indians.

PEN American panel in Manhattan, November 1994, on Indian Literature. N. Scott Momaday, James Welch, Gloria Miguel, Joy Harjo, and myself. Two or three hundred people in the audience. Mostly non-Indians; an Indian or three. Questions and answers.

"Why do you insist on calling yourselves Indian?" asked a white woman in a nice hat. "It's so demeaning."

"Listen," I said. "The word belongs to us now. We are Indians. That has nothing to do with Indians from India. We are not American Indians. We are Indians, pronounced In-din. It belongs to us. We own it and we're not going to give it back."

So much has been taken from us that we hold on to the smallest things with all the strength we have left.

Winter on the Spokane Indian Reservation, 1976. My two cousins, S and G, have enough money for gloves. They buy them at Irene's Grocery Store. Irene is a white woman who has lived on our reservation since the beginning of time. I have no money for gloves. My hands are bare.

We build snow fortresses on the football field. Since we are Indian boys playing, there must be a war. We stockpile snowballs. S and G build their fortress on the fifty-yard line. I build mine on the thirty-yard line. We begin our little war. My hands are bare.

My cousins are good warriors. They throw snowballs with precision. I am bombarded, under siege, defeated quickly. My cousins bury me in the snow. My grave is shallow. If my cousins knew how to dance, they might have danced on my grave. But they know how to laugh, so they laugh. They are my cousins, meaning we are related in the Indian way. My father drank beers with their father for most of two decades, and that is enough to make us relatives. Indians gather relatives like firewood, protection against the cold. I am buried in the snow, cold, without protection. My hands are bare.

After a short celebration, my cousins exhume me. I am too cold to fight. Shivering, I walk for home, anxious for warmth. I know my mother is home. She is probably sewing a quilt. She is always sewing quilts. If she sells a quilt, we have dinner. If she fails to sell a quilt, we go hungry. My mother has never failed to sell a quilt. But the threat of hunger is always there.

When I step into the house, my mother is sewing yet another quilt. She is singing a song under her breath. You might assume she is singing a highly traditional Spokane Indian song. She is singing Donna Fargo's "The Happiest Girl in the Whole USA." Improbably, this is a highly traditional Spokane Indian song. The living room is dark in the late afternoon. The house is cold. My mother is wearing her coat and shoes.

"Why don't you turn up the heat?" I ask my mother.

"No electricity," she says.

"Power went out?" I ask.

"Didn't pay the bill," she says.

I am colder. I inhale, exhale, my breath visible inside the house. I can hear a car sliding on the icy road outside. My mother is making a quilt. This quilt will pay for the electricity. Her fingers are stiff and painful from the cold. She is sewing as fast as she can.

On the jukebox in the bar: Hank Williams, Patsy Cline, Johnny Cash, Charlie Rich, Freddy Fender, Donna Fargo.

On the radio in the car: Creedence Clearwater Revival, Three Dog Night, Blood, Sweat and Tears, Janis Joplin, early Stones, earlier Beatles.

On the stereo in the house: Glen Campbell, Roy Orbison, Johnny Horton, Loretta Lynn, "The Ballad of the Green Beret."

The fourth-grade music teacher, Mr. Manley, set a row of musical instruments in front of us. From left to right, a flute, clarinet, French horn, trombone, trumpet, tuba, drum. We had our first chance to play that kind of music.

"Now," he explained, "I want all of you to line up behind the instrument you want to learn how to play."

Dawn, Loretta, and Karen lined up behind the flute. Melissa and Michelle behind the clarinet. Lori and Willette behind the French horn. All ten Indian boys lined up behind the drum.

My sister, Mary, was beautiful. She was fourteen years older than me. She wore short skirts and nylons because she was supposed to wear short skirts and nylons. It was expected. Her black hair combed long and straight. 1970. Often, she sat in her favorite chair, the fake leather lounger we rescued from the dump. Holding a hand mirror, she combed her hair, applied her makeup. Much lipstick and eyeshadow, no foundation. She was always leaving the house. I do not remember where she went. I do remember sitting at her feet, rubbing my cheek against her nyloned calf, while she waited for her ride.

She died in an early morning fire in Montana in 1981. At the time, I was sleeping at a friend's house in Washington. I was not dreaming of my sister.

"Sherman," asks the critic, "how does your work apply to the oral tradition?"

"Well," I say, as I hold my latest book close to me, "it doesn't apply at all because I type this. And I'm really, really quiet when I'm typing it."

Summer 1977. Steve and I want to attend the KISS concert in Spokane. KISS is very popular on my reservation. Gene Simmons, the bass player. Paul Stanley, lead singer and rhythm guitarist. Ace Frehley, lead guitar. Peter Criss, drummer. All four hide their faces behind elaborate makeup. Simmons the devil, Stanley the lover, Frehley the space man, Criss the cat.

The songs: "Do You Love Me," "Calling Dr. Love," "Love Gun," "Makin' Love," "C'mon and Love Me."

Steve and I are too young to go on our own. His uncle and aunt, born-again Christians, decide to chaperon us. Inside the Spokane Coliseum, the four of us find seats far from the stage and the enormous speakers. Uncle and Aunt wanted to avoid the bulk of the crowd, but have landed us in the unofficial pot smoking section. We are overwhelmed by the sweet smoke. Steve and I cover our mouths and noses with Styrofoam cups and try to breathe normally.

KISS opens their show with staged explosions, flashing red lights, a prolonged guitar solo by Frehley. Simmons spits fire. The crowd rushes the stage. All the pot smokers in our section hold lighters, tiny flames flickering, high above their heads. The songs are so familiar. We know all the words. The audience sings along.

The songs: "Let Me Go, Rock 'n Roll," "Detroit Rock City," "Rock and Roll All Nite."

The decibel level is tremendous. Steve and I can feel the sound waves crashing against the Styrofoam cups we hold over our faces. Aunt and Uncle are panicked, finally assured that the devil plays a mean guitar. This is too much for them. It is too much for Steve and me, but we pretend to be disappointed when Aunt and Uncle drag us out of the coliseum.

During the drive home, Aunt and Uncle play Christian music on the radio. Loudly and badly, they sing along. Steve and I are in the back of the Pacer, looking up through the strangely curved rear window. There is a meteor shower, the largest in a decade. Steve and I smell like pot smoke. We smile at this. Our ears ring. We make wishes on the shooting stars, though both of us know that a shooting star is not a star. It's just a sliver of stone.

I made a very conscious decision to marry an Indian woman, who made a very conscious decision to marry me.

Our hope: to give birth to and raise Indian children who love themselves. That is the most revolutionary act possible.

1982. I am the only Indian student at Reardan High, an all-white school in a small farm town just outside my reservation. I am in the pizza parlor, sharing a deluxe with my white friends. We are talking and laughing. A drunk Indian walks into the parlor. He staggers to the counter and orders a beer. The waiter ignores him. Our table is silent.

At our table, S is shaking her head. She leans toward the table as if to share a secret. We all lean toward her.

"Man," she says, "I hate Indians."

I am curious about the Indian writers who identify themselves as mixed-blood. It must be difficult for them, trying to decide into which container they should place their nouns and verbs. Yet, it must be good to be invisible, as a blond, Aryan-featured Jew might have known in Germany during World War II. Then again, I think of the horror stories that a pale Jew might tell about his life during the Holocaust.

An Incomplete List of People Whom I Wish Were Indian

1. Martin Luther King, Jr.
2. Robert Johnson
3. Meryl Streep
4. Helen Keller
5. Walt Whitman
6. Emily Dickinson
7. Superman
8. Adam
9. Eve
10. Muhammad Ali
11. Billie Jean King
12. John Lennon
13. Jimmy Carter
14. Rosa Parks
15. Shakespeare
16. John Steinbeck
17. Billy the Kid
18. Voltaire
19. Harriet Tubman
20. Flannery O'Connor
21. Pablo Neruda
22. Amelia Earhart
23. Sappho
24. Mary Magdalene

25. Robert DeNiro
26. Susan B. Anthony
27. Kareem Abdul-Jabbar
28. Wilma Rudolph
29. Isadora Duncan
30. Bruce Springsteen
31. Dian Fossey
32. Patsy Cline
33. Jesus Christ

Summer 1995. Seattle, Washington. I am idling at a red light when a car filled with white boys pulls up beside me. The white boy in the front passenger seat leans out his window.

"I hate you Indian motherfuckers," he screams.

I quietly wait for the green light.

1978. David, Randy, Steve, and I decide to form a reservation doo-wop group, like the Temptations. During recess, we practice behind the old tribal school. Steve, a falsetto, is the best singer. I am the worst singer, but have the deepest voice, and am therefore an asset.

"What songs do you want to sing?" asks David.

" 'Tracks of My Tears,' " says Steve, who always decides these kind of things.

We sing, desperately trying to remember the lyrics to that song. We try to remember other songs. We remember the chorus to most, the first verse of a few, and only one in its entirety. For some unknown reason, we all know the lyrics of "Monster Mash," a novelty hit from the fifties. However, I'm the only one who can manage to sing with the pseudo-Transylvanian accent that "Monster Mash" requires. This dubious skill makes me the lead singer, despite Steve's protests.

"We need a name for our group," says Randy.

"How about The Warriors?" I ask.

Everybody agrees. We watch westerns.

We sing "Monster Mash" over and over. We want to be famous. We want all the little Indian girls to shout our names. Finally, after days of practice, we are ready for our debut. Walking in a row like soldiers, the four of us parade around the playground. We sing "Monster Mash." I am in front, followed by Steve, David, then Randy, who is the shortest, but the toughest fighter our reservation has ever known. We sing. We are The Warriors. All the other Indian boys and girls line up behind us as we march. We are heroes. We are loved. I sing with everything I have inside of me: pain, happiness, anger, depression, heart, soul, small intestine. I sing and am rewarded with people who listen.

This is why I am a poet.

I remember watching Richard Nixon, during the whole Watergate affair, as he held a press conference and told the entire world that he was not a liar.

For the first time, I understood that storytellers could be bad people.

Poetry = Anger · Imagination

Every time I venture into the bookstore, I find another book about Indians. There are hundreds of books about Indians published every year, yet so few are written by Indians. I gather all the books written about Indians. I discover:

1. A book written by a person who identifies herself as mixed-blood will sell more copies than a book written by a person who identifies herself as strictly Indian.
2. A book written by a non-Indian will sell more copies than a book written by a mixed-blood or Indian writer.
3. A book about Indian life in the pre-twentieth century, whether written by a non-Indian, mixed-blood, or Indian, will sell more copies than a book about twentieth-century Indian life.
4. If you are a non-Indian writing about Indians, it is almost guaranteed that Tony Hillerman will write something positive about you.
5. Reservation Indian writers are rarely published in any form.
6. Every Indian woman writer will be compared with Louise Erdrich. Every Indian man writer will be compared with Michael Dorris.
7. A very small percentage of the readers of Indian literature have heard of Simon J. Ortiz. This is a crime.

8. Books about the Sioux sell more copies than all of the books written about other tribes combined.
9. Mixed-blood writers often write about any tribe that interests them, whether or not the writer is descended from that tribe.
10. Most of the writers who use obviously Indian names, such as Eagle Woman and Pretty Shield, are usually non-Indian.
11. Non-Indian writers usually say "Great Spirit," "Mother Earth," "Two-Legged, Four-Legged, and Winged." Mixed-blood writers usually say "Creator," "Mother Earth," "Two-Legged, Four-Legged, and Winged." Indian writers usually say "God," "Earth," "Human Being, Dog, and Bird."
12. If an Indian book contains no dogs, then the book is written by a non-Indian or mixed-blood writer.
13. If there are winged animals who aren't supposed to have wings on the cover of the book, then it is written by a non-Indian.
14. Successful non-Indian writers are thought to be learned experts on Indian life. Successful mixed-blood writers are thought to be wonderful translators of Indian life. Successful Indian writers are thought to be traditional storytellers of Indian life.
15. Very few Indian and mixed-blood writers speak their tribal languages. Even fewer non-Indian writers speak their tribal languages.
16. Mixed-bloods often write exclusively about Indians, even if they grew up in non-Indian communities.
17. Indians often write exclusively about reservation life, even if they never lived on a reservation.
18. Non-Indian writers always write about reservation life.
19. Nobody has written the great urban Indian novel yet.
20. Most non-Indians who write about Indians are fiction writers. They write fiction about Indians because it sells.

Have you stood in a crowded room where nobody looks like you? If you are white, have you stood in a room full of black people? Are you an Irish man who has strolled through the streets of Compton? If you are black, have you stood in a room full of white people? Are you an African man who has been playing the back nine at the local country club? If you are a woman, have you stood in a room full of men? Are you Sandra Day O'Connor or Ruth Ginsburg?

Since I left the reservation, almost every room I enter is filled with people who do not look like me. There are only two million Indians in this country. We could all fit into one medium-sized city. We should look into it.

Often, I am most alone in bookstores where I am reading from my work. I look up from the page at a sea of white faces. This is frightening.

There was an apple tree outside my grandmother's house on the reservation. The apples were green; my grandmother's house was green. This was the game. My siblings and I would try to sneak apples from the tree. Sometimes, our friends would join our raiding expeditions. My grandmother believed green apples were poison and was simply trying to protect us from sickness. There is nothing biblical about this story.

The game had rules. We always had to raid the tree during daylight. My grandmother had bad eyes and it would have been unfair to challenge her during the dark. We all had to approach the tree at the same time. Arnold, my older brother. Kim and Arlene, my younger twin sisters. We had to climb the tree to steal apples, ignoring the fruit that hung low to the ground.

Arnold, of course, was the best apple thief on the reservation. He was chubby but quick. He was fearless in the tree, climbing to the top for the plumpest apples. He'd hang from a branch with one arm, reach for apples with the other, and fill his pockets with his booty. I loved him like crazy. My sisters were more conservative. They often grabbed one apple and ate it quickly while they sat on a sturdy branch. I always wanted the green apples that contained a hint of red. While we were busy raiding the tree, we'd also keep an eye on my grandmother's house. She was a big woman, nearly six feet tall. At the age of seventy, she could still outrun any ten-year-old.

Arnold, of course, was always the first kid out of the tree. He'd hang from a branch, drop to the ground, and scream loudly, announcing our presence to our grandmother. He'd run away, leaving my sisters and me stuck in the tree. We'd scramble to the ground and try to escape. If our grandmother said our name, we were automatically captured.

"Junior," she'd shout and I'd freeze. It was the rule. A dozen Indian kids were sometimes in that tree, scattering in random directions when our grandmother burst out of the house. If our grandmother remembered your name, you were a prisoner of war. And, believe me, no matter how many kids were running away, my grandmother always remembered my name.

"Junior," she'd shout and I would close my eyes in disgust. Captured again! I'd wait as she walked up to me. She'd hold out her hand and I'd give her any stolen apples. Then she'd smack me gently on the top of my head. I was free to run then, pretending she'd never caught me in the first place. I'd try to catch up with my siblings and friends. I would shout their names as I ran through the trees surrounding my grandmother's house.

My grandmother died when I was fourteen years old. I miss her. I miss everybody.

So many people claim to be Indian, speaking of an Indian grandmother, a warrior grandfather. Let's say the United States government announced that every Indian had to return to their reservation. How many people would shove their Indian ancestor back into the closet?

My mother still makes quilts. My wife and I sleep beneath one. My brother works for our tribal casino. One sister works for our bingo hall, while the other works in the tribal finance department. Our adopted little brother, James, who is actually our second cousin, is a freshman at Reardan High School. He can run the mile in five minutes.

My father used to leave us for weeks at a time to drink with his friends and cousins. I missed him so much I'd cry myself sick. Every time he left, I ended up in the emergency room. But I always got well and he always came back. He'd walk in the door without warning. We'd forgive him.

I could always tell when he was going to leave. He would be tense, quiet, unable to concentrate. He'd flip through magazines and television channels. He'd open the refrigerator door, study its contents, shut the door, and walk away. Five minutes later, he'd be back at the fridge, rearranging items on the shelves. I would follow him from place to place, trying to prevent his escape.

Once, he went into the bathroom, which had no windows, while I sat outside the only door and waited for him. I could not hear him inside. I knocked on the thin wood. I was five years old.

"Are you there?" I asked. "Are you still there?"

Years later, I am giving a reading at a bookstore in Spokane, Washington. There is a large crowd. I read a story about an Indian father who leaves his family for good. He moves to a city a thousand miles away. Then he dies. It is a sad story. When I finish, a woman in the front row breaks into tears.

"What's wrong?" I ask her.

"I'm so sorry about your father," she says.

"Thank you," I say. "But that's my father sitting right next to you."

Ayanvdadisdi: I Remember

CARROLL ARNETT (GOGISGI)

Born in Oklahoma City in 1927, Carroll Arnett (Gogisgi) was an enrolled member of the Overhill Band of the Cherokee Nation. Educated in the U.S. Marine Corps, the University of Oklahoma, Beloit College, and the University of Texas, Arnett has published twelve books of poems, the most recent of which are Night Perimeter: New and Selected Poems 1958–1990 *(1991) and* Spells *(1995). He has been widely anthologized, and his work has been translated into French, German, Dutch, Frisian, Macedonian, and Hungarian. Arnett was planning to retire from teaching at the time of his death in 1997.*

"But first let me tell you about my people."
—GOYATHLAY

Nearly everyone from Oklahoma and many others from all over the country have Cherokee grandmothers. Mine was not a princess and never had a stitch of buckskin clothing. Her name is recorded in the family Bible as Tennessee Ellen Belew, more often spelled Ballou. She was born in 1858 in the back of a wagon as her people emigrated from North Carolina to north-central Texas, where her father, Aaron, came to own and operate a dry goods store in the community of Pilot Point. When she was about nineteen, Tennie, as she was called, had the bad fortune to meet, presumably fall in love with, and marry a young saddle tramp named James Cavett Arnett. He called himself Jimmy Cavett and stressed the first syllable of his surname. A small man considerably less than six feet tall, he appears to have been more devoted to bourbon whiskey and stud poker than to my grandmother or to punching cattle. After a decade or so of driving Herefords all the way from north Texas through Indian Territory to the railhead at Abilene, Kansas, he decided he could make more money if he had his own spread closer to the markets at Kansas City and St. Louis. Reminded that his full-blood wife could claim headrights to tribal land in the Cherokee Strip, he decreed that they would establish that claim and move to begin ranching near Oologah in present-day Rogers County, Oklahoma. This was done apparently in the early to mid-1880s. I do not know of an exact record. My father (Tennie and Jimmy Cavett's eldest son, Herschel Warren, called Jack) often reminisced to me that the ranch lay "halfway between Chelsea and Adair, the nearest post office being Catalee."

(My father, incidentally, was very much like his father in that both men clearly felt that their lives never afforded them what they really deserved. Enough was never enough. Both went to their graves miserably unhappy, and I can feel only pity for them. Both were pseudo-aristocrats.)

Jimmy Cavett, notwithstanding what I've just said, seems to have made a success of the ranch near Oolagah and should have had every reason to feel personal satisfaction. Father and son again alike, both these men had a lifelong restlessness, a kind of nomadic itch that had to be scratched. Maybe this was their own, innermost manifest destiny. According to my father's repeated account, on January 1, 1900, Jimmy Cavett sold his herd of two thousand five- and six-year-old steers to Old Man Nottingham at $42 a head. From Bill Strange he bought three new wagons, three sets of harness, three teams of mules, and six cowhorses and started with family, two brothers-in-law, and $60,000 in cash for Hereford, Texas. I have never heard any explanation for this baffling move, nor why he was headed for the remote west Texas panhandle. I can only conjecture that he might have wanted to get away from his wife's people, the "goddamned Indins," whom he despised for their clannishness, and get back to God's Country, meaning Texas, where the Rangers had virtually exterminated identifiable tribal people forty years earlier.

The fourth night out, the Arnetts camped above a tent town that would soon become Luther, twenty-five miles northeast of present-day Oklahoma City. Jimmy Cavett ran into a cousin, Bud Cavett, the town's tent-saloonkeeper, who invited Jimmy to have a drink and sit in for a hand of poker, both of which lasted three days and three nights and cost Jimmy every cent of the $60,000. He survived the loss, finally owning a handsome two-story house, a livery stable, and two pecan groves there in Luther. He never said much, but shaving one morning he cut his throat very nearly from ear to ear and hadn't a word to say to anyone after that, not even good-bye. My most vivid memory of the old man, my grandpa who died when I was ten, is of his white-swathed throat, he sitting immobile in the cane-bottom rocker in the front room's musty gloom, glaring back at the nineteenth century. He had owned a .44-40 Winchester Model 1873, which he used to pop coyotes and prairie dogs when he rode herd. I was told when I was seven that the rifle would someday become mine. It didn't. A year or so before his death he lent it to someone who lent it to someone who lent it to someone else. Then it was gone.

Once or twice a month on Sundays during the thirties my mother drove our family out to Luther to visit Grandma and Grandpa. The 1929 Ford Model-A was registered in my dad's name though he never learned to drive; he couldn't be bothered. So it was up to Mother to chauffeur us anywhere we went. I don't remember other children in the vicinity of Grandma's house. My sister, Martha, and brother, Milton, were six and three years younger than I, and I certainly couldn't be pestered with such little kids. I therefore had no playmates in Luther and only one at home in Oklahoma City, where Dad worked as an accountant for various small businesses. The one playmate, Charlie Mehring, moved with his family to another neighborhood when I was about eight, so I was pretty much a loner for much of my childhood and invariably on Sundays in Luther. While Dad and Grandpa conversed in private about God knows what, Mother would clean house and cook. Grandma, now in her seventies and losing her eyesight, would try feebly to entertain us three kids. When she thought my father couldn't hear, she spoke Cherokee to me; if he caught her doing so, he scolded, saying, "Don't talk that Indin trash to that boy."

After Grandpa died in May 1938 Grandma came to live with us in Oklahoma City until her death in September of that year. Ocular cataracts were considered inoperable in the thirties; if you developed them, you simply went blind. By the time she moved in with us Grandma's eyesight was so weak that Mother had to remember to serve her food on a plain dinner plate to avoid the embarrassment of Grandma's scraping away at some other plate's decorative design. Like most poor people, she had been brought up to clean her plate at mealtime.

My favorite cousin was Boyd Norman, the younger son of Dad's sister Bernice (accent on the first syllable), who for many years was postmistress at Luther. Boyd was a happy-go-lucky clown, a leaven in an otherwise austere bunch of kinfolk. His wit and perpetual good nature always made me glad to see him. I suppose as a lark, he signed a six-year enlistment in the Marine Corps soon after Grandma's death, and was assigned to a guard company of the Fourth Marines stationed in Shanghai. The Japanese were already rattling their swords in the zone they occupied around the city, and when Boyd came home on leave in 1940 I expected him to be concerned by the threat of Japanese military action. Instead he cryptically remarked, "Aw, the Japs are harmless; they're better than those filthy Chinese." This attitude was surely modified two years later. About a month before Pearl Harbor was attacked, the Fourth Marines were transferred to the island fortress of Corregidor in Manila Bay. When Bataan and Corregidor fell to the Japanese in May 1942, Boyd was among those forced to make the Death March to the prison camp at Cabanatuan. He survived almost four years there, barely. Less than two years after his repatriation, he died from wounds he had received as a prisoner. During those war years and certainly after his return home, Boyd became my first, maybe my only role model. I admired and emulated his joking, self-effacing courage. I still do. He managed to suppress a fit of laughter when he learned in December 1945 that I had enlisted for two years in the Marine Corps.

My enlistment was not altogether voluntary. After a bland high school career and graduation in June 1945, I was notified by the local draft board that I would be called for preinduction examinations sometime that summer. Deferments were available for those in college, and I chose this delaying tactic by enrolling at the University of Oklahoma. That fall semester was a farce. Like many another fresh-man away from home for the first time with few restraints, I partied way too much and studied hardly at all. My grades naturally reflected this. When Mother sent them to me in boot camp the following January, I was surprised by only two. Good high school English teachers had instilled an interest in language, so I took a beginning Latin course in addition to the required freshman English. At the urging of my advisor I also took a course in college algebra. Math had always seemed irrelevant, and this course was no exception. The instructors in both classes, however, were quite interesting. My Latin teacher was an attractive young woman whom every male in the room thought was super-sexy, while the algebra teacher was the spit and image of Humphrey Bogart. These personal attributes detracted greatly from my attention to formal instruction, and judging by test scores throughout the semester, I anticipated receiving as final grades some sort of *C* in Latin and some sort of *B* in algebra. It turned out just the reverse, and I've wondered all these years whether there was a clerical error.

I was still a virgin at eighteen partly because of my uneasiness about girls and what they might offer and partly because our family had no car during the war years. Dad's income was meager, and what little I earned from odd jobs quickly evaporated. The last car we had was a 1936 Chevrolet, which was somehow disposed of in the early forties. I doubt that it was worn out; more likely Dad had borrowed money on it, failed to make payments, and the car was repossessed. I don't really know. I do know that my firm impression from a limited high school social circle was that if you didn't have a car or access to one, you didn't get girls. So I concentrated on building model aircraft: Allied and Axis war planes. More than a hundred hung by threads from my bedroom ceiling. I awoke each morning to the Battle of Britain. I didn't learn to drive until I was twenty-one and out of the Marine Corps.

Two other related memories from high school. Two doors west of our house lived the Rogers family. Mother had told us they were Cherokee Indians. Mr. Rogers (Cyril) was a tall, dark-skinned patrician with iron-gray hair and a genial smile, always. He was the first Cherokee man I'd ever seen, and he was awesome. He exuded a quiet strength wholly absent in my father's flabby, mercantile arrogance. One Saturday afternoon he invited me over to his driveway to listen, together with his two sons, to the story of Ned Christie, the Cherokee patriot. I was profoundly honored at being included in the small audience, but was downcast a few minutes later when Mrs. Rogers called him to the phone, after which he had to leave immediately for an emergency in Tahlequah. The storytelling of course was never concluded. Over the years I thought of Ned Christie on the infrequent occasions when I encountered the name Ned, and wondered vaguely about his story. It was not until fifteen years ago when I first met Robert Conley in Tahlequah, read his poem and more recently his fine novel *Ned Christie's War,* that the full story was told to me in its heartbreaking magnificence.

Around the same time as Mr. Rogers's interrupted storytelling, I had the first of a sporadic series of dreams of Grandma Tennie. It was slightly scary because she appeared in what I construed as a light, swirling fog, and she called to me in a tone not of fright but of insistence. For many years I never mentioned to anyone this dream nor those subsequent to it, and I'm not at all sure I should be writing about it now. Yet I feel a compulsion to finish a story that wants to be told. From the first I understood that she was calling me even though she was not saying "Carroll." (I never had a satisfactory explanation from my mother why she chose that name, which, to this day, causes a third of my mail to be addressed to "Ms. Carroll Arnett.") In the dream Grandma called me by a word I'd never heard and could not find in any English dictionary. By the third or fourth occurrence it began to sound like *go-giz-gi,* and when I finally acquired a copy of J. T. Alexander's *Dictionary of the Cherokee Language* I discovered similar words meaning "smoke" or "smoking." At long last it got through my thick head that the substance swirling around her is not fog but smoke, and smoke that's not threatening but reassuring, sacramental. "Dumbass," I said to myself, she's naming you, she's giving you your real name.

The Marines in Vietnam had a routine that asked: "What's the difference between the Boy Scouts and the Marine Corps?" Answer: "The Boy Scouts have adult leadership." From the mid-sixties 'til the Gulf War this seems a valid distinction; in the mid-forties it would not have been. With few exceptions, the NCOs and officers I dealt with during my brief service were mature, highly skilled, and highly disciplined veterans of the Pacific campaigns. There was the ordnance captain who tried to raise hell because my platoon's rifles had rust pits in their bores when we turned them in at the end of boot camp, but there was also the sergeant (our senior DI) who explained, "Sir, these rifles were fucked when they were issued to these men, and they're in better condition now than they were then." The captain finally muttered, "Yeah, you're right, Sergeant. As you were." In addition to beating the draft board, I joined the Marines to escape my stodgy Oklahoma City upbringing, and that I did. But since my service career was neither so flamboyant nor so miserable as cousin Boyd's, I won't dwell upon it further. I'm quite aware that military pride disturbs the sleep of liberal academia.

After discharge in October 1947, I enrolled at Oklahoma City University the next January, thanks to the GI Bill. As mentioned earlier, I had good high school English teachers, but they did little to encourage strictly literary interests. Their assigned readings in nineteenth-century fiction and verse bored me. At OCU I was fortunate in taking a second-semester freshman English course with a young instructor named Robert Stockwell. Not only did he strike a spark that gave me an inkling of the hard pleasures of imaginative writing, but he also introduced me to T. S. Eliot and Hemingway, both of whom quickly became demigods and remained so for several years. That summer I took a creative writing course with Stockwell and he encouraged my efforts at serious fiction, pointing out that if I were truly serious, I had best prepare myself for employment that would provide livable income since writing literary fiction (much less poetry) would not. With this advice in mind I wasted time, but little effort, in two education courses. Pure Mickey Mouse.

By the spring of 1949 I'd had enough of OCU and was ready to transfer to a "good school." Stockwell's glowing recommendation probably influenced Beloit College's decision to admit me that fall. I've never regretted the move. The faculty there were absolutely competent, highly demanding, yet always ready to help the inexperienced gain experience. I worked like hell the four semesters I was there because the work was worth doing; I was learning—in and out of class—how to write. When I graduated magna cum laude, Phi Beta Kappa, in June 1951, the academic honors didn't mean much to me. The awareness that I'd begun to put words together in ways that showed me and others things I hadn't known before—that meant a great deal.

Sometime in 1948 I'd begun trying to write poems. I don't remember whether I showed Stockwell any; probably not. I was *very* unsure of them. Prose seemed as natural as talking because my prose was just that—talk, hopefully good talk, put down on paper. The poems I was writing were artificial, contrived, plain silly. About this same time I began reading Ezra Pound, whose *ABC of Reading* taught me more than any other single teacher ever has about what I needed most to learn. I well understand why Pound could not abide American universities, yet I wish that I and others could have sat and talked writing with him. He always warmed to *les jeunes,* as do I. The circle of lessons started by Pound was not completed until the mid-sixties—fifteen years after I left Beloit—when I turned to the words of my people, the Native people of this country. Once learned, the lesson became abundantly clear: all literature in all its forms is the constant renewal of emotional and spiritual experience by reenacting that experience in language, words that show through action rather than merely talk about or around that experience. Pound's war cry was "Make it new!" That's precisely what the ceremonial use of language does, over and over again. Sacred or profane, it's all *nigohilv atsehisodi,* "constant renewal."

At Pound's instigation I minored in French at Beloit so I could read Villon, Laforgue, Corbière, and later René Char and Max Jacob. I'd begun sending out my own poems to little magazines, and now added a few tentative translations from these French poets. A piece of mine and a translation were published while I was a senior. I mouthed Pound at every opportunity, and one of my instructors who had also noticed a metaphysical influence quipped: "Carroll's become punny-wise and Pound-foolish."

Leaving Beloit with a shiny new BA, I returned to Oklahoma City to stay with my parents and recover from the grind of senior year. The GI Bill's gravy train was all gone, and I realized I'd had it soft as an undergraduate, never holding even a part-time job but studying and writing full-time. When I found a job as a shipping clerk for an auto parts distributor, I told myself, you can't do this or live like these people do indefinitely. I wanted to work with words, not ball and roller bearings. In the spring of 1952 I was admitted to graduate school at (back again!) the University of Oklahoma, and was awarded a small scholarship, which decided me to go ahead with it.

OU had changed little in the seven years since I'd first been there. When I returned, along with Joy Harjo, to read and speak at Oklahoma Poets Day in 1988, it had still changed very little; perhaps it's the nature of land-grant learneries to fossilize. In 1952 I was the only self-proclaimed poet/writer affiliated with the English department, and though I didn't proclaim loudly I was reassured by the trickle of acceptances from magazines. I completed required courses and worked at a master's thesis titled *Three New Romantics: Richard Wilbur, William Jay Smith, Theodore Roethke.* My thesis advisor put me and the thesis through three complete revisions before it became apparent that I could revise till my eyes fell out and the advisor would go on finding nits to pick. Meanwhile a young fireball instructor, Bill Handy, was hired away from OU by the University of Texas in Austin. I'd come to know and like him during the first of my two graduate years at OU, and soon after he moved to Texas he began recruiting me to transfer to UT. "Forget the master's," he said, "go straight for the PhD down here." Bill, a former salesman, was enthusiastic about nearly everything, the kind of person who talks more with his hands than with his mouth. His rhapsodies about the writing program at Texas, the writers already there, and the splendors of Austin's social scene—all these had their allure, and I bought into them. I transferred to Texas in the fall of 1954, and assumed a somewhat fatter teaching assistantship than the one held at OU. The three central chapters of the ill-fated master's thesis were later published as critical essays in journals, thereby granting me at least mild vindication.

Texas proved to be as Handy had touted it. I soon met a half dozen writers, real ones who wrote rather than merely talking about writing in bars or at cocktail parties: the poet Fred Eckman, who's become a lifelong friend and mentor; the story writer Jack Watson; folklorists Mody Boatright and Americo Paredes. Frank Dobie had retired from the English department, but still strutted around the swimming pool at Barton Springs on hot afternoons. The novelists Bill Brammer and Larry McMurtry were not on the faculty, but often turned up at weekend parties. Bill Handy flaunted my burgeoning publications to the university's new provost, Harry Huntt Ransom, and introduced me to him. Ransom made it immediately clear that he was an academic empire builder. A short, stocky fashion plate wearing elevator shoes, his favored term of approbation was "Oh yes, top drawer, top drawer!" He'd been a naval officer during the war and now commanded his university as he would a heavy cruiser. He would brook no insubordination, none. I knew that when I had to buck him four years later. At our introduction he asked me to serve as student member of his newly formed Visiting Critics Committee, whose mission was to invite and celebrate the critical and literary luminaries of the fifties. I was truly abashed at the prospect of lunching with T. S. Eliot, Auden, and the quiet old gentlemen of the New Criticism, but lunch with them I did over the next several years. Most were really nice guys, a few were harmless; Auden was a flaming asshole, a butt-pinching blob of pomposity.

I applied for and accepted a temporary instructorship at Knox College. In every way Knox reminded me of Beloit, and the two years at

Knox were a welcome breather from the pointless strenuosities, political backbiting, and overall foolishness of the two universities where I'd wasted time since leaving Beloit. From the first time I set foot behind a lectern forty years ago I've told myself and later told administrators, Let's not forget, I'm a writer who teaches, not a teacher who writes. Administrators, of course, are troubled by this distinction, construing it to mean that I subordinate teaching to writing. Never, not once ever have I done so. Teaching has been my chosen profession, writing my given métier. I teach because I'm good at it and it almost pays the bills; I write because like the mountain, it's there. Neither thwarts the other, each balances the other, and maintaining balance is what a life is.

When I left Knox and moved to Stephens College in 1960, I had what even that early had become standard misgivings. Stephens's jovial president assured me that if things went well for all of us during the possibly three-year probationary period, I might consider this a tenure-track position. Wonderful. For four, not three years I taught five classes six days a week under a nervously happy chairperson, Ralph Something. Stephens was then still a girls' school and not one I liked. I was ready to leave in 1964 for a somewhat saner job at Wittenberg University, where, another four years later, I got virtually the same runaround: You know, Carroll, we'd really like to keep you on with us ... if only you had finished that PhD. Negative. Out of here.

At Stephens I wrote a story called "La Dene and the Minotaur," which *Evergreen Review* published and which became the first chapter of the novel *La Dene*. During six weeks of one summer, I also completed a marathon of forty poems that would constitute *Through the Woods*. At Wittenberg I finished the manuscript of *La Dene*, and in 1965 Jim Weil published my first skinny book of poems, *Then*, from his Elizabeth Press. If I've been less than blessed in my choices of paying jobs, I've been doubly blessed in my publishers. I've not had a serious rift with any of them, and Jim Weil and Joe Bruchac have become cordial friends as well as dedicated business associates. By the time I moved on to the New Division, an experimental program at Nassón College in Maine, I had published two collections of poems with a third in press.

Students at New D were largely latter-day flower children who'd decided to go straight, more or less; faculty came from social and political activists prevalent from the sixties on. With no rigid administrative structure to gainsay us, New D students and faculty ran the show, and we ran it with an exhausting exhilaration. Sixty-hour workweeks were usually capped by mellow weekend parties. Naturally, our having so much fun while learning so much provoked the jealousy of the hidebound First Division, whose enrollment declined each semester while ours grew, and since the First D controlled the college's overall budget, the decision came to cease funding the experimental program beyond 1969–70. That was that.

Central Michigan University hired me in 1970 to help build a graduate writing curriculum. I did so, and three years later was promoted and tenured.

Some Saturdays back in the forties I walked three miles out to the Oklahoma State Historical Society's museum a block south of the capitol building on Lincoln Boulevard. I wandered the halls wondering at the somber exhibits, pictures, murals depicting Oklahoma Indians before and after statehood. Not a one of them ever smiled. Most of the Indians I'd ever seen stumbled out of beer joints on Reno and California in downtown Oklahoma City; they smiled. One once tugged my shirtsleeve to complain of the law "forbiddening the sale of alcohol drinks to Indins," a law long unenforced but still "on the goddamned statue books." What had happened to those people embalmed in the museum displays?

In the mid-sixties I finally began reading any and everything I could lay hands on dealing with Indian, Oklahoma or otherwise: Grant Foreman's books, Muriel Wright's, Angie Debo's, later Dee Brown and Vine Deloria, on and on. And I learned. I really learned that my education, all American cultural education, is founded in a conspiracy both of silence and of lies—red, white, and blue lies. *La Dene,* the novel finished at Wittenberg, tells of a mixed-blood Cherokee barmaid whom I'd taught how to drive when I did that for extra money ten years earlier. In Maine I wrote a long poem called "Removal" that tried to render the agony of the Trail of Tears. I was trying—still am—to grow into what I still refuse to label "my heritage" because to do so seems presumptuous if not pretentious. Grandma Tennie gave me my name, and I'm eternally, lovingly, grateful for that, yet I pray she'll come again just to talk with me and teach me.

In July 1974 I was awarded an NEA writing fellowship. Amid the euphoria, I reiterated where the grant money would go: to buy back a piece of land stolen from Anishinaabe people. That November I paid down and moved upon what soon became the single most important thing in my life: fifty acres of pine, cedar, and maple in Michigan's eastern Mecosta County with an old two-story house and sundry outbuildings erected in 1892 (nearly the same year that Jimmy Cavett Arnett made a profit from, then abandoned his wife's headright land in Oklahoma). It took a while for the locals to decide this breed wasn't here to savage their wives and kids; nowadays my best bow-hunting neighbor provides his family and mine with venison and cautions poachers, "You better get your ass outa here before Arnett blows it away."

That summer, the Wounded Knee trials dragged on in St. Paul, and I was fortunate to be there in August when defense testimony began. Of more than two hundred witnesses subpoenaed, the fifth to be called was Gladys Bissonette, an Oglala woman who had been a cook in the Indian camp throughout the siege. As she came to the witness stand, she carried her grandfather's pipe and asked Judge Nichol's permission to take the oath on it rather than on the courtroom Bible. The judge replied, "That will be fine, Mrs. Bissonette." For about two hours she responded to questions from both the defense team and the prosecution. When she was excused from the stand, the defense lawyers quickly huddled with Dennis Banks and Russell Means, everyone nodding in agreement. Bill Kuntsler approached the bench: "Your Honor, if it please the court, the defense wishes to rest its case. We need call no further witnesses; Gladys has said it all." And indeed she had. Recognizing flagrant governmental misconduct during both the siege and the trials, Judge Nichols dismissed all charges and released the defendants. Now, twenty years later, I'm hard put to cite what was gained from the confrontation. The American Indian Movement is still as controversial and internally contentious as ever, and Judge Nichol's honest adjudication is a shining exception to the rule of corruption that eats like cancer at the federal court system. So long as the FBI is allowed to call the shots—missing most of them but still gleefully shooting—innocent people like Anna Mae Aquash and Leonard Peltier will go on being murdered or imprisoned on fake evidence.

For someone who's become a semi-recluse on these fifty acres, I have at the same time grown a little more sociable and was delighted to welcome White Roots of Peace, the communication group from Akwesasne, when they traveled through Michigan in April 1975. Philip Deer, the Creek healer, was with them, and at the request of the young Mohawk men he agreed to conduct a sweat in the small pine grove out back. I wish now I had sweated with them as they asked me to, especially since it was to be the only occasion when I shared Philip's company, but at the time it seemed better for me to stand security while they were in the lodge since we were troubled every so often by intruders who never saw any of the fifty posted signs that lined the perimeter. The Mohawks were kind enough to leave the lodge in place, but that fall poachers came in and kicked it down. Later, Gordon Henry and I built another at a more secluded spot.

If the first half of my life was spent rooting around to find which way to go, this latter half seems to have found the way, and if I stray from it—well, that happens too. Let me count the circles of my blessings. First again, this place where I live, which I've come to know and love much better than the back of my hand. Some years ago, Lance Henson walked with me into the cedar swamp that forms two-thirds of the terrain. Noticing that I carried a rifle, he remarked, "I thought you said nothing could hurt you out here." I answered, "That's right, but I didn't say nothing would try." Three exchanges of gunfire have taught me to be alert and armed. Don't want to miss anything. A second blessing is my family, particularly my six-year-old grandson, Jerad. He's a marvelous little boy and I don't use that adjective loosely; he's truly a marvel, wiser in some ways than his sexagenarian grandfather. I'm blessed by the Indian writers I've gotten to know and cherish as tribal brothers, sisters, most specially Wotkogee/Littlecoon/Louis Oliver. In the twelve years I was privileged to know Louis, he became my real grandpa, more so than the poor old man in the cane-bottom rocker who left behind only his initials. I wish Louis could have been at the Returning the Gift Festival in Norman in July 1992. It would have meant so much to him as it would have for us all.

Several years ago when I was in Oklahoma I drove out to Luther's cemetery to visit the graves of Grandma and Boyd Norman. It was a warm, sunny weekday in April, the spring foliage in full bloom. Bluejays and crows screeched from a field nearby. As I walked around the

Arnett and Norman family plots I rehearsed the names of those dead before I was born, who were therefore little more than faceless engravings in gray headstones. At the foot of Grandma's and Boyd's graves I stood and spoke without words to each of them, then bent to put down tobacco. Rising, I collected a dozen blackjack acorns to take back to Michigan and was soon on the interstate headed home.

BURYING PAPER

BETTY LOUISE BELL

Betty Louise Bell is an assistant professor of English, Women's Studies, and American Culture at the University of Michigan, where she also serves as the director for the Program in Native American Studies. She is the author of Faces in the Moon. *Currently she is working on a literary history of early Native American women writers, entitled* A Red Girl's Reasoning.

Always, I have trusted words. To shape, inform, and bring the world closer. Everything I know, I was proud to say, I learned from books. At the age of six, I remember declaring my ambition to be a reader. In a house where both parents were semiliterate, where I read and wrote letters for relatives who could not read or write, I knew no greater ambition than to read. And in the books I read, there were *real* families: families free of lasting poverty, alcoholism, and violence. Their houses were homes, their love clear and clean, their survival finally certain. Within Betty Smith and Victoria Holt, I looked for my life, for my rightful families, for the ways in which I might slip into my future. It was not a future of romance and rescue; it was selection, the overcoming of early obstacles, the primacy of the imagination in the constant and immediate fact of survival. And to survive, I knew, I would need to become someone else.

After we moved from Oklahoma to California, when I was eleven, I began to imagine the unspeakable hope of being a writer. In my house, in my family, it would have been ludicrous to speak it—more evidence of my uppity ways—but to strangers on the bus, to the children I baby-sat, I used the word "writer," intimating existing work and recognition. I listened closely to all confidences and heard plots in the most disorganized lives. On long walks in an affluent neighboring community, I walked past the houses my mother cleaned and knew that I, too, would one day live in a safe white house. And words would bring me there.

I do wish I could remember words, and the desire to possess them, as deliberate and intended. I wish I could claim an early steadfast commitment to the representation of Native peoples and their cultures. I wish I could remember my youth as a time of self-knowledge and activism and not a headstrong, reckless escape into anything and anyone but myself. I slipped into novels and felt myself free of ideology and culture. There, in Jane Eyre's victory over Rochester or in Maggie Tulliver's love for her brother, I found my life. Later, when I wrote on Charlotte Brontë, I developed the flulike symptoms of tuberculosis, and when I put pen to George Eliot, I suffered with migraines.

For me, words were neutral, without political or personal affiliations, as equalizing in their availability as death. And anyone who could learn to use words shared the privileges (with anonymity) of those who were born to them. My walks took me down Palm Drive, into the center of Stanford University, the home of books and learning, gentility and power. I passed through its quad without comment, no one bothered with a second look, I could have been anyone, just another child of privilege worried only about the larger questions of life: what books to buy, what clothes to wear, what food to choose.

Words, from the beginning, were material culture. They clothed, housed, and accessorized their host. They would make me attractive and chic, with just a touch of refined negligence to give me that casual and natural look. And, of course, their beauty would make me loved. They would prove that you could "make a silk purse out of a sow's ear." I needed only to look at the sloppy, gratuitous suffering of those around me to know that the words I sought did not come from *that* experience.

JACKIE KENNEDY

As a mixed-blood child with siblings darker than myself, the eyes of storekeepers, bus drivers, teachers skipped over me but rested, with judgment, on my mother or siblings. Alone, I was invisible. With no more substance than a ghost who has yet to live, I moved without seeing or being seen. No one, I believed, noticed my Goodwill clothes or winced at my mouth of decaying green teeth or recognized my mangling of unfamiliar white words. Once, sitting at the counter of a doughnut shop with my mother, dressed in her predawn cafeteria whites, the manager of a local store leaned toward us and said to my mother, "Your daughter reminds me of Jackie Kennedy." Of course, I looked nothing like the young wife of the president, the compliment was meant for my mother: she had raised a child outside of her class and culture, a child with manners and affectations more ambitious than her employer's children. My mother beamed on the manager and said, "She always wanted more."

While pregnant with me, my mother picked cotton, working her way through a life of ex-husbands and relocated children in southwestern Oklahoma. "We ate beans every day," she told me, "and sometimes we didn't even have beans." Listening to her, I wondered if she had resented my hunger, as insistent and inevitable as her own. I was a large baby, nine solid pounds, she was quick to add, and my birth threw my mother into near-fatal convulsions. From the beginning we were bound by hunger and violence and, in order to survive, one of us had to have *more*.

I wanted the common opportunities born from the common lives of privilege. I was not committed to excess, only enough: enough money to live without hunger, without fear, and so little did we know of the gradations of class that I could imagine satiation and safety only in extreme material privilege. On those long, trancelike walks, I imagined my becoming sudden and transformative, without accountability for where I came from or who I loved. When I was married, my ex-husband's grandmother (a first-generation German Jew) screamed at her first glance of my mother and sister. She was rushed into the maid's bedroom, and I listened while my new in-laws explained to her that "Betty wasn't like that." And I believed them. Just as I had believed my mother and aunts.

"You're different," the women in my family said, long before organized memory began for me. It was a source of pride with them, my difference. Before the age of two, they saw something in me (and insisted that I see it as well) that spared me from the usual dreams and destinies of mixed-blood women in Oklahoma in the early fifties. I was different: I would not repeat their hard shames of poverty, illiteracy, domestic labor, or too many husbands and too many children. I walked early and talked early, my mother says, on my feet and taking command before my first year. I remember it a little differently: always in search of my mother and finding her, reaching up and taking hold of the hem of her slip. Or hiding under her bed, waiting for her to return and praying that she wouldn't beat me for telling Auney she had hocked the silverware. I did get the beating, a beating that roared and tore through my mother's helplessness and left both of us bloody. Afterward she took me to bed with her and the next morning, I received my share of the pawn loot: a quarter to see a Ma and Pa Kettle movie.

"You were born stubborn. Had to do things your own way," my mother always insisted when I attempted to tease out an apology for the early burdens of child care and family survival placed on me. "You wanted to do them," she says and, in more forgiving moments, I think she may have been right. But, most of the time, I wonder how we survived, and I look for someone on whom I can settle my anger and grief. Those early books had taught me that suffering can be articulated and a cause located. It has taken me forty-five years to imagine that the neat plot of blame, of cause and effect, might not apply to *real* acts of loving and survival.

By the time I was five, I was baby-sitting my two younger brothers and pushing the tool kit up to the kitchen sink to wash the dishes. I worked to make sense out of our lives, to bring them into ordinary consequences, believing with the greatness of an innocent heart in the power of kindness over evil, in the rewards visited on goodness and in the certain return of love. If one loved enough—or suffered enough—justice would be realized. I believed, for it was so in the books I read, that I would be able to compel—to carry if I must—my siblings on the force of my own narrative.

I ALWAYS THOUGHT I'D BE ABLE TO BRING THEM WITH ME

I knew words would save us. Not my mother's words, certainly not the words of my community, but the literate, shaped words of novels. I fell into them and emerged, each time, with a new sense of how our lives could be better. The space of fiction allowed me not only to reimagine our endings but our beginnings as well. In its generous possibilities, there was every chance of early mistaken identities, unknown benefactors, and easy escapes. Like the children of Dickens, our personal histories could change on the revelation of a story. Indian histories, I knew from westerns, were much less flexible.

I knew the power of the story. My mother's face, when she spoke of her mother, possessed a strength and light that failed when she was at work or in the presence of my stepfather. Then she seemed pathetic in her willingness to humiliate herself while dishing out cafeteria specials to superior college students or writing, then denying it, I HATE YOU across the shoulder of my stepfather's picture. He beat her, regularly, with the leg of a coffee table, drawing screams and blood and then turning on her frightened children. When he was out of the house, she wrote her words across his picture, then told stories of retribution by mean Indian women. "Don't mess with Indian women," her stories concluded. And she'd look at me, to see if I understood that she had ancient hidden powers, if she chose to use them, and that I too shared those powers. We were not as we appeared to be.

I learned to believe in stories, not lives. For four decades, I actually thought one could choose between them. With an effective life story an individual could create a world from any perspective and find resistance within the imagination. My dissertation argued that the creative resistance of nineteenth-century women writers had provided them with a freedom beyond the physical or cultural worlds of Victorian England. As nobody's daughter, I read these authors and myself as privileged orphans, creating the lives that the fates had failed to give us. Women, I knew, subversively created more from less.

Ironically, my first novel came not from the canons of English and American literature but from the Oklahoma voices of my mother and great aunt. The novel came late and may not have come at all if it wasn't for Gerald Vizenor's generous and firm belief in my ability to write it. He taught me, through example and faith, the worthiness of ordinary Native lives and the value of all stories informed by love. During that year with Gerald in Berkeley, I began to remember the look on my mother's face when she spoke of her mother, I began to remember humor in the face of personal devastation, and I began to remember that I had had a life, not the life of Dickens, Brontë, or Eliot, but a life shaped and haunted by its own unwritten but not untold stories. Gerald knew the stories before I told them, and his appreciative laughter told me I might have an audience. Over cappuccinos and fresh rolls, in serious or funny talk, Gerald was the first person to value me for my actual life. A few days before I left Berkeley, I sat on a ledge outside of Peet's Coffee, mourning how much I would miss his brilliance and steady friendship. When I looked up, he had appeared on the street, twenty paces from me. We sat there in silence, sipping coffee and watching the negotiations of the homeless around us, until it was time to go.

I SAID TOO MUCH

The last time I saw my mother she handed me a spiral notebook in which she had written down the facts of her early life. As if she had a premonition that we would never see each other again, she insisted I read the journal right then. She escorted me to a bedroom and shut the door. I sat on the edge of the bed, nursing a sense of imposition and distrust, and began to read. From the living room, I heard rocking and belching, the sounds of her worry and ulcers. Quickly, I realized that these stories were different from the ones I had heard since childhood: these were the stories she could not tell a child, the stories of her life after her mother died, the stories of a nine-year-old mixed-blood girl taken into the bed of her white stepfather to negotiate shelter and food for herself and her two younger sisters.

Clearly, it was a long apology for the negotiations her own children had assumed. Generation after generation, the bodies of children had been used to secure survival. When I came out of the bedroom, she was eager for my forgiveness. "See," she said, "you're lucky, you had a mother." I put the journal down and walked out to the porch. Timidly, she joined me, and then, through angry tears, she accused, "I know what's wrong. I said too much."

She was right. I did not want my story, or the stories of my siblings, to be just a continuation of the well-known horrors of violence and power. To be, simply, a repetition of her story. I wanted words to strengthen my grievances against her and celebrate my difference. I was embarrassed by her untutored appropriation of words that were never meant to tell such stories. Clearly, my mother did not understand the delicacies of narrative and audience. And worse, she wanted me to value the ugly horror of our lives. Someday, she knew, I would write her stories, but never again would I hear them as I heard them as a child.

She had turned to the journal after her children were grown, after maturity and destiny had stolen her morning audience, but she never gave up the ambition that her children (especially myself) would know her. She, too, trusted words, and their ability to carry the spirit. They reached back, through generations of Scotch-Cherokee Bells, and returned with explanations for the present. My mother would have no more thought of trying to speak of her life without speaking of her relatives' lives than she would have considered consulting a dictionary.

BURYING PAPER

After we came to California from Oklahoma, I began stealing and burying paper. I was eleven years old and imagined that books were written in spiral binders on wide, college-ruled sheets. Luckily, the local Letterman's, a grocery store chain, had a large selection of binders and pencils. In winter or the heat of summer, I slipped along its aisles—a tiny child in a large coat—and stuffed my pockets, my sleeves, and the inside of the coat with all the things I craved: Hostess chocolate pies, Pepsi's, Hershey's chocolate almond bars, cans of Vienna sausage, cartons of pencils and notebooks of paper. And then I crossed the vacant lot next to the store and buried the paper and pencils I had stolen. I never took them home. At home, they would be taken from me, used or destroyed by four younger siblings. And worse, treated frivolously, as if their value were only immediate and their promise something to scribble across, tear out, and throw away.

Three decades after my Letterman's thefts, I still hoard paper. In my bedroom closet, I have enough computer paper to keep a small office going for a year: reams and reams of bright white laser paper, 24 weight, with and without three holes punched. There, stacked among expensive shoes and to the top of hanging skirts, is who I wait to become. There are the stories I lived while invisible: the stories in my mother's journal, the stories of abuse so severe the imagination stepped in and removed me from them, the stories of love and shame unraveling each other, the stories . . . ordered and known by narrative, compelled into meaning, and blankly waiting for a future, different me. To be opened and used by someone who has enough: enough distance from the past to now become it, enough white privilege to write of being Indian, enough acceptance to speak of difference. Can there be that much paper in the world?

A few years ago, I understood my stealing of paper, when I could have taken more Hostess pies and candy bars, as a desire for something beyond survival. Now, I know the burying of paper as another strategy in silence and survival, for what is more characteristic of survival—for the poor, the endangered, the abused—than silence? Finally, with a closet full of paper, there are still the books, the short stories, the poems—alphabetized by author and categorized by genre—to tell me who I am and to cover my own silence with their literate noise. And as I read I anticipate, through the common properties of the writer, the stories I wait to tell.

My mother did not have my faith or respect for language. Her scrawl punished and violated all courtesies of spelling and grammar. Her words appeared as she heard them, without apologies. She would stuff a six-page run-on sentence into the smallest, cheapest envelope she could find and then misaddress it. Delivery and audience did not bring her words together in never-ending connections—she wrote because there was something she urgently needed to say. She did not know that what she had to say could be reduced to narrative, style, or conscious intent. Such considerations were for her educated daughter, who would know how to write it and "make it sound good."

SIMPLE LEARNING

Girl, yer gonna learn, my mother warned. *I don't know what it's gonna take. But you gonna study on this hard.* This refrain surfaced from my mother every time I, by look or word, judged myself better than her or my surroundings. *You remind me of those Bells, with their noses so far up in the air that they can't walk without tripping over their own feet.* Yet it was the greatest pride of my mother and aunts' lives that they were Bells, a large family well known for its intelligence and courage. The Bells produced statesmen and warriors and, to hear my mother tell it, were the aristocrats of the Cherokee Nation. My difference, simultaneously criticized and encouraged, came from the Bells, from those I knew and did not know. Sometimes, at the kitchen table, my mother would pause in her talk, look at me as if for the first time, and say to her sister, *You see it, Rozella?*

I sure do.

It was that simple: in a particular light or mood, my face could move from uncommitted to Indian. Half a century of mixed marriages and displacement did not disguise the Indian blood when it chose to surface. As I grow older, I'm able to see it in myself and others. I have become one of the women who, taking a face in my hands, can see relatives in a child's eyes. Or hear them, within the pacing of words said and not said.

I still hoard words for a time when I might use them to free myself of what I feel and know. But, like flashes of Indian blood, my mother can enter and change those words at any time. Words, once loved because they allowed me the illusions of free will and absolute creation, come in her voice.

There was this boy, one of them poor Stamps boys. His momma was a full-blooded Creek and his daddy was some no-account. This boy, he was in my class in the third grade. Didn't have no shoes, just like us. Rozella and me. Walked barefoot everywhere he went. But he didn't seem to mind. He'd just come on into the schoolroom, his feet as black as the road. Rozella and me, we always took a rag to our feet 'fore coming in. You know yer Auney, she shamed real easy. Well, this here boy, Henry, I think his name was, one day this Henry come to school with a bad cold. His nose running something awful, and he's using the sleeve of his raggedly sweater to wipe hisself. Right on the sleeve, he wipes it. Well our teacher decides she gonna shame him. Right there in front of everybody. And she says to him, "Henry, what's that on your sleeve?" Henry ain't got no idea what she's talking about. And the teacher comes over to him, in front of all of us right there in the schoolroom, and points to his sleeve. Henry looks up at her like she's lost her mind, like he's just plain sorry for her, and says, "Looks like anyone oughtta know what snot was."

My mother loved that story. She whooped after every telling, her laughter repeating the victorious joy of the small and the poor over the sheltered and shameless.

I wanted to become a writer because I could imagine nothing that would take me faster and farther down roads closed to women, Indians, and the poor. I could create worlds, peopled by characters of noble intentions and worthy passions, where life was uncomplicated by negotiations of shame. If I failed, there was enough existing fiction to fill a lifetime of teaching and research. The closet of paper would fund the worthy pursuit of another's work and secrets, leaving only traces of my memory behind to mark the work. And my mother would not be there when the Indian flashed across my face and I said, as I once did, "No. I'm not Indian." Or denied, as I was never able to do, that I was a woman or poor.

I could *almost* pass. For decades *almost* was taken for a life; now, it's not enough.

In English I'm Called Duane BigEagle

An Autobiographical Statement

DUANE BIGEAGLE

Duane BigEagle (Osage) was born at Claremore, Oklahoma, in 1946. He has published nationally and internationally as well as in tribal newspapers, and in the following anthologies: From the Belly of the Shark *(ed. Walter Lowenfels),* The Remembered Earth *(ed. Geary Hobson),* Earth Power Coming: Short Fiction in Native American Literature *(ed. Simon Ortiz), and* Returning the Gift *(ed. Joseph Bruchac). He is a lecturer in American Indian Studies at Sonoma State University, a founding board member of the American Indian Public Charter School (Oakland, California), and winner of the 1993 W. A. Gerbode Poetry Award.*

Haway! Wazhazhe ninka. Nikashiga sanee. In English my name is Duane BigEagle. I am Osage, fairly traditionally raised near the Osage Reservation in northeastern Oklahoma. My heritage is mixed blood—Osage and Irish, Cherokee and Dutch, Scots-Irish and English. I am a poet, teacher, painter, traditional Southern Straight dancer and singer, as well as cultural activist. When I was growing up, nobody told me I had to specialize in just one occupation, so I've pursued everything that interested me. It seems more natural for me to see the connections between things rather than to isolate life's elements into boxes that never touch. Poetry is connected to politics, education, tradition, even science. I also tend not to make so many distinctions between the arts or between art and any other aspect of life. To me, self-expression, creativity, and spirituality are the important things and not which medium you use. This tendency to see connections extends everywhere, even across time. When I began to call myself a poet, it didn't seem enough for me just to do my own writing. I saw a broader definition of "literary work" and felt a responsibility also to be a teacher and to prepare, as best I could, the way for literature in the coming generations. This has led me to teach creative writing to young people since 1976 with the California Poets in the Schools program. In many ways, I see the definition of poet as going quite a bit beyond "writing." Coming from an oral tradition culture, perhaps the only true "publishing" is to have my poems made into songs and placed on an American Indian drum (i.e., made a part of the repertoire).

As a youth I was taught to value a connection with the land that sustains our lives. I learned early that individuality, creativity, self-expression, and love of beauty are essential to the survival of a whole and healthy person. And I experienced the roles that art, dance, music, and poetry play in the passing of culture from one generation to the next. These lessons and values have formed me and, I believe, have helped to sustain American Indian people for at least the last fifty thousand years (my estimate) in this hemisphere. I know they have helped us to endure and survive the last five hundred years. (They say the Aborigine people of Australia have the oldest continuous culture in the world at forty thousand to fifty thousand years, but I think American Indian cultures may also be that old. Some traditional stories say we've always been here.)

I often wonder what the Americas would be like if Columbus and the early settlers had been able to see and value our cultures and civilizations. I have to use plurals here because Native Americans are multiethnic and multicultural. Many non-Indians tend to group Indian people together as one instead of respecting each as belonging to a nation of his or her own. Groups of people spread out over a whole continent (or hemisphere) are going to develop differently and this is as true for American Indians as it is for Europeans, Asians, or Africans. Yet, within these differences, groups may share certain cultural understandings—most Europeans and European Americans share a common Judeo-Christian outlook. Also, it seems to me, there is a philosophy and set of values common to American Indians: reverence for Mother Earth, respect for elders, harmony with nature, respect for personal integrity and individuality, acceptance of the paradoxical nature of life, service and concern for the group or community, and spirituality as a way of life. So, if Columbus had spoken fluent Taino (or the Taino people fluent Spanish), could he have understood the civilization he faced when he stepped ashore? Do most Americans today really understand the original cultures of America?

Individuality is common in America, but the Native American version, among many tribes, is especially strong—and significantly different. My non-Indian students are often amazed when I tell them that my parents rarely told me what to do. In many tribes it's considered improper to tell someone else what to do—an invasion of their individuality, perhaps even a stifling of that individuality. I'm not speaking of the "I'm for me and the hell with the rest of you" kind of individuality—that's mere isolation, a denying of what you might call natural law, and leads, in my opinion, to spiritual (and cultural?) death. Rather I'm speaking of individuality as personal development, a flowering of a unique self, a discovery of your own, singular path in life.

Paradoxically, this kind of individuality is also good for the group. When you have strong individuals who know who they are and what they're about, they have more to contribute to the group (assuming, of course, that you have in place all the other interlinked values that form American Indian cultures).

I spoke above of natural law. I didn't mean Darwin's survival of the fittest but rather that all things are interconnected and that all actions have a consequence. See-ahtt, Chief Seattle, spoke of the "web of life" in his famous 1854 speech. A couple of years ago, I decided to buy a new car. In thinking about what kind of car to buy, it occurred to me that the air coming out of my exhaust pipe was more or less the same air that was going to go into my great-granddaughter's mouth. When I learned that a pound of pollutants goes into the atmosphere for every gallon of gas burned, I decided to get a car with good gas mileage. This is not so much a philosophy of "Thou shalt not" but more one of "What will happen if." And, as the poet Gogisgi (Carroll Arnett) said, "Everything, every single thing matters." Living in the modern (i.e., mostly Western) world is not an easy task for people with a traditional tribal outlook, but then no one ever claimed, even in the old days, that the Indian way, the good Red Road, was an easy path.

Another couple of points—when Columbus arrived, he brought a different kind of time, linear time moving at a fixed, measurable rate as opposed to cyclical (or "seasonal") time—time as continuum with no beginning and no end. This is difficult to explain so let's just say that time is relative (even Einstein said so) and things are done as they need to be done rather than because a clock tells us it's "time." Time is geared to the activity at hand. Past and future time may be deemphasized in favor of the present. And when I go back home, the old folks there seem to have all the time in the world. Columbus (and other settlers) also brought guilt. Every culture has a mechanism of social control—a way of getting the people to do "what's right" to keep the culture or society going. As far as I can determine, there was no such thing as guilt in this hemisphere before Columbus arrived. The mechanism of social control was shame.

There are many other differences—an emphasis on sharing, cooperation, and harmony; an egalitarianism which says that everyone is important and has a valuable contribution to make and a role to play;

an emphasis on courtesy and delicacy of feeling; a deemphasis of hierarchical thinking and materialism; and many more. In the old days it was customary for Osage people who aspired to be leaders to give away everything they owned three times in their life. It was felt that this brought them an understanding of the true value of material things and demonstrated their commitment to the tribe. All of these things I bring up so that when I say, autobiographically, that I was born at a certain place to certain people, you will have some understanding of what I really mean.

Actually, I'm not completely comfortable with autobiographical writing; it seems immodest somehow. And as a poet and an Osage born mid-century, there are many things in my life and in the lives of my relatives that could be confusing and easily misunderstood by those whose first inclination is to pass judgment or who didn't grow up in a conflict of cultures. Also, I'm not much attracted to the elitist "cult of the individual" that I find among many writers and critics in America (as if the bare facts of a life or a psychological profile could explain the "mystery" of writing, which may come as inspiration from our Creator or from some collective consciousness). Perhaps that kind of individuality came about in humans when people stopped holding things— land, tools, food—communally and started seeing themselves as isolated beings or families pitted against the rest of the world. (I wonder if this kind of thinking doesn't come in part from the Judeo-Christian precept that man has dominion over nature—an idea that is very foreign to most Native Americans. Human beings are not seen as separate from nature; it's like trying to have dominion over your own foot!). I don't know who composed most of the songs I sing when I sit around the drum—some of them may be much older than anything written down in books—but that doesn't decrease their lessons, power, and usefulness. They belong to all of us and there is a responsibility to see that they're there for future generations.

As a teacher, I do see a value in sharing my experience with young people in hopes that they can perhaps start from where I leave off and not go through every step of reinventing the bow and arrow. And, too, in my poetry I often use an autobiographical style; I tend to start from my own experience and let it lead the reader/listener out beyond to some other place I'm trying to go. Hopefully, if my poetry has been successful, an experience itself will have been presented rather than the particular facts of a life, which is most often autobiography.

But let me begin there, at Claremore, Oklahoma, in 1946:

> I remember the Indian Hospital
> where I was born.
> It's built around a courtyard
> with a garden and trees in the center.
> Years later I would go back
> and wait with my mother
> in the high ceilinged
> white walled reception room
> with dark wooden benches
> where the people sat.
> Through the arches of the courtyard,
> I could see the window
> of the maternity ward
> and the bush that bloomed
> in late Spring
> with fawn yellow flowers.
> They say a nurse held me up to that window
> the minute I opened my eyes ...

> (from "Birthplace")

I was born in May (Moon of the Delicate Rose, which is also known as Moon of the Killing Frost—paradox and contradiction were with me from the beginning) to Norman Ray BigEagle and Lillian Dorcas (Mc-Cuistian) BigEagle. Dad is the son of Harry BigEagle, a full-blood Osage (Osage Allotment #497), a member of the Native American Church, and one of the last of the Hominy District Osages to move into town (Hominy, Oklahoma) from his traditional village after the Allotment Act. This 1887 Act of Congress forced Indian people to stop holding their land communally and to divide it up individually— a very effective attack on ancient cultural practices and traditional Indian life. Dad's mother was Myrtle Louisa Goad, a tough, stubborn, Scots-Irish and English settler to Oklahoma from the Penitentiary Mountain area of Arkansas. "Nothing's more lonesome than the sound of thunder rolling over Penitentiary Mountain," she used to say. She was also an excellent maker of Osage meat pies, and people used to come from quite a distance to bring her buffalo and beef to make into this Osage delicacy. Mom is the daughter of an Irish farmer, William (Will) Washington McCuistian, who always planted two acres of corn next to the house and often spoke of "God L'Mighty." Some of my earliest memories are of running through those cornfields, whose stalks seemed to reach up almost to the sky. Mom's mother was Sylvia Josephine (Wheeler) McCuistian, of Dutch and Cherokee heritage, though no one on that side of the family talked very much about their Indian blood in the first half of this century. To my recollection, she was dark enough to be half Cherokee, but we'll never know since all of those records were burned up in a courthouse fire long ago. I remember that she used to sit on an old nail keg instead of a chair at the dinner table so she could have quick and easy access to the wood cook stove. As early as I can remember, I had people all around me using simile and metaphor; it was a natural way of communicating for both the Indian and the rural Oklahoma white sides of the family.

There were many interesting influences and role models around me as I grew up. I remember a red fireman's hat that I got for my fourth birthday and how happy I was to get it and how sad everyone else was because that was the night that my aunt Rosie (grand-aunt, really) slipped on a banana peel in a Safeway parking lot and broke her hip. Good and bad seemed to come together in big doses back then. Rosie had married a Wyandot-Quapaw man named Lee Stand who eventually passed away from the injuries he received in World War I. Rosie got a widow's pension but only as long as she never married again, which she never did. But that didn't stop her from living a full life; she just sort of had to do it under the table. She was one of my first examples of a nonstandard lifestyle—a bohemian we'd call her today. She had a daughter later (and a son from her marriage) and raised both children by herself in spite of the fact that she spent much of her life on crutches. She was an example of a strong woman and someone who met life's difficulties with courage, fortitude, grace, and extreme honesty. I can still see her thin frame, a bandanna around her head, moving across the yard to her '38 Buick, scaring the chickens out of the way with her crutch as she went.

It seems strange, and obvious, to say that my parents were an influence, but they were—more so, it seems to me, than was the case with many of my non-Indian friends. Their honesty, good humor, and up-rightness, their capacity for hard work and keeping busy, their ability to enjoy life without pretensions and without destroying anything, were good for me to see while growing up. They've always been my best friends.

I also encountered fairly early the work of John Joseph Mathews. Mathews was Osage and a Rhodes scholar. After his studies in En-gland, he was in North Africa with a group of scholars studying the Berber tribe. He tells the story of how the scholars were admiring the freedom and independence of the tribesmen as they rode their horses across the desert, firing their guns in the air in some ceremony. The scholars were lamenting how Western man seemed to have lost some of that vitality of life when Mathews suddenly realized that he hadn't lost anything, that he could see this anytime he wanted on the Osage Reservation. So he went back home to Pawhuska, the capital of the Osage Nation. He later wrote books about Osage life and was instru-mental in establishing the Osage Tribal Museum in the late 1930s. The Osage have a history of sending interesting people out into the world (the ballerina Maria Tall Chief was another) and it may be from this that I got the idea that it was proper for an Osage to be as comfortable in the drawing rooms of Europe as around our own campfires.

My parents were poor, and there are many stories behind that statement. They met hitchhiking, with little to begin their marriage except youthful energy and exuberance. They moved around a lot in search of work when I was little and I was often left with grand-parents.

TRAVELING TO TOWN

When I was very young,
we always went to town
in the flatbed wagon.
We'd leave as soon
as the day's first heat
had stopped the mare's breath
from forming a cloud
in the air.
Kids sprawled in the back
among dusty bushels

of corn and beans.
As we rode down main street,
the town revealed itself
backwards
for my sister and me to see.
We loved the brick and sandstone buildings
and the farmer's market
with its sawdust floor.
Best of all
was Monkey Ward
with its large wood paneled center room
and the little wires
with paper messages
that flew back and forth
like trained birds.
We finally got to Safeway
where Grandma did the shopping
and Grandpa sat outside
on the brick steps in the sunlight
watching all the grandkids.
From a shady coolness
on the other side of the street
the ice cream store
would call to us
with its banging screen door.
Grandpa always had money for ice cream
and we'd ride home down main street
licking ice cream
watching the town reveal itself
backwards again
in afternoon sun.

(NOTE: Many people in rural America referred to the Montgomery Ward store as
"Monkey Ward.")

There is not much I can say in words on a page that can even begin
to explain the richness of growing up with grandparents in rural
northeastern Oklahoma. Kids had a part in everything. I remember sitting around the yard with uncles, aunts, and cousins shucking corn and
cutting the kernels off the cob to can for winter, churning cream into

butter with a wooden churn, riding horses (and cows!) through the summer fields, going camping and to powwows and dances where the smell of wood smoke became inextricably mixed with the songs of meadowlark and hawk, singers and drum. In many ways I've spent my life trying to recover that heritage and feeling. People say being Indian is a lifelong learning process, and I'm still learning. I believe it is possible to hold on to much of traditional life in the modern world; most years I fly fifteen hundred miles in a modern jet to dance in our tribal ceremonies, parts of which are certainly ancient.

INSIDE OSAGE

The town crier's first bell sounds
calling dancers to get dressed
and head for the dance arbor.
Soon drums and singing
will float across these wide fields.
I sit for a moment
on a wood splitting stump
by the low concrete porch
and remember how the houses
are built practically on the ground,
and how the rivers and creeks
have their own distinct smells.
How it feels to be so far
from a main road
that you see fifty miles
across low hills and gullies
covered in prairie grass
rippling in a breeze
all the way from Nebraska.
Meadowlarks whistle sunlit melodies
and a single shrill hawk's shriek
arouses my heart.
Tourists may see gas stations, farms,
cattleguards across red dirt roads,
and asphalt highways
speeding through one street towns.
But if you look carefully,
you can find another land hidden here,

the invisible vertical to this horizontal world.
Rising up as a high school
in the middle of nowhere,
glimpsed in the blue flash of a thunderstorm,
it's an older land where war honors
are still being sung,
where cooking fires still send out
a warm invitation of good smells,
where eagle feathers stand upright
in fields of undisturbed snow.
I feel it at the dances,
on the evening of the third day
during the last songs
when the circle of women singers
stand up from their chairs
and sing behind the men
whose drumsticks swing up
like beating wings of an eagle.
Dancers circle, then face in to the singers
as a shimmering column
of sound and light
rises out of the drum
and races toward the sky.

When I was fairly young, Dad got a job as a mechanic with American Airlines and we began a slow spiral into the big city of Tulsa. By junior high and high school, I was in the Tulsa public school system. This was after Sputnik and the government was throwing tons of money into the science and math curriculums. It worked! I became enthralled with the modernity of science; I wanted to be an astrophysicist. I worked very hard from my first algebra course in eighth grade to the latest physics course as a high school senior. I worked so hard that I began to lose contact with my rural and Indian background (but I didn't forget). Everything around me—school, church, TV, friends—pointed away from that old-fashioned, so-called primitive life to a world of the new modernity. In the spring of 1964 I won a Santa Fe (Railroad) Foundation Indian scholarship to study physics at the University of California at Berkeley. The fall of '64 found me in the right place at the right time, studying Einstein and the theories of modern physics. We studied from photocopied texts; the curriculum was so new it hadn't been published yet. But something else was also going on. That fall was the beginning of the Free Speech Movement, the student strikes, and "sex, drugs, and rock 'n roll." It was amazing stuff for a young Indian kid from Oklahoma and I jumped right in. I had one hand around Heisenberg's Uncertainty Principle and the other hand around a picket sign. A cloud of smoke coming toward me on the street might have been tear gas or marijuana (or later, gun smoke). The politics of the student movement were every bit as stimulating and educational as the theories of modern physics. In all of this swirling excitement, I didn't notice that I wasn't learning anything about my own Indian heritage. But I did notice something unusual about some of those theories in my physics curriculum—I had heard them before. Many of the latest theories of modern physics resembled, and seemed to confirm, some of the most ancient teachings of American Indian philosophy and spirituality. This thought was influential for a young mixed breed seeking unity in his life.

MY GRANDFATHER WAS A QUANTUM PHYSICIST

I can see him now
smiling
in full dance regalia,
an eagle feather fan in his hand.
He's standing with the other men
on the grassy field
in front of the round house
on a sunny afternoon.

Scientists have finally discovered
that the intimate details
of our lives
are influenced by things
behind the physical world,
beyond the stars
and beyond time.

My grandfather knew this.

I got an excellent Western education at Berkeley. My scholarship didn't cover everything so I worked at the UC library for four years, which was fortunate since I read a great variety of books. I also got an education in realpolitik on the streets and I've tended toward activism ever since. When my second year began, the new physics curriculum wasn't ready and I realized I'd have to give up Einstein and go back to bouncing balls and thermodynamics. I decided to change my major and modulated through the social sciences to literature (an easy thing for a supple young mind). I was ambitious and almost had a double major in English and Comparative Literature when I decided I'd had enough, took my BA in English, and moved back to the country.

I ended up on a three-hundred-acre sheep ranch on a river by the ocean in northern Mendocino County, California. It was a beautiful place and I stayed there ten years. While there, I helped start a small press, the Ten Mile River Press, and for six years I had a weekly "Poetry on the Radio" program on my local FM station. I also began painting (mostly watercolors and oils) and teaching poetry to children with California Poets in the Schools. One of my favorite places to teach is in the town of Covelo on the Round Valley Reservation in eastern Mendocino County. It's a large, circular valley where many northern California Indian tribes were moved after gold was discovered and California became a state. The area is half Indian and half white and reminded me in many ways of Hominy, Oklahoma. I remember being surprised that, although the elementary school was half and half, when I went to teach at the high school, there were almost no Indian kids in the classes. Because of the cultural differences and other social and economic pressures, the needs of the Indian kids weren't being met and they dropped out. It hit me that if things didn't change, my children were going to be facing the same discrimination that my parents and I had faced. This was the beginning of my cultural activism. I've written about this sense of dislocation and loss, of being a stranger and invisible in your own land:

WAZHAZHE AIRLINES

Once I died in a plane crash
and when I got up, no one could see me.
It was a free flight
(Dad worked for the company)
but I asked for my money back anyway.
It didn't work, they couldn't hear me either.

I decided to catch the reservation taxi
and spend my French leather gloves
on a ride out to the bar on Eagle Creek.
The Indian bartender was off that night
and I had no money for a drink.
The only other Indian there
was Leroy Stands Tall;
he could see the shape I was in
so he bought me a beer
but he drank half of it
before he slid it down the bar.
I sat down in the corner
to write an autobiography
of my early years:
I was poor as dirt and my mother
was in love with a hitchhiker.
I'm blind in one eye
where my sister hit me with a park swing—
she didn't mean to, her little legs pumping
as she ran away from the neighborhood goat.
My legs are crooked
from a deficiency of early nourishment—
my parents fed me from a book.
My skull is flat in places,
we weren't allowed cradleboards then
so I fell down between the bed and the wall.
I'm tall because my father
just caught me by the heels.
I'm named after a paratrooper.
He was killed at the Battle of the Bulge,
which is why I'm so skinny.
I'm deaf in one ear and always turn to the left.
My lungs are immense
from carrying dead Indians around.
My ribs ache from laughing
at my reflection in the mirror.
My eyeballs got turned around
in the birth canal and stare
inward into a space defined

by superstitions of a summer night,
by dark birds against stars.
I don't know why I'm so alone,
I don't think I was born that way.
I have two sons—
both almost as old as I am.
All my first three wives
left me on the same night.
Being Eagle clan, I dream of fancydancing—
I've got the legs for it
from chasing girls across the prairie—
but my memory of the old songs
is drowned out by a century
of gunshots and car horns.
I love to travel: Pawhuska, Tulsa,
Flagstaff, Paris, Venice;
but I always come home.
Hon-monin, old Walks-in-the-Night,
follows me everywhere I go;
he has even less of a chance
than I do.
Some day my dad and I
will build an airplane so light
that it'll float.
We'll take my mother and sister,
all my wives, kids, relatives,
and all the People
and we'll fly back up to the stars
where we used to live.
All those holes up there in the sky—
that's where we'll find our refuge.

(NOTE: "Osage" is an English word; in our language, it's "Wazhazhe." Also, in one part of the origin story of our tribe, the People lived for a time in the sky to seek the counsel of the stars, moon, and sun.)

When I think of my influences, one of the greatest was simply the free time that living in the country gave me. In college I'd gotten in the habit of reading everything I could find by one particular author before moving on to another. I suppose I started with Dylan Thomas and worked my way around the European authors—Rilke, the French symbolists and surrealists, Mayakovsky. But I also read Li Po and the Japanese writer Kenji Miyazawa, William Carlos Williams, and the Beats in America, and, of course, all the other American Indian authors I could find: Simon Ortiz, Leslie Silko, Scott Momaday, James Welch, Louise Erdrich, and many others. One of the most important for me was César Vallejo, the half-Indian Peruvian writer. The publication by University of California Press of his *Complete Posthumous Poetry* in 1979 was a revelation and has influenced my writing since then. Caught in between Indian and Western cultures, he exploded into a whole new way of looking at and writing about the world. He is full of duality and paradox and thinks with his heart as well as his mind—a quality I admire. Dostoyevsky and Carlos Fuentes pushed me into writing fiction and two new novels have impressed me lately: *To the River's Edge* by Elizabeth Cook-Lynn and *Ghost Singer* by Anna Lee Walters.

In painting, my early influences were the work of the early Kiowa artists and people like Blackbear Bosin, Harrison Begay, and Jerome Tiger. I've studied the work of the French Impressionists and the Japanese woodblock print artist, Hiroshige. More recently, I've been impressed by Fritz Scholder, T. C. Cannon, Jaune Quick-to-See Smith, and the Lakota artist Robert Penn. The writer Barry Gifford has been a friend for over twenty-five years and the part-Mohawk Canadian writer Bill Bradd and I have edited each other's work for over twenty years. I've fallen in love with several women who are writers and artists and they have influenced me greatly; their contribution to my development as a human being and an artist cannot be overestimated. The sexism in America is evident when I walk into an English class and see twelve pictures of white male authors and one of Emily Dickinson. It's staggering to me what we've left unsaid and undone in ignoring the full capacity of women to contribute regularly and as a matter of course to all areas of society. I don't remember that so much on the Res. Osage women have always been strong leaders—and recognized as such even if they weren't always on the rostrum or Tribal Council. I was at a meeting in Pawhuska recently where there was a discussion of the word "chairman" and whether it shouldn't be "chairperson." The women nixed the change, they didn't mind "chairman" as long as they got to call the shots. There is some learned sexism (and racism too! Aren't all people a manifestation of *Wah-kon-tah,* the Creator, and therefore sacred?), but I think in most tribes there isn't so much hierarchical thinking and *everyone* is recognized as being important to the tribe's survival and growth.

In the 1980s I was active as an arts administrator and even served for a time as president of the board of directors of California Poets in the Schools. I also began to be invited to serve on grant review panels and arts planning task forces (for the California Arts Council, the National Endowment for the Arts, and local arts commissions). Again and again, I was struck by the Eurocentric bias of many of these agencies. Funds and resources that belonged to all the people were divided up in a way that gave European American artists and arts organizations a much greater share than their percentage of the population warranted. This is especially important in California, where 45 percent of the population are people of color (one in four Americans are people of color). Native Americans and other people of color were being judged by Eurocentric standards of excellence and, of course, we didn't measure up. The word "excellence" became a code word for "all white." (It's a bit like the new code word "colorblind." Colorblind means that you understand the various different cultures around you well enough to be able to judge "excellence" in their terms as well as your own. California is probably ten years away from being colorblind; America as a whole is more like twenty years away.) Just because we don't operate in a European manner doesn't mean that we don't have excellence.

I was raised with the idea that intelligence, imagination, creativity, and capacity for hard work are passed out to all groups fairly equally. (The idea that African Americans may be genetically less intelligent only tells me that the people who are advancing that idea have never spent any time around African Americans). In not supporting all groups fairly because of cultural biases, we fail to develop the full potential of all our citizens and we weaken our state and our nation. It occurred to me one day that an American Indian powwow is the cultural equivalent of a Beethoven symphony. Actually, I think it's stronger because more people are directly involved in the creative process as opposed to the passive appreciation of listening to a symphony. Participation in the creative process leads to greater creativity, and creativity, I believe, is one of the keys to survival and growth. In many tribes there is no separate word for art because art is so much a part of daily life; an arrowhead, a song, a ceremonial dress—their beauty is inseparable from their function and vice versa. In making these things we become more creative and that creativity strengthens our Nations. Everything is connected! I often gain strength from trying to imagine what life was like in more traditional times:

TWO HEART CLAN

Two Hearts are always first
to send blankets and food to a sing.
Two Hearts know that stolen objects
always go back where they belong.
Two Hearts keep silent when they have
nothing to say, but gossip travels like an arrow.
Two Hearts stay up late at a 49 dance
and wake up bleary-eyed with the sun.
Two Hearts bring venison at mid-winter
to the wind blown lodges of the elders.
Two Hearts die in heat-shimmering prairie grass
and are buried facing west
under piles of red rock.
Two Hearts raise the sun with their prayers
and call deaf-eared rain with gesture
old as rain itself.
Two Hearts never do what they're told
and their children grow up strong steady reeds
impervious to wind.
Two Hearts camp under late summer cottonwoods;
their gray smoke lifts
soft white seed to the sky.
Two Hearts read the winter in a spider web
leaping against its anchoring strands
in the first cool wind of autumn.
A Two Heart life is the journey of a star
from blue evening through black night
to red dawn's horizon.
Two Hearts know we all must pass from this world
yet they laugh, they laugh, they laugh.

This isn't a proper autobiography. The older I get, the less important my personal history seems. My culture, my perspective and experience, the times I've lived in, the ideas I've held dear and those I've fought against—these have shaped who I am. In many ways I've come full circle. When I first began writing poetry, I imitated traditional prayers, often repeating sections to the four directions (which got me rejection slips from European American editors: "Why all the unnecessary repetition?"). Now my poems seem again to be prayers, as well as pleas and meditations. I'll end with two examples:

PULL

I pull the shirt off over my head,
pull the covers up,
pull feathers from my fingers,
circles of smoke from my eyes.
I pull dawn from sleep and generosity
from the last bell of my strength.
I shake debt out of my shoe.
I lean back and loosen
the rope from around my neck,
from around my feet
splashing down shallow creek beds,
from around the spirits
flying back to their home in the sky.
I unbutton the top button
of the storehouse of linen,
the hiding place of all night dancing,
the pathway of necessity and tenderness.
I open the back door of summer night,
sip turquoise light
from the leading edge of storm
and pull long black hair
in writhing strands from the wind.
I pull names from silence,
a strong heart from laughter
and dreams from the nubs on raw buckskin.
I pull Native Nations and the good Red Road
from the spirits of the People
dancing and singing around me.
I grab time from the hands of the clock,
bend it into a hoop

and give this moment back
to the pure, bare, original day.

NOTE ON THE MODERN WORLD

A crumpled piece of paper
with symbols on it.
Canyon wall with symbols on it.
A skyscraper wall with advertising on it.
How small we are, how large.
Have I forgotten how to be noble,
how to walk barefoot?
What did we say to one another
before we sat in a room
isolated by TV?
I cross one leg over the other,
I sit civilized and mute.
Have I forgotten how to sit on the earth
and to sing and tell stories?
Are we grown too numerous,
will we forget who we are?
We can say—they were lucky,
they had rivers, canyon walls,
traditions old as the sun.
But we cannot cross back over
the confusion of days—
that time without memory or song.
It's buried in snow at Wounded Knee,
at Tierra del Fuego or on the Arctic Circle,
or lost across oceans in barren fields.
And we have our cities.
Cities fascinate and disturb me;
there are so many of us!
Confidently we march past one another,
we strive, we love, we work.
We're defiant, aggressive.
We spell each emotion, each nuance
correctly.
We've provided the spirits of the woods
with electricity,

put radios popping tunes
on the shoulders of shamans.
And when we blunder,
my god! it's genius!
We turn it into a million bucks!
How dare I complain?
How dare I remember
the blackness of sky
lit only by stars,
the white seed of cottonwood trees
floating on the wind
like light, aimless birds.
Of course I'm saying this
only because I'm poor,
or because my people
were once overrun
by a stampede of others.
But that's not it.
Allow me to remove my face.
Here, hold it by the ears.
Now you see the white bone
of skull and teeth.
Yes, this is the way I am,
full of kindness and contemplation,
smiling out at the world
from an elemental stance.
Now I see clearly
the twin globes
spinning in their sockets,
the many billions of us
spinning in our bodies
around the axis of our spirit.
Each day now we spin faster,
we wobble and sway
with the speed and wind.
The Stone Age and the next century
meet daily in our valleys and streets.
We are some of us so different
that not even gesture

can cross the great silence.
We are at all stages at once,
the ape and the space man
touch on the full circle.
The diametrically opposed meet.
Rich and poor
view each other's excesses
shamefaced and angry.
It is only natural
to meet life with such passion.
How can any one of us,
born as we are from contradiction,
escape the tide that flows
around and through us.
The day is about to end,
like a poor man
thrown out of his house,
like the sobbing of the earth
at the edge of the flood.
The light is turning dark,
the gods are stepping down,
changing places.
Between the walls of the canyon,
the river draws to itself
the domain of shadow and reflection.
How small we are, how large?

AUTOBIOGRAPHY AS SPECTACLE

An Act of Liberation or the Illusion of Liberation?

GLORIA BIRD

Gloria Bird (Spokane) was born in 1951 in Washington State. She is the author of The River of History *(1997), and* Full Moon on the Reservation *(1993), which won the Diane Decorah First Book Award for poetry. She has co-authored with Joy Harjo the anthology* Reinventing the Enemy's Language: North American Native Women's Writing *(1997). She is an associate editor for the* Wicazo Sa Review. *Ms. Bird lives in Spokane, Washington.*

"Between colonizer and colonized there is room only for forced labor, intimidation, pressure, the police, taxation, theft, rape, compulsory crops, contempt, mistrust, arrogance, self-complacency, swinishness, brainless elites, degraded masses. No human contact, but relations of domination and submission which turn the colonizing man into a classroom monitor, an army sergeant, a prison guard, a slave driver, and the indigenous man into an instrument of production.

"My turn to state an equation: colonization = 'thingification...'

"I hear the storm. They talk to me about progress, about 'achievements,' diseases cured, improved standards of living. *I* am talking about societies drained of their essence, cultures trampled underfoot, institutions smashed, magnificent artistic creations destroyed, extraordinary *possibilities* wiped out.... I am talking about millions of men torn from their gods, their land, their habits, their life—from life, from the dance, from wisdom."

—AIMÉ CÉSAIRE, *DISCOURSE ON COLONIALISM* (21–22)

I begin with Césaire as a springboard into my discussion of being Native in America because it is good for perspective. (Who knows the tactics of colonialism better than the colonized?) Also, as a Native writer I am intimately involved in evaluating the aftermath of colonization and its impact that cannot help but shape my life and my own perceptions of the world. The competing stories of the indigenous peoples' sense of tribal histories and the privileged, legitimized perspectives on national history are on a collision course. It is from this place that I write, digesting, and ultimately attempt to undo the damage that colonization has wrought. From the Third World, the war dance in the blood has been reawakened.

Placing my story on public display is not something I have undertaken lightly. I enter this discourse hesitantly, knowing that my story, my life, my words are all a part of a spectacle, a peering into Indian life and thought that is in a sense intrusive. I have agreed because of the opportunity this offers to counter some of the misrepresentations of "Indian" that are legitimized in academia and pop culture about Native peoples. To this end, I would like to place my story against the backdrop of colonial context to address some of the misperceptions about Native people that compose the construct of "Indian" in the mainstream. I understand that the Native Other when viewed up close should pose no threat in a system where all transferable signs mirror the image of *all that I am not.* And so I begin with the paradox of constructing an idea of "self" in terms that presuppose a colonial mental bondage.

How I have come to know myself as Indian is contradicted continually in mainstream pop culture, in commercials, in ads in magazines, and in film. I recognize that outside of my immediate Native community, images of Indians are not held up as either the ideal or a template for "beauty." From my perspective, then, I am continually forced to negotiate between *what I know* and what I am told about myself as an Indian. Neither do I believe that my dilemma in this case or my particular experience is unique to me. As an example, I recall a day when my oldest daughter, who was four years old, came home crying. She had been next door playing with a neighbor's child. They had been watching an old black-and-white western on TV. The neighbor boy pointed to the screen laughing at the hooting Indians being chased by cavalry and told her that she was an "Indian." I hugged my heartbroken daughter and said, "But you *are* an Indian." She told me right back, "But I'm not *that* kind of Indian." None of us are.

I attended one year at public school (one out of two years spent outside of the Bureau of Indian Affairs Indian boarding school system). In the Washington State history text, the history of Northwest Native peoples was given in one full paragraph that highlighted Chief Sealth, for whom the city of Seattle was named. Not only did it appear that we Natives of Washington State did not exist, but we also had not apparently made a contribution worth mentioning.

Having lived on reservations during the early part of my life, the areas of Native history and shared cultural knowledge were often assisted by *place.* With our grandparents, we, my younger sister and I, traveled to the reservation to picnic, to sit under the trees on blankets and listen to our grandparents talking. We often found ourselves above Tshimakain Creek, where the land sloped down into a brush-filled ravine surrounded by pine trees, a favorite spot of my grandfather. On the rise above where we sat to eat stood a pine tree that formed a huge Y. In the center of its branches, where the two arms met the trunk of the tree, a cradleboard lay on its side, the tree growing up and around it. It looked as though a great hand had forced the cradleboard straight down into the heart of the tree, the headrest jutting from one side and the footrest from the other.

The story is a simple one: *The people were running from cavalry, and a young mother placed her baby in the cradleboard in the Y of the tree to save it, running, leading the cavalry in another direction from her child. She never returned.*

Later, the story of Colonel Steptoe, defeated at the butte named for his humiliation, unfolds. In retaliation, the army killed the Indians' horses, approximately seven hundred animals belonging to the Spokanes. Though these two events may not be directly connected they are to my mind a reminder of our history, filled with violence and oppression. The Spokane were considered "hostile" as were all tribal groups who refused to sign treaties, an act of resistance that would inevitably lead to reduced landholdings and confine them to a reservation.

My grandparents would have been too young to have lived through those times. But maybe my great-grandmother, my *tu pi ya*? While we sat contemplating fried chicken and potato salad, swatting the ants from the blanket, my mind rushed forward to the conclusion of the story of the baby tied into the cradleboard, who cried into the night, rocking in the arms of the sleepless tree.

Once, on returning home, I went in search of this picnic spot, driving in circles and following dead-end dirt roads to rediscover the place rooted in my memories as cradling tribal and family history. The site was not to be found. I was told later that some young men out on a drinking/shooting spree had shot the cradleboard into nothing. How well we Indians have learned from the colonizer to devalue our history.

Take, for instance, then President Ronald Reagan speaking in Moscow in 1988:

Let me tell you just a little something about the American Indian in our land. We have provided millions of acres of land for what are called "preservations"—or, "reservations," I should say. They, from the beginning, announced that they wanted to maintain their way of life as they had always lived, there on the plains and the desert, and so forth. And we set up these reservations so they could. And we have a Bureau of Indian Affairs to help take care of them. At the same time, we provide education for them—schools on the reservations. And they are free also to leave the reservations and be American citizens among the rest of us—and many do. Some still prefer, however, that early way of life. And we have done everything we can to meet their demands as to what and how they want to live. Maybe we made a mistake; maybe we should not have humored them in that wanting to stay in that primitive lifestyle. Maybe we should have said, no, come join us, be citizens.[1]

That the then president of the United States could be as publicly oblivious to Native peoples to the extent that our citizenship was in question, and that our livelihood was perceived as "primitive"; to deny the United States' obligation to uphold Indian treaties; to offhandedly refer to Indian reservations as "preservations"; to suggest that it was a "mistake" to set aside these lands (conveniently forgetting that this was done in exchange for Indians' ceding larger tracts of land); to suggest that this was a pacification move on the part of the United States, "to humor them," meaning us, is an outrage. I view Reagan's ignorance of Indian history, and consequently American history, as a mirror of America's basic lack of knowledge about us.

Only last year, my thirteen-year-old son came home from school with homework in social studies in which one of his questions required his answering that *wampum belts = money*. Commodification of Native systems of documenting agreements is a gross misinterpretation. Though it is not surprising that the historical significance of tribal agreements are mediated through Euro-American standards based upon exchange value.

The commodification of "Indian" has also reached the dialogue of Native peoples themselves, exemplifying, at least to this writer, the extent of the colonization. That my tribal ID has currency value and that tribes are now in the business of selling memberships clouds further the issue of legitimate claim. There is an irony to the *buying into* the effects of colonization, such as oppression, dispossession, the inherited guilt and shame many of us have been made to associate with our being Indian. The commodity gain, the immediate profit, is an assumed access to Native spiritual and cultural knowledge, which I read as the paraphernalia of romanticism of Native peoples. This phenomenon *does* have an exchange value in a corrupt system.

I understand that the way I have come to know myself as Indian has been a process of socialization which includes a way of perceiving the world that is unique to the people from whom I am descended. This apprehension of the world is culture bound and serves as an axiom of how my perception differs from *the Other's* perception or *reality* of the world. As I see it, the difficulty of communicating is not so much a question of speaking across cultures so much as it is a problem of speaking across realities that are culture bound. It's always easier to move through the world oblivious. By that I mean that it is easier to rely solely on what can be seen, touched, and proven. The extreme of that seems to be manipulating those who live obliviously by becoming an Indian-on-call, where one can always claim to have had a vision or a shamanic ancestor, for example. It appears that the quickest way to "Indianness" is the path of least resistance.

For Native peoples reared in Native communities, it is easy to spot the impostors, whose claim to "Indianness" as a solid, unbending reality reeks of self-centeredness and currency. Neither does a brown face automatically assure "Indianness," only a shared marginalization. I hear the storm, and in that the outcry at "essentialism." Still, I believe it is easier on the reservation to talk about *being* Indian. As my mother says, "If you have to claim to be a medicine man, then you aren't."

There is a comic scene, for instance, in the movie *Thunderheart* where the tribal policeman (Graham Greene) informs the FBI agent (Val Kilmer) that he, Kilmer, has had a *vision*. Incredulous, Greene tells Kilmer how he's lived on the reservation all his life and has never had a vision. This seemingly harmless, near throwaway scene points to one of the conflicting representations of "Indian," and exemplifies the contradictions at work in mainstream consciousness about "Indianness." Which is that anything Indian is public domain property and that sacredness is not respected or is applied superficially and arbitrarily to everything. But, hey, we're supposed to be entertained.

The basic premise for the movie relies upon our buying into the idea that a young man of Indian descent who has been reared far from his origins—and who has learned early to be ashamed of his Indian father—begins having visions. The plot is to take, for all practical purposes, this white guy, a descendant of Indian heritage, place him on an Indian reservation where he begins *seeing* things, namely, the massacre of Wounded Knee, his people being chased by cavalry and shot down, and remnants of the people dancing the Ghost Dance. We witness his transformation from anti-Indian white who disclaims the people who live in Third World conditions in the middle of the United States ("These are not my people") in the beginning, to pro-Indian red in the end, befriending along the way the tribal policeman and a medicine man—who tells him that "Mr. Magoo is not to be trusted."

The backdrop to the plot are the issues surrounding American Indian Movement (AIM, aka ARM in the movie) activity on the Pine Ridge Reservation, and the death of Anna Mae Aquash, though all of the details surrounding these issues have been fictionalized. But perhaps the saving grace of this movie is that the FBI are not the good guys—and, in fact, are the criminals. The uncomfortable truth of this film, if there is one to be found, is the representation of Indians oppressing other Indians. The usefulness of this last configuration should not be underestimated nor the impact upon Native communities overlooked. I will return to this idea later, but I would like to digress to comment upon why I find the critique of Native representation useful.

I began writing as a poet, but received my degree in literature. Along the way, I have been influenced by the personal narrative writing styles of African American feminist writers, and began writing criticism that attempted to *read* Native American literatures as a product of colonization, looking at ways that Native peoples have internalized colonial attitudes and beliefs about themselves that appear in their creative work. Early on, I questioned the usefulness of this type of criticism and wondered whether or not it was self-defeating to criticize other Native writers. That process could be thought of as playing into the hands of the colonizer. I am still struggling with the moral dilemma this poses for me; aggressive criticism goes against the way I have been raised. I suspect this has a bearing on why there are few Native writers who write literary criticism.

My alternative was to practice what I preached in my own creative endeavors. I began writing prose poems in which I incorporate criticism of Native representation—knowing full well that there would be critics of both the form and content. It is not my intention here to argue poetic strategies. If anyone has the need to engage in that discussion, they may.

The issues of representation overlap with and are as complex as issues of identity. We are often caught between the crossfire of realism and perpetuating stereotypes, especially when it comes to sensitive subjects. For instance, in how we represent the problem of alcoholism in our work or, simply, in how we discuss individual family/tribal history. For me, being Indian in the United States is filled with innumerable complexities and mixed feelings, but ultimately I have to attend to the business of interrogating damaging stereotypes and representations of Indians for the sake of my children. I take this as my duty, which it certainly is, not only for my own children, but the children who are entrusted to me throughout the school year.

I relate my story to that of my family and the people I am descended from, and it goes without saying that I cannot separate my story from theirs. We are a rural, reservation people and nothing in my memory is sparked by a single artistic influence. But I should qualify that statement. The women of my family have all been beadworkers, including myself, although this is not out of the ordinary where I come from. I have always felt that my family's lives and stories, and therefore my own, are uninteresting, and that we are an ordinary people. I've taken a lot for granted, and it is only through time that I have been able to recognize and distinguish our particular difference.

My grandmother, aunts, uncles, my mother, my sisters, and our combined children are enrolled members of the Spokane tribe of Indians. My ancestors are the *slawtews,* or Chewelah, a band of the Flathead. Among the immediate family (mother, sisters, and our combined children), we represent an amalgamation of tribal groups, including: Flathead, Spokane, Sonoran Mexican Indian, Hopi, Laguna Pueblo, Santo Domingo Pueblo, Thompson (Canadian Native), Haida/Lummi, and Nez Perce. We, my family, are the products of the ongoing process of colonization by virtue of intertribal marriage.

In Chewelah, the night sky mirrored the bowl of the valley held between the dark, lush mountains. In summer, my sisters and I would camp out in our grandparents' yard, making our beds of blankets and sleeping bags in the soft grass. In the fifties, my older sister was in her early teens. She taught us to distinguish the Big Dipper and Little Dipper in the sky—empowering knowledge for the minds of young Indian girls, that. We were comforted and smug in familiar surroundings. Life was so simple. And as we lay beneath the stars, she taught us sappy love songs that she'd learned from the radio, and it didn't take much coaxing on her part. We sang loudly, wildly up to the stars: "Will I be pretty, will I be rich? / *Que sera, sera,* whatever will be, will be." In the morning we shook the earwigs loose that clung to the bottom of our damp blankets and watched them scurry from the sunlight back into the deep grass.

I look back on our lives, which from that early age were instilled with the conflicting values of the world we lived in. On the one hand we learned to appreciate the stories of tribal history and the landbase, to read the sky, to find food in the woods. But then again, we were not encouraged as women to aspire to more than becoming someone's wife, all three of us marrying badly. *Que sera, sera.*

From my family, I have been informed by two conflicting narratives. There is a story my older sister told me about a woman who was captured by "stick Indians" and taken to the woods, where she lived with them for years. One day, she walked out of the woods and back to her people. It doesn't matter if the story is true or not. The point is that the story became family mythology that touched my life.

My father also tells a story of his ancestors, who came into this country from Mexico. This story, too, may not be true. He tells of an ancestor who was the daughter of a wealthy man who did not want his daughter marrying a poor man with whom she had fallen in love. He sent her away by stagecoach, and en route the stagecoach was robbed of its wealth and of the daughter by the man the daughter was forbidden to marry. Both disappeared together. Regardless of the validity of the story, it informs me of that part of myself that I have inherited from my father. What I "read" in my father's story is the internalization of class distinctions that are made by non-Native peoples. It is the inverted story of the Indian princess all over again—everyone, my father included, wanting to believe themselves descended from royalty, or if not royalty, the next best thing, the monied. I can only speculate as to the source of that wealth in a land notorious for the exploitation of its indigenous people, and would not pride myself for having descended from death-mongers.

Though both my grandparents on my father's side were very dark-complected people, my father claims he is "Spanish, not Mexican." At other times, he has claimed that we are descended from the Aztec. In the former, he has learned to deny himself and the part of him that is indigenous, a complete contradiction of how he lives his life as an "Indian" (going to powwows, serving on the Indian PTA, fathering Indian children, and collecting powwow music). How his contradictory attitude impacts on my perception as his offspring is that I choose to accept his parents, whom I never knew, as Native Mexican peoples. As Indian.

These stories that have informed my life have also informed my dreamscape: where stick Indians live, and a former life where I was also captive of a Mexican husband, but ran off from the hacienda with the gardener. I have no doubt that stick Indians *do* live, and that the gardener in my dream of my former life explains the connection to the father of my older daughters, a Pueblo.

In my mind, I am not any more Aztec than I am "Spanish." In my reality, my father is descended from Mexican itinerant workers: Mexican Indians. In an old photograph of his parents, they are a dark-skinned people: his mother is very round, her body like a mountain, as solid; his father is a sinewy-bodied man, the product of hard work. By heredity, it could be possible to call myself chicana, though I have been socialized as Indian. This is how I know myself.

To return to the subject of Indians oppressing other Indians, as mentioned earlier, and how this has affected my life, I offer another story. On the reservation, tribal politics are not all that different from mainstream politics—which are bound to issues of power, how it corrupts, how it is wielded unethically. Back home several years ago, one member of the Tribal Council had pushed a law through that allowed the enrollment of children who had one parent of Canadian Native descent in order to enroll his grandchildren. Ironically, Canadian Natives are not considered Indian, in spite of the fact that several of the northern-border tribal groups have families on both sides. Take, for example, the Okanogan band of the Colville, the Blackfeet, the Cree, and Iroquoian peoples.

Enrollments are part of the public record and are published in the tribal newsletter. When my mother saw the announcement of the enrollment of this man's grandchildren, she began the process of application for enrollment for my children whose father is of Canadian Native descent. She filed the necessary paperwork, and was soon notified that the law had been rescinded. My children were enrolled two years later, only after she spoke directly to Tribal Council members, demonstrating through oral repetition of family genealogy how that particular tribal councilman's great-grandfather and ours were blood brothers and how we are related.

There are two parts of my life: growing up on the reservation and then my experience in the educational system, which has separated me from that earlier life. To be eligible to attend BIA boarding schools, you have to be an enrolled member of an Indian tribe. Maybe more to the point is that students come from reservations. Why so few "Native" writers have been educated in that system—uprooted from their homelands, people, and lifestyles—has never, to my knowledge, been raised. It brings up, for me, other related issues. For instance, that the inferior education of Indian children has never become an issue, and that issues of class are not acknowledged. Yet I ask those self-evaluating questions of myself. I look at my participation in the process of undoing the damage that colonization has wrought, and do not hesitate to question, "Am I the product of my own assimilation, the mnemonic device of hegemonic order?" in poem.

What have not been adequately addressed are the many differences between the People and ourselves, meaning Native writers, and these *are* issues of class. I have been educated in a system that is designed to deny us on many levels; but as a participant in that system, which has earned me a "site of privilege" from which to speak, however marginally, what have I become? And if the answer to that question remains continually out of reach, it does not keep me from asking of myself, because I *say* as I please, is this an act of liberation or the illusion of liberation?

In the United States, the existence of the BIA boarding school system is not common knowledge. In an undergraduate course on the Brontë sisters, we were discussing the repressed atmosphere of early English boarding schools. The instructor blithely commented on how that system was in the historical past, and assured the class that there weren't such types of schools anymore. I offered that, yes, there were, and in fact, in this country. I mentioned how I'd spent most of my life before and throughout high school in boarding schools that were very much parallel to the oppressive atmosphere of those we were reading about. I was a scholarship student and, needless to say, my comments were not well received in the posh, private school among the bright-eyed eighteen-year-old children of the upper classes, and earned me thereafter the contempt of my instructor.

To return again to the words of Aimé Césaire with which I began, I would like to point out that as a Native person, Césaire addresses the same underlying issues of colonization to which Native people often refer. Although I feel that this is, or should be, a beginning place only, a recognition of the submerged pain that we have inherited. Because in that recognition, perhaps healing can follow. I frequently come in contact with outside perceptions of Native peoples, and cannot help but notice how, in general, there is an unwillingness to interrogate the site of privilege as it filters down through the strata of Native lives in the process of colonization. It is not either bitterness or conflict that motivates my work, though I am sure that some will perceive the material as conflict-motivated. There is a correlation I would like to make between qualitative lived experience and quantitative learned experience that from a Native perspective I feel is missing in our, meaning Native writers', discussions. This requires a willingness to uncover the layering of stereotypes and romanticisms of the public "Indian." For me, what has worked is that through a discussion of where the personal, the public, and political arenas intersect in my life, I can make sense of what "it" means to me. The "it," the dance through the sawing jaws of colonization.

NOTES

1. From "President Reagan's Remarks and a Question-and-Answer Session with the Students and Faculty at Moscow State University, May 31, 1988," in *Ronald Reagan: The Great Communicator,* Internet (p. 10 of 12), March 10, 1998.

Rituals of Memory

Kimberly M. Blaeser

Kimberly M. Blaeser (Anishinaabe), an enrolled member of the Minnesota Chippewa tribe, grew up on the White Earth Reservation in northwestern Minnesota. An associate professor of English at the University of Wisconsin—Milwaukee, she teaches Native American Literature, Creative Writing, and American Nature Writing. Blaeser's publications include a critical study, Gerald Vizenor: Writing in the Oral Tradition, *and a collection of poetry,* Trailing You, *which won the 1993 First Book Award from the Native Writers' Circle of the Americas. She is the editor of* Stories Migrating Home, *a collection of Anishinaabe prose. Her poetry, short fiction, personal essays, and scholarly articles have also been anthologized in numerous Canadian and American collections including* Reinventing the Enemy's Language, Earth Song, Sky Spirit, Narrative Chance, Returning the Gift, Women on Hunting, The Colour of Resistance, New Voices in Native American Literary Criticism, Blue Dawn, Red Earth, Unsettling America, *and* Dreaming History. *Blaeser is currently finishing her second book of poems,* Absentee Indians.

· I

Memory begins with various wonders. For my friend Mary, it began with hair. Her hair grew tightly curled, so strong the spirals defied taming. Brushing and combing brought tears. When Mary tried to run her fingers through her hair as she saw others do, her fingers became hopelessly captured by the curls. Hair, she deduced, must grow in loops, out of our head at one point, back into it at another. Because her locks had never been cut, the loops never broken, her fingers became entangled in the loops.

Perhaps that story delights me because it stands as a wonderful example of our always innocent attempts to explain the world. Or perhaps because it seems a fine metaphor for the looped relationships of family, place, and community, the innate patterns of ourselves that always keep us returning. No matter how long our lives, no matter how far our experience takes us from our origins, our lives remain connected, always loop back to that center of our identity, our spirit.

I believe we belong to the circle and, for our survival, we will return in one way or another to renew those rhythms of life out of which our sense of self has emerged. Some of us have a physical place and a people we return to. We also have what Gerald Vizenor calls the "interior landscapes" of our imaginative and spiritual lives. Perhaps our strongest link to the sacred center, the pulsing core of being, is memory and the storytelling and ceremonies that feed it—our own rituals of memory.

My memories entangle themselves oddly among the roots of several cultures: Native American, perhaps foremost in my mind, but also a German Catholic background, the culture of rural America, the close looping of small towns in the Midwest, and what I guess could be called Minnesota wilderness culture. But these several cultures did not always exist in opposition or in isolation from one another. I re-member Memorial Day celebrations when my father joined the Le-gionnaires in their visits to all the graveyards in Mahnomen and Nay-Tah-Waush. Uniformed, sometimes sweating in the early sum-mer heat, they marched to the sites, stood at attention as taps was played, and then, as a gesture of salute to the fallen veterans, they shot over the graves. Each year, through late morning and early afternoon, we followed the men on these tours. We stood, moved to goose bumps by the lonely trumpet tune, scrambling with all the other children for spent casings when each ceremony was concluded.

The last site on their schedule was the Indian burial grounds close to the BAB landing. As a child I saw nothing unusual about a dozen American Legionnaires marching back on the little wooded path and paying solemn respect to those Indian warriors who later I would real-ize were really of another nation. On this march through the tall grasses and hazelnut bushes that crowded the path, my older brother and I often fell in step. Several times I marched beside Sig Tveit and his trumpet, his arm linked through mine. We stood, all of us—those descended from settlers of Norwegian, German, or other European origins, and those descended from Anishinaabe or other Indian people. Together in a moment out of ordinary time, we paused in the little opening at the wooden grave houses, oblivious to the wood ticks, which must later be picked carefully from our clothes and our flesh, oblivious to the buzzing of mosquitoes or sand flies, oblivious as well to the more trivial tensions of contemporary politics. We stood to-gether in a great ceremonial loop of our humanity, in our need to re-member our ancestors and the lives they lived, together in our desire to immerse ourselves in their honor, to always carry those memories forward with us, to be ourselves somehow made holy by the ritual of those memories. We emerged quiet from those little woods, from that darker place of memory, into the too bright sunshine of a late May day in the twentieth century.

And then we arrived back at the sandy beach. The men brought out beer from the trunks of their cars, laughter and talk sprang up, picnic foods came out, and people would disperse again—to their own fami-lies.

I don't know if the Legionnaires still march back into the woods each year. I like to believe they do. For that kind of experience has helped me keep balance when the strands of my mixed heritage seem to pull one against another. However unconscious, it was a moment of crossover, a moment when the borders of culture were nullified by the greater instincts of humanity to remember and to give honor.

Perhaps the Memorial Days of those early years have became one of the watermarks of my life because they brought to ceremonial focus the many tellings of the past that filled up the hours and days of my childhood. As children, we were never so much taught as storied. All work and play had memories attached.

A walk to the outhouse reminded my mom of her aunt Florence, who once had a premonition that included the tilted floor of the outhouse at the farm in Beaulieu, of her aunt Florence, who everyone knew saw things, of her aunt Florence, who, she would later say, I must have taken after. The pocket of my grandma's apron must have held stories, for she would often pause, her hand in the bottom of that pocket as if fingering something, and then exhale a laugh and begin the account of someone's foolishness while out hanging clothes or picking berries or gone visiting. I know that the kerosene lamp gave off bright memories, for whenever it was lighted someone began to tell a Star Bad Boy story. The casting of a fishing line carried stories as it arced across the water at Bass Lake, plopped into the lily pads at North Twin, sent rings rippling from the bobber on Little Elbow. How my mom came to get her name, the bold skunks at the farm, Ivan and Bill's return from Indian boarding school—the stories rippled out from each moment until the very air seemed rich with presence and each breath we took seemed to fill us with history.

So each year when we stood before those wooden grave houses inhaling and exhaling memory, stirring the past with our breath, the trumpet music sang stories, the gunshots sounded history, and we immersed ourselves deeply in the rituals of memory.

II

On Tuesday, September 13, 1994, my mom's lifelong friend, Darlene Hutchinson, died of lung cancer. Darlene and Marlene they were. Born one day apart.

On the phone. My mom tells me. They were called the Siamese twins when they were children, so attached they seemed to one an-

other, so much time they spent together, arms or hands linked. Together they went on relocation to Chicago. Both went to Montana.
Both had cancer. Hutch, my mom always called her. Margo, she called
my mom. On the last day of Darlene's life, my mom fed her. Why am
I thankful for this final looping as if it were of my own life? Why do I
feel such gratitude to hear my mother tell me Indian songs were sung
and an eagle flew over when her friend was lowered into the ground?
Why do the stories of that relationship tell me so much about who I
am? Late at night, long distance, we recall together their life as if we
both remember the smell of Chicago stockyards, war rationing, and a
forties adolescence.

In the timbre of my mother's voice I hear myself spoken.

YOUR OLD LOST LOVES

for I have left
the same handsome men
standing in photos
with that girl
from my past
seeing them grow younger
leaner, taller
each year
hearing their deep
fine words
in the rustle
of each fall's leaves
together
barefoot
we walk
country roads
ankle deep in mud
I turn to you
young laughing ghost
hubba hubba
never quite matching
your daring
ooh la la
I need those memories

fourteen kids
and no papa

some lovers I know
in stories
some by heart
for I stand
just as you did
on the same lake shore
watching darkness come
suns setting in unison
casting long shadows
one after another
across the years

old lost loves
you and I
clasping identical dark hands
smelling of clay and damp pine
hearing again
song of owl and loon
endless and lonesome
lingering night sounds
bouncing
echoing forever
back and forth
across a single lake
called time

We are built partly of memories, some secondhand. It must be this way. We have a place in our family, we are recognized in our community, and our identity is formed through storied relationships. I never saw my father's letters from Billings to Marlene "Little Eyes" Antell, wasn't around for my brother's birth during a New Year's blizzard, don't remember my first antelope hunting trip at three months old, but these accounts have settled into my very marrow. I know those times as well as I know the stare of that old cat Beasty with the two different-colored eyes.

Sometimes my own memories form the shadowy background, sometimes the crisp outline of the stories told about the times of my early years. Although he died before I turned three, I remember my grandpa Antell. The feeling of his presence. Stored flashes of his image. I see his laughing face tipped away from me as if I were on his lap reaching for him in some child's game and he is craning his neck to keep himself safe from a pinch. This could be any of many times I saw his face that way, or it could be the time, as my mother reminds me, I sat on his lap telling him a story when, worn out from the day's work, he fell asleep and I tried to pull open his eyes with my fingers: *"Open your eyes, Grandpa, I can't see you. Oh, dare you are!"*

In my clearest memory, Grandpa Antell is standing just inside the door of the old farmhouse. Backlighted by the sun, holding his cap by the visor, he is dusting it off against his work pants. As the dust and the halo of sunlight mingle they must fray the edges of his physical form, because he seems partly made of light, and I hesitate to approach him.

"Yes. The boys were like that, too. They'd come in jest dirty all over, but it was their cap they would brush off."

"I also remember another time at the farm, when Robbie and I and some of the other cousins were standing at the screen door half crying because something had had happened. We had to stay there in the house you said while you went with the grown-ups down to the barn."

"You remember that?"

"Yes."

"That must have been when Dad died. We went down to cover his body with sheets. It was really windy that day and all the animals had gathered round him, as if they were protecting him from the cold wind, we thought. You were only two and a half then.

"We always think Dad musta knew he was going to die, because of some of the things he said and how he began trying to get things fixed up to make it easier for Mum. He had gone to the dentist you know to have something done, and for some reason the dentist made him have his heart checked. He never told anyone. We found that out later. But he must have known."

Around my own sparse but clear memories, I have built a man my family remembers well as kind, gentle, too generous sometimes, but with that Antell stubbornness.

"He could be hard, too. One time some people had come visiting and had stayed

on and on, pretty late. I guess Dad was tired because he said, 'Come on, Maym, maybe we should go to bed, these people might want to go home.' "

The stories we remember and tell have a mysterious way of journeying with us. We become the stories we tell, don't we? They inhabit us. We become the people and places of our past, because our identity is created from their stories. Looped together: memory, stories, being.

Although I don't remember my Grandpa Antell with his team of horses, wasn't born yet when he worked at the CCC (Civilian Conservation Corps) camps, I've seen those pictures and heard those stories. So John Antell inhabits more than flashes of images in my mind, his life history is familiar territory to me, and he has been built—both his good and his folly—somehow into my own character.

Our familiar sense of identity we construct not only from stories and memories, but from the overheard declarations of adults. *You have your father's smile . . . high cheekbones just like your mother . . . your grandfather's quiet voice.* Over time, that recognition of physical or temperamental likeness grows into something else. When one day we find ourselves saying my father and I have the same skin, my mother and I have the same eyes, we may also mean I understand what it feels like to be inside that skin, to look from those eyes, because I have done that with them. We have become each other too many times to easily believe we are separate creatures. It is an inherited curse—or a blessing—of my family to imagine so well that we live the lives of many besides ourselves, to identify so closely that we experience moments of another's life—sometimes only with the mind, sometimes with the body as well.

For many years my mother and I would manifest with bruises each other's injuries. And I remember that Billings summer day, in a younger world. My mother, brother, and I stopped our games, feeling unexplainably sad. We sat huddled together trying to cheer one another up. And then my father came home from work early. His hand and arm were bandaged where they had been struck by the bed of a dump truck. Our unease, we knew, was tied to his accident. I could tell many stories of intuition, premonition, shared physical phenomena, too many for them to be coincidence or to have only so-called rational explanations. And though I, too, have been inoculated with the skepticism of science, for me these experiences transcend the simple logic of this world which says we are separate, and attest to the mysterious power of family relationships.

III

You might say I grew up in the eye of a hurricane. *Gah-wah-bah-bi-gon-i-kah,* White Earth. Poverty, violence, legal entanglements, political battles, racial tensions, and perhaps despair were whirling about me, within range of my vision, but I was in a still place, kept safe by those who were themselves so often pulled into those destructive winds.

Money was always scarce and food sometimes in short supply, but I was oblivious in my child's world of plenty. Stories of those early days often astound me with their grisly facts. Of course I remember that, when living with my grandparents, we had no electricity, no running water, only wood-burning stoves, but that was normal life to me—no hardship. The Minnesota winters made trips to the outhouse an unpleasant task, dreaded, but one that we faced with humor. My mother tells this story: One day she complained about having to go to the bathroom and teasingly asked me to go for her. Ten minutes later she looked for me, spotted the outhouse door ajar and my chubby legs dangling from one of the seats. Hauling water, kerosene lamps, wood stoves, winter drafts through the windows, even commodity food and the church poor box—these are not hardships for children, when the house is full of people, laughter, games, stories, and affection.

So when I am told of the way my uncles were burdened with hunting for food, how they hoarded shells, careful not to waste a shot on only one duck, I am astonished because I don't recall hunger. When my mother describes the one-room apartment she and my father lived in when my brother was a toddler and I was a newborn and how they had to keep milk for me in a neighbor's refrigerator because they didn't have one of their own, I wonder that they didn't find us a burden. When I remember how the four of us used to ride around in my father's dump truck, my brother and I crowded on my mother's lap or close to her side to keep away from the stick shift, *I* remember sitting high, gleeful and giddy, proud to be in that wonderful truck. My parents remember the embarrassment of having to take that truck everywhere because it was the only transportation we had. They remember the trip from Montana to Minnesota, the four of us crowded in the cab of that truck for seven hundred miles.

Many of the stories my maternal family tells of one another from those days are stories of the small heroic acts that seem to come naturally to those in want: how my uncle Bill worked in Duluth on the ships and saved even the oranges he received as part of his food to bring home for his brothers and sisters; or how, as children, my aunts and uncles worked throughout the hot summer in the huge gardens their parents had on both sides of the road by North Twin, only to watch my grandpa load up his horse and wagon with produce to take to the Peabodys and other families who, he said, had no one to take care of them. But the teller of each of these tales seems to regret only the sorrow and pain borne by someone else, seems indeed unaware of the way the story reflects the pitiful reality of his own life.

When I think of that era in my family's history, I often think, with a mixture of humor and sadness, of a pair of silver-colored overshoes. In those days people did not often get "to town." The village of Mahnomen, though actually less than thirty miles away from Nay-Tah-Waush and Twin Lakes, was a great distance from the Indian villages and the lives people lived there. So when someone was going into Mahnomen, they often performed small chores for others in the community as well. One winter my grandma sent money for a pair of girl's rubbers. On the return trip her neighbor brought her the boots, but they were ladies' overshoes, made for high heels. Just a young girl, my mother wore them that winter over her flat shoes, each step she took accompanied by the *squish* of the excess rubber beneath her feet. Exports from white America, she learned early, were often a poor fit for Indian lives.

Though not burdened with the same racial prejudice built into the reservation economy, my father's large farm family struggled through the years, too. When he tells stories of the childhood he accepted so readily, it is a hard childhood, but one left to me to regret on his behalf. My dad remembers fondly the syrup sandwiches he often took to country school and the happy times when he and his brothers and sisters would bring a potato, which they were allowed to place on top of the big wood stove and which would then be tender and hot by lunchtime. His stories are not tales of longing, simply memories of what was.

Isn't it our perception of just that hint of quiet nobility that makes the poor past a place we sometimes regret having outdistanced? But I don't wish to romanticize poverty. The knowledge of my family's struggles is a painful story I regularly long to rewrite, may indeed be the story I rewrite with my own life. Yet whatever the reality of our conditions when I was a child, whether living with my grandparents on the Beaulieu farm or later in Nay-Tah-Waush, or with my parents and brother in Billings or Mahnomen, I was safely insulated by the presence and affections of family.

When there were more of us in one house than there were resting places, we slept crosswise in bed. And now, years later, when we gather for holiday meals (although all of us live in separate houses now), after dinner we may still plop ourselves sideways across a single bed together to laugh and talk and sometimes nap.

IV

Indeed, although I remember crying when my mother had to leave me behind when she went to the dentist, and missing my daddy when he was working construction in Montana, I think the first real heartache of my life came when I had to leave that safe, still center to enter school. In many ways I have been homesick ever since.

Perhaps this is a strange, even dangerous admission for someone destined to end up in the college classroom. But the educational system undoubtedly has the potential, perhaps the intention, to tear us from our best, most innocent selves.

At the same time, education has saved me from repeating a scenario of young motherhood, abuse, poverty, and alcoholism, too often played out on reservations around the country. I earned the degrees that unlock many doors in America. Through my work I have met Indian people on a parallel journey, people with whom I share a common history. I have gained the tools to tell the stories that deserve to be told, that should be heard, and I bring them into my classrooms. I try to share my perspective—not just my academic knowledge. Many times I think I teach to undermine the structure of our educational system; many times I fear it is undermining my own most sacred center. It seems frighteningly symbolic to me that one of the first things government boarding schools did when Indian children arrived was cut their hair. Education has always been for me a dangerous cutting away. The academic perspective implies a distance, a distance that cannot be fully retraced. Looking back across that distance, I feel lonesome.

RITUALS, YOURS—AND MINE

I.

living by your words
as if i haven't enough of my own
ever
to make them stretch
that long distance
from home to here
from then to now
and all the new words
i've ever read learned
or shelved so neatly
can't explain myself to me
like yours always do

sometimes that one gesture
of your chin and lips
my memory of
the sideways movement of your eyes
are the only words
from that language
i can manage
to put things in their place

II.

walked in on you today
closed the screened door quietly
so you wouldn't notice
just yet
stood watched you
mumbling shuffling about the kitchen
your long yellow-gray braid
hanging heavy down your back

wanted to see you turn
just that way
hear that familiar exclamation
you snapping the dishtowel
landing it just short of me
shame on me for surprising you

you walk toward me laughing
don't change anything I chant silently
wiping your hands on your faded print apron
you lay them gently still damp cool
one on each side of my face
for that long long second

"When'd you come? Sit down, I'm making breakfast."
I watch the wrinkled loose flesh jiggle on your arms
as you reach to wind and pin your braid
hurry to find your teeth behind the water pail
pull up your peanut butter stockings
pull down your flowered house dress
and wet your fingers
to smooth the hair back behind your ears

III.

smoothing away time with the fluid line
of your memory
I am in place at your table
in the morning damp of your still dark kitchen
I wait for you to come

stepping through the curtained doorway
you enter intent on this day
restart the fire
fill place the kettle
pull open the kitchen door
inviting daylight to come
welcoming it into your house—
bringing it into mine.

V

"Indians," Ed Castillo says, "can hold more than one thing sacred." With school began my double life. I went to Catholic grade school, where I earned a reputation for being quiet, obedient, pious, and bright. I learned my Baltimore Catechism—*"Who made you?" "God made me." "Why did God make you?" "God made me because he loves me."*—learned my singsong phonics—*ba be bi ba bu, ca ce ci ca cu, da de di da du*—

studied my spelling—*i before e, except after c, or when it sounds like a as in neighbor and weigh.* In between school days, we gathered hazelnuts, went partridge hunting, fished, had long deer-hunting weekends, went to powwows, went spearing and ice fishing, played canasta and whist, learned the daisy chain, beaded on looms, made fish house candles, sausage, and quilts. No one then questioned the necessity or value of our school education, but somehow I grew up knowing it wasn't the only—maybe not even the most important—education I would need, and sometimes we stole time from that education for the other one. My parents might keep us home from school or come and get us mid-day for some more lovely adventure on a lake or in the woods. I'm still thankful for those stolen moments, because now I know by heart not only the Hail Mary, the Our Father, and the National Anthem, but the misty prayers water gives off at dawn and the ancient song of the loon; I recognize not only the alphabet and the parts of the English sentence, but the silhouetted form of the shipoke and the intricate language of a beaver's teeth and tail.

My life at school and in the Catholic Church is officially recorded and documented—dates of baptism, First Communion and confirmation, quarterly grade reports, attendance records—just as my academic life is later documented at universities in Minnesota, Indiana, and Wisconsin. But for my other education, practical and spiritual, I have no grades or degrees, no certificates to commemorate the annual rituals. I have some tangibles of those processes—a jingle dress, fans of feathers, sometimes photos—but mostly I have stories, dreams, and memories.

I remember learning the sugar bush in the spring woods, following you follow the visor of your cap as if it were a divining rod. Stepping high through scattered spots of deep snow, laughing, I struggle to lift my leg, but only my stockinged foot comes with, leaving in the snowbank one of the boots I borrowed from my auntie.

Late March, in the still freezing nights and warm days, the sap begins to run. Thawing. Melting. Sap, *drip,* sap, *drip,* sap, *drip.* Spouts and cans adorn the trunks of the trees in the maple grove. Bright sun shines and the sap glistens as it drips into the tin cans, each drop sending new ripples through the clear liquid already collected.

We walk tree to tree, you with the heavy bucket, me emptying the cans, together sharing a sweet sip now and then. You pretend to squeeze the trees, convince me to lay my ear against the trunk to hear the sap run. Then the festive boiling comes. We sit for hours by the fire, the big cast-iron kettle suspended and filled with gathered sap, pine boughs handy to prevent overflow. With maple tea and March woods, the world seems full.

Together we remember, as if we used them, wooden spouts for tapping, birch bark baskets for gathering. And then you tell me of the sugar bushes of your early springs. In the drowsy afternoon beside the fire, your voice seems a part of the steam that rises steadily from the boiling sap. *"We went with a team of horses then, and camped in the woods until the boiling was done. We laid trap for beaver and spent hours chopping wood each day to keep the fire going. When the sap was running good, you could hear a pounding all through the woods."* I listen carefully, then and now, as if I can still hear the echoes. And sometimes I think I do, and sometimes I think it's just my story heart beating on and on like sap falling drop by drop—sap, *drip*, sap, *drip*, heart, *beat*.

VI

If I have found a way to balance the various loyalties with which my child's heart was early impressed, it was partly my grandmother who showed me the way. She never talked about such things directly, but she lived them and we all watched. Converted by missionaries, she learned the rules of Christianity and followed the ones that were most important, but she still retained the mystery and humor of her Anishinaabe heritage. She knew Indian medicines for everything from cough to poison ivy, she attended at births and deaths, and when she visited she still spoke her own language. She would scold her children for card playing and talking "dirty," but we all knew about the hidden deck of cards in her sewing machine cabinet and my mother remembers Mum's feigned confidences about one downtrodden character or another who, she would whisper, was my mother's real father.

And then, of course, I remember her comments about hair, which she seemed to see as one of the physical symbols of Indian tradition. Her own was long, below her waist. She wore it braided and in a bun during the day, hanging down her back at night. I'd often sit before her as she brushed my own hair, hair that made me stand out as a child amid all my black-haired relatives for it was almost white at birth, turning to blond and finally to a burnished brown as I grew older. White Head, my uncles called me in teasing. But my grandma didn't seem to mind the color—it was long. When I started Catholic school, she used to ask over and over, as if to reassure us both, "Those Catholic girls have long hair, don't they?" "Yes, mostly, I guess," I'd answer, although I had friends in Catholic school with little pixie cuts. "They keep their hair long," she would say, dropping her voice in finality. When I was in second grade, Grandma came to my First Communion at St. Michael's in Mahnomen. Pictures show the two of us together, her with her flowered dress and long hair done neatly in a bun, me with my white frilly dress and my Communion veil—over my still long ponytail. New ideas, new rituals could be sacred, too, as long as they didn't sever us from the old people, old places, and good, older traditions.

Grandma Antell never heard the story of Mary and how she believed hair grows in loops, but I think Grandma knew those loops, too. Long hair rooted like memories. Fed from within, the layers cover me with a warmth and cascade about my life. And sometimes, when I pull my fingers through the curls—it reminds me.

Life Woven with Song

Nora Marks Dauenhauer

Nora Marks Dauenhauer (Tlingit) was born in 1927. Her books are The Droning Shaman *(poetry, 1988) and a series of* Classics of Tlingit Oral Literature, *co-edited with her husband, Richard Dauenhauer, and published by the University of Washington Press. With Richard Dauenhauer and Gary Holthaus she edited a special issue of* Alaska Quarterly Review *in 1986:* Alaska Native Writers, Storytellers, and Orators *(with a revised and expanded edition published in October 1999). She has published in many journals and anthologies. Her awards include a Before Columbus Foundation American Book Award and the Governor's Award for the Arts from the state of Alaska. From 1983 to 1997 she was principal researcher in Language and Cultural Studies at Sealaska Heritage Foundation in Juneau. She is now a freelance writer.*

FIRST MEMORIES OF ART

I know it was a wonderful day, sunny, by looking at the green leaves that curtained the space between a spruce bough and the surface of the earth. The earth I could smell was an open one. I could see silhouettes walking and bending over at intervals. I felt I knew them. I could see bundles of turf rolled up like bales of cotton, at least three of them. One slightly to my left, another at an angle to the right of me, I could see only a crescent section of the last one, with shade-filtered light. I could make out the brown earth that I smelled with roots that looked like a giant drawing of a being with its veins exposed. The two or three people who were bending and walking at intervals were cutting and pulling the veins. The people were my grandmother, my aunt, my father's older sister, and a teenage girl named Shaa X̱aatk'í. When they were done, they unrolled the bales of turf to cover the bed of roots.

At a later time in my life this haunting image kept coming back to me. I asked my mother if she remembered such an incident in my early life. After thinking about it, she told me I went with my grandmother to pick spruce roots near Elfin Cove. My grandmother Eliza and Auntie Anny, with my mother's cousin Alice, were picking spruce roots to weave into spruce root baskets. This is the earliest I remember going for natural materials to be made into art.

Another time, it was midday. My grandmother was sitting in a nest of timothy grass near a playhouse. She looked like a little girl getting ready to go into the playhouse. She was so tiny she'd fit in nicely. She seemed to have the grass tangling around her fingers and hands. I could smell the strong, fresh grass. I could also hear the snapping of them as they broke. Beside her was a pile of grass broken at the joints. She kept on breaking these grasses at their joints. In the next image I remember the grasses in a pan with water. They looked like logs lashed together by loggers in a bay. The house was filled with the aroma. In my next memory I see the grasses lashed together, hanging up to dry on nails on a wall. Next to them were coiled in figure eights the spruce roots for baskets.

The winter was cold. We were living somewhere in a tent. I could hear my grandmother's squeaky thumb and index finger moving along a weft of a spruce root basket. My grandma Eliza always moved slowly in whatever she did, but she was steady. Her baskets were always rising in beauty. My auntie Anny wove fast, and her work always looked the color of cockle flesh. When Grandma and Auntie wove they both made squeaky sounds together. Next to them were coils of split spruce roots and split timothy grass to run around the baskets in geometric prints, row upon row.

My auntie Jennie was a beadworker and skin sewer. She was very good at keeping children quiet too. Early in my life she made dolls for me that we kept in a raisin box. The dolls were made from old cloths that had drops of seal oil on them. They smelled like seal oil and raisins when we played with them. We gave them names and carried on dialogue as the dolls' voices; they came to life as our relatives. I have many fond memories of Auntie Jennie, such as these, from various periods of my life. From time to time, they find their way into poems.

MY AUNTIE JENNIE'S BED

She always slept on a bed
with many pillows,
small ones, large ones,
old and new.
Once in a while
she made me sit among them
and made me play rag dolls
with dolls made of old rags
from whatever she decided
was good for dolls.
My dolls would always smell
of raisins and seal oil
because I kept them

in a Sun Maid raisin box.
She would help me make the dolls
talk to each other.
On occasion
she would have the dolls go fishing
or picking berries.
Each doll would have a Tlingit name
and the families would have names too.
She taught me how to give names
to Tlingit dolls.
I now give names to my grandchildren
and nieces and nephews.

Once when Auntie Jennie was beading moccasin tops, she made me strand red and white beads onto a thread. She drew a strawberry on a tiny moccasin top with a pencil. Then she showed me how to bead the strawberry: first outline it, then fill it in with beads. It looked wonderful, even with all the knots and tangles of threads on both sides of the top. She said, "Even when strawberries are ripe they're never the same size or look the same." She cleaned it up and made a moccasin with it. In this way it became real.

My father logged yellow cedar from many areas. He looked for trees that had a nice grain. He was a grand carver. He carved for four shops and the Alaska Native Arts Co-op (ANAC) Cache. He made miniature totems and life-size masks. In the boat or house or tent, every corner would have the scent of yellow cedar. He carved a lot, so all of us children learned to steer clear of his work area, especially where he kept his razor-sharp knives and the liquid paint he used on his totems and masks. When he began painting, his totems took on a new look. His masks took on a very mystic personality: the Kooshdaakaa, (Land Otter Man), the Frog Man, Fish Mask, Blackskin, and the Lady, all representing stories I heard falling asleep.

During the day, focus was on the work to keep alive and warm. After the evening meal all of the men who were along hunting or trapping participated in storytelling. This is when I would be pulled in and woven along into the stories. I imagined every incident or tragic ending. I usually fell asleep listening to the storytelling.

When I would waken, my grandmother Eliza and Auntie Anny would be weaving their baskets; when I went to sleep they were weaving. I sometimes thought they never slept and wove all night. Auntie Jennie was one who sewed. She never stopped her sewing either; while she sewed she hummed through her teeth. She never seemed to tire.

At times I'd watch my father line up his miniature totems all painted first with black lines, then the blue lines, then red lines, some brown or some yellow. Then he would pack them in a box with newspaper or magazine pages to keep the paint that hadn't dried yet from touching the other totems. Then he would take the totems to a merchant who bought them and sold them to tourists. When my father was in a hurry, my mother helped him paint the totems. They laughed at how their work appeared to them.

After he sold them, he would bring down to the boat or the house at Marks Trail groceries and a box of day-old pastries for treats, and for adults to eat with tea or coffee. My father loved wine. He sometimes made enough money to buy this too, which sometimes ran away with him. Other than this, he was a wonderful father.

My father was the youngest of four brothers. Every one of them was a carver and boat builder who came from a long line of artists and boat builders in Hoonah. During the winter, on bad days when they couldn't go out to hunt or trap, the men would carve something, after taking care of the camp's shelters and wood. The women took care of food and clothing. At times they made warm, thick mittens and insulators to wear inside shoe packs for when the men hunted in freezing weather. They mended shirts, coats, sweaters, and pants for both men and children in the evenings.

GAMES AND CHORES

On bad-weather days we would stay inside the tent, which the wind would puff up and deflate. I still love to listen to the wind rustling through the trees around us. Because our indoor living space was so crowded, we enjoyed outdoor activities. If we kids dressed warm, we got to play out in the wind. At such times we created many ways in which to play. One of them was playing with the wind. We would see how much we'd have to push if we ran against it. We'd talk to each other but our voices were blown off with the wind. We let it carry us along, then we'd turn and run against it.

On nice days we played with boats we made from driftwood. These are called *kooxwás'* in Tlingit. We waited until the tide was over the gravel above the seaweeded beach. We played with bubbles as the tide came in. I know some children would have loved playing on the beaches we played on with our driftwood boats. We had so much fun. We would tie a yard-long string to the bow of the boat, then tie the end to a stick about a yard or more long. Then we dragged the boats by the end of the sticks, taking them into coves. We acted the roles of the boat captains, deckhands, and cooks. The captain would say to the cook, "Got some coffee down there?" Cook always answered, "There's a little left. I'll make some more, do you want the last of it?" Captain answered, "Yes!"

At times our play crew unloaded salmon to a fish buyer. The fish buyer would ask the captain, "How's fishing today, Alex?" He'd answer, "Not bad." All this dialogue went on in Tlingit. When there was a monolingual, English-speaking captain, we imitated the language by what it sounded like to us because none of us could speak English. We spoke only in Tlingit.

During severe cold spells we played two-people string games called *tleilk'óo* in Tlingit. We passed the forms back and forth. Our favorite Tlingit game was the one called *k'ich'óo*. We played it similar to a dice game. This game was taught to us by our uncle John. He carved an object that looked like a tiny chair, one and a quarter inch square. We would throw this on a flat surface and call out which way it fell, sidewise with the back down or in a sitting position. You'd win if the chair landed in a sitting position. We played this while the wind whipped everything around us. We also played a wind and whistle game called *xoon kayénaa*. The wind and whistle toy was made like a big button, with two holes and a strong string drawn through them, then tied at the ends. To play you twisted away or toward you the two-hole object while holding the strings on each end. When the strings started to twist up, you started pulling on each end at once and relaxing after every pull. Each time you pulled on the string, the object made a wuffing sound from the wind it created. We took turns on the game, passing the object from one to the next child. We were allowed to play this one only when it was wet and rainy: the belief was that the toy was an instrument to start the north wind and rain, so we didn't play with it too much. We played this game after our chores were done.

One chore was to roll up our beds when we got up in the morning. On good days we'd shake out our bedding outside and air them. After breakfast we gathered driftwood that was twisted along the beach by waves for the tank stoves my father and uncles made for the tents to cook on and to keep the tents warm. On wash day we carried water for the wash and everyone washed their clothes and bedding and dried them in the sun and wind. On cold days the wash froze.

During the summer on nice, sunny days my father took us on the home fishing boat to anchor off a stream where we could wash all our soiled clothes. We would bring along bar soap, washboards, and washtubs. We all washed and dried our clothes on hot rocks, and the heavy clothing, like jeans, we hung on low-hanging tree boughs. Because it was sometimes so hot, we didn't have to warm the water on a fire. If we left it in a washtub it warmed enough to wash in, so we filled every container first. Mom washed Baby's clothing and hers and father's. All the kids who were able washed their own clothes, and the little ones helped by washing their own socks. In some cases the older ones helped them to wash them over again. When all the wash was done we would wring our clothes out into a giant quilt, and the trees seemed like they were hung with flags.

The subsistence lifestyle that our extended family followed required us to be self-sufficient. My father learned to do makeshift welding if something important broke when we were living in remote camps. Folk medicine was also important and kept us alive. Some of these memories took shape in the following poem.

GRANDMOTHER ELIZA

My grandmother Eliza
was the family surgeon.
Her scalpel made from a pocket knife
she kept in a couple of pinches of snoose.
She saved my life by puncturing
my festering neck twice with her knife.
She saved my brother's life twice

when his arm turned bad.
The second time she saved him
was when his shoulder turned bad.
She always made sure
she didn't cut an artery.
She would feel around for days
finding the right spot to cut.
When the doctors found out
she saved my brother's life
they warned her,
"You know you could go to jail for this?"
Her intern, my Auntie Anny, saved my life
when I cut a vessel on my toe.
While my blood was squirting out
she went into the night
and cut and chewed the bark of Devil's Club.
She put the granules of chewed up Devil's Club
on my toe before the eyes of the folks
who came to console my mother
because I was bleeding to death.
Grandma's other intern, Auntie Jennie,
saved our uncle's life when his son
accidentally shot him through the leg.
The doctor warned her, too,
when he saw how she cured.
Her relative cured herself of diabetes.
Now, a doctor keeps on asking,
"How did you cure yourself?"

BOAT BUILDING

When my uncles and my father built their boats, they bent and steamed the prow, keel, and rib planks. Of course, this method wasn't new to them. Before any English or Russian sailor appeared on the horizon, our people made great canoes, some seagoing and others for rivers, light enough to portage over glaciers, then on the return to come out under glaciers. They were made from cedar logs, then steamed open with hot rocks and water.

My father had a hot water tank he put over a fire with water inside. First he steamed the ribs, then he steamed the planks to curve and fit to the ribs of the boat. I never questioned the way they did this, but now I often think about it. It was natural for them to build their boats in this way. I never thought my father did high-tech boat building with innovations of his own. My father built Grandma's boat. He built Auntie's boat. He built a boat for himself and my mother when they got married. He, with his brothers and nephews, David, Willie, and Horace, rebuilt many boats. He rebuilt mine—a dinghy about eight feet long. I fished many summers. Each time they refinished an old boat, it took on a new look, and became more handsome, as all the grime fell from its face.

Getting ready for salmon seining was very complicated. Before fishing, my father and brothers began mending their seine net. A seine is a net used to catch salmon from seine boats. The seine is the one that is called purse seine. The smell of the web was very strong, smelling of tar. Nowadays, from time to time, I smell it in my mind. I know my father sometimes talked about putting his net in a mixture called blue stone. It was some kind of a chemical bath designed to keep the jellyfish away. They mended their webs by using a shuttle with web mending line in it. They measured each mesh from cross corner to cross corner, four and one quarter inch for each mesh, called *waak* ("eye") in Tlingit.

In early spring my father cleaned the bottom of the boat. This involved scrubbing off all the barnacles that grew on the hull of our boat. After the scrubbing and cleaning, Pop and his crew painted the bottom with copper paint up to the water line. Occasionally we helped with painting. If we didn't, it was because we didn't do a good job.

Our extended family used to fish off several boats. For safety, we usually traveled together in a small fleet of two, three, or four boats. The crew consisted of my uncles, my father's sister's sons, and my brothers. Some of my childhood memories of our boat are worked into poems.

A POEM FOR JIM NA<u>G</u>ATÁAK'W (<u>J</u>A<u>K</u>WTÉEN)
MY GRANDFATHER, BLIND AND NEARLY DEAF

I was telling my grandfather
about what was happening
on the boat. My father
and his brothers were trying to
anchor against the wind
and tide.

I could smell him, especially
his hair. It was a warm smell.
I yelled as loud as I could,
telling him what I saw.
My face was wet from driving
rain.

I could see his long eyebrows,
I could look at him and get
really close. We both liked this.
Getting close was his way of
seeing.

MUSIC AND SONG

When Saturday came and seine boats appeared around the point at Icy Straits cannery, after unloading and cleaning the boat and sitting down, Pop and his nephews and sons would bring out their guitars on the deck of the *New Anny*, tied to a float. The music carried on the water, an acoustic for their music. Many young fishermen still remember this even today. I asked my mother where they learned to play. She said, "Your father and his brother took lessons from a Hawaiian who lived in Juneau. He also taught your dad and his brother to dance Hawaiian hula." My father taught his clan sisters so they could dance at his brother's memorial.

The family was very musical. All my aunts and uncles sang in the Russian Orthodox Church. They were also ceremonial singers for potlatches, called <u>K</u>oo.éex' in Tlingit. My oldest uncle composed songs in Tlingit. He composed them for his brother's children. We still sing them today.

As I look back on my youth and childhood, I realize how much songs and music formed a good part of our lives. My extended family and my father and aunts all composed Tlingit songs. Most important of them was Shkík, my aunt Mary's mother, and the grandmother of my cousin Elizabeth Govina. Shkík was a shaman (*íxt'* in Tlingit). She had many spirit helpers and songs. Her spirit helpers are still singing today, through the visual art pieces depicting those spirits that my father carved as ceremonial commissions. Mrs. Lindoff, who was Aunt Mary's aunt, also composed many songs, as did her brother, Johnny C. Johnson. One of the most popular is about Tlingit elder Amy Marvin, and it is still sung today by the Hoonah Mount Fairweather Dancers.

On my father's side, my uncle Jim Marks composed songs about the women he loved. His brother John also composed songs. My father's clan sister by the name of Lxook composed many songs that are still sung in Hoonah. My paternal grandfather, Jakwteen, came from a river where you could hear the people singing above the noise of the river. He composed, as did his relatives from Chilkat. His cousin John Mark, and Jack David, my auntie Jennie's brother, were song leaders. A relative named K'eedzaa composed one of the favorite songs performed by our family dance group today. One of my mother's relatives, K'uxaach, builder of the Canoe Prow House along the Alsek River, also composed many songs, but we have been able to save only two of them.

Lullabies were an early part of our lives as children. When we were old enough to stand, my grandfather would sing lullabies to us and we would dance to them. My cousin Betty, who was the oldest of the grandchildren, danced every time our grandfather started to sing. One time he told her, *"A kínt iyahán, Chxánk',"* literally, "You're not standing close enough," a euphemism hinting that one needs to improve one's dancing. Little Betty took him literally and thought she should move out a little, until she had moved so close to the stove that she was nearly burning! One of my uncles composed lullabies for the girls in the family, and sang lullabies for the boys. He had nicknames by which he called all the boys.

As we grew older, work songs became part of our lives. Whether we were cutting up salmon or picking berries, you could hear my aunts and grandmother singing. Today, I sing these lullabies and songs for my grandchildren and great-grandchild. Here's one of my favorites, which I translated into English.

> Let's go up the hill,
> little girls.
> I thought I saw
> elderberry blossoms over there.
> It was her gray hair
> that I saw,
> that I saw
> there.

This is the art I grew up with. My whole family is artistic. My brothers are still carvers and my sister Florence and my mother are still artists in beadwork. My mother had a one-person show of her art at the Alaska State Museum in March 1988, entitled "Wax, Facets and Felt: Beadwork by Emma Marks." My cousin Betty, Uncle John's daughter, had a Tlingit art shop on the dock in Juneau where tourists disembark.

SCHOOL AND CHURCH

Our family has lived for five generations on a small piece of land on Douglas Island, across the Gastineau Channel from Juneau. There was no road when I was a child, so we had to walk along the beach for about half an hour to meet the school bus. Taxis would also drop us off at that point. Before the Juneau-Douglas bridge was finished in the mid-1930s, the family would row across the channel to shop, go to movies, or to church. The family believed in a higher power, and my uncle set aside time for prayer wherever we were. On Sunday, we all rowed across for services at St. Nicholas Russian Orthodox Church. Whenever we were in Hoonah, we were also active in church activities, especially meetings and choir practice. Often these were held in the clan houses. When we went to church school, I tried to learn to read Russian prayers. As I look back on things, I guess I had the desire to go to school all along.

But going to school wasn't easy. During my childhood, truant officers often detained families such as ours, forcing them to settle in towns.

This made it impossible to pursue the traditional seasonal subsistence economy, so elders were suspicious of school authorities. When we stopped in Hoonah or Juneau on the boat, my father and the rest of the family hid the children from the school authorities. My brothers, sisters, and I were so restless we were like bees in a beehive, ready to drone out of the boat the minute we were allowed to go outside.

At one point while we older children were going to school in Hoonah, we took our little brother Raymond along. We never heard the end of that all during our growing up! Whenever we got to Juneau, the family would have liked my father to stay for a little while longer, and settle down for the rest of the winter. Eventually, we children ended up in school full-time. For me, at the age of eight, it was my first exposure to English, having grown up until that time in a culturally conservative, monolingual, Tlingit-speaking environment. I have mixed memories of school. The first memories are of being rapped across the knuckles with a ruler for speaking Tlingit, and of always being blamed and punished for reasons I didn't understand, for which I didn't know enough English to explain or defend myself. I could defend myself pretty well with my fists on the playground, though. I used to beat up boys for hitting me with snowballs and for teasing me. I even chased them into the boys' bathroom to beat them up! Usually they became my friends after I beat them up.

When I turned sixteen, I was all set to go to school at Sheldon Jackson School in Sitka. I had money that I made from my first job in one of the canneries that I was to work at throughout my life as a mother and housewife (more about this below). But when my grandmother got wind of my plans, her only comment was "She might as well take my head with her!" And that was the end of my education for many years.

Our first to graduate from high school was Horace Marks, my cousin; then there was Ron Williams, another cousin; and my brother Alex Marks. There were many others who followed. Some were kids from *New Anny*, others from my uncle's boat, *Urania*.

I would like to note here that Horace went on from high school to become the Alaska Native Brotherhood Grand Camp secretary in the late 1930s and early 1940s. He was also involved with the forming of Indian Reorganization Act councils. His older brother, Austin Hammond, gave us wisdom to continue into the twenty-first century. He went on to be the leader of Raven House and an officer in the Salvation Army. When asked how he could be both a leader of Raven House and a leader in the Salvation Army, he responded, "God made us to be Tlingit and to continue our culture." He didn't see the need to abandon our culture. Several years ago he set up a culture camp, Lkoot Kwáan ("People of Chilkoot"), where our youth can learn about being a good human being. He left to us of the Lukaax.ádi clan a trust of Raven House for us to continue to practice our culture. To help our education in Tlingit culture, language, literature, and use of land, Austin and his brother Horace found a moviemaker to document his argument for Lukaax.ádi land in Chilkoot. The state had withdrawn many Lukaax.ádi sites, mostly historical, around Haines. With the help of my father's third-grade education from Chemawa Indian School, and with his own Tlingit knowledge of land ownership, my grandfather Jim Nagataak'w applied for ownership to the land my family lived on. He and my father camped at the door of BLM (Bureau of Land Management) until the bureaucrats tired of them and started proceedings for them to gain title to the land now called Marks Trail in Juneau (named after the logging trail blazed by my grandfather). They applied for land in 1916 and received the deed for it in 1921. My father and grandfather stood at the government door until they softened their path to their land. Most of my grandfather's original land was lost to the miners, but what remains is one of the few parcels of land still in Tlingit possession.

Up until the 1960s Pop and Mom raised us on native foods. They supplemented them with Western foods bought with totem pole, seining, beadwork, and basketry money. Seasonal cannery work was also a major source of cash income for the women, and most of us worked in canneries for many years. I guess we had fun. But, in retrospect, it is sobering to be more conceptually aware of the discrimination we all experienced, especially segregated housing. The white women's bunkhouse had showers and toilets, while the Indian families lived in cabins with no toilets or running water. But this experience, like others, gives rise to poetry.

SALMON EGG PULLER—$2.15 AN HOUR

You learn to dance with machines,
keep time with the header.

Swing your arms,
reach inside the salmon cavity
with your left hand,
where the head was.

Grab lightly
top of egg sack
with fingers,
pull gently, but quick.
Reach in immediately with right hand
for the lower egg sack.
Pull this gently.

Slide them into a chute to catch the eggs.
Reach into the next salmon.
Do this four hours in the morning
with a fifteen minute coffee break.

Go home for lunch.
Attend to the kids, and feed them.
Work four hours in the afternoon
with a fifteen minute coffee break.

Go home for dinner.
Attend to kids, and feed them.

Go back for two more hours,
four more hours.
Reach,
pull gently.

When your fingers start swelling up,
soak them in epsom salts.
If you don't have time,
stand under the shower
with your hands up under the spray.
Get to bed early if you can.
Next day, if your fingers are sore,
start dancing immediately.
The pain will go away
after icy fish with eggs.

TLINGIT RENAISSANCE: TLINGIT LANGUAGE
AND ORAL LITERATURE RESEARCH

In 1968 my uncle Jim Marks passed away, leaving my aunt Jennie Marks as a widow. She set aside this retirement stage of her life to teach us Tlingit dancing, and we formed the Marks Trail Dancers in 1969 or 1970. She taught us our Lukaax̱.ádi clan songs and we danced to them. We became a popular group.

Pop got excited and made me a rattle. Mom was also excited and made us dance jewelry and tunics. I made button robes for friends and fund-raisers. Our brother John and Mom made ear yarns for dancing our special dances. My father and mother, with the help of my brother, made a set of Raven wings and headdress in which my daughter Le performed the Raven dance.

Mom made me a dance tunic that I still wear. My father later made me a headdress called G̱eesán Shakee.át and sent it to me for Christmas. I unveiled it at Auntie Jennie's memorial. By this time we were splitting off into educational institutions. My friend Rosita Worl went to Harvard. My daughter Le also went off to Harvard. After my children were out of school, I completed my GED and went off to college at Alaska Methodist University (AMU) in Anchorage, where I received formal training in linguistics and folklore. I graduated in 1976 with a BA in anthropology with a concentration in Tlingit literature. At AMU I began the literary work that is now finding its way into publication some twenty years later.

While I was at the university I read *Beowulf* and *Njal's Saga*. They seemed so Tlingit to me in their concern with funerals and family trees. I read Homer, Ferlinghetti, e. e. cummings, Basho, John Haines, Gary Snyder, Dennis Tedlock, and Han Shan. They became some of my teachers. I transcribed and translated Jessie Dalton and the rest of the oratory delivered at my uncle Jim Marks's memorial as a directed study with R. L. Dauenhauer, who would later become my husband. I realized later that these Tlingit orators had become my instructors in Tlingit literature.

Later, as younger Native American writers began to appear in print, I became excited and inspired initially by their work, and subsequently by meeting in person Simon Ortiz, James Welch, Joy Harjo,

Luci Tapahanso, and others. I also began to discover the work of earlier Native writers such as D'Arcy McNickle.

Following my first year at the university, I was hired by Dr. Michael Krauss of the University of Alaska Fairbanks to do fieldwork with Tlingit elders in southeast Alaska, as a project of the Alaska Native Language Center (ANLC). These elders also became my instructors as I worked with them. Some of them gave me advice when I worked with them, others told me off. Working with ANLC helped me to be in the right place at the right time, and tape-record many elders who have since passed on. We are still working with this backlog.

After finishing my BA degree, I continued to work on Tlingit with my husband. Most of this work was an overload, done late at night, in addition to our regular jobs. In 1983, we decided to move to Juneau to be closer to our family, and to devote ourselves more fully to Tlingit. My husband resigned his university position in Anchorage.

After we moved to Juneau, jobs opened up for us at Sealaska Heritage Foundation (SHF), an Alaska Native nonprofit organization, where I was principal researcher in Language and Cultural Studies from 1983 to 1997, working primarily with transcribing, translating, and publishing Tlingit oral literature.

We bought land uphill from my mother's beach property on Douglas Island, across from Juneau. The land we bought was originally part of my grandfather's land that was taken during the gold rush and eventually subdivided by the descendants of the original miner. At that time, Natives were not able to file claims, but miners could claim Native land right up to the houses the Natives occupied. We bought it back, built our house, and built a new smokehouse on the beach.

CONCLUSION

My life now is in many respects the opposite of my childhood. Then, we lived much of the year on our boat and in hunting, fishing, and trapping camps in "the bush." We came to town only for provisions. Now it's a treat to go out on a boat.

Coming to town in my childhood put us into contact with whites.

With this contact came our first experience with racism. From the first time I saw white hate I experienced racism as a white-hot whip that can bring you to your knees with one strike. As a child, the stares of white children were so hot and cruel that I cowered and wanted to hide and never come out again. I tried to shield my little brothers I was baby-sitting with my arms. I had nowhere to run with them. The boat we were on had dried up on the tide flats, and it was too high for me to take them down from it. So we stood and took the rain of spears from their eyes until they left us alone because the tide was coming in and they couldn't taunt us anymore. Up to now, after many decades, I'm still stinging from their white whip. These patterns still exist, they are alive and well today, and it hurts to see my grandchildren experience them. This was a negative aspect of growing up, and I try to be assertive today to help defend our youngest generations from the same patterns of abuse.

On the positive side, all through my childhood I was surrounded by artists at work. It was a necessity to bring groceries into the house. I'm sure my father was influenced by his mother's brothers and uncles. He didn't try to make a first-rate piece of art for a tourist sale. The market didn't give him the price he wanted for it. Only after the 1944 Hoonah fire was he commissioned with his brother Jim for first-rate pieces, when he carved the Mount Fairweather Hat and Mountain Tribe's Dog Hat mentioned above. He put his heart and true talent and inspiration into such clan commissions, which yield more cultural significance than cash income. Following the Hoonah pieces, he made other clan commissions, including a Frog headdress for Lillian Hammond of the L'uknax̱.ádi (Coho Salmon) clan, and a rattle for Austin Hammond, steward of Raven House in Haines, Alaska. As I see my father's work in ceremonial use today, I'm sure it will stand the test of time.

We will keep singing my uncles' songs. We will wear my mother's beadwork, which improves with time. My brothers and sisters all have her beadwork. She made them as gifts. My children, nieces and nephews, and grandchildren all have her works of art. She made beaded symbols for a vest for my husband, which he treasures. I'm also lucky to have one vest made with her creations. My mother has strung many glass beads and sewed beads throughout her life.

I am what I am from my family of artists and friends, from books and professional colleagues, and most important, from my husband and partner in my profession, Richard.

Thanks to the editors of the following journals and anthology, in which the four poems included here (and which are from a forthcoming volume) were first published: *The Wicazo Sa Review, A Journal of Indian Studies* ("Poem for my Grandfather" and "Salmon Egg Puller"), *Rolling Stock* ("Grandmother Eliza"), and *From the Island's Edge: A Sitka Reader* ("My Auntie Jennie's Bed").

The Good Red Road

Charlotte DeClue (Kawashinsay)

Charlotte DeClue (Kawashinsay) was born in Enid, Oklahoma, in 1948 to an Osage mother and a Kiowa father. She has been a social worker, worked in bingo halls, raised children, taught writing, and given performance poetry readings throughout the United States. Her work has appeared in a number of anthologies and literary journals, most recently in New Letters. *She is currently working on short fiction and has recently released an audio tape (from Howling Dog Press) called* Ten Good Horses.

Chotsi Little Star is my name. When I was very young, my uncle, Thatcher Bowlegs, gave me a naming ceremony. I was given the Indian name, Kawashinkashinsay, Kawashinsay for short, which means "ponytail." I was also given two ponies, Smokey and Daisy. They accompanied me when I hired on to do a children's television show in Hollywood. Recently I have been working on a series of autobiographical accounts of my early days as a child actor. They refer to a context I have long outgrown, although in writing them, I am forced to relive them. Hollywood was hard for a child; I learned that there were a lot of people there who did not like children. They treated horses badly in Hollywood, too.

My family kept a book called *The Good Red Road*. It was the job of my mother, and the other women in the family, to inscribe passages in the book. It read like a family Bible. But it was a good source of learning since many of our family members were scattered throughout the countryside. We even "went abroad," so to speak, traveling, coming home, and transcribing our experiences in journals and diaries.

When those experiences made reference to Wakontah, the Great Spirit, or any of the great mysteries we inherited from our spiritual clans, those would go down in the "book," *The Good Red Road*.

It was there I learned the value of writing in a language I would eventually inherit from the non-Indian world. But it was for our people that we first wrote.

Indian people have always formed a valuable audience for self-expression, mine included.

It is for my people I write, and to my people I dedicate my work.

In the course of giving readings around the country, young professional "skins" will come up to me and ask, "How do you do it?"

The first thing I tell them is that you have to believe in yourself, because if you don't, there's nobody else who will. My acting, my experience with dance, I've learned as much or more about life from them than I have from literature or engagement with the "literary profession."

But the model of other writers *has* been important to me. It was the work of Simon Ortiz that influenced me to become a writer. Simon had just come of age as a poet when I began to read him, and I forced the faculty then helping me design independent reading course work in Native American literature to include his work along with the fiction of James Welch and N. Scott Momaday.

I want my art to stay alive; I want it to reach the audience it was intended for, an audience of Indian people. That way there will be another generation of Indians who will not only be strong in their art but strong in their identity as tribalists, too.

We are a tribal people.

A few years ago, I did a residency at a high school in Anadarko, Oklahoma, which has a large population of Indian students. One of my colleagues at that time, a well-respected playwright named Linda Poolaw, asked me what I thought she might offer these students. Linda is a Kiowa who had attended school in Anadarko, and I suggested that she just tell them what it was like for her when she was in high school. She brought tears to my eyes as she recounted her experiences of those days, and how she first learned what it meant to be Indian.

"You know how I found out I was Indian?" she asked an audience of Indians and non-Indians. "By getting my teeth kicked in for being one." Another colleague in Anadarko told of his encounter with a group of white students at a local Dairy Queen who had refused to sit down next to him, an Indian. I have such stories, too—like the time I auditioned for and won a role as the voice of Beetle Bailey for a syndicated cartoon. At a state speech tournament, I gave the same performance that had won me my role and got disqualified for not meeting the tournament "standards." Later, I was told by several of those who had supported me that I had been denied my first-place ribbon not because of my talent but because of my race.

No wonder we question whether things today have really changed.

Fortunately, Indian teachers and parents see the real value of our work as Native writers. They see that, after all, we are just carrying on a tradition taught to us by our ancestors . . . that we are valuing who we are as Indian people. We Native writers are role models for future generations.

When I was very young, I had an incurable habit of trying to imitate the world around me. If I saw a rabbit running across the field, I would try to jump like her. I learned to climb trees by watching squirrels. Riding horses came easiest when I found out what it felt like to be on all fours. My problems started when I began to imitate the people around me. It seemed I always chose to imitate just those things people wanted to hide about themselves.

For example, there was the time my big brother got fat and tried to suck his stomach in, especially around girls. He got mad one evening when I strutted around the dinner table like the cockeyed rooster who was always showing his chest off in the chicken coop.

Soon I learned that my antics could get the attention of my elders. In Wa-zha-zhe society that meant approval, as most elders were proud of their children.

When company came over I would get them to pay attention to something I had just learned or accomplished

"Watch this," I would insist as I clicked my tongue and pranced around like when we trot dance.

"Oh, yes," they'd say, smiling. Which meant I had really achieved something.

Every little achievement meant something I could use to impress my elders. It was a little like putting notches on a *coup stick*.

But every phase has its ending.

One day my mother took me to visit the home of a Ponca family down the road. There was a very old woman, the grandmother, sitting outside under an arbor. Most Ponca children were good at about everything, especially softball. So there wasn't much I could do to impress her.

There was something I did have to show off. I had lost my four front teeth. So I casually walked up to the old woman, pulled my mouth back with my fingers, and said, "See."

Her face lit up and she started laughing.

"See," she said back to me. She was toothless.

Such a story has to happen only once in your life. It resulted in my being sent to my room, where I had to sit in the corner and think about what I had just done.

My mother, who never spanked us or raised her voice, had her own unique way of proving her point.

"Have you thought about it?" she asked me through the doorway. For the life of me I couldn't think what I had done wrong.

The spider crawling up the wall to build her web provided the answer. "You mocked your elders," the little spider said as she watched her shadow fade into the corner of the room.

"Have you thought about it yet?" my mother asked one more time. Sitting in the dark was not pleasant.

"Yes," I said meekly.

"What was it, then?" she quizzed.

I sucked in my cheek and sighed, resigning myself to her wisdom. "I mocked my elders," I answered.

For giving the right answer I was allowed out of my room. I emerged, feeling like a wounded coyote crawling out of its hole.

From then on there seemed to be a part of myself that never felt completely understood. I think now it must have been that part of myself, and the need to express it, that influenced me to write.

It has been a long, hard road.

My mother, who never allowed anyone to complain, would have said, "A long, hard road, huh? So is being Indian."

Most of the Indian people I grew up with were highly motivated, always dancing or singing, always scribbling pictures with chalk or pencil, always telling stories. They were naturally expressive people. Most of what they expressed was a reflection of their world, a natural world filled with mystery and beauty.

As tribal people we grew up with talent and ambition. Most of us have gotten an education, made our mark on the world, and settled in places that are familiar to us. These places we call "home," whether that is a reservation, a small Oklahoma town, or a big city.

It is all the same—indigenous territory. We are nothing like the stereotypes thrown at us in B-rated western movies or early-day

American novels. It is a wonder we survived at all without losing our sense of identity.

For me, writing became just another way of expressing my identity as an Indian woman, and exploring that part of myself that has always needed to be understood. But it was those early learning lessons that shaped how I felt about the world. No wonder; I had some very good mentors.

Everything I learned as a child became a preparation for life. Even combatting the racism and insensitivity I encountered in school was like sitting in the corner of my room until I had learned the right answer.

During a workshop that I was giving for the Indian Education Program in Oklahoma several years ago, I noticed one of my students, a ten-year-old girl with a very troubled look on her face. We had been discussing books about Indians.

"What's wrong?" I asked her.

She shook her head and I told her to think about it and tell me later what was bothering her.

At the end of the day she came up to me, tapped me on the arm, and said, "I'm from Skedee." Skedee is a Pawnee settlement not far from where I grew up.

"Ah-ha," I said, thinking she was about to tell me about her people.

"Those books over there at that place," she said, pointing in the direction of the Norman Public Library, "they lie about us."

"Yes, some of them do," I reassured her. "Now, tell me how they lie."

It didn't take her long to correct every misconception ever written down about her people. Something even white academicians have never been able to do.

That is why it is important for us to develop talent in our children. They will one day be the next generation of Indian writers and artists, who will continue to correct the mistakes of the past.

I see my generation of Native writers as a transition linking the past with the present. One day our children will be the contemporaries and we will have become the "ancestors."

In the process of developing my work as a writer I find I am oftentimes at odds with the label "Native American writing." Even though it connects us with a community we value, it often becomes a box that is too confining and restrictive.

When I first started submitting my work for publication I was an undergraduate at the University of Missouri in Kansas City. I was told by the writing establishment at the time that my work was "too ethnic" for consideration. I was determined to prove them wrong. I would submit my work with only my name, making no reference to my race, wanting my work to be considered on its own merit without a label.

Even though the response to my work was favorable, editors would write back with "We like your work, but is there something we should know about you?"

I would respond, "If you are asking if I am white, no, I am not. I am Osage from Oklahoma."

If it had not been for presses like Strawberry Press, which published my chapbook, *Without Warning,* I would have spent my entire career having to explain myself. There has been a sufficient amount of good Native American anthologies and publications that we should be able to be considered serious writers, apart from the label. What we need is more people who are willing to publish us independently of the label.

The young girl from Skedee had not learned to label her thinking. She had simply begun by asking herself the right questions and providing the answers. Hopefully she and her peers will be accepted for their ability to think apart from so-called mainstream society. After all, how can we move forward if we are not allowed to challenge existing conceptions of ourselves as Indian people?

All you have to do to test the sincerity of a person who says they are sympathetic to our literature is to watch them wince when you use the word "Indian" instead of "Native American."

Recently I got involved in a discussion with an editor from a national review magazine. During our conversation he used the term "Native American" at least a dozen times. He went so far as to nearly correct my reference to myself as Indian, as if I no longer had a right to define myself or my work in my own terms. At the same time he objected vehemently to my reference to him as a "white man."

It reminded me of an editor from Chicago who wanted me to change the term "white" in one of my poems ("Voices") because he was afraid it would be offensive to some of his readers. I refused. He published my poem anyway.

No longer should we have to be told that we need to change our language in order to conform to a white audience.

I write for myself and the people I know and care about. In most instances those are Indian people. But I have learned that most people just enjoy a good story, a strong poem, an entertaining play. Most people who come to hear me read are simply interested in hearing what an Osage woman has to say. Few of them sit and make distinctions about me based on the color of my skin.

Indian people appreciate writing they can identify with, in the same way as non-Indians. Indians remain our most valuable audience.

My work as a Native writer has involved me in issues that have ranged from religious freedom legislation to debates on the exploitation of indigenous cultures. Those issues are important to our survival.

I am more likely to read a book about women's health care than a book about the Ghost Dance religion, especially by a non-Indian author. When I first heard Rita Dove read her poem "Parsley" on public television, I was stirred by her understanding of the genocide against her people. Yet I am rarely asked about my impression of the work of an Afro-American woman poet. I have been asked to review books on such things as "The Religious Practices of Native Prisoners in Nebraska," but rarely am I asked my opinion about Fassbinder, whose films I enjoy. My non-Indian colleagues will invariably bring up the most recent book they have read about Indians. But they never involve me in discussions about Shakespeare, which I devoured in high school, learning to recite Portia's speech.

Few white scholars are interested in hearing how I won a Jim Thorpe athletic award when I was fifteen, and how it felt to be forced to compete in a segregated field separate from white students. Or how I had to design my own course work in college in order to study the work of Native writers because such literature was not included in the curriculum.

Most of us are multitalented and skilled in a variety of areas. Yet I have encountered people who are surprised to find out that Maria Tallchief, one of the originators of the American School of Ballet, is a member of my tribe.

It reminds me of when I heard Buffy Sainte-Marie, a recording artist from the Cree Nation, speak on behalf of her people during the

Longest Walk in the late seventies, a walk across the country to protest anti-Indian legislation. She said, "Indians have to be 200 percent human beings. We have to be 100 percent good in the white world, and we have to be 100 percent good in the Indian world."

We should no longer have to prove we know what we are talking about. Our contribution to the field of literature merits consideration of us as writers first. If the label "Native American writing" is to remain meaningful, we need to take it back and redefine it to fit our needs and the needs of our communities.

One of the most influential experiences in promoting my work *Ten Good Horses, Stiletto 2* (Howling Dog Press) was a series of readings I did at the Denver Center for the Performing Arts. Not only was it a chance to work onstage at a major performing arts center, it gave me the opportunity to confront some serious issues. It was the fall of '93 and the city of Denver was in the midst of controversy over censorship, a situation that was becoming volatile.

Seeing my reluctance to get up on stage and read my work, Jimmy Baca, the Chicano poet who I was honored to perform with, said to me in his determined way, "Charlotte, you get up there and you tell them how an Indian woman sees the world."

I read my poem "Visiting Day," which is my response to the treatment of Native people behind prison walls. I talked about the fishing rights struggle in Wisconsin, demonstrating how it felt to be jeered at, spit on, and called "squaw" by white supremists. Most important, it gave me a chance to read my poem "Four Hands." It is a poem that talks about my friendship with a young man from the Yanomami Nation in Brazil who was sold to a carnival and put on display in a freak show.

It is that poem, "Four Hands," that I have dedicated, on a tape I recently made, to Rigoberta Menchu, a Nobel Peace Prize recipient. Rigoberta is a woman of great power and beauty, whom I have been able to share conversations with during her visits to Oklahoma. She has taught me that spirituality is a universal language. A language that remains a focal point for political organization in our communities.

As a Native woman I write to survive, to keep something alive. Which means I do not necessarily write for the whims of a consumer culture. But writing is more than an expression of something we struggle to keep alive. It is a tool for healing and learning.

When I wrote the poem "The Pox" it was at a time when the Columbus Quincentennial Celebration was taking root in 1992. For a long time I had buried inside myself the loss of a baby brother from a disease I believe we inherited from a previous generation. There is documented evidence that the U.S. government purposely infected military blankets, east of the Mississippi, with smallpox, and shipped them to the Osage tribe. This disease, not present before colonization, killed many of our people.

In writing the poem, I was able to touch the grief inside myself that I had buried all those years and to lay his spirit to rest. Each time I read it I am reminded of the peace I have found in the healing influence of poetic reasoning.

Writing has been for me a way of reclaiming what has been lost, or buried, or held secretly inside. A way to touch that place that struggles for light when there is only darkness; for warmth when there is only a cold, unresponsive world. It is the hand that reaches through barbed wire and iron bars toward the freedom we once shared as indigenous people of this continent. It is a way of reclaiming the stories and history of our people.

Perhaps the young girl-child in my workshop will become a writer and correct the books that "lie about us." As I told her, it is just as important to tell the truth as it is to know where to put your next comma.

"Besides," I told her, "how many people know how to spell Skedee?" Maybe one day I will be the toothless elder demonstrating my accomplishments.

That is who we are ... forever ... and ever.

A Journey to the Heart

Anita Endrezze

Anita Endrezze was born in Long Beach, California, in 1952. Her books of poetry are at the helm of twilight *(Broken Moon Press, 1992), which won the 1992 Bumbershoot/Weyerhauser Award and the Washington State Governor's Writing Award,* Lune D'Ambre *(Roget, 1993), and* The Humming of Stars and Bees and Waves *(Making Waves Press, 1998). An artist as well as a writer, she has had exhibitions in Wales, England, Finland, and the United States. Her short stories and poems have appeared in many national and international publications.*

The faces of my ancestors are both luminous and shadowy. I'm standing in a long line, holding the memory of their hands. My own hands are bone and muscle, sinew and threadlike veins of blood. We're dreaming about one another or maybe playing a game of "telephone," hundreds of years old. You know, where one person whispers a message or story to another, who then whispers it to the next person in line. *Pass it on*. Perhaps the message is changed slightly, but constantly, until it has created a new language, a different shape of itself. Or maybe the words become the dimple in your mother's cheek or the stubborn cowlick in your sister's hair. Still, there is a connection of breath, heart, mind, and spirit.

Not one of my immediate ancestors was a professional storyteller, yet all told stories about our families, and, collectively, the stories of their lives have influenced me.

I'm half-Indian and half-white. Most people assume it's my mother who is Indian. Not so. My mother's grandparents came from Vinica (Slovenia), Fai Della Paganella (alpine Italy), and Curciu (Romania). For sociopolitical reasons, they all probably spoke German in addition to their national languages. They were two men and two women, traveling individually from their small villages to the end of the earth: Butte, Montana. They came in the late 1890s: Johanna Ostronič, Joseph Kambič, Elizabeth Yaeger, Eugenio Endrizzi.

Like many young men, Eugenio Endrizzi intended on working for a few years in America, making his fortune, and then returning to Italy. In Butte, he met Elizabeth Yaeger and they married and had children (my grandfather, William Eugene "Papa Billy," was one of them). Eugenio had sent his family back to Italy but he was killed in a mining accident on October 11, 1905. He was thirty-eight.

I have a copy of the newspaper article about his death. The headlines read: DEAD MINERS CARELESS. Below that it says, "Endrizzi and O'Neill failed to follow instructions of the shift boss."

Further headlines add: CRUSHED BENEATH TONS OF ROCK IN SPECU-LATOR MINE.

The detailed article goes on to say that "suddenly and without warning, an immense quantity of rock came down from the hanging wall and caught O'Neill and Endrizzi. One of them spoke a few words after falling, but the other appeared to be dead."

I'd like to think it was my great-grandfather passing on that message, speaking his last few words. What did he say? I'm still listening. Maybe my son was learning as he arranged his rock collection. The beauty of each rock was formed under certain immense pressures in the heart of the earth. Each rock exists, singular in its own beauty, and ageless. Like people.

Eugenio's widow and children returned to that raw city of bricks and trees burnt leafless by the sulfuric acid in the air. Butte was a city of great wealth, vitality, and death. A town that heaved itself up and out of the earth, home to immigrants from Ireland, Italy, Scotland, and Scandinavia. My mother was born there.

Her name is Jean and she is Papa Billy's daughter. She's fair-skinned with amber-colored eyes and blondish brown hair. I have photos of her when she was a little girl, wearing her blond hair in a Dutch-boy haircut. She's told me how she played on the mine tailings.

Shortly before World War II, she moved to Long Beach, California, and worked in the naval shipyards, drafting. She was very good at it. The blue lines were clean, neat, and precise.

My father, Alexander Raymond Diaz, was Yaqui. A full-blood with a dark, moon face, and hair so black it shone blue at times. When he met my mother he was a divorced motorcycle mechanic for the Long Beach Police Department. After they were married, they tried to buy a house but because he was Indian, no one would sell one to him. And because my mother was a woman, she wasn't allowed to buy one either.

I wrote about this in the following excerpt from "La Morena as the Sad-eyed Jaguar Priest." *La Morena* means "the dark woman" and is one aspect of the female presence in many of the poems and prose poems I have included in a new book I'm working on about my family history. The title of the manuscript is "Throwing Water at the Moon, Fire at the Sun." I am also related to the Moreno family.

After my father was discharged from the service, "They gave him a piece of paper: a treaty between him and the government. He was honorably discharged into the rest of his life. He folded the paper carefully into a square animal that had yellow eyes and the soul of a jaguar priest."

Then my father married his first wife. "She worked in the fish canneries, slicing open the pale bellies of tuna, pulling the guts out until the front of her apron was bloody. She had two children, then he left her.

"He got married again. Tried to buy a house. 'Here's my discharge papers, see?' he said, unfolding the yellow-eyed jaguar animal. 'I was Honorable. I can use the GI Bill to get me a house.'

"The man who sold houses laughed. 'You're an Indian!' The yellow-eyed animal crumbled into dust. The paper fell from Dad's fingers.

"So, my mother tried. 'I'm not an Indian. And I've got a job.' She looked at the house with its white trim and oleander bushes with yellow eyes and the cracked sidewalk that swam up the street like a gutted tuna and the street that opened into the ocean where war was over for a little while.

"The man who sold houses laughed. 'You're a woman!' He got into his car and drove away, leaving my parents standing somewhere on a lot of nothing.

"Then they saw a woman wearing a black sheath dress, her body like a slim knife, and black high-heeled shoes with small buttons shaped like white horses. Her skin was the color of Los Angeles and she smelled like citrus before the trees were cut down to make room for the tract houses. She stopped in front of them. Her eyes were the sad eyes of a Jaguar priest reduced to licking the spilled blood of tequila off the velvet floors of the El Torro bar in Tijuana.

" 'Someday, your daughter's going to write about this,' La Morena promised. 'Doesn't matter if she gets it the way it really happened. Nothing happens the way we remember it.'

" 'Yeah?' challenged my mother. 'What happened is that we didn't get the house.' "

While collecting stories for my book, I asked relatives for their memories and discovered that people remember things differently. One story may be told three different ways, filtered by individual perceptions and by time. I was intrigued by something Stravinsky said, that "one lives by memory, not by truth."

My father's parents, Carlotta Ramos and Emiterio (Meetah) Diaz, were Yaquis from Sonora, Mexico. It was a terrible time. Just before my grandparents were born, over one hundred Yaquis were burned in a church in Bacum, one of the eight Yaqui pueblos. This is what happened: six hundred men, women, and children surrendered to a Mexican colonel, who ordered 450 of them into the church. The others were let go. He kept ten leaders as hostage and promised that if there were any attempts to escape, all hostages would be shot. He trained his artillery on the church door.

During the night a disturbance broke out. The colonel killed the hostages and shelled the doorway. Fire started in the church. One hundred and twenty Yaquis were killed.

RED AT BACUM (MEXICO)
1868

1

there are red clouds
of smoke
and splinters of bone

there are green palm
fronds smoldering above
the shattered altar

there are nails exploding
out the end of cooked fingers
there are 120

ways they died, alone, together
in front of the cross   praying
or spitting at it   skin sizzling

red mouths blood gun fire
red wine sacramental robes
red falling   red shredded

2

the next day hummingbirds

took the hair from human skulls
to weave nests

for tiny shells, heartbeats
they like anything red
fire

embroidery thread on white cotton
a small gold cross still glowing hot

among Bacum ashes[1]

There were constant battles against the Mexican government and
the soldiers, the *federales,* who enforced the tax collections and took
away Yaqui rights and land. Reprisals against the Yaquis included de-
portation to the Yucatán, slavery, rape, murder, and starvation. My
grandfather, Meetah, was just a boy when he saw his father murdered
by Mexicans. Meetah escaped by hiding under the porch and later
walked north. In "Bones Resembling My Grandfather" ("Throwing
Water at the Moon, Fire at the Sun"), I relate how he "scooped up
handfuls of mud and made a turban of wet earth" as he crossed the
Salton Sea. This is how he avoided sunstroke.

In 1886, when Carlotta was a child, the Yaquis suffered a defeat
against General Carbo. Two hundred Yaquis died and two thousand
became prisoners of war. Diseases claimed the lives of many civilian
Yaquis. Many Yaquis were settled in the eight pueblos, under the control of the government, but the majority left the Yaqui Valley, seeking
work and freedom. Some fled to the rugged Bacatate Mountains. They
raided the Mexicans and the pueblo Yaquis.

In 1900, General Torres battled the mountain Yaquis and killed
four hundred men. Many others committed suicide by jumping off
cliffs. Over a thousand women and children were forced to march
down the trail. Most died along the way. This is called the Massacre of
Mazocoba. Only eighteen *federales* were killed and sixty wounded.
Thirty-five guns were taken from the Yaquis during the "battle."

By 1907, Yaquis were a cash commodity, selling for sixty pesos a
head to the henequen plantation owners in the Yucatán and the sugar
fields in Oaxaca.

Many Yaquis left Mexico at this time. Most fled to Arizona,
refugees from their native homeland, always hoping they would be

able to return. My grandparents (separately, since they were not married at this time) went to California.

Although Yaqui history continued hand in hand with Mexican history (in 1910 the Mexican Revolution changed the country), my grandparents had removed themselves from those dangers and begun to merge with American history and culture.

The Arizona Yaquis continued with their own culture more strongly than the California Yaquis. In 1978, a small reservation, the Pascua village, was established. (My grandparents, however, never lived on a reservation since they were deceased by that time and my father, who died in 1979 in Tucson, hadn't health or energy to establish enrollment.)

My grandmother Carlotta came to the United States before 1916 (when my father was born here). As astute businesswoman, she later owned property in several counties: produce fields and houses for field-workers. She carried her money wrapped up in her shawl. My father remembered the early days, though, when they all had to pick lettuce and strawberries and walnuts in order to survive. They went as far as San Francisco, working in the fields.

Carlotta's father, Pedro Ramos, had been a merchant in Sonora. He had a caravan of burros loaded with supplies that he traded and sold along the coast near Guaymas. One possibility is that he was also a smuggler, perhaps a gunrunner for the Yaquis in the mountains.

Pedro was murdered, "shot by Mexicans dressed as Indian," according to family legend. This phrase always made me wonder until I learned more about Yaqui history. I think that the mountain Yaquis had a disdain for the pueblo Yaquis and would've characterized them as "Mexicans dressed as Indian." In other words, the pueblo Yaquis may have dressed like other Yaquis but were really Mexican at heart, living and accepting Mexican rule. Or perhaps he was simply shot by Mexican bandits.

In any case, his wife, my great-grandmother Estefana Garica, marched to the local law authority. With a gun on each tiny hip, she demanded that he find the killers or die himself.

Another story is told about her. She had a tooth pulled—and it was the wrong one. She swore she'd kill the "dentist."

My Yaqui grandmothers were strong women, educated, clever, and fearless. Carlotta was also graceful, exceedingly beautiful, and kind.

She fed hobos, loved music (playing the twelve-string guitar), and sang. She was only four feet, eleven inches tall, with masses of dark hair piled up on top of her head. Her eyes were deep black. I have her photo on my office wall, next to one of her husband, Meetah. He's posed stiffly in a suit, with a shock of unruly hair escaping out from under a dark hat. He didn't like Mexicans. He lived his life like an Indian, he'd say to anyone. He could easily lift four hundred pounds, according to my father. Meetah was five-ten and stocky. As a young man, he trained horses all over California and Arizona. He died from a hit-and-run accident in the middle of the night in Long Beach, California, on September 19, 1937. He'd probably been drinking. I wrote about it in a story called "Grandfather Sun Falls in Love with a Moon-faced Woman" ("Throwing Water at the Moon, Fire at the Sun" and published in *The Carolina Quarterly*, vol. 50 no. 1, fall 1997). The story is actually a retelling of an old Yaqui story about the sun falling in love with the moon, but I wove it into our family history.

"He was probably drunk, you know, on maize mixed with water. That night, that night, he fell in love for the first time in this life. It was not the first time he drank to forget the long journey, the tramping through alkaline dust white as ground bones, the mud packed on his head like a beehive." He saw a beautiful woman one evening and asked her to marry him. She agreed, but only if he would find the perfect gift, one that would fit her precisely.

But he could never find that gift and she left him. He married an "ordinary, beautiful Yaqui woman." Still, he could never forget his first love, a woman so changeable that she was never the same size from day to day. Once, "the strap of her red dress slid down one shoulder. She canted one hip, angling her ankle until the high-heeled shoe slipped off and the small space between heel and earth was like red earth and roses. He wanted to kiss her heels, let her walk across him, the way he walked across Sonora." Another time, she was so thin that "she had no hips, just two sharp plates of bone. Her belly was an empty cup."

On his last night, "he was Sun, hot and feeling the blood pounding his feet. He danced in the street, watching the headlights give him a stage. He bent over, waiting for the applause, bottle in one hand." And "when the car hit him, he thought it was love again. A big punch to the solar plexus. A real jab to the heart." He saw the woman, the moon-faced woman, floating in the bottle, "saw her, full and round and womanly. He lay with his head on her lap. He lay with his head on the curb."

Meetah owned a junk yard, which now is just part of the neighborhood across the street from the Long Beach Community Hospital. His was a long journey, from a boy witnessing his father, Valentino, murdered by soldiers, to a man living not far from Hollywood, town of illusions and fantasy.

Valentino also dealt with *his* father's death. Valentino and his brother and father had been up in the Bacatate Mountains, hunting for honey, when something happened. I don't know what, maybe a heart attack or a fall down the mountain trail. The boys had to bury their father there among the red rocks and crumbling earth.

Diaz is not a Yaqui name, but one given to our family. It is a Mexican name, most specifically that of the Mexican president Porfirio Diaz, who was in power from 1876 to 1910. Sometime during that period, we acquired that last name. I was born Anita Diaz.

Life was hard for my ancestors. They didn't live long. But I know about them through the stories we still tell. There are not enough stories; I always want to hear more. I want to understand them and learn more about them and myself. I want my children, Aaron and Maja, to know them also. That's why I write and paint, to *pass it on*.

My father never spoke Yaqui. When he was young, he was ashamed of being Indian. He didn't want to listen to the old stories. And yet he liked to tell us about what life was like "in the old days." My younger half-sister Rondi told me how he'd go skinny-dipping in the ocean and the police would take his clothes. He traveled with his family in a buckboard wagon into Los Angeles. He was, she says, great at storytelling, funny, and generous. Rondi says, "I see him both with eyes of an adult and memory of a child. When I was little, he was wonderful. He'd sing for me and let me blow up the muscles on his arm by blowing hard on his thumbs." But he also ran around with other women and was a "happy drunk." He was married three times (my mom was the second) and had six children plus several illegitimate ones. My older half-sister Mary Francis has only good memories of him. My full sister, Barbara, remembers him not at all.

I wish I spoke Yaqui. I'd have to go to Arizona or Sonora to learn it.

No one speaks it here in Spokane, Washington! I know only a few words. I enjoy learning languages. I've studied Latin, Spanish, and I speak, read, and write Danish. I can also read Norwegian. The history of words is the history of people. People define and are defined by their language. If you study languages, you learn about war, religion, adventure, and spirit. I think it's very interesting that scholars studying Indian languages today are coming to realize that the great diversity of languages in this hemisphere supports the idea that we've been here a lot longer than the accepted, academic starting point of 11,500 years (the Clovis timetable). In fact, recent research has agreed that Native people have been here for about 45,000 years. The voice of a people truly is their history.

Yaquis have had centuries of contact with Europeans. The first Spaniard went through in about 1533 on a slave-raiding expedition. Another explorer, Francisco De Ullora, saw "naked people" and smoke signals on the beach as he sailed up the Sea of Cortez (1539 to 1541). There have been periods of relative peace, but consider this: at one time, there were 30,000 Yaquis living in eighty rancherias. Three hundred years later, there were only 10,000 left. For better and for worse, the Spanish-Mexican culture, language, and religion have influenced Yaqui culture.

The Yaquis have lived near the Rio Yaqui in northwestern Sonora for thousands of years. In fact, one name given to us is Hia Hiaqui, which means "People Who Shout Across the River." Another name used by native speakers is Yoemem. It means "The People."

There is an ancient story with several versions about the creation of the world and the Yaqui people. The spirit being is a woman called Yomumuli, whose name means "Enchanted Bee." In the short story "The Humming of Stars and Bees and Waves," I interwove the mythical (Yomumuli) with the present (an old woman who's considering what it's like to be half-Yaqui).

"She knows that her tribe believes in dreams, but since she's only half-Yaqui, she doesn't know if the dreams believe in her."

I think a lot of mixed-bloods feel this way.

The story ends with these words: "These are my ancestors, my future." I mean by this that we are all connected, formed under pressure, individual in our beauty and grimness, and timeless.

In another short story, called "There Was a Yaqui Woman," the main character is a woman faced with deciding whether she wants to continue with her marriage. She's Indian; her husband is white. His family is racist and she can't take it anymore since it's now affecting her children. She doesn't have much faith or self-confidence, but as she and her husband argue, she thinks:

"I didn't know my tribe's language. Neither did my father and he was a full-blood. Lots of Indians were forced to speak English; that was not their disgrace. No, it was to their credit that they still believed in themselves, that they still passed on their stories.

"The stories were my lifeline to the past. They defined my awareness. While shaping words to my children as I told them the old stories, the words shaped me."

She tries to explain how she feels by telling her husband a story, but he has no patience. "You go off on some Indian story that doesn't have a point to it," he says in exasperation.

She decides, at last, to be strong for herself and her daughters. She can hear her dead grandmothers "stomping their feet like horses. They like a good fight." So over his objections, she tells a story that tells him what she's going to do, and it's an old traditional Yaqui story. The stories have shown her a way.

I have always told stories. Life is a strong vision of words and images.

When I was born, "I was born / with one leg twisted / toward the womb. / Was I dreaming / of running away / from life?" (from the poem "I was born" in *at the helm of twilight,* Broken Moon Press, 1992). I wore a cast as a newborn but my leg has always been a little weak. In spirit, though, I'm strong.

My maternal grandmother, Ann or Nana, was also a quiet woman. Deeply religious, she tried to get me to go to Mass. My mother wouldn't let her. Even so, I grew up with ideas and experiences in both Catholic and Protestant churches. Nana was ninety-two years old when she died in 1994 and she taught me a lot about patience. She was a nurse in a time when nurses were instructed how to formulate their own disinfectants and told how to prepare a kitchen for a woman's birth labor. She was born in Butte, Montana.

She was a good shot; they called her Annie Oakley. But she was also fearful, didn't like taking risks, avoided changes. I have tried to follow my mother's example of saying yes to life's possibilities. Still, I can understand my grandmother. In her lifetime, the world went through tremendous changes.

Her husband, my Papa Billy, was a steamfitter by trade and an inventor by inclination. He invented an ore classifier used in the Montana mines.

He had a rock collection: stunning purple crystals and clusters of yellow crystals that caught and refracted the light. We set them all on our mantel. Blue-green rocks we were warned not to lick (copper). Solid "fool's gold" or pyrite, which made our children's eyes glitter. Heavy chunks of lead. I learned the names of rocks before I learned my multiplication tables.

Although Papa Billy's father had been killed in that mining accident, he was fascinated with the deep earth—and the deep sea. Papa Billy invented a nuclear-powered submarine with a conical hull. I still have all his patent drawings. I can see his drafting table, set square in the golden light of a lace-curtained window. Pens. Straight edge. Crumbly erasers. A small penknife to sharpen thin-leaded pencils. The implements of his creativity were just as exciting to me as his creations.

My parents' marriage was very troubled. We lived for a while in Merlin, Oregon, near Grant's Pass. My parents logged their land. I remember napping in a tent covered with crawling caterpillars. I breathed the close, green-tinted, pine-scented air. I heard the milky sighs of my sleeping baby sister, Barbara.

It was a place of violence, I've since learned. I wrote a poem about it that appears below.

My Little Sister's Heart in My Hands
Part One: Rogue River, Oregon, 1856

"I promised to give you some of our experience in hunting Indians—
a kind of game not often treated of in your journal—
and as the sport has become rather universal
on this coast, every bit of experience will be of service
to the amateur or professional hunter . . .
A large herd crossed the mountains last winter . . .

We have caught a great many females or squaws and young,
but the bucks have generally made their escape . . .
You must [as a hunter] vow vengeance
against every Indian you meet,
but never molest any
except peaceable Indians,
who are unarmed,
and expect no danger;
this is a gallant thing,
when done in the face of public opinion,
law and order.

If an Indian is a prisoner
and charged with some offence,
you go up to him very fiercely
and say, "You d—d scoundrel,
why did you steal my pantaloons?"
The Indian does not understand
a word of English, but thinks
it's something terrible, looks scared,
and shakes his head. This is proof
positive
of his guilt
and you haul out your revolver
and blow his brains out.

He can't help himself,
for his feet and hands
are tied.
You have done a determined thing,
and henceforth
a made man."

              from an editorial, *Porter's Prairie,* May 28, 1856

            PART TWO: ROGUE RIVER, 1956

We live not far from the Rogue River
where Indian babies were thrown into bonfires.
I'm too young to know this.
Every night, though, I hear black snakes in the grass
sliding through the meadows toward the river,

their long black bodies gliding, glistening like tears.
Under the pear-shaped stars, in the orchards of womblike fruit,
I hear cries, weeping. I hear Sally Bell's voice:
Soon . . . some white men came.
They killed my grandfather
and my mother
and my father.
I saw them do it.
Then they killed my baby sister
and cut her heart out
and threw it in the brush
where I ran and hid.
My little sister was a baby,
just crawling around.
I didn't know what to do.
I was so scared that I guess
I just hid there
a long time
with my little sister's heart
in my hands . . .

PART THREE: ROGUE RIVER IN REVIEW, 1996

I have a baby sister.
I have a daughter.
I have a mother.
I have a grandmother.
I have felt their hearts beating
under my cupped hands, against my cheek
as I loved them, as I slept.

A long time have we hid
with our hearts in our hands
with the soft red rivers
flowing
from one to the other.
You can't say you didn't know.
Not now. Not now.
And though some have died
not hurting anyone,

they are *this* voice, *this* poem
untied, and henceforth,
determined
that the truth
will blow your brains out.[2]

NOTE: *Sally Bell was a Sinkyone Indian woman and her report was recorded in 1935.*

My father scared me. We finally left, my mother secretly stealing away with us girls. We moved around a lot after that. From birth to age eighteen, I lived in thirteen different houses. I went to a different school every year from sixth to twelfth grade. In "Housing Dreams" (*The Humming of Stars and Bees and Waves,* a book of poems and short stories, Making Waves Press, 1998), I say, "There's no rhythm / to moving / except the moving." And "we moved / because we were nowhere / better / than tomorrow."

For many Indian writers, place is vital. For me, it's been thought and feeling. It's been four generations on either side of the family since someone has died where they were born. We have been rootless for over one hundred years. And yet that restlessness, or desperation for something better, has given us a vitality, a sense of adventure. I've lived in Hawaii, Oregon, Washington, and California. I've visited France, England, Mexico, Canada, and Denmark. My husband is from Denmark. My children have a great sense of the world.

I've grown up knowing my connections in the world also, the countries my ancestors came from, the people still living there.

WRITTEN IN A SPRING STORM

I can't sleep tonight.
As I lean out the window,
my hair feels heavy, tropical
full of flowers fragrant as vanilla
and parrots' wings.
Here among the green hills:
sensual thunder, lightning
illuminating my long eyes.

Generations of women
have plaited their hair

into mine. *ko'oko'im. Tucson.*
Durango. Fai Della Paganella.
Semic. Curcui. Val di Non.
Vincia. Butte. Mezzo Lombardo.
How many have sat, alone,
in their white gowns
brushing their hair
at night?

I put down my comb.
Looking down the far road,
there is only the darkness
of widows' veils, falling like rain.
Men die young, or leave,
or never arrive at all.
Centuries of waiting,
the woman's arm on the sill,
her eyes looking into the distant storm.

What I've inherited from ancient women
is a patient restlessness.
When my hair gets too long,
I cut it. Ruthlessly.

When my heart gets too heavy,
I hold my hands out
to lightning.

Now when I read that poem, as a mixed-blood, I think how much you can spend your life doing a fancy two-step between different cultures and family members or lovers who don't understand you. You need to learn to grab that lightning and throw it back. I've learned to be more assertive since I wrote that. I'm less passive in all my relationships.

There's a legend in the southwest about a woman called La Llorona, the Crying Woman.

In Mexico and the Southwest, there is an old story about a spirit woman who wanders the desert looking for men. She is very beautiful and sad. When men approach her, trying to help, they are captivated by her beauty and she destroys them. Some say she is seeking revenge for all her children who were killed by the Spanish conquistadors. Others think that this is a metaphor for the destruction of Native cultures and that she is Mexico personified. It's also been suggested that she is Mal- intzin (or La Malinche), an Aztec sold as a slave to the Maya and later sold again to Cortés. They say she drowned her son when Cortés wanted to take their son back to Spain and leave her in Mexico. In my version, I've put her in the modern, urban world. She has just finished presenting her work before an audience and is answering their ques- tions. Perhaps she is now a poet or artist?

> Thank you. Now maybe you have some questions
> you'd like to ask me?
> But first let me tell you about my hands
> which were once white flowers
> and now are rain.
> They have the distinctive fragrance
> of a woman plucking eucalyptus leaves.
>
> A good question: how do I get my ideas?
> I wander the streets looking
> for some man dumb enough
> to come out in the dark,
> when he knows there are ghosts shaped like maggots
> and things without any feet
> and humans stiff with vomit huddled in doorways
> and I loosen my hair
> and weep like an owl.
> I wear a gown he can see through
> so of course he follows me anywhere,
> my beautiful face suspended
> above a neck slender as a candle
>
> and he follows, stumbling
>
> hands outstretched like a comic-book zombie.
> Usually, I take him to the reservoir
> although the lake is more traditional,
> and I watch the black waters reflecting the moon
> until my eyes are swollen with tears.
> I slither into the water;
> he wades toward me, his mouth gaping like a loony.

The water turns into blood and he's wading up to his hips
in blood, he's drowning in blood.
He thinks this is a Stephen King movie, but it's not.
I'm real. The last thing he sees
is my face looking like a horse's head
stripped of its flesh.

Next question. Am I rich?
Where my mouth was there is fire
and my tongue which was the milky tongue
of many generations
is a bag of dust.
I am not a metaphor for all the Indian women
who have suffered. I'm as real
as your denial, your ignorance.
I am as rich as my daughter whose body was smeared
by the white liquids of men
as my son who suffocated in the red dust of TB
as my baby whose body shook in the black fires
of prophetic dreams
as my unborn whose body was a window for the blue doves
as my twins who slaved in the Durango silver mines
and who whored at the gates for a mouthful of corn
and as rich as the miscarried who died with burning sores
and as fortunate as their children who became instead mimosa
and the strange laughter in the wild wind.

Another good question: Am I famous?
I come from the center of red hands
and my voice is known
in the roots of grass.

Last question, please.
Yes? What's my next project?
Actually, I've been working on this
for some time: my hands are full of syringes.
There are humans substantial as rags
who suck on my cocaine breasts.
I wipe the pus from the cracks
in their tongues and give them blankets
of paper. I wear my skirt clear up

to my ass so they can see my blood-dark body
and I hook them, flashing
my long red fingernails
that used to be rain
but now are thicker, saltier,
because one's lifework must evolve.

I'm confident of the universal impact
of my new work.

Well, I'd like to answer more of your questions
but there's moonlight twitching out of my hair
and some of you are ready for a fix, aren't you,
and some of you have appointments with the dark
hands of strangers so I want you to know
that I've worked through my feelings of revenge.
What I do now, watching you carve up your skin
into totemic white snakes,
is nothing personal:
history was legend is Art.

Thank you for inviting me,
but now, as you know,
your time is up.[3]

In this poem, a beautiful woman is being interviewed and reveals the justified anger of her genetic memory. Even though hatred has warped her, she feeds on it. Anger that rages into hatred is not courageous; it's a fist against life and bruises the soul. The poem is also about women who were abused and are now abusing themselves, and the diseases of the Europeans that destroyed 90 percent of Native populations. In addition, the poem is about the warping of myths in our lives.

My grandmother Carlotta was raped by Mexican soldiers. From my book in progress, "Throwing Water at the Moon, Fire at the Sun," is the following poem.

ANGELINA

No one talks about her: *Angelina*. Her name sounds pretty, like the gold-gilded statues with wings and red-rouged cheeks I see at mass. *Angelina*.

She didn't look like my father or the rest of them: Johnny, Kuti, Pilar.

Kiko. But she was my grandmother Carlotta's child: blue-eyed, blonde *Angelina.*

Not a miraculous conception, life embedded spiritually in Carlotta's womb, not that, not that.

Carlotta was raped by Mexican soldiers, back when Yaqui hands were cut off and nailed christlike to boards, rows of hands, palms out, fingers curled slightly

so that you can see the nails hammered through the palms and the ragged edges

of the wrists. So you can see all the hands that once smoothed a baby's hair

and patted tortillas and dug, broken nailed, into the earth for *plata.* Quotas of silver, and if there wasn't enough, then you were truly empty-handed.

But Carlotta kept her hands. And her baby. *Angelina,* child born under the severed

stars of the Mexican Revolution, small angel wrapped in shawls,

named *Angelina* because her mother refused
to let evil win. Later, Dad says no one talks to Angelina anymore,

ever since she wouldn't accept five one-dollar bills
when my father tried to pay her back the five-dollar bill

he had borrowed in 1942 to buy my brother medicine.
This was forty years ago. And when I ask about Angelina

no one remembers her, or will tell me why they have a blue-eyed sister,
or why she held them in such enmity, or was it just contrariness,

or where she is buried with her hands folded loosely
so that anywhere I walk I may be walking on an angel,

knowing that the heart of an angel can become friable,
easily crushed by the boots of this world.

A bad thing happened to Carlotta, but by all accounts she was a good and kind person. *She* was not the bad thing. She was stronger than that.

I have been asked by the editors to write about Indian identity. In the first drafts, I did comment, stumbling here and there. I didn't say anything important or that couldn't be said better by others. Knowing whether someone is Indian or not may help me find a connection with that person, a sense of familiarity and acceptance, but more important to me is learning whether that person has a good heart. In Yaqui, it is said, "Nejpo wa itom jiak Yoémia si túu jiapsekame." In Spanish it is: *Soy la tribu Yaqui de gran corazón.* And it means "I am the Yaqui tribe of great (good) heart." As an individual Yaqui, that is my goal, to have a good heart, to be kind and loving. It is the individuals that make up a tribe and an identity. I'm not an enrolled member of the Arizona Pascua tribe. I've never tried to enroll, but I may someday.

Those early ancestors of mine, those "naked people" sending smoke signals from the white beaches to the white sails of a creaking Spanish ship, sent the very human message *we are here*. In the face of the unknown, humans have always left their mark: handprints on cave walls, painted suns on rocks, flute solos to the stars. Sometimes words are not adequate for communication. Elements must be transformed: mineral pigments into paint; sound into song; fire into smoke.

When words fail me, turning as elusive and annoying as smoke, when I need to touch, then I paint or make baskets. I can work with texture and color that becomes almost immediately visible and tangible. It pleases me to have something I can *touch* after working so much with words and thought. The struggle to put ideas into words is itself important to the formation of a writer's vision and growth. Painting uses a different set of tools (brush, paper, paint, water), but the struggle is still there.

I try to combine the visual aspect of painting with my writing. I try to develop color and texture with words. The following excerpt is from a short story called "Ponies Gathering in the Dark" (*Ploughshares*, spring 1994, and *The Humming of Stars and Bees and Waves.*)

Under the house, the ancient continent measured the journey of clay animals: giant beaver, tiny horses, elk, intricately scaled snakes, vast bears that had clawed the horizon to shreds. There is a memory of ice animals walking into the sun, their bones crushed under the weight of frozen moons. And there is the tribe of obsidian, those sharp-headed old ones, who danced around fire, singing the hunt before iron.

Long ago, the beavers built their lodges here, when the marshes were thick with mud and sweet rushes. In the middle of winter, the oldest would tell about First Beavers, giant creatures that gnawed down trees the size of night.

The story is about a medicine man who is trying to find a cure for the sicknesses that are overpowering his people. While in a sweat lodge, he had a vision of many people:

"But what astonished him most of all was that he knew they were his children. Their skins were pink, white, brown, golden. Their eyes were the color of rocks: jade, obsidian, slate, amber. Or else the color of trees: green, yellow, brown. Some even had eyes the color of sky, water, or thunder. And their hair was the color of iron, bear, fire.

"He saw them playing, laughing, arguing. He watched them dreaming, the soft dust of meteors sifting down through the roof to cover their faces with cool fire, their calm hands luminous, reaching out."

Here, he sees all of us mixed-bloods, living and dreaming, continuing life.

This story, which relates how one certain site has changed throughout time, has a less obvious message: wherever houses are built in this country, there is a memory, a history, of Native peoples and animals. Early European immigrants thought our land was a wilderness, with no sense of history or landmarks of civilization. However, this truly was "Indian country," for no group of people can survive for generations without seeking out the possibilities of their surroundings and understanding the plants, animals, and environment. Now we know that the life of the earth came first, with its tribes of rock and fire, and then came the clans of animals. It's good to remember that there is a history before humans, too.

In the Aztec creation myth, Hungry Woman falls from the spirit world and creates the foundations of the world with her body. We are like her. Our bones are part rock, our hair part grass, and our tears are part ocean and human feelings. Our link to the world of animals and plants and minerals is one we should never forget.

In the Yaqui story of creation, Yomumuli creates everything out of love and joy. She guides both people and animals and offers them free will within a set of moral laws. Those humans who couldn't agree with her prophecy of the future were free to leave and go into the desert or the sea, where they became ants or dolphins. But it is said that if you are lost at sea, the dolphins will help you back to land because they remember the time when we were all one people. And if you are lost in the desert, the ants will also help you, remembering the time when we were all related.

I recently made a pilgrimage. Thanks to Artist Trust, an arts organization of Washington State, I was able to travel to Sonora, Mexico. The grant covered my costs and I traveled lightly, eating one meal a day (shrimp or fish soup with lobster fresh from the sea), walking with my day pack along the highways, flagging down buses. I hiked along miles of white sandy beaches, rode a horse into the desert, and entered the warren of small shops in the old shopping district of Guaymas. Everywhere, I looked for faces I would recognize. Faces of people who might look like relatives. And I found them, on street corners selling oranges, riding the buses, or driving taxis. In my broken Spanish, I told everyone I spoke to that my grandparents came from here, that I was a Yaqui. And they all smiled, welcoming me. We talked about the ancient red mountains, the turquoise sea, the fields of strawberries. I saw the Bacatate Mountains where my great-grandfather died. I saw Bacum. I saw Vicam. I saw the Rio Yaqui as it flowed toward the sea through fields of maize. On its banks was a restaurant called the Rio Yaqui selling Tecate (beer) and seafood.

In Ciudad Obregon, I visited the Yaqui Museum. Everything was in Spanish, but I can read it better than I can speak it so there was no problem. I read how Yaqui cranial capacities are larger than other area tribes and I grinned. We always knew we had a bit more potential than others! I also viewed an old canoe, made of wood and very heavy-looking. A boat fit for the ocean or a rough wild river.

I took lots of photos. Now, home again, I'm painting from them, interpreting vision and symbol and reality. I'm synthesizing experience with art, preparing to pass on my ideas to others. My trip to our tribal homeland was a journey to the heart.

NOTES

1. Published in *The Carolina Quarterly*, vol. 50, no. 1, fall 1997.
2. Published in *Lost Rivers*, Making Waves, 1997.
3. Published in *The Kenyon Review*, vol. XIII, no. 4, 1991.

SELF-INTERVIEW

HANAY GEIOGAMAH

Hanay Geiogamah, born in 1945, is a member of the Kiowa Indian tribe of Oklahoma. He has Delaware heritage on his mother's side. Geiogamah studied journalism at the University of Oklahoma in Norman in the late sixties. As a National Indian Youth Council member, Geiogamah organized the first American Indian theater company at La Mama Experimental Theater Club in New York in 1972. His subsequent work in the Native performing arts in this country has focused on play production, arts advocacy, university teaching, and founding the American Indian Dance Theater in 1987. More recently he has been involved as a writer and producer of television and films in Los Angeles. Mr. Geiogamah is a professor in the School of Theater, Film, and Television at the University of California at Los Angeles and is planning to produce a slate of low-budget feature films on American Indian themes over the next five years.

OCTOBER FULL MOON

I know the only time I'll see it all
as dazzlingly clear and calm as I've ever wanted
is when I plunge, fully clothed, except for my shoes,
through the flowing push of the clear stream,
down as close to the rock-strewn bottom as I can manage,
and there, on the night of the full moon of October,
forget the foul air of the big shit city,
where Indian fools go to die,
look up, through the silver eddies,
and tell myself, if the excitement lets me remember:
Here it is, Geiogamah!

I started working seriously toward becoming a creative writer by first working as a journalist. This is a decision I'll always be glad I made because the organizing requirements of news reporting and writing form the basis for the most urgent need of all writers—discipline. I've been a writer now for twenty-eight years, and I'm still not as disciplined as I need to be, but I'm a lot more focused and self-directed now than I was ten years ago and eons beyond where I was twenty years ago. But I still haven't gotten there yet, and I've stopped trying to blame this on some vague, inner restlessness that supposedly affects the Indian or other such fantasies. No, man, it's my responsibility, and that's it. (All this to say that this essay is very difficult to write!)

Journalism taught me how to conduct interviews, and I always liked the process of preparing for and conducting a one-on-one interview. I felt I was more in charge than not, and I definitely thought I was smart, cool, sophisticated, and on top of it. Mostly, I wasn't, but that's what I thought. In the past several years, the situation has reversed itself somewhat for me; because of my work in theater, films, and television,

I now get asked for interviews. It's not the enviable position some people might think—not at all, and if you're the interviewee, you always ask yourself: Why in the hell is he/she asking me that? And, Didn't this person do any homework? And when you read the final article, you cringe, wince, and duck. At last, here's a chance to interview myself, to get some of it right! Can I? Is this fair? Can I tell the truth? Keep it short, simple, not ramble? (The editor said I could even include some of my own poetry, if I dared.) Here goes:

1. When did you start to write, and what caused you to want to write?

I was born in southwestern Oklahoma in the summer of 1945 and grew up in the Indian agency town of Anadarko. Because most of the state of Oklahoma had been taken away from the many tribes who had either migrated to the area or had been forcibly moved there by the federal government when the place was called Indian Territory, all prior to 1900, we Oklahoma Indians, unlike Indians nearly everywhere else in the United States, didn't have reservations to call home. We Kiowas, like all other Oklahoma tribes, once lived on a sizable reservation that we shared with the Comanches and Kiowa Apaches, but after 1900, the tribal landbase was reduced to scattered 160-acre allotments. It was on an allotment near the little farming town of Gotebo, Oklahoma, that my father, Claude Geiogamah, Sr., was born in 1915 to my grandfather, Henry Geiogamah, a keeper of one of the tribe's Ten Grandmothers medicine bundles, and my grandmother, Bey-Topi, the daughter of Buffalo Tongue, one of the last angry Kiowas. If you've read Alice Marriot's *The Ten Grandmothers*, you have a notion of what Kiowa life was like in the area in the 1910s and 1920s. Change, change, change, and more change.

When he was only six years old, my father lost his father, which was a deeply traumatic experience for him. Soon thereafter, he and my late uncle, Judson Geiogamah, were sent to government school at Riverside, near Anadarko. The Geiogamah family was presided over by my two aunts, Florence Geiogamah Redbird and Anna Geiogamah Morrison, both of whom took turns in looking after my father and uncle over the next twenty years of their lives. Both of these full-blooded Kiowa men never really had much of a home after my grandmother remarried. They worked in WPA programs, did farm labor, moved about from Anadarko to Lawton to Mountain View and Gotebo. Sometime in the 1930s, Uncle Judson received severe head injuries when a horse bolted on him and trampled him, leaving him with brain damage that afflicted him for the rest of his life. As the elder son, Uncle Judson inherited the keepership of the Grandmother bundle from his father, and when he died, very sadly, in 1958, my father became the keeper.

In the very late 1930s, my father met my mother in Anadarko, and they were married and in early 1941 began having a total of eleven children: eight daughters and three sons. For most of his early life, Claude Geiogamah, Sr., had not been able to enjoy a stable home environment, had not been exposed to Kiowa religion or language or culture on a daily, sustaining basis. But because he was an Indian in an area where about twelve tribes confluenced, he held on to his Indian identity and Kiowa-ness pretty successfully.

Having settled in Anadarko, with a population of 5,200, half of whom were Indians, my family became "town Indians," and the gulf between where we lived, on Texas Street, and the open country around Sugar Creek, eight miles south of Gotebo, two miles down the road from Rainy Mountain, and about sixty-five miles from Anadarko, was pretty wide. It was nearly impossible for us town Indians, on visits to Aunt Florence and her family at Sugar Creek, to imagine *ever* being this far out in the country. And our country relatives were *so* Indian, *so* different from us town Indians. They ate cow guts—bote—and liked it. They were browner than us. They went to the bathroom in a little outhouse, way off from the main house. They spoke Kiowa!

In Anadarko, one developed an affinity with all the other town Indians, whether they were Kiowas, Caddos, Wichitas, Cheyennes, Delawares, Comanches, or Apaches, and an acceptance of and tolerance for other tribes were easy to come by, indeed were a sine qua non for being there. No question that the whites were in charge. We Indians all stuck together—always. Because nearly all the Indians were poor, except for those whose parents worked for the Bureau of Indian Affairs, it was necessary to find ways other than nice clothes and cars to achieve any degree of status or self-respect. Being smart in school helped, playing sports helped, even being pretty and handsome helped. My family was very poor, so I dreamed a lot, and somehow, when I was twelve or thirteen, I began turning my dreams into stories and writing my stories into words. I gave these to my teachers, who were all encouraging and helpful and supportive, and that, I guess, was the beginning of my writing thing. It was only a matter of a few years before it would occur to me that I could—should—be writing about my life as an Indian, as a Kiowa. A place like Anadarko certainly provided (and is still providing) a lot of subject matter. It is a unique place in this world.

2. Why do you choose a professional career in the performing arts?

At some point in my mid-twenties, about 1973, I recall consciously deciding that I would go ahead and pursue a career in the theater. I thought I could pull it off. I'd been somewhat successful as a journalist, but the arts and especially theater at that time seemed to offer more challenge and excitement. I was naive enough then not to give much thought to any monetary aspects of this decision, and I was mostly unaware that I was consigning myself to twenty years or so of poverty. I had had one modestly successful theater production in New York (from which I didn't earn one dollar), and the flash of that warmed my enthusiasm enough that I gave up a career-track job in public relations in Washington, DC, to move to the lower part of the Lower East Side of New York City, into what they call a railroad flat, and join forces with a small band of Indian actors to set off on a fabulous journey to create an Indian theater.

I always believed, and still do, that the Lord will provide. A good friend taught me that. Trust. He will come through. Meanwhile, my fellow Indian theater artists and I would be in the avant-garde of the quest to find new forms of Indian expression, new ways to examine Indian cultural, social, and political issues, new sources of creative energy, new forms of wit, humor, and intelligence! The bills would be paid. We would become a line item on a foundation budget. *How can they not go on funding us? We are Indians, man! The original owners of this country! They owe us!*

Looking back, I'm astounded at how strong the force that gripped me was. In the avant-garde of the Indian arts! A wide-open future! Wow! Three years after our 1972 launching of the first professional Indian theater in New York, I was flat on my ass in a dilapidated rented house in Oklahoma City, and the theater company had all but dissolved, the fervor was all dissipated, the energy all burned out, there was no funding, and the sun was going down fast on the future.

There wasn't very much in the experience of growing up Indian in Anadarko, Oklahoma, that helped to flush the country bumpkin mentality and naïveté from my mind and my way of doing things. It seems that as my awareness of being an Indian grew, as a kind of parallel development with what was happening with Indian people in the rest of the country in the early sixties, a few reality connections didn't get synapsed in my head. My brash enthusiasm and intense, energetic push never led me to actually lie or to deliberately misrepresent the facts, but there were plenty of occasions when I felt I was crossing my fingers behind my back, like when I ardently declared to the people at the National Endowment for the Arts in Washington and the Ford Foundation in New York that, yes, Indian people wanted and needed an Indian theater to illuminate and ennoble their lives, to set the record straight, and to lead the way to the future. I had convinced myself that I believed this, deep in my heart. Then I landed square in the middle of the full-fledged responsibility to prove it and to produce the goods that would make it all real. But I was trying to become an Indian artist. I had to take lots of risks.

Bumpkin mentality or not, in the three wild years that all the Great Work was being done—the avant, man—we actually managed to do a teeny bit of some pretty good stuff. We weren't fully aware of this at the time; few artists ever are, are they? My instincts, which had not withdrawn completely and which I still trusted when I could think clearly enough to do so, told me that we had caught a glimpse of some wonderful light, had seen some amazing colors, and had heard some lovely sounds. I saw that in our first one-act productions we had brought to theatrical life some vivid aspects of Indian character and mores. We had begun the process of dramatizing Indian strengths and weaknesses of character and community. We tackled issues like alcoholism and the way it is a catalyst for our cultural and moral degeneration. We enacted situations of Indian-to-Indian perfidy and of confused identity. We celebrated our cultural institutions—we put a forty-nine celebration onstage with all its wonderful energy, singing, dancing, bawdiness, and violence. We used song and dance and storytelling tradition to tell a tribal myth of creation. We gave wild comic life to Coyote. To me it was clear that all of my experiences as a Kiowa, as an Indian, for the preceding twenty-seven years of my life in Oklahoma could be an almost endless source of rich creative material. We were only scratching the surface, and the larger possibilities were visible, real, not pipe dreams.

The Indian shows we created in the early seventies are available and are still being performed. Since this period, I've been slowly, calmly trying to produce new productions, to produce movies, trying to present Indian dance in new contexts, to make new music, to encourage actors and writers. I've sifted and refined thoughts, ideas, and reflections, hoping once again to access those beautiful visions and wonderful sounds I heard when I was buzzin' in the seventies. Somewhere in that cool glaze are the shapes and forms of our future culture: revitalized and reinvigorated art forms, new styles, new rhythms. I guess I'm seduced. A lot of the giddiness is gone, and the sense of responsibility that comes makes a great stabilizer. In my daily mantra, I ask for patience, determination, fortitude, and more patience. Bottom line? I still believe a true Indian theater is going to happen.

WHEN THE SPIDER VISITS

The spider glided with magical smoothness and silence
all the way down from the ceiling,
leaving his secret hideout.
He landed firmly on my right shoulder.
Then he marched unhesitatingly across my chest,
over my thumping heart,
down the side of the sofa, onto the floor,
to a new hideout?
My small, uncertain voice at once
gave thanks for the bounty of ideas
he was bringing with him
all the way from his ancestors,
whom my people knew and respected
so surely.
When he had gone, I ran
for water,
repeating "Thank you, a-ho" to the friend
who had chosen my heart
to cross over.

How does a man make certain
that he will remember
such a wondrous occurrence?
The old ways of recording special times and marvelous occasions,
bright colors and paints on skins, dried and stretched,
is softly, respectfully forgotten.
I found him again, in a radiant corona,
waiting calmly to help me record
the blessings
in colors deep as a movie's,
and to write the promised joys and good fortunes
across the days and years
of all my hopes, and fears, and dreams.

3. What cultural assets do American Indian people have?

I have heard my Kiowa relatives talk about the beautiful music, flute melodies and vocal chanting, that would suddenly break the silence of a summer afternoon in the yard surrounding the Geiogamah home at Sugar Creek, a short distance from the famous Rainy Mountain. This music is part of the medicine that blesses a home where one of the Grandmother medicine bundles lives. I have never heard this music, but I want to, and I pray that some day I will. If this good thing happens, I will have heard something that my grandfather and great-grandfather surely heard. That will be a special occasion like few others.

Indian people have lost so much over so long a stretch of history—their homelands, much of their languages, their hope, their self-respect. I think we're making some progress in recapturing and restoring a lot of the intangibles, and in some places we're even buying back parts of the land! The one resource I think we've always had that's been banged and battered but never destroyed is a deep and abiding sense of identity, which is the basis of our strong reverence and respect for our cultural heritage. A lot of this is probably because of the oral traditions that were and to a large degree still are our primary means of communicating from one generation to the next.

In our own voices we tell each other, our families, our children, our friends, and our fellow tribesmen who we were, where we came from, what happened to us on the way, why this and that are the way they are.

We hear and take part in these stories, and they identify us, connect us, empower us, and guide and remind us. These stories are dances, rituals, ceremonies, customs, and traditions. They are instructions, regulations, and laws. Coming from our elders, from our mothers and fathers, from our artists and storytellers, from our medicine people and spiritual leaders, our stories become the fabric and patterns of our culture. Few other cultures in the world are so flexible, so accommodating, so generous. Our culture protects us and heals us, and out of this rich and complex inheritance, we gain strength to do all the other work we find before us.

The truth of this is visible in all aspects of the work we have done over the past seven years with the American Indian Dance Theater. In 1986, when twenty-four gifted dancers and singers and I came together to forge this company, most of us were familiar with the dances and songs pretty much in a powwow or public ceremonial form and context. We had not given much thought at all to adapting the dances for the concert stages of live theater and taking these performances into theaters all across America, to Europe, Africa, Australia, and Asia, to share with hundreds of thousands of people who knew very little about Indians. As artists, the performers of the American Indian Dance Theater have discovered that it's definitely possible to do new things, to try an old dance step in a new context. They're not afraid to make new songs, to step in a new direction, to experiment, to play, to push boundaries. The original source material comes alive and works right along with us. When I was six or seven years old and I watched the war dancers at the annual American Indian Exposition in Anadarko and heard the singers' voices rise and fall in full-throttle unison, I felt that in some way I was part of the singing and dancing. The energy, the thunder, the strength and power of the movement touched me and made me feel a part of the community, of the unending flow of creative energy. Forty-five years later, I know that at seven years of age I was beaming into the right wavelengths.

4. *What are your thoughts about the current community of American Indian writers, their strengths, their challenges?*

We Indian people are blessed with the presence of many creative writers who are dedicated to presenting our stories and views of life to readers around the world. There are dozens and dozens of Indian poets, at least one in just about every one of the five-hundred-plus tribes. There are novelists and essayists, historians and journalists, even a few playwrights and screenwriters. I think most of them are dedicated to their work, their craft, and to the responsibilities and challenges that come with the profession.

The output of all these creative minds is prodigious, especially from the poets. It's not so great a picture, though, when you add the accumulated work of Indian writers to the output of all the non-Indians who are busily churning out hundreds of books on Indian subjects. The reading public which buys all the published books about Indians—by Indians and non-Indians both—seems to have an enormous appetite for works on the subject, because dozens of individuals, most of them non-Indians, make comfortable livings off their book sales, their lecture tour fees, teaching salaries, seminars, and guest appearances. The bottom line, profits-wise, gets bigger and bigger.

I wonder what will happen if and when the pro-Indian reading public's appetite wanes, and the Indian as attractive subject moves to a secondary or lesser position in the limelight. Who will be left standing? The Indian writer or the successful non-Indian writers? My guess is that a Tony Hillerman, whom I don't think cares much about real Indian issues and concerns, can withstand even the most withering recession and drought that could hit and cripple the Indian vogue. Could James Welch, Leslie Marmon Silko, or N. Scott Momaday survive? What would happen to their sales, which are already specialized by their intense Indian focus and distinct writing styles?

Welch, Silko, Momaday, and others like Louise Erdrich and Linda Hogan are as gifted and capable writers as any Tony Hillerman or Lynn Andrews or Jamake Highwater (remember him?). Some of the Indian writers today, in my opinion, are ready to shine and illuminate Indian life in the nineties and beyond. How are these writers going to be able to compete with the non-Indian Indian writers? How will they find their audiences? How will they connect with the Indian audience? How will they define and expand their vision?

In Los Angeles just now I'm working with a Ho-Chunk writer named Joseph Brown Thunder on a couple of screenplays that we are determined to get produced. Joseph is in his late twenties, and he is as good a screenwriter as any of the others in his age group or in all the ethnic groups represented in the business. He knows it's a very tough competition, and he has no dreamy-eyed notion that he's going to be successful simply because he's an Indian. His principal strength is that he is a good storyteller, and he can spin and color his stories the way Indians know them. He's one of a very tiny number of Indians who are writing television and film scripts, aiming at the potential audience of hundreds of millions of people. This, I strongly believe, is a creative area where our talents should explore and move into before the non-Indians establish a dominant control of the turf. Erdrich, Harjo, Alexie, Whiteman, Momaday, Paula Allen, and many others should check out this scene real soon. Film and television writing could help pay all the bills and enable those Indians who are good at it to succeed and still have enough quality time to keep working toward that break-through masterpiece of a poem, novel, essay, or play. It's the future, and in this onrushing future, I think we can do some great work, create some beautiful films, all in our own style, words, and genre. The creative context will be collaborative, communal, family, if you like. The first all-Indian movie is gestating, and many more will surely follow.

5. *What do you hope to accomplish in your filmmaking work? What are your strategies?*

Right now I'm working toward the goal of helping to start the formation of the American Indian cinema. I say starting the formation because I don't think a full-blown Indian cinema will exist for at least another ten years because the creative and physical process of making movies and television shows is just so complex and time consuming. It's quite enough to hope that perhaps three or four all-Indian film and television productions will have been completed by then, and by all-Indian I mean that these works will be written, directed, and produced by Indian creative artists with casts of American Indian actors.

These productions will be financed with money raised by the Indian producers, hopefully from Indian and tribal sources, and will be presented under the auspices of American Indian film production companies. It's unrealistic to think that there'll be an all-Indian studio or network, but I'm certain there'll be several operating Indian production companies that will be staffed with Indian professionals.

With adequate financial backing today, now, I could produce one moderately scaled feature motion picture or television movie of the week. I've been a producer on six productions over the past five years, and I have enough capability accumulated to produce a film, which, obviously, I intend to do.

The first step is to line up an Indian writer to write the script. Then I hire an Indian director, from among the two or three who could really do it, to direct the project. I staff the production crew with at least 75 percent American Indians and cast the roles with all American Indian actors. I hire experienced non-Indians to help me arrange distribution of the completed product (this aspect of the process is crucial), and I hire the best post-production personnel my budget permits. I use every resource I have and can muster to promote the film and get it seen by as wide an audience as possible.

After this first film, I go right on to a second production, then a third, and on like that. I overlap and juggle and shift and work both ends from the middle to maximize the lead time it takes to develop a project and get it before the cameras. Time is really an urgent factor in this work.

I'm not too concerned about encountering a shortage of good material because I know how many thousands of stories American Indian writers have access to and could create that could be adapted for scripts.

I must apprentice as many Indian directors as I can recruit and guide them through the learning and training process. I ask for financial backing for all this from the studios, from the networks, from cable stations, from the tribes, from the reservation bingoists, conglomerates, speculators, the Pequots of Connecticut, the Missions of California, from the Corporation for Public Broadcasting, from the Germans, the Japanese, even the Australians. I solicit rich people, wealthy Indianophiles, stars, captains of Indian industry, and anybody who shows the least flicker of sincere interest.

THE DREAM

The young man followed the path of his dream.
The earth was calling him.
He walked for many seasons.

He heard sounds no other one had ever heard.
He knew the Creator was guiding him.
Each time he washed, he would be new again.
"A-ho. Thank you. A-ho."
In his sleep he saw the world ahead.
The dream path stretched on,
and the road got shorter.
He felt prepared.
And then he saw the gift.
And he knew that he would be the first one to make the
sound that he heard in his dream.
He would have the honor of bringing this gift to
the tribe.

6. *How would you assess the current American Indian acting pool?*

Ten years ago there was a small community of American Indian actors scattered across Indian Country. Most of them had limited experience on the screen or stage, but they were filled with determination, drive, and enthusiasm. I'd say at least half of these pioneering Indian thespians were hip enough to know what the show business term "paying your dues" means, and were prepared emotionally, mentally, and physically to knuckle under for the long run. There were maybe twenty or so of these individuals then, ladies and gents who had what it really takes to be a professional actor. I'm not talking about good looks, high cheekbones, long, silky black hair, statuesque posture. All these help if you have them, but they aren't the core requirements the noble profession of acting demands.

Those who will make it as actors usually have an inner sense of self-respect, a fair degree of intelligence, and genuine interest in life, other people, other cultures, and perhaps the great issues of the day. He or she is neither petty nor shallow and is not driven by greed and egoism. There is also present a sense of being an artist, a sense of awareness that being an artist carries with it a mantle of responsibilities and challenges. These artists also have a vigorous sense of adventure, an honest humor, and an attitude of respect for the spirits and the mysteries and wonders of life. I'm not saying that all Indian actors must possess all these traits and characteristics. But the actors who become really good actors display a good number of these attributes. They are like priests, shamans, healers. They are good people.

Will Sampson was one of these artists. When he passed away in 1987, I wrote this about him:

Will Sampson was probably the most celebrated American Indian personality of this half of the 20th Century, and he was a star who never let you know he was a star.

In a period of just about two years, 1976–77, he became the most renowned American Indian performing artist to ever work in the industry. He was honored by many tribes, and he counted as his personal friends some of the most famous and powerful people in the business. But never, not ever, did one hear him brag about his status or talk in power-tripping terms about any clout or special influence he had. Nor did one ever see him act in public in a manner that was anything less than warmly gracious, accessible and compassionate. He was a first-class Indian gentleman.

Will's interests were not centered in the performing arts only. He cared deeply about the Indian people of this country, cared about their health problems, cared about alcoholism, drug abuse, delinquency, lack of educational and employment opportunities. Always, if his name could help a just and good cause, he would lend it—the best possible use of one's celebrity status.

Who are some of the working actors today who are in this category? Tantoo Cardinal is one. She is a lovely lady, a professional, a good spirit. Jane Lind is one of our best actresses, hands down. There's a fellow named Michael Greyeyes who has star quality. August Schellenberg has it too. Wes Studi has become a wonderful actor, and Kimberly Norris is heading toward leading-lady status. Joseph Runningfox is capable of excellent acting, and Gary Farmer is one of the best. A newcomer named Loren Cardinal will be working for a long time to come.

There are lots of bright new faces coming into the scene: Bryan Frejo, Ryan Black, Irene Bedard, Georgenna Lightning, Jon Proudstar, and Adam Beech. All of these people have demonstrated that they can do it, that they can deliver the goods and make people suspend their disbelief and like it. They have trained, studied, worked their voices, worked out, auditioned, waited patiently, been rejected, lost out on a great part, and kept going dutifully and humbly. And nearly every one of them is a nice person and is enjoyable to be with and be friends with.

About one thousand others are aspiring and have their sights set on the bright lights, fame, and fortune. Unfortunately, however, the majority of these Indian aspirants have little talent, maybe none, are motivated by narcissism, ego, greed, or selfishness, and think that their good looks or their fast talk or their bright smiles or Indian blood will do the trick. The good ones, the ones who have studied and trained and been in plays and taken class after class after class, you'll see on the screen, or on the stage, or right there in the middle of the tube. There is no other way.

7. *Do you have any advice for young Indians aspiring to show business careers?*

I answered part of this in the preceding response, but I'll paraphrase part of it again to drive home a point. If you want to be an actor, major in theater at a good college or university. Play every role you can get cast in, every race, gender, type, or size. Read all the plays you can, Shakespeare, the Greeks, Williams, Pinter, Mamet, Albee, Shepard, all of them. Do not automatically reject cultures other than your own. To study them is to illuminate your own culture. Prepare for the long haul, and factor in taking a lot of shit and encountering major disappointment after major disappointment.

If you want to be a director, study everything and get your mind and your life organized. Learn at least one foreign language. Travel abroad. Keep expanding your mind in every direction. The concept of "Indian time" will not ever be acceptable. Probably a stint as a director in the Indian theater will help as preparation, and formal study of the directing process will definitely be good. Start learning how to get along with all kinds of people. Study art and painting and all kinds of music. Learn how to get a great number of people to do what you tell them to do without hating you or resenting your asking them to do something. Start making choices, decisions, and sticking with your choices. Know when to switch and reverse. Learn how to take charge and to stay in charge. Start directing as early as possible. Save all your money and produce a small film all your own. Remember the Hispanic director Robert Rodriguez, who hit it big with his little $7,000 first effort? Keep yourself balanced, treat yourself with respect, and trust your inner voice and instincts. Get an apprenticeship as soon as you can.

If you want to be a screenwriter, learn the format and the tricks of the trade. Both television and movies have their own unique requirements for writers. Character, dialogue, and structure really count, so absorb all you can about these elements. Shape your stories into filmable ideas, strong visual images, graphic shots that tell the story with a minimum of words. Learn word compression, thought compression, and emotion compression. Plan a good spec script, write it, and circulate it to all possible patrons. Learn the art of patience and suspend your ego, possibly for good. You won't snag an agent until you get somebody interested in your script. And don't forget that you are an Indian, that you come from a sweet, humble, and decent community of people, that you are speaking for these people, and that you have a tie to them and a responsibility that must be upheld.

If you do all this, you should be OK. Make friends with the right kinds of people, not just anybody who says hello to you.

If you want to be a producer, that will take a while to break into, but if you can raise five or ten million dollars and get a good script and persuade some good actors to do it, and get the right director to sign on, you're in.

If you want to be in Indian show business for the glamour and glitter, for the fame and the adulation, for the power and the glory, it'll be all the harder for you. For whatever reasons, it's just harder if those are the things you're after.

OUT OF ME

Took a look at what's inside,
saw the ugly things that hide in me,
inside of me.
I asked myself: Am I strong?
Can I knock out all that's wrong in me?
Out of me.
Be a better man for all,

answer to the spirit calling me,
calling me.
I saw a path not walked on.
I heard a song not yet sung,
I felt a fire burning in my head.
I smelled the cedar burning,
I saw the colors strong and shining,
a circle round and perfect here,
inside of me, inside of me.
I think I know what's in me,
I know I feel it now,
it's coming out of me,
coming out of me,
coming out of me:
A bird of beauty hovers over me.

8. *What do you see as the role of the tribes in the future development of American Indian culture and the performing arts?*

I used to think I had some reasonable, workable ideas about this, but now I'm not so sure of what I think. Maybe I'm just reacting to a personal sense of having been pretty much neglected by the tribes and the major Indian organizations over the past twenty years, a stretch of time when I would have taken just about any handout from anybody to get the rent paid and to put something to eat on the table. Fighting off bitterness is a very important aspect of being an artist, so I just fight it off and keep looking ahead.

I know as well as anybody how difficult the whole show has been for all Indians, especially for the tribes and their leaders. The mighty monolith of American indifference and mean-spiritedness is a formidable reality that can take away all the joy in life if one spends all of one's time resisting it.

In spite of how hard things have been and how much time the effort to cope has absorbed, I still feel that some kind of formal attitude, policy, program, or protocols that the tribes could sponsor in behalf of the many artists who are working and struggling to bring honor and beauty to the people would be a wonderfully encouraging thing.

I recently wrote that to nurture the new generation of artists and communicators, a complex support network (cash grants, housing, materials, spiritual support and guidance, honor, respect, and employment) must be established by all the tribes to assure development of the artistic elements of tribal life. Public and private arts funding for American Indian artists in terms of money per capita is far below what has been disbursed for non-Indian arts projects. It's imperative that the tribes find ways to allocate resources and funds to support their creative members.

With tribal support will come an expansion of the professional expertise base. Actors, directors, designers, technical personnel, administrators, managers, and producers are all positions that, when employed, generate both income and tax revenues as well as prestige and a stronger sense of community for the tribes. Synergy—very simple, and not so hard to accomplish.

If the tribes become more supportive and tribal leaders develop a clearer understanding of the importance of this artistic investment and the good it can do, Indian creative folk will be better able to make their essential contributions to tribal life. It appears that now, more than ever, Indian people need the artistic elements of life, which bind them together, unify their style into a living force, and give them strength and pride as a people. Wonderful artistic traditions were developed and nurtured in the past, when the tribes supported their artists and gave them love, respect, and inspiration. Does any of us not hope this will be the way it is in the future?

END OF THE FREEBIE ERA

Don't let me in for free, I don't need that kind
of break, not anymore.
I want to pay to see the show. I have some money now.
How much does this cost?
I need to pay my own way.
I am going to face the honest challenge.
I want to learn more as a paying customer.
And you? Are you with the press?
Are you a special guest? Or a parent? Or a friend?
You shouldn't expect freebies from us anymore either.
See the box office staff for your bill, please.

*9. What are the problems at hand for the continuing development of a vital,
healthy American Indian culture, as you see them?*

Sometimes I get this unpleasant notion that we Indians are maybe a
little too busy being Indian these days. (I know that the zealots among
us will pounce on this immediately, but I'll say what I have to say anyway.) We may very well be overdoing our thing. Or we might not be
applying our intelligence and our energies in the right ways to the
right goals and projects. I realize that every Indian demands equality,
respect, and to be heard and understood. Each Indian has a right to be
proud and deserves a measure of dignity. But somehow, through an
odd quirk of the respect factor, I think our eagerness to be accommodating, respectful, and fair to one and all contributes to the excessive-
ness I see all around today.

There's a lot of narcissism in Indian life today. There is a lot of ex-
hibitionism, self-centeredness, and selfishness. Occasionally one
senses an excess of smug self-righteousness. There is discernible a lot
of egoism and a lot of slackness. There is a puzzling amount of idle-
ness and a plentiful supply of self-appointed experts.

There is too much powwowing; the volume of all powwowing is
staggering. I know full well that we need to sing and dance and celebrate, but this much?

There is a lot of visiting, moving about, restlessness, and coming
and going. There are still too many telephones disconnected because
of unnecessarily unpaid bills. There is a good deal of striving for the
limelight, and numerous hokey raconteurs and pompous spokesper-
sons. And there is a lot of impatience and perhaps unrealistic expecta-
tion.

The concern is that these distractions of excess and the energy they
drain from the good work will continue to drag and drain and mislead
a lot of talented and sincere people. Real problems could result.

Everybody has needs, everyone has weaknesses. I'm a weak person
when it comes to saying no. I want to do the best I can. I believe all of
us Indians want to do the best we can. We all respect our parents and
grandparents and our elders and tribal ancestors. I don't think there
was a lot of excess in the things they did, and their wisdom and their
ways got us to where we are today.

10. *What alterations do you make on your personal history, assuming you could do so? And why?*

I can't change the past, and I wouldn't want to because its lessons, good and bad, have taught me all I know. Maybe, however, I can do something about the future if I stay positive. I'll look after my health closely, keep an open mind, learn new things, and trust in the Creator. I feel fortunate that the old home place south of Gotebo, in Oklahoma, is still in our family, the place where my father grew up and my Kiowa people lived. If I'm fortunate, I'll build me a house out there and retire there. That little quiet corner of the world provides an image that illumines my life and offers a spiritual goal.

SUGAR CREEK

Sugar Creek, brown, and red, and forever.
Kiowa people know you well, the earth
respects you.
Uncle said, A crocodile lives in there.
Sister and I believed him.
Grandma washed clothes in there.
My aunties helped her.
Daddy and Uncle swam in there,
summertime of 1920.
Turtles sulked and hid in there,
my cousins caught them.
Sugar Creek, right south of Highway 9,
Grandpa Henry heard your voice while he was praying.
Tipi sat close to the bank, the people gathered.
Rainclouds made the lime marks fade,
the bull frogs flourished.
Sugar Creek, the clan lived there,
next to Lone Wolf Chapel.
Sugar Creek, in blazing sun,
the cows come running.
I want to come and try to pray,
and know your comfort always.

The Grandmother will always live there, at Sugar Creek, and her sisters will always be nearby. The beautiful music that the Creator and the good spirits make to adorn their homes will always be there too, ready to puncture the silence and enchant and carry the blessings. Rainy Mountain will be there too, a mile down the road. My father and uncle climbed its gentle slopes many times when they were little boys. I vowed that I will climb it too. That feat will be something to write about for sure! A-ho.

ENTRIES INTO THE
AUTOBIOGRAPHICAL I

GORDON HENRY, JR.

Gordon Henry, Jr., is an enrolled member of the White Earth Chippewa tribe of Minnesota. He is currently an associate professor in the English Department at Michigan State University, where he teaches Fiction Writing and American Indian Literature. Henry has published poetry and fiction in numerous anthologies of American Indian Literature, including Earth Power Coming, Earth Song, Sky Spirit, Songs from This Earth on Turtle's Back, *and* Native American Literature. *In 1994 he published his first novel,* The Light People, *which won an American Book Award in 1995. He lives in Big Rapids, Michigan, with his wife, Mary Anne, and his daughters, Kehli, Mira, and Emily.*

"Live in the nowhere that you came from,
even though you have an address here ..."
—JALAL UDDIN RUMI
"Autobiography is the subject of personal logistics of knowable
selves. How does one put I where one is or was? One needs a
center, around which to build. The center is rarely an I."
—FROM THE UNCOLLECTED WRITINGS OF
BOMBARTO ROSE, MIXED-BLOOD, OJIBWA

EVOCATION: From the wisdom of forebears to the clean clear northern
streams, among Mississippi mothers and Otter Tail Pillager fathers, farther
back beyond the current conventions of names and numbers, beyond the skins
and skeins of dark heavy liquid, let me be in honor of those who came before,
of the first bringer of light, of the charge of creation and the spark of Creator,
let me live in a good way with the gifts of creation.

THE FIRST DOOR: I AS NOT I

I am not:

postmodern or modern; a sign, or a signifier, between signifieds;
surreal or existential; neo-traditional or beat; transcendental or
metaphysical; confessional, shaman, warrior, or sun priest; trickster,
nationalist, exile, or anthropocentric; psycho-dramatizer, or dish-
washer safe, microwaveable, sunday supplement collector plate; sell-
out, or shade; or shadow chaser; or orphan boy, pop icon, trapper,
trader, weaver, stone carver, powwow investor; or an angel looking
backward; or an arboreal rodent, road kill, or coyote, totem taster, clan
speaker, band stander, or dream song; sonnet carrier, villanelle revival-
ist, or windigo washer; fumigator, suicide doctor, freeze-dried mystic;
or the lone ranger lover, heaven seeker, or hell raiser; church leveler,
drunken wonderer, sneaking, creeping, powwow playboy; or two-

thirds higher honor song singer; or hotel lecturer, casino medicine keeper, or shelling-shooting, crow or weasel; otter; or turtle, better or worse, water spirit, star gazing, anthropological shape shifter; or check-out-line half-breed hero, or formula detective, divided between ordinary and nonordinary; or authentic, natural, unnatural, deconstructive, white hating, eros, or ethos; or pathos; or apollonian, dionysian, radical; or card-carrying, blood quantum physicist; or an apple, delicious, golden, or rotten, or otherwise; a tomahawk, hair splitter, polemicist; or a two-stepper, ten steps from a twelve stepper; or thunder being; or light being, writer of wrongs; or prepackaged, beadworking, pipe carrier; or pipefitter, ironworker; or artificer; of law and politics, of extraterrestrial intelligence; or medicine wheeler, spokesman, or blackjack dealer; or chaos theorist, social contractor under federal control; or a plains clothes wardrobe keeper, sign wearer; or a graffiti artist; or epidermal epistemologist, with nobody home, with an idea, an ego, or a paper skin, or a well-read skin, or next of skin, intellectual, personal mythologizer disguised as a historian; or a *jessakeed, wabano,* or a crystal gazer, or a new age bookseller, with a men's movement mind; or a biological timekeeper, a one or only, to be believed or not, to be forgotten, or a presence in absence, an absence in presence, intense; or a psychic autobiographer; or an archaeologist on the fringes; or a firekeeper/doorman; or a burnout, exclusionist, a disillusionist; or a sounder of the senses; or a sensual geographer; or a contradictor; or a great *waboose*; like, or as the king of ghosts; or a star lake ricer, an either/or demanding, neither; or a word waster, a word recycler; or an apocalyptic, problematic poser, or a wholly imaginative, word charger, gnostic; or a list maker, cataloger; or a horoscopic, celestial reflector; or a sacred mechanic, in the absence of culture; or a technological nightmare, flood recollector; or a little person, on familiar terms with cultural giants; or a winter tongued salamander, licking the sky; or a relativist; or a roadman, morning star man; or a hanger-around the fort, fetish hanger, with a broken chevy; or first person, omniscient narrator of second or third person confluences of consciousness; or a hyper-essential, parabolic, metaphrastic, *nabi;* or a cherokee or a sioux, lakota or dakota; or house blesser, prepackaged strawberry mist; or a car fragrance; or a savior; or a minority; or canon fodder; or a fry-bread concessionaire; or an ethnic festivaler, wild ricer; or *pinik naboop;* or a fighting illini, an eagle or a hawk; or a peacemaker, a professor of any kind of highly classified studies; or a synecdoche, collective or unconscious, anima or inanimate; or an actor, or a plotter, didactic, or mimetic, or metahuman, onamatopeia, or polytheist, or an agnostic; or a death song poet; or a prophet; or a pilgrim; or a ghost supper waiting to happen, pure spirit; or a nascent name on the material precipice; or a materialist with secondhand clothes, or a euromuse looking for a place to land, or shall I claim more simply, I am not any of the above, on any line, on any form, to be signed below, or signified as other, with any other signifier between terms and conditions, esoteric to names, spiritual or otherwise, exoteric to names, European or otherwise, or shall I claim more simply: No, I am none of these.

These are just some of my relatives. Some of them are buried between memories of falling leaves; some live as we speak; some of them are on the road; some have traveled many roads: some of them not good, some of them red, some of them not red, many of them red, not good, many of them good not red, many of them both or neither. Still they are my relations and for them I am thankful.

The Second Door: I as Traveler I

I am a traveler:
outside White Earth, a child
nearly dead from lack of air,
in the heavy embrace
of pneumonia,
in Philadelphia projects;

One who fears superman,
One who fears zorro,
a gunfighting son
of a Bear totem father.

I am a traveler:
in the hands of sisters
in Catholic services,
in schools where the mist
takes the shapes of children
and eats lives whole and complete
in cursive and the arrangement of
letters.

I am a traveler:
one mistake from perfect
on a dirt diamond
in a bay area park,
where still train cars are
the main attraction;
in an oceanside elementary
school where velocity
times memory is the
spelling game rocket
with your name on it;
in a classroom where everyone
wants to reach the flat moon
on the flat wall
from the flat earth.

I am a traveler:
like Anishinaabe
grandfather Joe V.,
the dead pow-wow
dancer inside
the wooden box,
like all of us
who are outside
White Earth.

I am a traveler:
to the door of
Brunette, the old Native man
at the wood pile, smoking
half and half,
the old Pine Point man
driving cousins and
double cousins to Shell
Lake;
the old Pillager companion
of the old woman Obahbaum
who sees father
in son, who hears
mother in daughter

who embraces
us and covers us with that
thick warmth of quilt
when we come in frozen
from nights of speaking
with sister speaking with stars.

I am a traveler again:
to that pacific rock
where Zawquod hooks
up with Enterprise squadrons
and heads for the Gulf
of Tonkin;
where we go with Castro
from lessons on perspective
to shake mangoes down
from the tree of the grouchy
old Chammoran man;
Where Wilma V. drives us
into the bush to find
bicycle thieves;
where the girls of the
island pay brother to
watch the corrugated metal
outhouse door
and kill shrews while they
piss;
where brother Bonehead beat
the hell out of two Cabreras,
in boxing matches set up
by their father;
where brother Mukwa
found WWII shells in
Sumay caves.

I am a traveler:
to White Earth again,
briefly,
where to everyone's
amazement brother K

drove one over the
left fielder's head
and silenced laughter
at Naytahwaush;
where after proving we could
memorize the apostles' creed
we fought with the heavy
sheriff's heavy son
at pine point during
recess from confirmation
practice;
where we found names
mossed over on brush covered
graves in the bush
near rush lake;
where we speared suckers
trapped gophers and sold the skins
to the old man
across from Grandma Marie's;
where we shot uncle's pistols,
recoiled and raised dogs
under the dead
Pontiac;
where the Loon mother put
out a chimney fire by herself
while we stood in our pajamas
with Irene V. calling to no one
into nowhere
for help.

I am a traveler:
wandering in and out of
north suburban schools
where we talked of organizing
an Indian student walkout
with Chickasaw Boston
and Skenadore, only to
realize we had the necessary
federal blood quantum,
but not the numbers, so

we returned to geometry;
where *Bury My Heart at Wounded Knee*
was required reading for
smart kids;
where we continued
to wander in and out of
north suburban factories,
universities,
thunderbird drunk and in trouble;
where we guzzled and smoked
against the wall of the Teepee;
where rats ate holes
in our bread and the Greek landlord
raised his kids on our rent
and his kids raised German Shepherds
to attack Blacks;
where we worked slowly
and stupidly toward a
first degree in the wrong lodge,
in the wrong field;
where we became
an expert on Ceta
guidelines in two weeks
at the Big Fort job service;
where we made plans
on a park bench, near a Great
Lakes harbor, to leave
for Morroco with a one-eared
woman;
where we became expert
in time and materials
on the Commonwealth Edison site,
where we stopped the old carpenter
foreman, who went one too many
rounds with Joe Louis,
from going a round
with a local union man.

I am a traveler:
who married in a mill town along the

Rock River, not far from a stone
Blackhawk, carved into a cliff,

I am a traveler:
to Michigan to
a more advanced degree
in the wrong lodge;
where a shield teacher
came to us out of Ironwood,
where words and memory
saved Little Star from death
in Ann Arbor.

I am a traveler:
to Red River to
a more advanced degree
among Dakota and Turtle
Mountain people;
where Red Owl and his brother
took me to sweat
where old man Four Star
and his son
took me to sweat;
where Eagle Heart
and his brother
and Crossing Wind
opened their doors to me;
where we met Winona
at land recovery meetings;
where we drove into badlands
and told stories among
schoolchildren;
where we went to namings
again and again.
where Rainbow complicated her own
birth by reaching out too soon;
where we learned of the thirsty
dance, where travelers gave us
thunder songs.

I am a traveler:
to Eagletown
where we sang with two crows
a couple of times;
where we tried to write
substance abuse reports
in the early morning, before
the BIA phone rang;

where we tried to work with
public schools at the Saginaw
Chippewa tribe;
where we planted corn
and ran on the road
all summer in the humid
air;
where we fasted
and forgot about writing
novels, poems or essays;

I will be a traveler:
every year
from the year
young thunder woman arrived
in Mecosta County to this year
in Spanish cities.

I will be a traveler:
to the thirsty dance lodge
where we lead scouts,
wrapped in willow,
to the ceremonial center
where we dance in place
where we look to the center,
the center we try to
remember, to heal those
others we love,
when the idea of self
becomes too much
for others

to carry, when we know
we are truly home.

THE THIRD DOOR: I AS ALTER I-AN AUTOBIOGRAPHICAL META-TALE ON WRITING

Not long ago White Crow stole my camera—an old Canon with a fixed aperture. In the long run that was not so bad, but I could not present people with certain proofs, the proof people want from pictures without words. So I wrote words as if they were pictures in still lives like

The moon stops the night
traveling low in the tissue
of clouds
the glass is out of
reach of the hand turning
over.
In morning
The head is framed by
window by deep August
light, crossing through the
play of leaves.

Then—and this was before White Crow stole my camera—some woman in a graduate school fiction workshop said, "Why don't you write about Indians having their land stolen?" So I thought, Pictures aren't good enough; people not only want to see, they want to know something about the picture. "What does the one who makes the picture think of the picture" was the question I had to ask myself. Being of sound mind and limited vision, this presented problems for me, since it was after all difficult for me to see anything with clarity, whether it was part or whole, stationary or moving. So I tried again.

Vision and breath
travel away in the smell
of rain.

Next to a pick-up
an old man stands
sleeping drunk,
leave him,
there is the liquor
store, jukebox shadows
of music . . .

I tried to put myself in the picture, but I was unclear and still there was no stolen land in the poem. Then some road poet, bear writer—who I will call Spotted Eagle—told me "it's all metaphor." That was good because I was naive enough to believe him and that was good because it made me forget the focus of the woman in the fiction workshop. So I turned my head again.

Rice Lake loons call
the distance darkening,
in whatever was dream
fading,
as crows lift piece
by piece from the dead
on the side of the road.

When I showed my work to Spotted Eagle he said, "That's good, you've got crows and you've got road, keep putting those in and people will say they're metaphors." So I camped at windows, watching for crows, looking for metaphors. I saw sunflash in violet and green on the wings of one crow on top of Ramon's Mexican Restaurant, but I knew they'd nail me in writing workshop if I used the word "violet," so I refrained from opening any stanza with what I saw and I turned over poetic words in my mind. (I thought of a word I'd seen in a writing workshop, iridescent for the colored light on the wing, then I thought green? Cedar green? No, lighter and streaked with light and other colors.) By then I knew I was in trouble and I was losing all interest in writing, when I met White Crow at a poetry reading. The reading itself was uneventful—four people read and five people listened. But after the reading White Crow said "Creeley," and Spotted Eagle, who read with us, said, "Whitman." Thinking it was my turn I said,

"Williams." They both turned, at the same time. "Yeah, Williams." I felt good and started humming "I Can't Help It if I'm Still in Love with You," while they went on: "Rexroth," White Crow said. "Neruda," Spotted Eagle replied. It went on like this for a long time, each poet talking about his influences, style, and appearances on the page. I listened for a while, until I grew sleepy. I drifted back to the car hoping Spotted Eagle would follow soon, since we had to return from the university town we were in to the university town we came from. After a handrolled velvet smoke I fell asleep in the back of my blue Nova.

I dreamed as I still do of my father's life. How he told me of the last time he saw his father.

I was in the backseat of the car. We were riding outside the reservation. My father told me to go to sleep. That was the last time I saw him.

Then I was with my father on the reservation, in the rooms where he slept, in the house of the old people, my great-grandparents. There was a past I couldn't live in, a past of languages and words I never learned, a past of words my father couldn't share. So as a child I was never a speaker and the comfort I received grew not out of words, but out of the resilience of a Native presence of my father's grandparents and their ways. They took him in and raised him when my father and his brother and his sisters had no one else. And I saw the face of the old ones then. When I stopped thinking of myself I knew who I was and where I came from and I believed in this dream the way I believe that the spirits of the ones who raised my fathers raised me up. So I wrote

Wake chants circle overhead, like black crows watching her will stumble through weak moments. Like when she heard the carriage outside and went to the window with his name on her lips. Or when she looked over in the corner and saw him sleeping, with his mouth open, in the blue chair, next to the woodstove. She saw them, dissembled reflections on the insides of her black glasses.... The old woman dreams she is up north, on the reservation. It is autumn. Pine smoke hanging over the tops of houses, leaves sleepwalking in gray wind, skeletal trees scratching ghost gray sky ... Out the window, he lifts the axe. (He is young.) She watches as it splits a log on the tree stump. He turns away and starts toward the house. (He is old.) He takes out his pipe and presses down tobacco. She goes to the door to meet him. She opens the door. She tries to touch him. He passes through her, like a cold shiver, and walks into a photograph. . . .

(from Sleeping in Rain)

Then I was a boy again. Outside my maternal grandmother's house, at the place where we lived when we returned to White Earth. I stood in the grass, watching shadows grow long into the road. The old woman was watching me from a window, her head framed by the light in the kitchen. (She told me later she saw me talking to myself.) I was alone, wrapped up in a game I made up. In the game I took two small men, each made of molded plastic, and I put them in a box. I cut a hole in the box. I called it a door. Then I talked to myself and I sang to myself and I shook the box as I watched the shadows grow into the road. In time one of the men would fly out the door of the box and the man who stayed inside, I called him the winner. In time I brought other men into the game and I gave some of the men names, sometimes the men in the box would fly out of the door simultaneously, so I would send them back to try again, until one or the other was left inside. I can't remember when I quit playing that game.

I told White Crow of my dream in the Nova, but he wasn't interested. Then I showed him the words I wrote. "It's fiction," I said. "No," he said. "It's more like poetry. It's not realistic. There's too much I and the prose is weak." (Later, most of the people in the fiction workshop agreed with him.) "Try this," he said, "after you write, put your papers on an ironing board and run them under an iron. Not a hot iron, but a warm iron. If you make the iron too hot some words will stick to the metal, but if the iron's too cool the words and paper won't get flat enough." Flat, I thought, seems right and White Crow seems believable. "But," I said, "won't the words have a metallic trace to them?" White Crow blinked twice, once with light, once darkly. "Yes, but that's what you want, flat and a bit of iron, or aluminum." Also he said, "The iron brings out the material in the paper. The warmth of the metal helps the paper remember its life as a tree, as material. You follow?"

I don't remember going home after that. After a few more months, I got pneumonia for the second time in my life. My life turned then. I completed my master's degree and I went to Ann Arbor to start on another degree. But some element of my sickness held on. I had no desire to live or write. People entered my life and after speaking to an elder from Ironwood, I knew I had to get away. I had become part of other people's sickness as well; my first daughter, Kehli, almost choked to death while I partied with friends.

I decided then to leave Ann Arbor. When my wife and I were packing our things White Crow knocked on the sliding glass doors. As I carried boxes out to the U-Haul White Crow said, "Stop, I'll get a picture of you guys in front of the apartment." Then he picked up the Canon from the table and we stood there waiting. I remember thinking: it won't come out right; the light is no good and he doesn't know the camera. He took the picture. After a few minutes he left and we went back to packing.

My family and I went on to North Dakota. Later on, in the spring, when my wife and I wanted to take a picture of a double rainbow, we realized that we had no camera. It wasn't in the unpacked box marked miscellaneous and it wasn't in the closet, with the boxes of pictures.

But North Dakota was good, with or without the camera. I gradually felt myself healing. I wrote nothing for years, until I gave in to giving up writing. This led me to

How Soon

The story goes from in a rainfall
to sister walking a field
browned autumn. And when she arrives
winter has come, so the old man
rises from his chair, picks up
matches, pipe and tools, and
walks out to begin again.

The sculptures grow by the day,
birds in ice, recognizable
eagles, a bear who began
as a man in a moment of dance.
He does this in ice, all

winter carving at dawn,
carving at dusk.

And sister after walking a field
browned autumn arrives, watches
from the east window, waits,
goes out to him in spring,
taps him on the shoulder,
and points to the pools
of water he's standing over.

I also met new teachers outside of the university. An elder named Francis Cree took the time to meet with me, whenever I went up to Turtle Mountain. From him I learned strength and acceptance. He brought me into ceremonies, he opened his ceremonies to me and taught me. At the same time I started working as a writer in the schools in North Dakota. I traveled all over the state, teaching poetry and telling stories, many of which were about creating stories. Through Francis, through storytelling I grew to recognize the gifts of creation. I saw my wife and children anew. I began to understand the deep and profound ways of seeing that being in ceremony involved. These ways of seeing and understanding helped me to recognize the stories in all things; these ways of seeing helped me to try and see the cumulative past in the being present. My life opened and kept opening. At one ceremony I was given a gift.

The Story of a Blue Man

As Strawberry (or He Who Walks Behind the Buffalo) prepares to cut me, Little Boy walks up and hangs the beaded man around my neck.

After the ceremony, I receive instructions: feed him sweet things, put tobacco out, ask about him often. I do these things and I carry the man with me everywhere.

Sometimes when I think I've lost him, he turns up inside a shirt I've left in front of the mirror. Once I found him hanging from a willow branch, after I spent a morning gathering wood. I've given him peaches and strawberries in summer. I've taken him to see moss covered stones and to the creek where my children play.

When I think about him, I know that I am part of a larger family: I am part of Little Boy's family, Strawberry's family, Eagleheart's family, White Earth families, Vizenor families, and Henry families, the families of Bellangers and Fairbanks, the families of Minogeeshik, and Oskinaway, the families of those who came before us in words and names, the families of those who will come after.

For years I never saw White Crow, though I thought I saw someone who looked like him at a conference in Wisconsin. He was sitting at a table with a couple of Oneida women. Live birds in cages were singing over their heads, so I couldn't make out their conversation. I almost went up to him—to ask him about the old Canon—but a Cheyenne River poet going in another direction asked me to go to the casino with him, and I did.

I eventually left North Dakota and returned to Michigan. Since then I've worked for two tribes and two universities. Since then a third daughter has come among us. Since then I've given a beaded man to a Tuscarora elder. As for White Crow I've seen or heard nothing of him for a long time. I don't know that I'll ever see him again. If I do see him, I'll tell him to keep the camera. In some ways I believe the old Canon has always been his and he should keep it.

FOURTH DOOR: I AS STILL OPEN I-FROM SPAIN, 1994

In the metro station at Moncloa, we pass immigrant African vendors. They sell Winstons and beaded jewelry. People walk quickly by us, sometimes nudging us wordlessly. As we ascend the steps into the sunlight, I am thinking of smoking, looking for the old man at the top of the steps. I know he'll be there at a card table, selling gum and lighters. I need a lighter. I approach him and ask for a lighter. He holds one up and grinds his thumb against the metal lighter wheel, igniting a spark. Then flame shoots up, straight, orange and yellow. At this moment I long for home, for the moments before the sweat fires at Turtle Mountain, where Francis and Louis tell stories, where Houle and Ecklebecker trade insults, where Old Eagle and I sit in silence on stones, listening, remembering, and looking forward to more stories.

"Vale?" the old man says, as the flame draws into disappearance.

I take the lighter from him. *"Vale, gracias,"* I say.

"Megwetch," I whisper later as I take a smoke and think of many people, of many families, of home.

INVOCATION: May the children grow strong with their gifts and dreams. May those who have inspired us continue to inspire. I give thanks for this moment, for the good words and works of those who came before us, for the Creator and creation.

DISPLACEMENTS
PERFORMING MESTIZAJE[*]

PATRICIA PENN HILDEN

Of Dutch, English, and Nez Perce descent, Patricia Hilden has a doctorate from Cambridge University, and has taught at Cambridge, Oxford, and Emory University. She is currently professor of Ethnic Studies at the University of California, Berkeley.

Her scholarly publications include work on French and Belgian labor history, as well as work in Native American history and culture. Her recent book, When Nickels Were Indians *(1995), is an autobiographical reflection on growing up Native in California in the sixties and an examination of questions of identity more generally.*

*This essay owes its existence to: Timothy J. Reiss, to our talking circle, Dean Bear Claw, Chris Eyre, Bill Gossett, Shari Huhndorf, Carol Kalafatic, Harriett Skye, Miryam Yataco, and to Rainier Spencer, Arnold Krupat, and Alfred Arteaga.

September 4, 1977: I got lost. Somewhere between the Oakland airport and London's Heathrow, everything shifted. At school in Cambridge, then living in Paris, Oxford, Brussels, and, most recently, Atlanta and New York, I looked for direction but found only low skies, a sun rising and setting in wrong places: south in England, New York, and northern Europe; over land, not water, in Georgia. ("I could never live on the East Coast," said a friend. "The sun sets *on the wrong side.*") Now, wanting to go somewhere in Manhattan, I have to go outside (down elevator full of strangers, through a grim dentist office apartment lobby to a black asphalt drive joining the four great gray blocks of the deceptively named Washington Square Village), arrange myself facing the direction my mind (only upon considerable reflection) tells me is "uptown"—north of where I am standing—and then think hard about which is the east side, which the west. Even then, I am never really sure. "Lost" lurks around every corner . . . is virtually certain at subway stops, where time underground erases the tenuous hold on geography painstakingly established before setting out.

I stayed lost, got used to it, in fact, until last May. In Berkeley, Julio Ramos introduced me: "This is Alfredo Arteaga, Pat, from L.A. too, Chicano, even Indio, too." Alfred, *el poete* himself, looked at my blue eyes with that familiar "Oh yeah?" expression. Then, a little aggressively: "Do you remember when Ritchie Valens died?"

I did: Ritchie Valenzuela (before angloization), though older, was from my neighborhood. The day of his death, our principal suspended classes. "La Bamba," "Come On, Let's Go," and—over and over and over—"Donna" played over the school's loudspeakers as those who had known Ritchie, and lots who had not, cried and cried and cried. We were young: it was our second collective encounter with death by airplane. (Two planes had crashed and fallen on the playground at Pacoima Junior High two years before, killing Ritchie Valens's best friend. Staring out the window during my seventh-grade student government meeting, I had seen the planes meet in the air, had watched them fall, had wondered at the smoke rising in a tall column above what I did not realize was another junior high school. Those of us from that neighborhood, bused across town, where we had already begun to unlearn our "street" Spanish in favor of "smart kids' " French, were put back on buses and sent home.)

I was, I knew instantly, looking back into Alfred's brown eyes, hearing the familiar sounds of the right Spanish—caló, L.A. Spanish, not the lisping oddity of Castilian—home again. The sun, magnificently orange and pink and blue and lavender, fell straight into the *right* sea. Morning came from the east. And the sky resumed its identity: vast and much, much bluer than the skies over Europe, over New York, over Atlanta.

Kwame Anthony Appiah: "There is a piece of Akan wordplay . . . *'Esono esono, na esono sosono'* . . . which being translated reads, 'The elephant is one thing and the worm another.' "

Despite rediscovering home—for a time at least—I was not all the way home. Though cross-bloods, though Angeleno/a, Alfred and I were not the same, not even the same Indios/Indians, or even the same "discovereds." Some things matched: some Anglos "collect" Latinos, as as they like to collect Indians. Relationships—love and friendship— trick Chicano/as they often trick us as desire takes on politicized racial longings. Love across ethnic lines—easier but still complicated—is similarly vexed. But there are also dissimilarities. *"They,"* for one thing, want to *be* "Us": they want to touch us, enter our lives and spirits—and when they can't find us live, to dig up and collect our dead.

(At a recent film festival in New York I rediscovered the extent of this white desire. I wrote about it to Alfred: "It was worse than I imagined: a handful of Indian filmmakers and discussants facing a sea of THEM . . . : an auditorium filled with ethnographic filmmakers, collectors, teachers . . . Not one without more racist bones than most indigenous bodies contain . . . [We know this, thanks to the bone collections cherished in museums all over America. . . .] They wouldn't talk about the topic of our panel presentation, the politics of making films in indigenous communities. . . . Instead, it was all about their insatiable curiosity about Indians. As Dean Bear Claw put it, 'Before chairs, how did you people sit

down?' . . . It got worse when we were taken to lunch. People in suits literally took over the restaurant, pushing and shoving. All of us ended up having to add ourselves to already crowded tables. Almost as soon as we sat down [two of us together, the third trapped across the table] they began touching us . . . patting our arms and shoulders, laughing too loudly at everything we said, murmuring 'oh aren't you funny'. . . . I employed a Medusa gaze to stop them patting me on my cute little native head. S. and I then retreated behind what Wendy Rose calls the 'potted plant mode,' successfully removing ourselves from the loud, aggressive 'networking' all around us. But across the table, our friend was still being groped and patronized. . . . She would say something and they would all look at each other [anglo girls on the school playground] and agree that she was just the funniest, cutest little Indian they had ever met. S. and I came close to reaching across the table and removing some of the fondling hands. . . .

"Oh lord, rage on rage on. . . ."

Before going home to California in May, there were hideous months in New York City, where, remembering what must be remembered to write these thoughts, dreams stole my nights as the horror of the place captured my days. One dream came every night—suitably accompanied by sound effects in the ominous, concrete city dark: sirens, small explosions, sounds of windshields shattering, shouting, cries, the endless wail of car alarms.

A dark-haired evil woman announced that she had located the "remains" of a man in the water of a wide river, just across from where I lived. I knew whose body it was: my gentle young husband, who, having fallen in love with death, committed suicide. But she and other white people would not let me claim him. They insisted the body was to go into a museum; that they had the right to use it as they wished because it was an Indian "unknown." The dream was a horror of anguished frustration as I tried repeatedly to claim him and they refused.

A haunting dream: memories of his life and terrible death, memories of my helplessness, all awash in a collective memory of tribal bodies, thousands of them, claimed and stolen by the invaders' descendants for their museums, their collections, their scientific academies. It was a dream of my grief, and a dream of grief shared.

(Nothing about the new Heye Center of the National Museum of the American Indian assuages this mourning. Five hundred artifacts from the collection of the rapacious George Heye, are presented as "gifts," lifted intact from their bloody

history, given by Native America to "all of us" as most of the comments in the visitors' book—hundreds penned by the children whose overwhelming presence is inevitable when Indians are involved—claim. Entombed in that vast monument to U.S. economic imperial might, the marble and gilt Customs House, are eons of tribal sorrows and secrets.)

By April, it was time to get out. The semester ended, we rang up Avis, the first step in the rescue.

Early one May Sunday morning, we headed for Penn Station, climbing down the stairs to the Long Island Railroad, which would carry us to the car rental agency in Westbury. Everywhere, men, black and white, old and young, sprawled on the steps. The smell of urine, scent of New York, overpowered the constricted space as we climbed carefully down and around body after body. Not sufficiently practiced at life in this place, I kept looking: "Is he dead or alive?" Watching anxiously for movement, the slightest lifting of a chest . . . THIS MORNING'S DEAD PERSON: NEW YORK.

We got the car. We headed West. Three long days later, I was home under the wide skies. No people. No people smell. There, in California, I finished remembering: I wrote you a letter.

In our New Age, Native America has become a spiritual theme park as thousands of white self-exiles, carriers of a (contagious?) marginalized modern consciousness, frantically pursue something to fill their emptiness. Indians—as individuals, as collectivities, as disembodied words and even fashion accessories—are hapless destinations.

The tribal world braces itself. *They* are coming, fat with their conviction that their experience of their culture's death agonies renders them fit companions for those they name "marginals," those "exiled" from what they all see as "real history"—the long (upward) trajectory from the Enlightenment to the troublingly "fragmented" and uncertain present.

(At the new museum, a friend and I posted ourselves near a "sacred circle" built into the floor and spotlighted. A sign explains that Indians have many such "sacred places" where they go to seek visions. Visitors are invited to stand for "a few moments in silence" in the museum's hyper-fake circle, where they may experience this "Indian" peace. Many visitors took advantage of this offer of quick, painless enlightenment, though men shuffled into the circle with

embarrassed expressions while women positioned themselves unashamedly under the artificial "sun," assuming beatific expressions which followed their faces through the exhibit's exit doorway.)

Just as Native America turned a baffled face to the first invasion, and amused expressions to generations of anthropologists, so now it turns its collective gaze (old people sigh and shake their heads: "white people are funny") to encounter this age's incarnation of the Indian researcher, seeking scholarly enlightenment in the name of cultural studies. Unlike their forebears, these culture analysts no longer lust after intricate diagrams of kinship relations or titillating details of exotic sex practices. Rather, they want tribal people to move over a bit (sometimes quite a lot) so that they can share the cultural space they have defined (from a distance) as this strange condition called "exile."

But of course no tribal person recognizes herself in this state. The closer come the refugees from urban modernism, arms outstretched for the pseudo-collegial embrace, the farther backward moves the Indian . . . until, in fact, she vanishes once again, over the shifting postmodernist horizon.

The seeker, however, is untroubled; it was not she he wanted. Rather he wanted what she leaves behind: her shadow, her representation, ready for freezing into the background portraits with which these "exiles" decorate their lives. Natives once again resume their historical destiny: "primitive" yardsticks against which the (post) modernist subject measures himself. Soon, the portrait's caption, "Marginality," assumes life, assumes permanence; forever (again!) hung on those vacant walls, coloring the empty lives of the self-described, self-chosen "postmodernists."

But although representation suggests that they are now really *truly* vanished, we know Indians are still around. So where are the "real authentick Indians?"

Letter to Chris

17 July 1994
Davis, California

Dear Chris,

That night at Pane e Cioccolato, you were angry. You had just finished reading some of my book and wanted to talk. "Don't worry about your blue eyes and light complexion. Don't talk about it," you said. You don't want me to be self-conscious when we go together into company. My attitudes, you told me with unusual seriousness, were wrong. They cut me off from you. By considering how I look to most white people, I am not just giving in to their racism, I am also suggesting to you that we are not the same, not as related as we feel, one to the other—across generations, across gender, but *not* across race.

And you are right. You and I and most of the others of our group *are* relations: all mixed blood, all condemned to live crossing back and forth across the worlds.

(Months later, Alfred writes: "Kind of like the problem of siendo xicano *and yet eeking out some performance of self over and against and between two nations. . . .")*

What makes our group of fragments, Indians in New York, assembled by pure accident from all across the Americas, an "Us"? Dozens of things, whirling around in concentric circles, stars in the constellations of identity, of its community—things Anglos seem to know nothing about. The moccasin telegraph hums: "Whom do you know?" Telephones connect the "ins," exclude the "never heard ofs." Anagrams from the old days link: OEO, EOP, Upward Bound, IYC, NCAI. Or there is AIM, there are Indian centers, there is Wounded Knee, the Trail of Broken Treaties, Alcatraz, Washington fish-ins. There are academic and artistic worlds: historians, writers, artists, scholars, filmmakers. "Do you know?" "Do you know?"

There are relations: my sister or brother, my cousin, my parents. There are the histories: who are we? where did we come from?

But you are also wrong.

We know it every week, when we walk together out of the decrepit NYU building. Inside, around that table, sometimes smudged, sometimes not (our practices are quite random), we are kin. Outside—stopping for coffee—we are immediately divided by the gazes of passersby. W. becomes maybe "African Something"? or East Indian? or Mexican? or . . . ? Three of us become white: that Shari's blue eyes have an obvious Yup'ik shape, that Bill's manner has Apache written all over it, that all our teeth are . . . *teeth!???* You, Harriett, Dean, and Carol are the "Indians." Miryam is Indian too—but not "North American." The rest of us?

(Another restaurant: we began to discuss—again—this persistent, gnawing issue of crossed blood—prompted, again, by white reactions to us. I discovered

that I was the only one who knew the markers with which the children of 1950s Los Angeles were classified! No one else, Crow, Yup'ik, Osage, Cheyennel/Arapaho, Andean, Lakota, had ever heard of "shovel" teeth, cheekbone to chin measurements, hairlessness, hair texture. . . .

So: Los Angeles, in the fifties as now a hotbed of race warfare, had evidently taught its children (Alfred knows these markers too) how to see their "correct" racial slots while elsewhere identity had come not from physical appearance but rather from family, from community, from place.

Indeed, in the post-war years race identification was taught not just in Los Angeles but all over California: in the 1960s and 1970s we used to play "race": aviator glasses were the real test. If they didn't leave wide red gashes on your high-cheekboned face, you weren't a "real Indian." Or peanut butter: if it didn't lodge itself behind all your front teeth, you were as fake as someone who wore a beard or full mustache, who had hairy legs or arms.)

By 1994, when such superficial racial classification was practiced everywhere, our external and—consequently—internal selves seem implacably divided. Our "white" experiences of race are thus always different from yours.

Take that plane flight from Atlanta: you and Harriett and I, traveling back to New York. Sitting directly in front of us were three French tourists, one shockingly kitted out in "Indian" vestments: a T-shirt bearing the face of some generic (unrecognizable to us) "chief," a heavily riveted black leather belt, black trousers, beaded headband, choker, Navajo silver bracelet. They spotted . . . *you,* Chris, not me, not Harriett. Assuming no one around them spoke French, they began, in high excitement, to speculate about what tribe you might be from . . . *"un vrai Indien,"* they murmured joyously, sneaking glimpses of you through their armrests.

You, oblivious, continued to nod and drum to the music in your ears. Their voices and their gestures grew more obvious. I intervened, leaning across to tell you, in carefully enunciated, loud English, to notice the people in front of us, the European "wannabes" in their ridiculous costumes. You began to watch them back. Soon, you whispered, "Wait 'til you see the guy's jacket!" As indeed Harriett and I soon did as he stood to don it before landing. It was magnificently absurd: black leather, hung with large feathers, decorated with intricate beadwork. Along the arms, more feathers, these fake, embossed in the leather and painted purple. We all laughed; Harriett, Lakota-style, decided to confront the man once we were all off the plane.

At the baggage turnstile, these strange tourists gathered as close to us as they could. Harriett went to engage them—introducing herself with customary graciousness, and adding, "Standing Rock Lakota." They treated her courteously, but it was clear that they wanted something more than a light-skinned, light-eyed woman, however "real" Lakota. They wanted you, your long black hair, your black eyes, your dark skin. I saw them coming and turned to warn you. You, however, had already disappeared—into the crowd, safe from their rapacious tourism.

Or during that condescension session at the film festival. I had a choice. I could have slipped into a white role that would have transformed utterly their collective reaction to me. My Cambridge don mode, equipped with degrees and credentials, would instantly have halted the groping, the collecting, the patronizing giggles of amazement that we Indians could not only talk, but could even use our knives and forks. I could effectively switch "races"—to *my* hyper-Anglo side—where I would be left alone.

(This, too, is complicated. Once again Alfred prodded: "Was this occasion the first time you appeared in New York as an Indian?" he asked. "Haven't you lived there slipping in and out of racial conflict all along by playing Anglo when you're with Anglos?" "Of course," he wrote, "I know and you know that this choice is solely your desire not to be mistaken by people you don't know for a wannabe, a white person with a rumor of Cherokee blood in a great-grandparent or two. But it is surely still a choice you have habitually made that has protected you from the rapacious collecting instincts of Anglos.")

There is still another side to this. When *you* go among Native people, you do not have to carry credentials. Your looks (and, to a lesser extent, your sex) win you instant acceptance. No one questions your claims. No one asks you to *make* claims. Never for you the experience that happened to me when I met a very famous Native performer for the first time. She instantly dragged me into a women's restroom, where, looking me up and down, she demanded, "Who are you?" It took me a moment to figure out that she wanted my tribal background. I told her. She continued to peer closely (much too closely—but she is New York and I am not) and at great length at my face, my body, my hair. At last she pronounced her verdict: "I see it," she told me, "inside those blue eyes and that light skin I can see it." She took my arm to signal this acceptance, pulling me back outside.

Within or without Indian Country, then, my acceptance is harder earned, borne more lightly, more timorously. It is a fragile thing—carried inside, for years almost never outside except with other Native people who know me.

Of course it is not up to you to make me feel better about it, or—something that happens in spite of us—lend me racial credibility. I am fully aware—we all are—that those of us who look "white" enjoy choices others—you—don't. But there are many times when I wish that I looked what I am, that everyone could see what I saw looking at you that first time in my living room in New York: the same face, the same bones, the same hair, the same *soul* (the same big "Indian ears"!), all externally different only because of color.

Another airport, this in *our* home country, out west. It was, in fact, Portland, where the terminal was awash in Oregon Trail celebrations. Videos played, over and over, scenes of courage on the trail. A voice repeated: "Brave settlers carrying out the destiny of our great nation."

For sale everywhere were dozens of Indian artifacts. Behind one shop counter, a giddily cheery (or did she just seem that way after the aggressive nastiness of New York?) woman assured an overdressed anglo couple that all the goods were "genuine," made by "real Indians." When they had finished their buying, the woman turned to me. I was standing next to a display of jewelry decorated with the Columbia River petroglyphs, drowned forever by the Celilo Falls Dam. She bragged about the success of that project, which had supplied electricity for Portland's growth. She was *boasting* to me—child of the people whose ancient art these pictures were! Child of the people whose sacred places, whose fishing grounds, whose lives had been swept away by the white greed for electricity. . . . This would not happen to you. (Or would it? Behind my blue eyes, I don't know.)

Of course there are still more intricate complications in this matter of Indian identity—some we meet in the same way.

No Turning Back Our parents and grandparents chose the white road. Turning Back—retrieving our tribal selves, rediscovering lost relations, learning language, learning the origins of the behavior we learned from the old people around us—is it fake? isn't it wannabe? Can it only be thought "authentic" if one accepts the essentialist view (that of the last century's racist scientists) that Indianness is carried just where *they* said all along: in the blood?

But *is* this journey into a collective past necessarily artificial? Are we not making a simple journey home, finding our people, finding ourselves, together?

Perhaps. But still, we mixed-bloods, we displaced thousands, know that we shall never return all the way home. We have no home.

"To be Hopi is to be *at* Hopi," Angela wrote. But you and I have never felt this connection, both of us growing up far, far from the tribal people from whom we both come. As I grew up in Los Angeles knowing more about being Navajo—or Hopi—than about being Nez Perce, so you learned more about being Modoc or Klamath than about being what you are. So what does the tribal community mean to you? Is it a pan-Indian world? where "traditions" are the ragged remnants of Gerald Vizenor's "survivance"? Is it a world defined—and limited—by the physical markers of race? Is it the most recent eliminator of outsiders, tribal enrollment?

You will forgive me if I "go academic"?

You have read about the enrollment attacks on certain well-known writers, artists, filmmakers, political militants. In their haste to exclude, attackers get confused, muddling "real" fakes with those whose blood quantum is insufficient for particular tribal enrollment—or who did not get enrolled at some point when no one was counting red blood cells. Ward Churchill goes to war with Tim Giago: accusations fly back and forth. Accusations and counter-accusations grow increasingly ridiculous: hair dye and sunglasses worn indoors . . . skin coloring, pancake makeup, braid ties, ponytails . . . whose are *real*?

Rational voices intervene: from the Southwest comes a letter deploring the self-destructiveness of harsh identity politics: "From . . . *Indian Country Today*," writes Kelly Begay, "I have learned about new efforts directed toward describing and limiting the definition of 'Indian.' I can tell you that I'm truly alarmed at what seems to be a concerted drive to create an exclusionary class of people who by their own doing will undo themselves in the end (and destroy all Indian people in a few generations). . . . Any legal definition of any person, place, or concept also creates a concomitant drawing of parameters which not only protect, but exclude as well. If only the legally defined Indian can call him or herself Indian, then all the rest (who might be full-blood but unable to fulfill tribal blood quantum requirements) are left out in the cold."

Begay suggests criteria for "Who is Indian?" "First and paramount, anybody who states that he or she is Indian or descended from Indian people should be considered to be socially identified as Indian. This is the same right and courtesy which is extended to Jews, Irish, French, Italians, Blacks, Hispanics, Asians and any other group. And, importantly, any person not asking for services which require them to be enrolled should not be prosecuted or persecuted by any group whether that group be Indian or non-Indian. They should have the legal right to be just who they say they are...."*

But alas, like most things, it is more complicated. What about people who "discover" possible Native roots just in time to publish books on Native subjects? Who then become both scholarly authorities and "Indians"—or "mixed blood," as those with dubious claims usually classify themselves. This might not pose problems (except of satire) if Native voices were being heard. But when a Euro-American represents herself as Native when she is not (not by blood *or* experience *or* community), in settings lacking genuine Native voices, then it *is* surely a problem—of ethics, of integrity, of the silencing (again) of America's tribal people.

Not everyone who claims to be Indian receives equal scorn, however, even from those most rabid in their pursuit of "wannabes." When two of the Kennedy children, Robert Kennedy, Jr., and Kerry Kennedy Cuomo, visited South Dakota in May 1993, *Indian Country Today*, vociferous in its protests against "wouldbes," reported with approval Kerry Kennedy Cuomo's revelation that "As she was growing up and people asked her what she wanted to be, she would always reply, 'I want to be an Indian.'" The origins of her desire were the presents Robert Kennedy brought back to his children after trips West. "The gifts," the paper reported, "were ceremonial bonnets and other Indian artifacts and he would tell them the story behind the gifts." The Kennedys were welcomed with "A special spiritual ceremony . . . held for them at the home of Tim and Lynn Giago. . . . Oglala spiritual leader Rick Two Dog conducted a sweat lodge ceremony for the Kennedys and for Lynn Giago and was told by *Tunkasila* of the names they should be given." Robert Jr. was given the name "Spotted Eagle, his son [it's Indians, bring the kids!] Bobby Kennedy III was named White Buffalo Boy, Kerry Kennedy was named Good Earth Woman. . . ."

*From *Indian Country Today* (Sept. 15, 1993): p. A6

Of course there is nothing intrinsically wrong about any of this: Oglala Lakota people have every right to share sacred ceremonies with outsiders, to name them, to honor them with eagle plumes. But one doubts that less prominent wannabes, ordinary folks who declared that various artifacts given them in childhood had made them "want to be Indian," would have received welcome and acceptance from those who have been among the most vigorous in their pursuit of others much less "white" than the Kennedys.

All this identity policing was, of course, prompted most recently by implementation of the Indian Arts and Crafts Act. And there is another "identity" act (this one touching closer to all our homes) that similarly poses myriad problems for would-be purists. It, too, was motivated by good intentions, in this case to stop the drain of tribal children "adopted out" to white families.

(The adoption rate was staggering: Euro-American would-be parents, it seems, lusted after Indian children as much as they desired to collect Indian grownups. In the year the act was passed, Native American children were being adopted at a rate twenty times higher than the national rate. Not surprisingly, the phrase "adopted out" is common to all Indian families, including mine, from which several of my father's cousins have disappeared, their existence noted only by those ominous, foreclosing words.)

But the effects of the 1978 Indian Child Welfare Act have been more mixed than most hoped. Adoptions continue as month after month court cases, riddled with identity confusion, surface. One recent story may be typical. It involves a child of a white mother who gave the boy up for adoption when he was one day old. He was adopted by white people who took him home to their Idaho dairy farm. *The New York Times* reported that although the boy's father, an "Oglala Sioux Indian," "has never seen the boy or sought custody," the tribe has brought suit to reclaim him for his Indian relatives and to bring him to Pine Ridge.

This five-year-old is one half Lakota. Other children in similar cases possess less tribal blood. In Oregon, a twelve-year-old who is one eighth Cherokee is being taken from people who have raised him from infancy because "he belongs with Indians." This is not a tribal claim: rather, the state of Oregon is making a decision based solely on its interpretation of the law.

Who wins in such cases? Does the issue have to do with blood? The half-white child, after all, is half-white while the Cherokee boy is only one-eighth Indian. Does white blood not matter then? Moreover, would the people claiming a child with one-eighth Indian blood allow that same child to enroll if he/she were not an adoption case? And what about children with even less "pure" blood? Most tribal members, as everyone knows, are themselves possessors of mixed blood. If a man whose "blood" is primarily Mexican (though of course some of that blood is probably "Indian") fathers a child with a woman with one-sixteenth Indian blood, what does that make the child? And where do looks matter? If the child "looks" Indian, will he/she be more accepted in the tribe than a child whose genes coughed up white markers? We know what the outside world will do and say about it. But what about the blood-conscious Indian world? Is the white-looking child, raised with a white family but "returned" to tribal life on a reservation at age four or five or twelve, ever going to belong the way a child might who "looked" his/her Indian heritage?

These are not easy questions to answer. The world of identity politics is complicated and vexed. Shari and I share two identities as a result, including that of America's "in group." We recognized this mixed-blood bond at once when we met the first time. Her blue eyes looked into mine, then at the brown hair, the lightish skin.... We both thought, You, *too?*

(We could solve problems as they do in Europe, where "hobbyists" gather at summer campgrounds to play Indian. They keep their games "authentic" by employing stereotypical markers. One rulebook, for example, prescribes an "Indian way of speaking": sugar is "sweet white powder," coffee, "black drink," tea, "yellow drink." Participants name themselves "Eagle Feather," "Grey Owl," "Bird On His Leg" and wear elaborately "authentic" beaded and feathered costumes. They must, moreover, wear long black wigs with "appropriate headdress." Nonconformists become "half-breeds": "anyone who looks like an Indian in his [sic] behavior and appearance, but wears short hair, mustache, or beard, or whose clothes show him to be a White person.")

In our relentlessly "real" world, where politicians, fearful of the inexorable (re)"coloring" of North America, have begun proclaiming the necessity of "reasserting *American* culture and civilization" (Newt Gingrich's thinly disguised whites-only politics) it is an essential but fraught tie, this mixed-blood tie, artifact of racism, of an identity-shattering American history.

It holds inside it a hiding place—a place where we cross-bloods belong, with you, but also (not more intensely) with each other.

It is to this self—hidden from most of the outside world—that we most often flee. We may protect it too vehemently. Are we Vizenor's "freebooters of racism"? Do we tumble *too* heedlessly into a heavily romanticized "Indian Country"? Do *we* demand that "res" people stay as *we* need them to be? our romantic, nostalgic past? untouched, unchanged, unchanging? Do we, who move freely in and out, educated and credentialed, desire a red road fixed in concrete, an alternate path we can take (drive down) when, from time to time, *our* "modernist" (or, for some, postmodernist) world overwhelms? Does our blood quantum distinguish our sentiments from those of our white wannabe colleagues? Or is it something else?

I think of a cartoon I saw recently in *The New Yorker*. It shows two cows and a pig standing in a field gazing into the sky watching a third cow jump over the moon. The pig turns a questioning face to one of her bovine companions who explains, "It's a cow thing. You wouldn't understand." Whatever our blood, we Indians are all cows, and we do understand that, if nothing else. To paraphrase a most untribal poet, "We *must* love one another or die!"

So you are right.

From our native land in the west, I send you these words.

Love,

A Soul
Like the Sun

ROBERTA HILL

*Roberta Hill is a member of the Oneida Nation of Wisconsin. She is
a professor of English and American Indian Studies at the University
of Wisconsin, Madison. Her books of poetry include* Star
Quilt *(1984), now in a fifteenth-year edition,* Philadelphia
Flowers *(1995), and* Excerpts from "Your Fierce Resistance"
(1992). Her poetry has appeared most recently in Reinventing the
Enemy's Language, Tamaqua, *and* Pemmican, *among others.
Her poem, "In my voice," is included in the St. Paul Poetry Garden,
a collaborative sculptural project located in downtown St. Paul,
Minnesota. Her fiction has appeared in* Talking Leaves: An An-
thology of Contemporary Native American Short Stories,
and in Sweetgrass Grows All Around Her. *An essay also ap-
peared in* Speaking for the Generations: Native Writers on
Writing. *In 1993, she received a Lila Wallace–Reader's Digest
Award, which gave her time to complete a biography of her grandmother, Dr. L. Rosa Minoka-Hill. That manuscript was one of two
winners of the University of Nebraska's Native American Prose
Award; it will be forthcoming from the University of Nebraska
Press.*

In her essay, "Site of Memory," Toni Morrison shares her method of "literary archeology." She gains access to hidden, undisclosed lives imaginatively by finding an image; then believing in the floodwaters of memory, she traces that image back to its truth. My life as a writer has been to seek and discover the moral vision of my heritage by paying attention to the world and the images that come as I dream of it. My practice of this search has also been shaped by the conversions of previous generations and by a longing for knowledge of my ancestors' ways of life. I felt ripped away from generations past.

My writing emerges from a similar act of imaginative archaeology. On the most immediate layer, two generations before me, are choices my grandmother made when she converted to Catholicism and raised her children with a firm belief in that faith. The choices I've made come from feeling an undisclosed turmoil that keeps traveling down through generations and which has never been easily shared even among those who most deeply feel it. I feel at times as if my most meaningful truths have been locked up in a vortex somewhere inside my dreams and that I must continue to search for a way to break through into that pattern where truth becomes evident and more easily lived. There has been no name for the secret gaps in our history. The pain that accompanied it was too dreadful to discuss and the means for overcoming it continues on a parallel course; it is the desire to become whole and complete and aware of one's passage from those most ancient mythic roots to the present moment.

I gained a love of language because the Catholic Church had fastened a powerful hold on my childhood imagination. Not only did the Church give me a love of ritual—that male voice chanting Latin's round and ornate sounds into the echoing caverns of the church ceiling—it also injected me with a sense of shame. By second grade, I learned that people had within them more than one floor. Their souls contained basements, where sins lurked in the gloom of furnace fires. Even if we all tried to live on the main floor of our daylight consciousness, or in richer moments in the choir loft, surrounded by angelic flutterings, the basement was still the grounding space and it gathered murky sins. The only way to reach the high altar of heaven was to learn how to speak in the right way to a priest. Learning to confess was my earliest training for learning to write. The right words in the right order was the only way to reach the ear of God.

For that first confession I carried the weight of my wrongs like a sack of pebbles against my ribs. Even if I sucked in my breath, held my diaphragm tight against my stomach, the painful catch remained. One Saturday in November I sat in the pew at St. Patrick's school. I was a second-grader learning to make a first confession. Sister Catherine's chubby fresh face peered at each of us from the frame of her black habit. The boys then the girls said aloud to the walls of the schoolroom, "Forgive me, Father, for I have sinned. This is my first confession." Then we were to tell the priest all the sins we committed, according to their proper classification: mortal or venial. Mortal sins brought terrible pain and blotted out God's voice. They could send a sinner to the fires of hell forever. Venial sins smudged the window of a sinner's soul and could be cleaned more easily. Confession cleared up both kinds of sins and made your soul shine in the sun. Sister Catherine helped us practice by having us walk up to her gray metal desk and whisper into the starched white cloth over her ear.

While each of us solemnly proceeded one at a time to the desk, the rest fidgeted in our seats and colored pictures of Spot and Jane running down a sidewalk. I smelled the sharp green as I filled in the trees. When Sister wasn't looking, one color in the ensemble, usually an oddly mixed one like magenta or chartreuse, rose from its spot and belted out a song. No one heard the singer but me. I favored Prussian blue because it sang deeply felt melodies in a minor key. The song lyrics had words like "midnight" in them and shivered through me like winter trees in twilight. Smart students said the alphabet backward but I got stuck between the mountains of "m" and "n." At last the bell rang and I put on my blue wool coat with brass buttons and worried as I tied the scarf tight around my neck. Could a person flunk confession? Could I be driven away from the Church and made to suffer a pagan life?

Pagan babies looked more like me than my fellow students did. The Indian, African, and Asian babies had forlorn expressions with brown, thin limbs, curly or straight black hair. In my own line of ancestors, I knew there lurked a quite recent line of pagans and felt at times tempted to ask about them, believing that the conversion of my grandmother proved our family worthy. What kept me silent about the gaps in salvation? Such a distinction among human beings eventually led me to reject Catholicism and seek out Longhouse beliefs. Unable to conceive of the question, the child I once was walked down the hall bustling with older students and stepped down the stairs into a brisk wind.

My mother was ironing when I got home, and the smell of steam melted with the smell of cookies. I sat at the kitchen table and ate a coconut bar. Outside the two neighbor boys walked in and out of their house. They rode in cars and fixed things for their mother. Pleasant and easygoing by nature, both were friendly to me, not like the neighbor boys at the house we lived in the year before. Those boys from the Catholic school tied my big sister to a tree one Sunday morning, trying to burn her up in a pile of leaves. In the backyard of this house along the fence lived a similarly vengeful boy with auburn hair and freckles. He snarled at all of us "dirty Indians" and shot peas at my mother's sheets in the summer.

It would be simple to live if a person were all soul. The baggage of bodies complicated life. If Sister Catherine taught me how to care for my soul, my mother watched over my body. If one of us girls was constipated and dared to admit it, we had to drink "Black Draught," a purifying concoction that came from the Deep South in a yellow box with black letters. I'd blow up before I'd admit to constipation. Because I was so thin, my mother spooned a lime-green syrup down my gullet to kill the great tapeworm coiled inside me. When the worm wiggled, I touched myself and that was why I had too many sins to confess. I figured it would take days to count them all. I swung my leg against the chair as I muddled over sin and wages. The pebbles of my many grievous faults mashed the cookie inside me.

That night when I lay in my bed and looked out the door toward my parents' bedroom, I felt the cold sheets and the bumps in the mattress. In the dark the deep green walls fell toward the street forever and the closet and dresser stood in precise shadows, strengthened by their secret spaces. I feared my body and the powerful feelings that charged me with pleasure and guilt at the same time. My mother was getting ready for bed. A wash of light streamed around the now-closed door.

My fingers stroked soft hidden places until the devil poked his head from the closet door. I saw the mirror-colored reflection of his eyes in the closet door, opened just a crack. I squinted and saw the red embers sparkle from the engines of hell. I lay trapped between the desire to explore and the emerging awareness of shame and moral danger. I ran through the hall into my mother's now-dark bedroom. She wasn't asleep but resting on her bed. I slipped through the door frame to ask if I could be with her awhile.

I entered the room my father had painted in sky-blue swirls. On the ceiling and walls whirlpools spun in the dim light from the hall. In day or dark the room contained the expansiveness of swimming under the ocean. He painted the swirls to compensate for this house that neither of them wanted. It was the only one they could buy. The Realtor who showed them a house on Ashland Street told them it was sold when my father came to sign papers for it. My father carried in his bones the burn of such discrimination. Eventually, they bought this house on Hazel Street on the West Side. The swirls in the bedroom compensated his pain and made the room their own. I've felt the same detached quiet under a summer sky.

I padded around the walnut bedpost. The room smelled of old wood and the warmth of bodies pressed into comfortable quilts. It held the scent of adult intimacies and the security of their presence. To the right of the bedpost rose a mahogany highboy with more drawers than I could count. In my mind the highboy with six rows of drawers across and five down held both our family's and my grandmother's presence. The scrolled brass latches on its giant bank of drawers clanged lightly when I opened them. Some drawers fooled me into thinking they were stacked separately but when I opened them, the stack became a shoot that held canes and umbrellas, much too deep for me to reach the bottom. The top drawer held my grandmother's necklaces of wooden beads and cones with fluffs coming out of them. I found my mother's things in one of the drawers, pictures of her nursing school days and mysterious medical tubes and nozzles. The highboy stood for tradition

202 · *Roberta Hill*

and the concealments and surprises a child finds when snooping around where she's not supposed to go. Its massive mahogany bulk grounded my life.

I was the awkward, gangly albatross struggling to rise over the edge of her bed. I floundered across it like a jetty, heading for the spot near my mother's outstretched arm. The blanket had white nubs and fringes, ticklish and warm as solid seafoam.

I thought my parents met on the Caribbean Sea because she loved seafoam candy and he painted the rhythmic blue waves of this room where they loved and tormented each other with love's denial. Their marriage was sometimes the Civil War and sometimes Reconstruction. Together they were the North and South Poles: Choctaw challenging Oneida-Mohawk; Philadelphia Quakers contemplating the gaiety of those Louisiana French. They loved and understood the deep poverty of their childhoods. Sometimes their love sustained its calm by the recognition of my mother's obvious bad health. My legs grazed the edges of the bottom sheet and I wiggled toward her for warmth.

This bed with its turned posts could keep me from drowning in guilt and shame. Why couldn't I be good? Her breathing labored, still she welcomed me under her arm. Dare I ask her about the place that tingled? Would she, like the Father Above with his cloud-white beard, point an angry finger and send me back to bed? My mother's hair shimmered auburn gray in the dark and she looked old at thirty-two years. Whenever she worried, her chin filled with small dimples. Her gray eyes closed when I peeped up to see if she would talk to me.

We did not know she was dying from cirrhosis caused by malnutrition in her girlhood. A registered nurse, she must have known that jaundice and physical weakness signaled a serious liver disease. She died the following spring. That night we lay together, listening to the train thunder along its track behind our garage. Perhaps she was sleepy or in pain. She did not speak and silence rose like a channel I would have to cross.

"Mom?"

She murmured a response and I asked her about doing bad things, and about touching where a person wasn't supposed to touch.

"All children get curious about their bodies."

I heard the whistle of her breathing and waves of shame covered me. I longed to find a way out of this dilemma on that muted night.

"Why is it bad?" I asked.

"It has to do with the sixth commandment and not committing adultery. I guess if you get used to that pleasure, you might not stop when you get older. You might run off with someone you weren't married to," she said.

"I try not to, Mom, but I can't always stop. Do I need to count up all those times, every one?"

"You can try," she said.

When I closed my eyes and tried to count back to the very beginning, I felt fires from hell rake my eyelids and the devil getting ready to poke me with a glowing brand. I scrinched my eyes trying to remember the very first time I discovered that feeling in my body. It always filled me with breathlessness, the same as seeing flowers up close. It must have been before Danny who lived upstairs taught me how to kiss and whistle in one lesson. Was my blood somehow to be blamed? Was there something in my most secret self preventing me from claiming beauty and goodness? Would the path of my life be made of thorns and brambles?

"Am I bad?" I whispered, unable to fathom the end of the abyss of my sins.

"Don't fret so about it," she said, sleepily. She was the same woman who had locked me in the garage after giving me a whipping. She could be kind and quick to rage. I choked on the need to tell her and felt the power of shame bolt my chest and throat to the bed.

"How can I count it all?" I sobbed. She lifted her head to see me crying and curled under her arm.

"Gather all the little ones and count it as one big sin," she said, lying down again. Her Southern accent lulled my fears of dying suddenly without forgiveness.

"God knows you. He is merciful."

She assured me a mortal sin was different, like oranges were different from bananas. I settled into the relief she offered and then felt panicked by the thought that she could die without forgiveness. "Remember keep holy the Sabbath" blazed under my eyelids.

"Mom?"

"Now what? Can't you go to sleep?" she asked.

"Remember the Sunday we got ready for church, but you said we weren't going? Mom, that was a mortal sin. Should I tell that one?"

My little sister and I had put on our navy-blue suits, looking like potential nuns. We dawdled and fought and she grew tired from the chore of getting us ready. Then she decided we weren't going to go because she was too sick to hurry us along. We cried and cried because we felt we were bad.

"That's my sin because I decided we weren't going," she said. I saw the big stain floating over her heart in the dark, a luna moth with furry wings of doeskin brown. It thrummed against my chest until I couldn't swallow any more fear.

"Promise me you'll go to confession, so you won't go to hell if you get hit by a car."

"Yes," she whispered. I kissed her goodnight and felt her chapped lips scrape against mine. Perhaps at the time, I sensed her illness. Fear of her dying seized me and I clutched her and made her promise me she wouldn't die. She told me she was born in the year Halley's comet came and that she planned to live until she was seventy-three, long enough to see it come again. I believed her.

Just as she alleviated my shame and fears that night, she drove herself to clean and work and care for us, unable to trust my father with household chores. Her perfectionism and denial of her needs kept her from going to the hospital for years. Perhaps she knew what was sapping her strength and killing her. At that time there was no cure. Her family was her joy, her burden, and her death. By the time she had to go into surgery, it was too late.

I stayed in my cocoon near her and watched her drift to sleep, her mouth slightly pursed open, her breath whistling lightly as her chest rose and sank in the dark. When I snuggled down, my tired eye motes danced in sparkling patterns like slow-motion fireworks and I felt as if the jetty of my parents' bed could sustain me in all storms. I dreamed of dahlias with their ruffled, frivolous manners, and the way they grew along a fence nearby in the warm days of September before I went to school. Their petals flounced like crinolines and made me want to leap and spring, whole and complete in the purity of both body and soul, free from the notions of sin. The dream gave respite from the feelings of shame and my fear of going wrong in the dark.

After several more weeks of instruction, just before the beginning of Advent, we walked through the dim church past the candles flickering in their red and blue jars before the statue of the Virgin. Our shoes clicked on the church floor even when we walked on tiptoe and Jesus looked lonely, seeing us come with more sins, the pale muscles of his arms and hands cold in the shallow light.

I remember my feet in their scuffed brown oxfords and my girl-friends' feet in penny loafers and white anklets. Because I could not understand at the time that the feeling of my difference was due to racial prejudice, I always felt the same raw exposure grating through me. I knew that even though the sister said that Jesus loved us all the same, I existed with other Indians behind a pane of glass and never could break through to intimate understanding. In two long rows with the boys on one side and the girls on another we walked toward the confessionals in the front of the church and bowed our heads. My hunter-green jumper had stains on it from grease and paste. My hair bounced about my head in a mess of brown curls. Sister Catherine with her chubby pink cheeks ran to the front of the pews, raised her long black sleeves and lowered them in one motion. As if made of one body, we swished into place.

She reminded us again of the tortures of hell. We had to confess every little half lie because it wounded him in his heart. Her black sleeve swept in one gesture toward the shadowy cross and we knew he heard. I thought about those touches beneath blankets late at night when lights dimmed and the hymns we made up funny words for. Every one of us was a sinner.

For a moment I wished my mother were here to help me count. I wished instead of telling a priest in a confessional I could tell my mother and be washed clean like she washed me clean as a baby. Why did we have to tell a man the most intimate struggles with our girl bodies? Counting didn't matter to my mother. Why did it matter to the priest? What was more important—the telling or the counting? How could I say it in the best way?

I smelled the faint residue of frankincense and the sweet smell of old prayers. I saw sins fall like chestnut-colored leaves my friends and I gathered for bonfires my father set in the fall. It sounded odd to think of sins like leaves, yet it made sense to think of them that way. A re-newal of life. Old leaves into buds. Then it was my turn. I stepped through the pew and scrunched over the feet and knees of friends and enemies and opened the door with its black velvet curtains and shut myself into the dark, cushioned closet.

My voice seemed dry and scratchy as I began, "Forgive me, Father, for I have sinned." In the echo, I felt God was there inside the folds of black curtains. I knew everyone outside might be straining to hear but the velvet led me to somber thoughts. Trapped with my life, I peered at the brass grate and heard the priest whispering absolution to the girl in the other confessional. My knees burned and stuck to the kneeler. My breath swooshed like the wind before a rain, louder than I had ever heard it before. Was heaven like this spot of grainy light?

I got sins piled high as rockets, I wanted to say. Instead, I did as I was taught and then told every sin I could remember and counted the troublesome secrets as one. The priest listened on the other side of the brass screen. Even with a deep squint I saw little of his outline and only heard his voice. My heartstrings began to play "Turkey in the Straw," my father's fun-time tune. I waited. Could he be tallying my sins?

"For penance, say five Our Fathers and five Hail Marys and make a good Act of Contrition," he said.

I prayed because I wanted release from wrong and shame. I wanted the pane of glass to break as I listened to his intoning *"Absolvo Mei,"* the prayer that washed me clean. My soul chimed with its brightened bell. Now I could accept poverty and hunger. I felt forgiven even when the hem on my jumper tore beneath my shoe as I got up to leave. As I opened the door to the stares of others, I felt like leaping and laughing. I grinned at the next sorry sinner going inside the confessional.

The gold tabernacle on the altar glistened in the sacristy in front of me. For a moment, I wondered whether a ray of light would strike me dead because I turned all the little sins into a big one. We had heard the story about how a murderer came into the church to confess. He struggled—go, *no*, don't go—and was about to leave the church when a beam of light flashed from the tabernacle and struck him dead instantly. I waited for the beam to find me but nothing happened. My mother knew how God did things. I knew then I would probably be bad again. After all, wasn't I smiling during penance? My lips just curled up without my help. I looked at Kitty and Christine. Kitty folded her hands tightly and her long ringlets of blond hair bounced as she prayed. Christine looked even more than ever like Rose Red from the fairy tale. Her black hair was pinned back with a barrette. She always looked neat, even at the end of the day. I thought I saw the Holy

Ghost flying past, reflected in Judy's glasses. I wanted to die right there, where heaven was assured. But Sister Catherine looked over our second-grade faces, motioned once more with both arms for us to rise, and made us walk slowly out into the bright sunlight of a troubled world.

I learned from those moments in the velvet dark that words held power. I searched for truth to come with the right sounds to bring comfort and restoration of the feeling of wholeness and peace. To create with language is to be absorbed by the spirit and to connect with the numinous presence at the deepest heart of our human lives. Even if we do not succeed in the act of writing, dancing, telling a story, singing a song, even if the piece does not engage others as we hope, it restores balance and eventually brings joy. If we desire it, the practice of an art opens us to growth and recovery.

Perhaps my resistance and confusion toward Catholicism grew from this first encounter, for by the time I was seventeen, I stopped going to church, much to the chagrin of my father. What I learned of self-righteousness and arrogance, of judgment without compassion, of intentional rejection by those who claim love as a central value is another story. But I knew at seventeen that the Church had aided in the conquest and control over Indian people. I knew that in the name of Jesus an institution had killed millions of indigenous people. I knew that some members of that faith had also put their lives on the line to keep Indians safe but that the central aim was conversion. I could not separate into little drawers all the contradictions. If we turn as we age toward a greater acceptance of ourselves as human beings, I now see the wealth of ritual and spiritual nourishment such a faith could offer a person who had been torn away from his Indian traditions. I see how its meaning supported my grandmother's needs. I see also how similar the belief in the power of language is to Longhouse ways and other Indian traditional values.

In a long poem called "Under These Viadocks," I imagined a girl who keeps dreaming of her ancestral past. The events of the past unexpectedly bring her images of the truth, which no one mentions because the grief is still too fresh and painful. The syncretic image in both histories is the white bird. White birds flew through the trees and spoke to Good Peter on that April day in 1792. The Oneidas were alarmed by what the birds said. Good Peter acted unwisely in dealing with John Livingston, who came to make deals for Oneida land. In Catholicism, the white bird as Holy Spirit symbolizes peace, wisdom, and enlightenment. The white bird the girl sees in church led her

Over the mint green near St. John's head
it guided her back
to a chip of sky where a priest had come
just for the evening. He helped
the women whose brothers were gone,
offering beads for a memorized song.
He felt what is common to most of mankind—
fear of the unknown and the sublime.
"These old women are witches.
They cannot remember when to say Jesus
and will not surrender to the good word."

The old women nodded, yes, they knew evil.
It's a dog with strange eyes that bites
without warning.

Working their art, the old women walked
the sunlit woods, knew each plant,
knew dock from mallow. Making magic
of seeds, they spun them round until
the wings carried away pain. One by one,
the sick revived and laughter came,
or the final shudder and more tears.

But now chains of guilt and fear
are hurled across a lovely world
and grandparents stand before the pit,
lean over the pole and are hit
on the head. They fell so deep only earthworms
know where they lay. The worms carry back
wisps of their hair. See it float
on the moonlight when summer is gone?

The sister is angry. She wants answers now.
"Who is the martyr? They pulled out his nails."
The girl can't remember but stares at the clock
and wishes a fog could bury this school.
Fog meeting fog over fences of exile.

In the poem I allude to a number of historical events that are often unknown by most American readers. In the conversion process, communities were torn apart and the knowledgeable men and women were sometimes accused of witchcraft and killed. The Jesuit missionaries who went into Longhouse territory for the purpose of conversion were killed because of the hostilities created by the French, yet they are considered martyrs for the faith. This title subverts a discussion about their ultimate purpose, which was to aid in the incorporation of Longhouse people and their land into the fur trade. The elders who died as a result of witchcraft scares are never considered martyrs in the historical accounts.

What sustains me through these images is the knowledge that I can continue to seek and learn from the Oneida culture. Due to the intense social challenges of the 1960s and the determined efforts of many Oneida and other Indian people, we feel ourselves rooted in the stories of what happened before Columbus and in the stories of what will happen after the Americas are renewed.

The Peacemaker and his helper, Ayowatha, established the Confederacy before the arrival of Columbus, and the practice of its principals continues today. Some of the ideals of the Great Peace have been incorporated into American ideals of democracy; however, the Great Peace brings a larger and more complex energy to bear than the making of a country called the United States. A number of Longhouse or Hotinonshonni leaders have spoken and written about the meaning of our traditional ways of life, including Oren Lyons, Audrey Shenandoah, John Mohawk, Jolene Richard, Mike Mitchell, Dr. Carol Cornelius, Dr. Robert Powless, Doug George, and others.

One of the central images of the Great Peace is the white pine with its four roots branching out to the four directions. At the local level, the Oneida's now have an elementary school which teaches Oneida cultural concepts and stresses learning the language. Within these concepts is an awareness of how human beings and the other lifeforms follow natural laws to continue life. Genevieve Gollnick, the school superintendent, who also developed the curriculum, incorporated the ideals of reason, peace, righteousness, and power into the educational plans for the school. Learning to respect one's own life and that of others, learning that people have the capacity to reason together in order to prevent hostilities, learning to be responsible and cooperative in order to reach a consensus, learning that power grows from the expression of unity—these are concepts informing the educational plan of the school. Internationally, Chief Jake Swamp reinstituted the practice of dedicating a tree of peace in various places all over the world. He has dedicated trees in Albany, New York; Geneva, Switzerland, and Minneapolis, Minnesota. There is also a tree of peace in Madison, Wisconsin. The pine tree reminds us of the principles of the Great Law, which supports the continuation of life. It reminds us to guard against the egotism and violence of modern culture and to recognize how we need to respect and be responsible for the continuation of life.

When I consider my writing, I see that I still seek for the means to understand my people's ways of life, the stories given me and the people and experiences that are gifts. We are in the process of revitalization and it takes many hearts, hands, and eyes to accomplish this, especially in a world where the dominant system is to extract resources and pollute rivers, to store spent fuel rods in "safe" containers on great bodies of fresh water like Lake Michigan and the Mississippi River system.

As real, actualized human beings, we have a responsibility to maintain peace as a practice so that the beings who surround us with this shared gift of life can also continue with their responsibilities. In the dynamic understanding of life as a gift that must be maintained through expressions of gratitude, the Peacemaker instituted the process of being good relatives to each other. In this way, we support the complex nature of the earth's ecosystems. In congressional and other political debates, most Americans consider argument to be a form of verbal warfare. In the view of Oneida culture, language is a gift. The words that we share and exchange with one another balance what we take to sustain our lives. What a radical transformation it would be if the practice and actualization of peace, of making relations, of participating in a system where people were free from want, and where ceremonial life rested upon the ideal of justice and goodwill happens to the world. I believe that is the transformation we are experiencing and which is part of my writing and the writing of so many others, especially other Indian writers.

A century ago tremendous institutional and social stress was placed upon indigenous people to become Americans. The oppression of our ways of life was constant through the nineteenth century, and by the emergence into the twentieth century, Indian people knew they had to live in a "modern" world. However, our ties to the homeland of New York State were never forgotten. From the arrival in Wisconsin through the 1870s, tribal secretary John O. Powless recorded where and sometimes how the people died. Reading through his account, I saw the progression from Oneida Castle, New York, to Duck Creek, Wisconsin. I felt the strength of purpose to make a community here and felt in some small way how the Oneidas witnessed this change. The struggle to recognize our stories has reached another turn in the cycle of time.

Oneida people now speak of revitalization. In such a historical moment, it is easy to ignore and to deny the necessary choices of recent past generations, like those of my grandparents, who from need, necessity, and lack of alternatives became Catholic or Episcopalian or Methodist. In the process of growth and renewal, I hope we can understand and accept all these avenues of struggle and not become smug with our newfound knowledge. To be aware of how we are limited and to be vigilant in order to maintain our choices is crucial to our continued growth as people who value life in all its expressions.

My Mothers,
My Uncles, Myself

LEANNE HOWE

LeAnne Howe, an enrolled member of the Choctaw Nation of Oklahoma, was born in 1951. In addition to being an author, lecturer, and playwright, she has published legal essays and written scripts for public television documentaries. Her stories have appeared in many magazines such as Callaloo, Story, Fiction International, *and* Cimarron Review, *as well as anthologies such as* Spider Woman's Granddaughters, Seventh Generation: An Anthology of Native American Plays, *and* Earth Song, Sky Spirit. *Her plays have been produced around the country and she has received a number of awards and fellowships. LeAnne Howe has taught at Carleton College, and is currently on the faculty at Grinnell College.*

My mother walked her shoes off on the bare floors of the boarding-house in Edmond, Oklahoma, as she carried me in her soft round belly the final three weeks before I was born.

Auntie Mm's was a holding pen for pregnant white women and unwed Indians. Local church women preached to the women of Auntie Mm's on why they shouldn't give up their flesh and blood to adopting families; why they should have remained celibate; and why men with grace and the courage would someday come along... if they were good.

In 1951, in Oklahoma, in that time, there was a difference between being "a woman in trouble" and "a big-bellied Indian." When my mother speaks of this time, she waits a moment. There is silence. Then she clears her throat.

"Those church ladies made the white women mad," she remarks in a low thin voice. "One older pregnant woman hollered at those church ladies. She said it was the men who put us here. Go talk to the men."

My mother omits how she felt. I am supposed to know. I have learned the language of silence that she speaks. Non-Indians may think I mean "reading between the lines," but it is more than that. It is the language that cannot be verbalized. It is codified and understood by the listening heart and becomes clearer as the listener grows older.

Belly Mother is Choctaw. A full-blood. When she knew I was coming, she went to her older brother for help, and together they found Auntie Mm's.

About this time, a family from Stonewall, Oklahoma, had heard that there was a famous Indian lawyer living in their midst. This family of Cherokee women wanted an Indian baby so they went to him. The lawyer began to ask around.

"Is there anyone who will give a baby away?"

Although he never said so, my uncle must have heard this message floating in the air around Tannehill, the small community of Choctaws where my relatives lived just outside McAlester, Oklahoma. So my uncle contacted this Indian lawyer about his sister, the one with the growing belly who was swelling out of her shoes in Edmond, Oklahoma.

The circumstances must have seemed natural for the Indian lawyer and my uncle, although they never said so. It was an old-time trade between Indian families: one had something, one wanted something. To add to the accord, my father was part Cherokee, at least that's what he told my mother the night they made me.

On April 29 at 3:26 A.M. I arrived. The baby born before me was blinded when someone put the wrong solution in its eyes. With me, however, they were careful. I was lucky. I was healthy. My trade could be executed.

Five days later, my Cherokee mother tenderly folded her arms like a basket and carried me away from the whites of disgrace. In the photographs taken on that day, Basket Mother holds me in front of her body like a prize. And it has been in her arms I have stayed. Periodically, though, I return to lay my head against the belly of my mother, relearning old rhythms.

This is my story. This is how I came to have two mothers: Belly Mother, the one who carried me inside her, and Basket Mother, the one who carried me in front of her. Looking back on all these loose pieces of memory thread, I realize I weaved them into the wholeness that is me. And I see the symmetry.

DO YOU SEE WHAT I MEAN?

As I thought about my identity as a Native writer, as a Choctaw woman, it became clear to me that "everything does matter." When I write fiction, poetry, or history (at least the kind of history I'm interested in writing), I pull the passages of my life, and the lives of my mothers, my mothers' mothers, my uncles, the greater community of *chafachúka* ("family") and *iksa* ("clan"), together to form the basis for critique, interpretation; a moment in the raw world. My obligation in that critique is that I must learn more about my ancestors, understand them better than I imagined. Then I must be able to render all our col-

lective experiences into a meaningful form. I call this process "tribalography." Whether it be fiction, poetry, a play, or history, American
Indian writers and storytellers create tribalography to inform ourselves, and the non-Indian world, about who we are.

I am part Cherokee and I was adopted by a Cherokee family, although I am wholly Choctaw. What I mean is that until the twentieth
century, Choctaws were matrilineal by custom and laws, meaning that
we traced descent through our mother and her relatives. The French
colonial records are full of discussions in the early eighteenth century
on how simplified Choctaw culture was in terms of identifying kinship: a child made belonged to its mother and her kin. The French
were astonished at this cultural difference between themselves and the
Choctaws, so they wrote about it. Even as late as 1906, the Choctaws
were still trying to apply this old tribal custom to maintain cultural
identity. In that year the Choctaw and Chickasaw Freedman's Association argued to a committee of U.S. senators that they were entitled to
Choctaw allotment lands. The Freedman's Association based their
case on the fact that many of their members were illegitimate descendants of Choctaw fathers and black mothers. Melvin Cornish, who was
the attorney for both the Choctaws and Chickasaw nations, pointed
out that according to the tribal customs, illegitimate children always
followed the "status of the mother," meaning they were the children of
their mothers. Congress took the argument seriously and closed the
rolls to the Freedman. In other words, motherhood mattered in deter-
mining who and what the tribe was all about. There is one more thing:
mother's brother mattered too.

Uncles matter in Choctaw culture, in ways that are different from
European American "uncle ways." In those eighteenth-century French
colonial records there are clues as to how different the role of "father"
was from "uncle." Uncle was responsible for the education of his sister's children. He also fulfilled the disciplinarian role, which is a little
bit different from European Americans' "uncle" role. Fathers loved
their children and could play a Peter Pan kind of role, never disciplin-
ing their children, *especially* the girls.

In my own case I have found it very interesting that my uncle
helped with my adoption. When I returned to my Choctaw family and
reintroduced myself as a young adult, I visited my uncle's house first,

telling myself into existence like a storyteller returning from a long journey. My uncle nodded and listened to my narrative, then sent me to my mother's house. At that time, I didn't know how to spell "matrilineal kinship system," but after studying our history, it seems to me that our culture is not dead and gone to "acculturation hell." What I had been doing "naturally," meaning that I identified as entirely Choctaw because my mother is Choctaw, was historically "the way we were." Today (at least on paper), our identification system is open to children whose mother *or* father is Choctaw.

When I was growing up there were no men in my life except Basket Mother's brother. At the time of my adoption in 1951, I had a father, but I can't remember a single thing he ever said to me. The main reason for this, I think, is because I was very sickly with scarlet fever as a small child and always in the care of women. Later, I was hospitalized with rheumatic fever, and again, always in the care of women. After almost two years in bed, when I'd recovered enough from disease and overmedication, my adopted father tried to kill himself. He was hospitalized for insanity and never returned to our house. Later he succeeded and that was the end of him. As a result I grew up without a male voice in my ear. I grew up believing women are in charge of everything. I think a poem I wrote called "Evidence of Red" explains, even as a child, that I thought that women had power.

> First, the night opened out.
> Bodies took root from rotting salt
> and seawater into evidence of red life.
> Relentless waves pumped tidal air
> into a single heartbeat.
>
> In the pulp of shadow and space,
> water sucked our people from sleep.
> That's how it all began. At least
> that's all we can remember to tell.
> It began with water and heartbeat.
>
> In minutes we tunneled through
> corn woman's navel into tinges
> of moist red women and men.
> Yawning, we collected our chins,
> knees, breasts, and sure-footed determination.

A few thousand years before
Moses parted the Red Sea, and a
God with three heads was born in the Middle East,
the Choctaw people danced
our homeland infra red.

Finally when the stranger's arms
reached to strangle the us,
Grandmother eavesdropped
on the three-faced deity
who said that Chaos was Coming.

When he turned his lips and tried to kiss her
she made it rain on him.
"Maybe you've forgotten,
you were born of water and woman,"
she said, as she walked away, laughing.

(from *Nebraska English Journal, 1994*)

ABOUT MY MOTHERS' MOTHERS

Basket Mother is an artist. When life seems to fall down around her, she paints up a beautiful sky on canvas. Her stories tend to be visual, not verbal. However, my Cherokee grandmother taught me the power of a good story. I've wished many times that I could remember how she said what she said in Cherokee. When she spoke the language her voice resonated like the wings of hummingbirds.

"Come and eat." "Come and sit by the fire." "Let's go outside and have a smoke. Wash your hair in rainwater."

When she had a story she would say, "Do you hear what I hear? Listen! ygiea. e-e."

I am not able to write in Cherokee or make her words come alive on paper. But I remember her voice and how she cocked her head side to side just like a bird.

"Do you hear what I hear?" Then she would begin.

"I don't know if you remember old Lum Jones?" she'd query again.

"I was standing right here when I saw the Angel of Death appear on Lum Jones's front porch, go inside his house, and before I knew what happened, it had snatched him up through the treetops. Whoo-ee, that is the truth!" (I'd heard this before but every time she told it, I'd be scared.)

Of course, everyone in the family testified that Lum Jones was as dead as Andrew Jackson right after Grandmother saw him being pulled up through the elm tree. It was a fact. She could see life and death and I was told not to be afraid of living or dying. That was the lesson.

I learned that she knew what she was talking about. One night while I was in the hospital with rheumatic fever, I overheard someone say I was dying. Later my grandmother appeared to me, first as a huge bird hovering over my bed, and then as if at the same time she was standing with her hand on my forehead. She said a few words I couldn't understand. Then she left. I have written about her in *Indians Never Say Goodbye*, combining her visit to my hospital bed and her story of the Snake People. Both are very real experiences and important because just as I became a part of my adopted Cherokee family, she became a part of my story. However, as I explained, I couldn't or didn't learn Cherokee, and have since learned a bit of Choctaw; thus all the second-language texts in my work are Choctaw.

There she was standing over me. She inched her face close to my face. She put her hands on my face. I remembered her immediately, but did not speak. My eyes blurred. They were hot and heavy. It hurt to look at Ain't Sally. It hurt to see.

I closed my eyes. I felt her cool touch. She chanted. "You will be well. You will not die. *Chim achukma taha che.* You will be well. *Chi pesa taha che.*"

She sang to me. Then I heard her leave.

A woman whose bed was surrounded by white partitions moaned again. This was not a new sound. It was a constant. Her breath whistled irregularly. There was no escaping the whistle. The whistling sounds were everywhere in the white room. Then they stopped.

Another woman in another bed called out. No answer. She pushed the bell. Women wearing white dresses came into the room. They pushed the partitions back. They said the whistling woman was dead. I went back to sleep. Before the hospital. Before rheumatic fever. Before the dead woman. I had met Ain't Sally. I was seven years old.

Ain't Sally was an ancient Indian relative who lived in Hayrick, outside of Dublin. A place of the Snakes. A place of memory.

Once a base camp for nomadic tribes following buffalo, once a county seat, Hayrick, Texas, took its name from a solitary mountain standing in the breadth of open grasslands. Only a state government road sign remains, marking the place of Hayrick. Marking the sign of the Snakes.

The only time we visited Ain't Sally, I rode in the back seat of our green 1950 Chevrolet, and listened to my Indian grandmother tell stories about our family. Chapters went like this:

—Life in a Dugout.

—Making Lye Soap.

—How Grandfather got VD.

I don't remember much of the drive to Hayrick. We drove the rural roads of West Texas. There were two lanes of dust and dirt, stagnant, green-belted river beds, and one-lane bridges.

When we arrived at Ain't Sally's the old woman ambled out of a rusted screen door of a paintless wooden house. Breasts sagging, her thin body lacking in strength seemed unable to support her weight. She wore a sleeveless dress which revealed naked brown skin, skin that was no more than a sheath for aging bones. Hairless underarms.

She fed us saltine crackers and cold squirrel dumplings. She asked me questions. She asked me about my secrets. I don't remember having any to tell. She told me hers while I ate.

She said I reminded her of someone she'd seen a long time ago. I remember dancing for her. I told her I was a bird. The manbird. A hunter. I danced around the kitchen table and sang and pretended to be Pow-Wow Dancer. A bird of dance. A bird of rhythm. . . .

. . . As we walked farther from the house, I remember a hot gusty wind picked up her voice like dust tendrils on bedrock and blew it away from me. I ran to catch the sound. I found Ain't Sally sitting on a granite rock.

—"Indian girl. *Alla Tek*.

—"Come and see, on our land, the four winds of the old days will blow through our hair." Then she tugged at my black braids.

—"Come and visit the Snakes, *Alla Tek*.

—"When I was your age they blew across this place like red dust devils on flat neutral plains.

—"Can you see them?
—"Do you hear the Snake People calling us?"
—"Yes. Yes. I can see them. I hear them. They are naked and wild. Their eyes, like black grapes, shining in the Sun, stare back at me.
—"They're hungry."

I watch the Snake People eat the fleshy intestines of my uncle's butchered cow. I taste the hot blood, roll it around on my tongue and remember. It makes me sweat.

I watch the Snake People play games around the carcass. And before we walk back into the house, the old woman and me, she ran her crooked fingers across my eyes and said:

—"Indian Girl. *Alla Tek.*
—"The ghosts of your ancestors will visit you there."

(from "Indians Never Say Good-bye,"
Reinventing the Enemy's Language, 1997)

The Snake People my grandmother told about in her story were Comanches who'd travel across her great aunt's land. When Grandmother told me that story for the first time we were looking across the same land she'd seen as a young girl with her great aunt. Today the Snake People live on in me through her stories. I didn't know it at the time, but Grandmother was coding her family in my head and teaching me how to communicate after she was gone. When she ended a story, she'd squeal, "Whee-e-e-e, that's enough, I can tell you no more today." Then she'd whistle at her birds. Then she'd have a smoke.

There were many different birds in my grandmother's head. She said so. Sometimes she sang them there. At her death she said the birds never stopped chirping in her head. Kept her up all night. Made her ears ring. And it is their music that she died hearing. Not our voices.

When I want to be in touch with her I tell her stories.

"INDIAN WOMEN DON'T DOCUMENT CHANGE; THEY MAKE CHANGE"

I am paraphrasing a Rayna Green-ism[1] in her 1980 article, "Native American Women."

So far I have been writing as if growing up in a house of women was no big deal. Who am I trying to kid? Life was complicated. As a young adult, dealing with two families was not easy, particularly when they were so similar: both Southeastern Indian tribes, both matrilineal, both believe they are the real people! Everyone else is the "Other." As I said, growing up in the sixties, I was not able to verbalize this because I didn't know the meaning of matriarchy, even though I lived it. In short I didn't handle it very well. My biological sister and I led very similar lives even though we lived apart. And sometimes I felt shame at being adopted.

When I married in the late 1960s, I began making change. Two of them. Both boys. (This year my sons are ages twenty-six and twenty-eight, and I have two granddaughters, ages one and four.) As a mother of two babies, I wanted my children, but not my husband. I also realized that both my mothers really never had men in their lives for long periods of time. I was following the same pattern.

By the time I was twenty-three, a young divorced mother with two sons, I entered college and my life became more and more schizophrenic. I wanted to be a mother, a student, a lawyer, a writer, an Indian in a job where I didn't have to ask, "Can I freshen up your coffee, hon?"

In an early poem I wrote, "Coyote Dancing with Twisted Sister Running," I am trying to reconcile my past and present, my multifamilies, and as I said earlier, render a meaningful critique. (About myself.)

I

My life is made up of 30-minute intervals.
30 minutes to get dressed,
30 minutes to drive to work,
30 minutes to eat lunch,
and thirty minutes to watch the daily news
Coyote mother
is this what you had in mind
when you moved your pups to town?
I learned the language
I learned how to blend my colors
to match the grayness
I learned how to dance their way

II

Ah but,
She-za-tickle-to,
ain't that the name of a quarter horse?
A black-haired horsewoman
nasty dancing with
fat fingered midgets
and slender black winos
drunked up, fucked up
sweatin' the blues
A wild thing
She-za-tickle-to,
swiggin' slugs of Jack Daniels
a switchblade strapped to her thigh
teasin' the regulars
trying to pick fights,
passin' for white,
passin' for Lebanese,
passin' for Jew,
just passin' through
Coyote woman
where are your pups now?
No doubt skulking from the German Shepherds
and trying to remember ...

(from *Coyote Papers*, Wowapi Press, 1985)

Today, if I had to say one thing that is changing in fiction about American Indians, it is that it is okay to write about the urban Indian experience. More than okay. It has become necessary. At the time I began writing fiction, in the early 1980s, it wasn't. Most of the material being written was about reservation Indians, their politics, their problems, events that happened somewhere "out West." This left *me* hungry both as a reader and as a writer of fiction. So I wrote about that invisible fence that surrounds urban Indian communities in American society: the city. I wasn't very successful. I was told that my writing was not about *real* Indians, that no one wanted to hear about urban Indians who'd "lost" their culture to the city. I wrote *Biodegradable Indians,* which was published in a chapbook. No other editors besides Roxy and

Judy Gordon would touch it. I received a lot of feedback, but most people were appalled at its grittiness. I wrote in the piece, which was from the streets and Indian bars in Oklahoma City,

> It was the night of the crescent moon, Christmas Eve, 1980. Harry Bull Coming's big night. Wearing a buckskin shirt and moccasins, with an Eagle feather tied to one of his long black braids, Harry Bull Coming was about to make his debut as a professional comedian at the Red Race Hideaway in Tulsa, Oklahoma.
>
> For the twenty-two-year-old Indian, this was the most important night of his life. This was the night he'd rehearsed in his dreams. This was the night he would speak to his ancestors for counsel. This was the night he'd gamble the respect of his father.
>
> The Red Race was one of those places white people never go unless they want to get cut. The bathrooms worked only part time. There were pictures of naked blonde women plastered to the walls with their "scratch and sniff" decals torn off, and occasionally you could find personal items at the Red Race.
>
> It wasn't unusual for bar owner George Billy, a Choctaw from McAlester, to find a pair of false teeth or partial plates on the concrete floor, accidentally puked up along with the liquid dinner of some daring romantic who'd stayed too long listening to B.B. King and the blues.
>
> But nobody seemed to care or worry about missing teeth at the Red Race. For urban Indians, the Red Race was one hangout where would be warriors fought old battles and tried to remove the cosmic brain scars of the last century. . . .
>
> (from *Coyote Papers,* Wowapi Press, 1985)

My recent fiction involves late-nineteenth-century history. In *Hope at the Reservation,* I've written about a Choctaw boy in 1889 who was a captive of a cross-cultural experiment in education.

My interest in this area began when I joined the University of Iowa's Office of International Education and Services. In 1990, I was producing media aimed at educating the university and local community about the issues of cultural diversity. I worked with foreign students from eighty-nine countries and had a chance to see how international education theories and paradigms had changed, and also how ignorance about people who are culturally different continues to be perpetuated in and out of the classroom.

Hope at the Reservation has characters I am excited about. Dusky Long Gone Girl, as she is nicknamed by Hopaii Iskitini, is desperately trying to stay in school to escape her roots as the granddaughter of a slave. Hopaii Iskitini, or Hope, as the school faculty renames him, is just as desperate to leave school in order to stay Choctaw.

Hampton Normal and Agricultural Institute founder General Samuel Armstrong thought that if he put blacks and Indians together in one school, he could cause their good characteristics to rub off on each other. He founded the school to provide training for the newly freed blacks in 1868. While Armstrong believed his greatest calling was working with Negroes, he decided that his work with Indians might prove even more rewarding. Thus he developed what became known as the Hampton Method, placing blacks and Indians together in the first cross-cultural educational experiment.

In a generation of Civil War heroes, the general stood apart, a man who raised self-determination to an art form. While he fed the freedmen with government rations, he made them pay for it, "like men." To defend himself from being branded a white speculator, he wrote a newspaper editorial saying that "feeding Indians at agencies is the 'Old Contraband' system perpetuated, with the same wretched results—breeding beggars."

After three weeks at Hampton, the Episcopalian minister learns that money talks. General Armstrong agrees to take Hopaii Iskitini, but not his two sisters. When the Episcopalians, and the two girls pulled the springless wagon out of Hampton's yard, Hopaii Iskitini runs after them.

"*Tek Ishke*. Mama's girls," screams Hopaii Iskitini. Pisatuntema, his youngest sister, stretches her arms towards him. She tries to jump from her seat, but Mrs. Spencer grabs her. The eight-year-old girl yells for her brother, "Hopa-a-a-a," releasing the "a" when she runs out of breath.

Hopaii Iskitini runs faster. Tears stream down his face as he tires to catch the wagon rolling down the road.

George Lincoln, a full grown black man who was a janitor in the Indian boy's dormitory, tackles Hopaii Iskitini before he reaches the wagon. The black man holds the boy on the ground until the screaming girls are out of sight.

"Mr. Lincoln let up me," shouts Hopaii Iskitini trying to put his new English words together. *"Ia, ia, ia ia, ia!"* Suddenly the boy begins to shake all over. His mouth opens, but there are no sounds.

George Lincoln picks up the short stocky boy out of the dirt. Hopaii Iskitini peers around the yard for his sisters. They are gone. Above his open mouth, the boy's eyes flutter helplessly, then he falls.

The black man sinks on his knees with the Indian boy in his arms. "It's all right boy, I know how you feel," he says. "Everything's gonna be all right," soothes Mr. Lincoln.

"I know how you feel. I know."

George Lincoln repeats these words fitfully again and again like a hymn as he cradles the Indian boy's head to his chest.

(from *Hope at the Reservation*)

"O-MISHKE A NUMPA TILLOFASHIH ISH HAKLOH. ATTENTION, LISTEN TO MY REMARKS!"

"Educative theater" was meant originally to change the view that the target groups had of reality; to have an audience consider things in a different way than they were used to. Of the two plays I have written with Choctaw writer and poet Roxy Gordon that were produced, we were trying to achieve an ideal relationship between entertainment and teaching about American Indians.

Big PowWow was produced in 1987 by an African American theater company, Sojourner Truth Theater, in Fort Worth, Texas. The central character in *Big PowWow* is Blossom Bird Song, a contemporary urban Choctaw woman with a lot of problems to solve. Not only is she ignored by mainstream society, her "silences" are misunderstood at times by her own people. It is her voice, her theatrical litany spoken, at times, almost mantralike that forces the other characters to pay attention to her remarks:

(Forcefully and with power)
"I wanna go get my kids."
"I want my kids."
"You can stand here talking all night, but I am going to go and get my kids." *(end of act one)*

As far as we know it was the first collaboration in Texas that brought an all–American Indian cast together with a producer and director who are African Americans. While Sojourner Truth Theater does not think of itself as an indigenous theater company, we found that our collaboration was successful because both American Indian cast and playwrights and African American producer and director believed we had a kind of social responsibility, or, rather, social orientation, to show our social realities and how we find ways to deal with them.

For me this means that a woman's voice is centrally placed in my work. It is purposeful, and I am striving to combine my perception of what matters and meld it together in past and present.

As ambassadors and representatives of their families and *oklas* ("people"), historic Choctaw women were representatives of the "Word" and were as important as men. I have learned by studying the morphology of the Choctaw language that there is something mysterious about *nuk* or *nok*, which has to do with breath and mind. *Nukfoka* means that one is endowed with knowledge. *Nukfoki* is a teacher.

In the mid-eighteenth century, the French traveler and adventurer Jean-Bernard Bossu makes an interesting comment concerning Choctaw women speakers. While he applies his French cultural bias, writing in his journal that women loved their husbands so much that they followed them in battle, there may have been another reason: Choctaw women spoke the words of power.

"Some women are so fond of their husbands that they follow them to war. They keep by their sides in combat holding a quiver of arrows and encourage them by crying out continually that they must not fear their enemies, but die like true men. So fond of the men that they tell them they must die like true men."[2]

There are many examples of Choctaw women as ambassadors in the French colonial period. While they have been overlooked by historians, they are nevertheless important. One such instance is contained in a letter dated February 1746, from M. de Louboey, the King's Lieutenant of Mobile, to Jean Frédéric Phelypeaux, Count de Maurepas, Minister of the Marines and the Colonies from 1723–1749. In this letter it is clear from Louboey's point of view that the peace mission succeeded because a Choctaw woman was involved as ambassador or giver of the "Word" in the negotiations between the French, the Choctaws, and the Chickasaws.[3]

My great-grandmother's Choctaw family name was Anolitubbee, meaning "tells and kills," a storyteller who killed. My adopted Cherokee grandmother made sure that I would become a storyteller. In a way I am the bridge between blood and adopted community. By tradition and birth, I am a storyteller. I hope that I am doing what all my ancestors want me to do. In a way I am trying to tell you now, what I know from my breath and mind. I am trying to become a *Nukfoki,* and breathe on to the page the events that mattered, or shaped my life as Native Daughter, as Woman, as Writer. At the same time, I believe that my life, and the thing which helps me tell stories, can be revealed only because of my ancestors' lives. In a sense I am telling you about our lives, and together we are changing at once. This is what these women, my mothers, my mothers' mothers, and my uncles did for me. This is what I am doing for you. This strength is conveyed in my poem "*Hashi mi Mali.*"

I

Each morning, *Hashi,* the stark red creator rises,
swelling,
she passes over the ground, spilling a drop or two of her blood which
grows the corn, and the people: Choctaw that is we.
Naked, she goes down on us,
her flaming hair burns us brown.
Finally, in the month of *Tek Inhashi,* the Sun of Women,
when we are navel deep in red sumac, we cut the leaves and
smoke to her success. Sing her praises.
Hashi, Creator Sun, won't forget.

II

When *Ohoyo Ikbi* pulled
freshly-made Choctaw
out of her red thighs,
we were very wet, so
one-by-one,
she stacked us
on the mound,
and *Hashi* kissed our
bodies with her morning lips
and painted our faces with afternoon fire,

and, in the month of *Hashi Hoponi*, the Sun of Cooking,
we were made

III

It is said that
once-a-month warriors can kill a thing with spit.
So when the soldiers came,
our mothers stood on the tops of the
ramparts and made the *tashka* call
urging their men on.
Whirling their tongues and hatchets in rhythm,
they pulled red water and fire from their bodies
and covered their chests with bullet-proof blood.
And when it was over,
they made a fire bed on the prairie that
blew across the people like a storm;
melded our souls with iron.
And in the month of *Hashi Mali*, the Sun of Wind,
we listen for the voices
that still urge us on
at sunrise

(from *Gatherings: The En'owkin Journal of First North American Peoples*, Vol. IV—1993)

"Whee-e-e-e, that's enough, I can tell you no more today."

NOTES

1. Rayna Green is director of the American Indian Program, National Museum of American History at the Smithsonian Institution. *Native American Women* appeared in *Signs: Journal of Women in Culture and Society*, 1980, vol. 6, no. 2. The University of Chicago.

2. Jean-Bernard Bossu's *Travels in the Interior of North America, 1751–1762,* Norman: University of Oklahoma Press, 1962, p. 163.

3. *Mississippi Provincial Archives: French Dominion, 1729–1748, Vol. IV,* Rowland, Sanders, and Galloway, Louisiana State University Press, 1984, p. 260.

A Moment
in My Life

REX LEE JIM

Rex Lee Jim (Navajo) was born in 1962 into the Red House clan. He was born and raised in the Rock Point Community in Arizona, where he still lives. He teaches at Diné College in Tsaile, Arizona. In 1986 he received a BA in English from Princeton. In 1989, Princeton Collections of Western Americana published his Navajo-language book of poetry, Áhí Ni' Nikisheegiizh, *under the name Mazii Dinéltsoi. In 1994 the same publisher brought out* Saad.

When I realized that everything matters, I immediately knew that my destiny was completely in my control. Medicine people have known and talked about this personal power ever since I was a child. I didn't start school until I was rather old. I knew I was older than most of my classmates when other kids began to kid me about "the dumb kid who went to school with kids younger than himself." This label was baffling to me because I knew I had better grades than all of them. Proof was right there on my report cards. And I spoke up in class and participated in all activities. There were times when my speaking up got me in trouble and earned me a position kneeling outside the classroom, facing a blank wall. I even scrubbed the girls' bathroom with a toothbrush a few nights, after everyone else had gone to sleep. I didn't learn at that time that living an honest life could mean punishment. Regardless, my honesty taught me to leave a girls' rest room spotless.

I learned how to kneel, too. I often thought about this kneeling when I was taken on Sundays to the local Lutheran church in Rock Point, Arizona, and was asked to kneel and pray. While the Sunday school teacher prayed about the welfare of my future as a good and loyal Christian, I thought about the callouses on my knees. I came to realize much later that my honesty at that time was a virtue bestowed upon me by my childhood innocence, and that adults, no longer being innocent, despise honesty. Especially a child's honesty. I guess I now believe the adage "The truth hurts." However, as I believed at the time, and came to realize again only much later, "the truth hurts" only for those who do not know themselves. Today some of us have risen beyond ourselves, and we eagerly embrace the truth when we find it, for we constantly search for our wisdom in the everlasting intelligence.

Before I started Western schooling, my grandfather had pointed out this road to me and guided me for some time. I remember standing by my grandfather early in the morning. We stood facing the east. His patients stood to his left. We had just finished the morning and closing songs of the Blessing Way ceremony. As much as I wanted to stay up all night long, I fell asleep just past midnight. My grandfather woke me up for the last twelve songs. "My grandchild, wake up. Our grandfathers, the gods, are upon us. Wake up and let us go greet them." So I stood there facing the east. I remember cocks crowing at nearby hogans, perhaps a mile or two away. Sounds go far in the early dawn. Occasionally dogs barked and sheep bleated. And the sound of a jet echoed into the western horizon. Stars began to fade and the east began to rise with a quivering streak of white. Silhouettes of tamaric and greasewood and rabbit brush and tumbleweeds and yucca began to define themselves in dew and snow, shimmering in faint light. And the wind made the plants whistle and the bushes whisper. At the edge of this beginning, there was a moment of silence. From the center of this silence my grandfather's hand rose, took a pinch of corn pollen from his bag, put some on the tip of his tongue, took out another pinch and placed it on his head just a little beyond his hairline and where his hair parted, took out another pinch and with one motion gently made a road of corn pollen ahead of him, and only he knew how far into the future his thoughts went. As his right hand began to make the road, his voice sounded, *"Są'ah naagháí bik'eh hózhóón nishłǫ́ǫ naasháa doo."* It was magical for a child of four to hug his grandfather's right leg and see the world come to life with his grandfather's prayer. The world came alive exactly the way the words in the prayer described it to become. Magic! I stood there in awe and knew that the patient was restored to health and was now in spiritual wellness with his world. I was to see this creation many times for the next several years. Before Western schooling, everything was possible because I knew that if I should so desire, I could create my own world through my prayers, prescribed or personal.

Są'ah naagháí bik'eh hózhóón nishłǫ́ǫ naasháa doo. Understanding this formula empowers me to design the life that I desire. I am fortunate to have heard this declaration of personal achievement when I was a young child, and to have seen it in action. Unfortunately, many years had to elapse between those childhood days and the time of my recognition, acceptance, and application of the formula again. Here I do not offer a Navajo definition of the formula. I simply share with you how I interpret and use the formula in my life. It is one Navajo's experience with *Sa'ah naagháí bik'eh hózhóón*. In one poem, I referred to the formula as "May I be Everlasting and Beautiful Living."

Sa'ah naagháí bik'eh hózhóón nishłǫ́ǫ naasháa doo. When I sit on top of Hamburger Rock, I immensely enjoy the beauty of the landscape. I can see the Carrizo and Lukachukai Mountains to the east. I can see canyons and mesas and plateaus and washes and cottonwood and dark patches of greasewood decorating the space between where I sit and the mountains. To the south I can see the square outline of Round Rock sitting on the horizon and darkened shadows hiding in alcoves at the bottom of Bending Rock. To the west I can see Black Mesa streaming to the north and painted clouds hovering just above it. And to the north, right below me, I can see a deep cut in the earth known to me as Window Rock Canyon. A picturesque panorama this may be, but the immense joy I feel comes from my having explored the finer crevices of those canyons, climbed and fallen from those cottonwood branches, touched, smelled, and nibbled the different plants, jumped down from wash banks of several feet high to sand dunes fanning out at the bottom. To understand and use *sa'ah naagháí bik'eh hózhóón* in the way that my grandfather brought the world to life with it, I felt that it was imperative for me to explore the finer crevices and do some more jumping before I took a view from the top. So here is a quick analysis of the formula.

Sa'ah naagháí bik'eh hózhóón nishłǫ́ǫ naasháa doo. In short, this declaration of a healthy and wealthy lifestyle means to me the beauty of life realized through the application of teachings that work. Literally, *sa* means old age, *ah* means beyond, *naa* means environment, *ghái* means movement, *bi* means to it, *k'eh* means according, *hó* means self and that sense of an ever-presence of something greater, *zhóón* means beauty, *nishłǫ́ǫ* means I will be, *naasháa doo* means may I walk. This may be stated in the following way. "May I walk, being the omnipresent beauty created by the one that moves beyond old age." Now we all know that we are born into this world and we live for some time and then we all die.

In this analysis, I have concluded that those who have died of old age must have done something right to reach old age. For Navajos, death of old age means dying at the age of 102. My question is, What did this person do to live for so many years? So today when an elder says, "Let me give you a word of advice about life," I sit up and listen with all I've got. Often these advices begin with the phrase *"Ániid naasháádą́ą́'* ... ," or *"Ániid nijigháádą́ą́'* ..."—"When I was young, moving about ... ," or "When one is young, moving about ..." This introductory phrase shocked me into the reality and power of the moment. I immediately realized that in order for me to reach old age, the quality of my action in the moment was of utmost importance. Suddenly *sá* no longer meant old age in terms of years; *sá* came to mean quality. *Sá* is quality. Quality of ever-improving spirituality, quality of physical growth, quality of social flexibility, and quality of mental processing. *Sá* is the quality of ever-moving human wellness, and therefore a process of a healthy and wealthy world. I have come to realize that those who reach old age not only believed in quality, they also had a definite purpose in life and a definite plan to achieve it. *Sá* is also this definite purpose, the burning desire that is within man's soul. *Sá* is that goal for which purpose man is born into this life. Reaching *sá* is a lifelong goal for the individual, and an everlasting goal for a people. One only needs to define *sá*.

Ah means beyond. Beyond what? Continuing with our analysis, *ah* would indicate going beyond old age. As stated earlier, we are born, we live for some time, and then we die. It is true that our physical body dies and returns to dust. What happens to the soul or spirit, I will not discuss here. What I would like to point out is that what passes beyond death and on to the next generation are those advices dearly given by those sowers and reapers of everlasting life. *"Shicheii kójíníí nít'éé'* ... ," or *"Shimásání kójít'íí nít'éé'* ..."—"My grandfather used to say this ... ," or "My grandmother used to do this. ..." Today's teachers reach back into the past, beyond the present and this world, to bring into this world and present methods that work in creating a life that vibrates with happiness. Effective teachings defy death. They become traditions and are the foundation of effective living. Effective living demands constant improvement, and this means change. Embracing change that raises quality of living means raising your standards. Often good people remain good people. "I'm living a good life. I'm fine." Such remarks stunt people's growth. Why not live an exceptional life? Why not do things exceedingly well? Why not? *Ah* allows us to go beyond that quality that *sá* determines. *Sá'ah* takes us from what is good to what is excellent. *Sá'ah* elevates us from the mundane to the divine. *Sá'ah* makes us realize that we are spiritual beings having human experiences, and having a most wonderful time being human. *Ah*, then, is that element of the phrase that gives us courage and faith and forces us to take action. *Ah* allows us to take the dive and let go, to forgive American armed forces for past delusions and show them the way to glory during World War II. *Ah* drives us to find meaningful communication with the gods in what others consider meaningless grunts, and compels us to create sand paintings out of the desolate and harsh desert. *Ah*, then, is that sigh that creates inner peace.

Naaghái is a movement of a particular entity, a movement of the unity of something physical or conceptual and the environment in which it exists. Inherent in this word is that whatever moves, moves by itself. It is an ever-moving, living entity. This phrase encompasses the idea of the ripple or dominoes effect. A thought or an action touches every other part of creation. This natural law does not allow for isolation of events. *Naaghái* puts the idea of interconnectedness and global interdependency into motion. In the case of our analysis, we will place the perimeter of this motion to our sphere of personal influence. In other words, we will apply the natural law of *naaghái* only to the things that we can change. It is only natural that when we have high expectations and constantly exceed those expectations, the people we come into contact with and the environment in which we move will change greatly, and all for the better. I stated earlier that people who reach old age have definite plans for achieving their definite purposes in life. *Naaghái* is putting this plan into action. Let me state here that *naa* means the natural order of things, the universal laws in motion, nature at her best. By observing these natural laws and the results, one may come up with a personal, family, tribal, or national plan. Knowing that the influence of your actions goes beyond yourself allows you to plan well, to think of others, humans or otherwise. Consequently, when quality moves from goodness to excellence, *są'ah* moves beyond itself and becomes part of that natural process. With its movement, *są'ah* harmonizes all that it touches, and thus creates beauty.

Bik'eh means according to what just went before. In this case it refers to *są'ah naaghái*, just discussed. Following *bik'eh* is the word *hózhóón*. *According to*, then, is placed so that the *hózhóón* comes about because of *są'ah naaghái*. In this position, *bik'eh* becomes a function of transition. It becomes the means of achieving *hózhǫ́*—beauty. *Bik'eh*, then, is the embodiment of the natural law that allows us to begin at the beginning and end at the ending, our mental initiative resulting in some form of physical reality. *Bik'eh* reminds us that there are natural laws that we must follow. We must plant in the spring and take care of our crop during the summer if we are to reap our harvest in the fall. We should not expect to enjoy our crop a week after we planted it. As there are natural cycles in nature, there are natural cycles in human interaction. This universal law also applies at a very personal level. The whole notion of treating others the way you would like to be treated becomes concrete reality when this natural law comes into effect. When *bik'eh* is in motion, it forces us to abide by principles that have come before. These principles may come in forms of natural laws that we have no control over, or as products of our desires and plans for achieving our goals. The former we must respect and the latter we can and must control. *Bik'eh* ensures that all our actions are accounted for. Because of this natural law we learn to be responsible to ourselves and to others.

Our responsible actions bring beauty into this world. This beauty comes about because of following the laws set forth by *są'ah naagháí*. Fortunately, how *są'ah naagháí* is formulated is within our complete control. By exercising this responsibility, we design our own lives. We bring beauty into this world. The beauty comes from within us. *Hózhóón*, then, is our inner self singing and dancing in the physical world. *Hózhóón* is much more than our inner beings. *Hó* refers to the self; linguists also refer to it as the fourth person. While *hó* refers to the self, it also connects itself to the ever-presence of everlasting intelligence. It is this ever-greater source that allows us to harmonize with the rest of the universe. *Hó*, then, is our own unity with the gods, infinite intelligence, God, the Great Spirit, or by whatever name you refer to this natural greatness. Acknowledgment and acceptance of ourselves the way we are, then, is also acknowledgment and acceptance of the gods. What the gods allow us is not to remain the way we are. The gods have endowed us with the power to transform ourselves into their own images, which ultimately reflects what we see as ideal, what we strive for. *Hó*, then, is the universe in motion with each and every one of us at the center of the movement. *Zhóón* simply means beautiful. It could mean harmony, balance, equilibrium, calmness. It could mean whatever pleases an individual. *Zhóón* can only be defined by an individual, moment by moment. I find delight and a certain calming down in walking in a sandstorm just before sundown. Others may consider this rather uncomfortable. *Zhóón* to me is that evening walk. On the other hand, I will not find it to mean *zhóón* just right after a nice hot bath, or right before a ceremonial meal or dance that is to take place that evening. *Zhóón*, then, is ever-changing and so we must constantly search for it or create it. Its ever-changing nature allows us to flex our muscles, keep our senses sharpened, venture beyond our curiosities, play with children and laugh with them. *Zhóón* becomes a lifelong search.

Są'ah naagháí bik'eh hózhóón nishłǫǫ naasháa doo. May I walk, being the omnipresent beauty created by the one that moves beyond old age. May I be Everlasting and Beautiful Living. May I be every teaching that ever worked and continues to work, and the ever-increasing positive products resulting from applications of these teachings. Moving! Walking! May I move with the one that moves beyond old age. In becoming one with the one that moves beyond old age, may I walk with the past and the future in the present. May I be of everything.

> *Są'ah naagháí bik'eh hózhóón nishłíįgo naasháa doo*
> *Są'ah naagháí bik'eh hózhóón nishłǫǫ naasháa doo*
>
> *Tsíłkééh doo tídílnéehii nishłíįgo naasháa doo*
> *Ch'ikééh t'áá ałtsxóní náádleełí nishłǫǫ naasháa doo*
>
> *Tádídíín ashkii nishłíįgo naasháa doo*
> *Aniłt'ánii at'ééd nishłǫǫ naasháa doo*
>
> *K'os diłhił t'áá shee náhoodleełgo naasháa doo*
> *Áah diłhił t'áá shee náhoodleełgo naasháa doo*
>
> *Niłtsą bikạ' t'áá shee naałtingo naasháa doo*
> *Niłtsą bi'áád t'áá shee naałtingo naasháa doo*
>
> *Hózhǫǫgo naasháa doo*
> *Hózhǫǫgo naasháa doo*
> *Hózhǫǫ naasháa doo*
> *Hózhǫǫ naasháa doo*

May I be Everlasting and Beautiful Living, walking
May I be Everlasting and Beautiful Living, walking

May I be Unwounded Male Youth, walking
May I be Everchanging Female Youth, walking

May I be Pollen Boy, walking
May I be Ripener Girl, walking

May Dark Clouds continue to blanket me, walking
May Dark Mists continue to blanket me, walking

May Male Rain continue to shower me, walking
May Female Rain continue to shower me, walking

May I be Everlasting Beauty, walking
May I be Everlasting Beauty, walking
May I be Everlasting Beauty, walking
May I be Everlasting Beauty, walking

This poem is a view from the top. It is a spiritual emplacement of that panoramic view I described from the top of Hamburger Rock within myself. It is the cohesive wholeness within me that allows me to boldly dissect *sạ'ah naaghái bik'eh hózhóón* into its different parts, and an attempt to identify, define, or interpret them to fit into the broader picture which I would like to paint. It is a summation and wholeness of all the pieces in my life. *Sạ'ah naaghái bik'eh hózhóón nishłǫǫ naasháa doo.*

Sạ'ah naaghái bik'eh hózhóón nishłǫǫ naasháa doo is a becoming. Changing, improving, becoming. For one reason or another, when I am young, walking, I may never listen to my elders. Whatever they say, I may tend to push aside by saying, "That's old stuff. That's outdated. Don't be superstitious, Grandpa." Suddenly when old age makes its presence known, I may end up saying, "If I could only live my life over again. If I only listened to my elders then. Grandma knew it all along. If they only told me this. If I only realized this when I was younger." Earlier, I stated, "Unfortunately, many years had to elapse between those childhood days and the time of my recognition, acceptance, and application of the formula again." Well, the time came when I had to say, "If I only listened then." I may have been the first multimillionaire medicine man now, with a business network consisting of selling special healing herbs, sold by subscription only; sweat-lodge programs, personalized to your taste; television programs, even a late-night show. Let your own imagination run; it should be more interesting. Well, you never know, I may still become one.

In the meantime, let me share with you some of the advice that I should have listened to and followed. The second part of this writing will focus on that "magic" that I remember my grandfather performing. This magic takes place only after there is complete personal understanding of the concept of *są'ah naagháí bik'eh hózhóón*. Only then could it be applied effectively, with faith and responsibility.

"Get up. Your grandfather, Talking God, is coming. Go meet him. Run to the east. Run for health and wealth." Teachings from my grandfather would echo in my head. I would turn over and cover myself up. I had a hard time getting up early in the morning. Because of my work and late meetings, I came in late and needed to sleep late. I came up with all types of excuses to stay in bed. The sun would rise and warnings from my mother would fade with the morning dew. Then one day I decided to wake up early in the morning and watch the sun rise. I rose at least an hour before sunrise and I wandered there at the edge of dawn, rubbing my hands together and blowing on them every now and then. My breath was warm and it brought life back into my hands. Blowing on my hands made me think about my breath and life. My breath and my hands. I stood there, blowing on my hands over and over. I faced the east and stood there in silence. I remembered how my grandfather's words brought the world to life. The physical world was still there, all it needed was affirmation in human words. It was this human voice that brought reality and joy to the human experience. After so many years later, I finally stood where my grandfather stood. I prayed and the world came to life. And my grandfather, Talking God, was right there with me. I suddenly realized that he appears only to those who call on him. He does not intrude on human life, only when he is asked to.

I started playing with Talking God. I asked him to do this and that and he did this and that. I laughed in the dawn and the dawn laughed with me. I prayed that I would live upon this beautiful land, and the land emerged out of the darkness and covered herself with rabbitbrush, mormon tea, sagebrush, tumbleweed, rice grass, snakeweed, greasewood, and in the distance, dancing, were tamarack bushes, cottonwood trees, and Russian olive trees. I prayed that I may walk the earth enjoying good music. Sheep and goats bleated in the corral, horses neighed in the distance, a cock crowed at my mother's house, birds chirped and their wings gave voice to the air, and the wind rose and whispered to the plant people and they danced with me at dawn.

Even a coyote howled in a nearby canyon. I prayed that may the coyote's voice bring the rain, and I heard the thunder rumble somewhere to the west. Somehow I realized that my praying was simply a description of what was actually happening. However, what was amazing was that sense of timing. Somehow it seemed that I knew when to pray about the birds and the wind, and in what order. It seemed that my words came out before the physical events took place. The prayer appeared almost like a perfect execution of a plan made by the natural world and a human voice. It appeared that my voice and the natural world became one and the same. When I thought of this and the possibility of truth in it, I felt so happy and powerful. And this time when the sun rose, I cried and prayed. I was so happy that I don't even remember what I prayed for and about, who I prayed for. What I remember saying and what has been most moving and meaningful for me is *"Sạ'ah naagháí bik'eh hózhóón nishłǫ́ǫ naasháa doo."*

Since then I have prayed as often as possible at dawn. There are times when I still sleep in. I no longer feel guilty about letting the sun rise before me; after all, I do best when I get my rest. The prayer becomes even stronger when there is faith. Believing that your words will bring the world to life is *sạ́*. Knowing that your words will bring the world to life is *sạ'ah*. When you pray, there is movement of sound, then *sạ'ah naagháí* comes about. Your understanding of this concept then demands of you to create beauty in this world in a responsible way. Praying, then, is *sạ'ah naagháí bik'eh hózhóón*. When others ask me why I always smile and seem to enjoy whatever I do, I remember that morning when I prayed and played, and I answer, "I pray and I play."

The other day one of my students asked me about praying. I said, "This is what I am learning." When you get up early in the morning and go outside to pray, you tell your body that you are in control. In doing this, you have already claimed victory and the rest of the day will simply follow. I told him that talking with the gods is like dealing with teachers. The English teacher demands an outline for an essay, so the gods demand an outline for life. I explained that defining for yourself and understanding *sạ'ah naagháí bik'eh hózhóón* is your living infrastructure through which you will achieve whatever you desire. I briefly explained to him what is written above. Then I told him that every morning, or every time you pray, when you say, *"Sạ'ah naagháí bik'eh hózhóón nishłǫ́ǫ naasháa doo,"* you reaffirm your goal for life and beyond, and empower yourself to take action. So this is how I start my prayer.

The morning prayer is an affirmation of my life philosophy, followed by my outline for the day. This outline must take me closer to my lifelong goal. For example, I may pray in this way. "May I be Everlasting Beauty, walking ... speaking only kind words, corn pollen being my thoughts and words, relating well to all my relatives." When I am out doing things during the day, someone may step on my toes and I may feel like lashing him with my tongue, and he may rightly deserve it, but there will be an inner guide ready always to inform me that I have made a deal with myself and the gods early this morning. "Remember this morning? I remember you praying to say only kind words and treat all people with the respect that you would like to be treated with." In this way, our prayers keep us in line and keep evil thoughts from standing in the way of achieving our goals. Then I asked my student if he at one time bought something because he thought it was different, only to find out after the purchase that others had bought it, too. I told him that those others probably had whatever he bought before he even laid eyes on it. By buying it, he told his mind what was important to him, and the mind told the eyes to look for objects similar to what he bought. So he ended up seeing others wear or use whatever he bought. When I pray I tell my mind exactly what I want.

Then I continued with the essay analogy. The more detailed your outline for the essay, the better the essay will be. The teacher will be more than happy to give you that *A* that you work hard for. In the same way, the more detailed your prayer is in the morning, the gods will be more than happy to let you have whatever you desire from the day. Ask and you shall receive, Christ taught. Ask specifically and intelligently, and you may have your heart's desires.

Then I reminded him that he must also pray in the evening. The evening prayer is just as important. In this land of abundance, we simply grab and take. We need to pause at the end of the day, reflect on the day, and give thanks for our achievements. That moment of gratefulness is calming for the human soul and pleasing to the ears of those who give. I told my student to express his gratitude for anything, that this moment was entirely his. This moment of praying will allow him to think about his day. Soon he will learn to be grateful for what to others may seem ridiculous. But then, what is ridiculous about life?

One evening I was going for a walk and came upon a pile of horse manure. It was all dried up. I kicked it around. I got a stick and poked around in it. In fact, I sensed a certain power surging through me. Later that evening, I thanked the gods for sharing that pile of horse manure for me. Yes, I admit, it sounded ridiculous to stand out in the open, facing the emblazoned western outline of Black Mesa, and praying, "Thank you for letting me come upon a pile of horse manure during my evening walk." I'm sure even the gods chuckled. Actually, I didn't even use the word "manure." Nevertheless, I had forgotten the event for several months. Then one day, I was asked to give a lecture on the Long Walk to a class of Navajo students. I was also to say a few words about *ha'ahóní*—fortitude and faith—to the students. I thought about what I would say. Nothing seemed to fit; the words were all too dry and boring. I thought about calling and canceling. Finally, I decided to give the oral version of the textbook. When I arrived, I asked the students to kneel around me. I knelt down and made a dome shape with my right hand and placed it in the middle of the circle, and said, *"Ałk'idą́ą́' chąą' sitłéé', jiní."* All the students started roaring with laughter. The teacher stood there, gaped. "A long time ago, there was a pile of manure, they say. They also say that the person sat like this and did this." I continued to kneel, re-formed that pile of manure with my hand, lifted my hand and poked my right index finger into the pile, and finally took a scoop out and put it in my mouth. The laughter slowed down and others went "Yuck!" I felt that horse manure power surge through me once again. I stood up and said, "That is the genesis of the contemporary Navajo." Then I vividly described the conditions at Bosque Redondo when Navajos were captives there. I explained that in order for our ancestors to survive so that we could be here today, they had to poke through horse manure graciously offered by the soldiers' horses for undigested corn, which they collected and ate. For the next forty-five minutes I had those high school students in the grip of my hands, and while I held on to them, they laughed and felt pain, they experienced misery and learned about the power of hope and faith. At the end of the day, guess what I did? Yes, I once again gave thanks to the gods for having come upon that pile of horse manure. In that pile of manure I have learned much about my history, hope, faith, fortitude, and love. The greatest lesson from poking in that pile is the knowledge that in every negative circumstance, there is to be found a seed of great potential power. And this time when I prayed I didn't feel ridiculous. And I will give thanks again upon publication of this writing. So I advised my student to be grateful during the evening prayer.

I also explained to my student that although we pray in the morning and know that the gods are with us, we can only do so much and take so much. This is simply the natural law in motion. So we may not accomplish everything, or we may encounter problems that we couldn't get rid of, or say things we didn't mean. The evening prayer is also a time for purification. It is a time to say, "I did my best. Still, here is all this trash that I still have. Here, Lord, take it for me." In this way, you take out all negative things from your mind and body. When you go to sleep, you may have wonderful dreams about your sweetheart, instead of having nightmares. At this time, my student said, "Hmmm, maybe I should try this." It is also a time to ask for courage, fortitude, and persistence, especially when you have a tendency not to complete what you determine to do in your morning prayer. This may be due to fear, procrastination, or lack of direction. When you let go of the garbage, you will sleep and rest well. In the morning you will be up bright and early, eager to design your day.

I informed my student that there are other forms of praying. The morning and evening prayers are personal prayers. They must be part of your daily life. Of course, you may pray any time you want, to address a specific problem or just to be thankful. Then there are prescribed prayers that medicine people know. Learning to recite these prayers requires many years of dedication. These prayers are so powerful that their uses in supplication must strictly adhere to proper intonation, enunciation, and sequencing as given by the gods themselves. Along with these prayers are also prayers and songs to call back the forces released by earlier prayers. These prayers must also be given only at certain hours of the day, during certain rites as required by particular ceremonies given to counteract specific negative forces. They must be given only after certain stories take place or events happen. Otherwise, either the prayers are useless or you unleash forces that are beyond your control, which eventually will destroy you. So I encouraged my student to concentrate only on personal prayers for now.

Well, stop beating about the bush. What is your point? Is this essay about praying? It may be. What has praying got to do with your writing? Isn't that why you were asked to contribute to this book? Because you are a writer? I guess. Perhaps I'm just being Navajo, or simply following a tradition. I have to come around in circles and warm up before I make my point, which is at the center of the circle. I want to make sure that my point is a bull's-eye.

sdnouS, telosadi nda uto fo rrdeo, ear selsanemgni.
isolated, in forever are or meaningless beginning words, whether, the,.

Sounds, isolated and out of order, are meaningless. Words, isolated, whether in the beginning, or forever, are meaningless. In short, anything out of context is meaningless. I keep it simple. I am a simple man. My elders tell me to keep it simple. The *it* refers to communication. I don't get any more complicated than that.

My writing? I write to make sense out of sounds and words and paragraphs and essays and dissertations and books. I write to make sense out of my experiences, thoughts, emotions. I write to make sense out of the right brain and the left brain. I write to make sense out of reality and what's not for real. I write to make sense out of who's American Indian, who's Native American, who's the First American, and who's the indigenous person. I write to make sense out of who's Navajo and who's Diné. I write to make sense out of this writing. I think—or am I feeling it?—the bottom line is that I write to communicate with myself. That's why I write mostly in Navajo. I only wish I could have written this in Navajo. Well, I guess this writing is good for my English, anyway.

If anyone else makes sense of what I'm writing about, then it's great. I won't be the only one making sense out of my world. Perhaps I may help others make sense out of their worlds. If the sharing of my experience—in thought, flesh, or spirit—takes place only in this minute communion, then I am making my connections. So let me share with you a personal experience.

It's somewhat funny to know that the very personal is also the most common and therefore universal. This was written after a younger brother of mine died in a car crash involving alcohol. We were to become men together.

I know that I am a man.
And I know that I shouldn't cry.
But I also know that I must become a man.
I know that I must cry.

The other day I cried.
I cried when I went walking early in the morning.

I cried because I no longer understood the world.
I cried because you were no longer there with me.
I cried because when I cried, no one heard me.
I cried because I could no longer hold your hands.

I cried because I could no longer hold my brother's hands.
because when I did I became gay.
I cried because I was no longer allowed to hug my father.
because when I did I committed incest.
I cried because I was no longer allowed to shake my nephew's hands.
because when I did I enjoyed child molestation.
I cried because I was no longer allowed to touch my son's hair,
because when I did I raped.
I cried because I was no longer allowed to become a man.
because when I tried the world turned me into a woman.

I cried because I was no longer allowed to enjoy nature
on my morning walks because when I did I committed an act
of blasphemy against the civilized God.
I cried because I was no longer allowed to step on dry twigs
on my morning walks because when I did I killed living
things that provided knowledge for progress.
I cried because I was no longer allowed to watch eagles play
on my morning walks because when I did I only saw eagles
become shadows of crows dancing on barbed wire, claws bleeding.
I cried because I was no longer allowed to help ants travel quickly
on my morning walks because when I did the only distance I
found was my index finger swelling quickly.
I cried because I was no longer allowed to find peace
on my morning walks because when I did the grasshoppers
continued to fight and stripped corn husks blew away.

I cried because this morning when I awoke
I found myself alone and shivered at the touch of cold

contours of sheets that screamed, "She has been gone for hours."
I cried because when I had dinner with my parents last night
you accused me, "You are running around on me."

I cried because last night I did not dream.
I cried because today I cannot dream and when I
do I am afraid I will not know how to return from fantasy land.

I cried because I could no longer dream.
I cried because I could no longer understand why shadows shifted.
I cried because heat waves and sun rays brought tears to my eyes.

I cry because the earth shimmers and the sun glitters.
I cry because the rainbow sparkles and the lightning flashes.
I cry because the world cries with me.
I cry because I know that I am a man.
I cry because I know that a man must cry.
I cry because I want to become a man.
I cry because I am a man.
I cry, "This moment is mine."

Giving order to these sounds and words empowers me to rise above and beyond myself. Words uplift me to heights from which I transform myself into a power that transmutes any experience into an energy which I may direct toward a definite purpose that I desire to achieve. I am the maker of my own destiny. From this height, I know that words, knowledge, thoughts, emotions, experiences are all important. Isolated and dormant, they are useless. They are potential power. What is more important is knowing how, when, and for what to use this power. Therein lies our personal power! From this height, everything matters. Everything matters!

May I say farewell, for now, with the following poem.

I

rise

early in

the dawn when

dew drops just begin to shake

their sleeping bones.

I

rise

at the beginning of
a new creation and move
in the belly of an unknown day.

I
rise
to claim the day
in the wake of mystery.

I
rise,
Sun Carrier,
warrior,
to meet you so you may
hear for yourself my declaration.

I
rise
to light the world with my smile.

I
rise
to bless the day with my eyes.

I
rise
before you,
Sun Carrier,
father.
Listen.
My thundering laughter
proclaims,
This day is mine!

On the Tip
of My Tongue

An Autobiographical Essay

EVELINA ZUNI LUCERO

*Born in Albuquerque in 1953, Evelina Zuni Lucero is Isleta
Pueblo on her father's side, and San Juan Pueblo on her mother's.
She studied at Stanford University in the early days of its Native
American Program and later completed an MA in English at
the University of New Mexico. Her fiction has been published in*
Blue Mesa Review *(University of New Mexico Press, 1989),*
Northeast Indian Quarterly *(Cornell University, 1991),*
Women on Hunting *(Ecco Press, 1994),* Returning the Gift
(University of Arizona Press, 1994), Native American Litera-
ture *(HarperCollins College Publishers, 1994), and* Native Roots
and Rhythms *(Southwest Learning Centers, Inc., 1998). Lucero
has taught at the University of New Mexico, UNM-Valencia
Campus, and the Institute of American Indian Arts. Her novel,*
Time and Chance, *received the 1999 First Book Award by the
Native Writer's Circle of the Americas and is forthcoming from the
University of Arizona Press.*

For generations, Pueblo people have lived as farmers, moving with the rhythms of the seasons, in love with the soil, with hard work and tenacity, with the fruit of that hard work. We are generally known as peaceful people. Peaceful, I suppose, as in settled, but not as in docile. We can be diplomatic but we know when to fight. We have perfected the skill of looking like we're cooperating when all along, within, we are resisting, subverting, maintaining who we are in the face of demands to be otherwise.

In my veins flows the blood of two tribal peoples. One river courses through me, diverging, converging, moving constantly.

I do not speak my native languages, either Tiwa or Tewa. English has become my medium of communication, but it is not my mother tongue. I cannot think of it as part of me, as a heritage, a legacy. After all, English has been used as a tool to assert domination, to define Native people as less than, as inferior, filthy savages, good for nothing, words that construct a hostile world we have no place in. I feel deeply the loss of my native language. But having acquired the skills to manipulate the English language, I write to give voice to Native experience, to tell who we truly are, to make my words strong. To sing out: We are *People*. We call ourselves "the People" in our Native languages, but it obviously must be said in English—and said many times— before it will be heard.

Growing up off the reservation, I did not have a traditional upbringing yet grew up with a solid Indian identity. However, returning home years later raised feelings of displacement. I came face-to-face with difficult questions: What was my role as an Indian person who's been inside the Indian experience yet outside the reservation community? How was I to use my background to contribute to the community, to integrate myself and not separate myself from the people? My secure sense of being was deeply affected by these questions. I have come to realize the disquietedness I felt arose from the pressures by the dominant culture to eradicate Indianness through the educational system, the social-political structure, and language. It seems I have spent a good part of my early life trying to hold my own in the face of these pressures, and my adult years working out answers to the questions. It is in struggling to communicate this experience in my writings that I feel a sense of vindication for the dilemma I faced through no choice of my own.

What I know about the lives of my grandparents, my parents, and consequently about myself, about who I am, comes from family stories I accumulated over the years, then pieced together. I filled in the unstated, gauged the depths of shadows, gave them shades of meaning, and came to my own conclusions.

I was born in Albuquerque in the fall of 1953 at a time of no particular importance. Isleta Pueblo, the village of my father, was once surrounded by the waters of the Rio Grande, and in the 1950s, Isleta retained, at least metaphorically, the characteristics of its Spanish name, meaning "little island." Isleta largely remained insulated against the pressures and demands of the dominant culture, though the outside world was already nudging in changes. It was the last decade in which changes came slowly

My mother is from San Juan Pueblo, one of the eight northern Tewa-speaking pueblos. My parents were children of the day school and boarding school era, and it was at the Albuquerque Indian School they first met. At school, they were subjected to the oft-cited repression of their native language and forced acquisition of English, and teaching emphasizing cultural assimilation. My parents went through a series of name changes as they grew up, another reflection of colonization through language. My father grew up at Isleta being called by his Tiwa name, Kim-mu, which means "lion," a beautiful, more personal name than his name of record. José Abelicio is his Christian name, a Spanish name, but he went by a much shortened, more English—palatable version, Abie or Abe. My mother's given name was Katilda, but when she attended Catholic school as a child, the nuns maintained they could not spell such a name, so they renamed her Christine. Ironically, it is her Tewa name, Quah-Povi, which means "beads flower," that she uses most frequently.

The Indian school provided my parents with much more education than their parents had received, and with that they ventured out of their pueblos. A few years beyond high school, they dated, and then married during the turbulent years of World War II.

The years of their early adulthood were affected by the social and political forces moving American society, larger forces beyond the pueblo boundaries that brought changes no one could have anticipated. New Mexico was largely rural then, and economically depressed, Albuquerque not much more than a railroad stop. The pueblos were self-contained communities, relying primarily on subsistence farming. Employment opportunities for Indians didn't become available until World War II broke out. For Povi, this meant a food service job at Los Alamos National Laboratory, the birthplace of the atomic bomb. Later, she was employed in defense work in Albuquerque on an assembly line; my father joined the Air Corps and was eventually stationed at Lowry Field near Denver. Knowing my father was soon to be sent overseas, Povi traveled by bus to Denver, where they were married in a justice of the peace ceremony, a simple civil ceremony that haunted her years later because of its lack of blessings of family and church.

When my father left for the southwest Pacific, my mother returned to her parents' home in San Juan. My father was a member of a B-24 bombing group, the tail gunner and nose gunner, flying fifty missions altogether before he returned home the year before the war ended. He speaks very little of his military experience though he was a designated "hero," with an array of medals and news stories of his missions. One morning Povi's father woke her, worriedly saying, "Hurry up and get dressed. There is a policeman at the door asking for you. What have you done?" The policeman at the door turned out to be my dad in his military uniform, home from the war.

As with other Native Americans, serving in the war had widened the world for my father, exposing him to a totally different experience outside the pueblo, a totally different lifestyle requiring different skills. My father was a strong and determined man. In the military, he saw he was just as intelligent and capable as any man, any white man. He realized the importance of education as a means of acquiring a good job and knew what he needed to do. Against the will of his parents, who saw no value in further schooling, he attended the University of New Mexico on the GI Bill. Farming was how his parents knew to live, and that's what they wanted for him. So my father along with others began a departure from the traditional pueblo livelihood. Some went to college on the GI Bill; others acquired vocations and went into building trades.

My parents settled at Isleta in a two-room home in the village given to them by my grandmother, to which they added as their family grew. During the years my father was in school, they struggled financially. My father worked part-time and Povi worked at the Bernalillo County Indian Hospital as a nurse's aide. Although my mother is not as well educated as my father, he could not have accomplished what he did without her. They are opposites in some ways yet complements in ways that count. He is intellectual, she artistic, but they both shared the same dream.

My parents knew no other way to live except to work hard. They were raised during the Great Depression in extreme poverty and hardship, and their childhood experiences ingrained in them a strong work ethic. After my father obtained his degree in business education, he began working for the Bureau of Indian Affairs, first at the Southern Pueblos Agency in Albuquerque and then in Gallup. According to historian Joe Sando of Jemez Pueblo, the BIA was the only place pueblo college graduates of that time could find employment in New Mexico.

By the time I was born, the fifth child in a family of seven, my maternal grandfather, Demacio Cata, whom we called Papa Cata, came from San Juan to live with us. San Juan is one of the eight Tewa pueblos in northern New Mexico near Española, a beautiful place, peaceful and serene, full of deep silence. Or maybe that is just my subjective perception because I associate the area with my grandparents and those characteristics with them.

Papa Cata was a tall man with strong features, born sometime in the 1890s, and named Tompayo, meaning "Dawn." It's a name of personal significance to me as the dawning of my memories begins with remembrances of Papa Cata working around our house, cooking, taking care of me and my older brothers and sisters. I remember him combing my hair, his gentle touch as he braided my hair as his was braided and wrapped in the style of the men from the northern pueblos. He bathed me, dressed me, watched over me, and took me almost everywhere with him. In snapshot memories, I remember walking the village with him, my hand in his, and riding the Albuquerque city bus that included Isleta in its daily route. He talked with my mother in Tewa, the sound of which I have always associated with the gurgling of a mountain stream. And my last memory of him—I must have been four years old—is of him stuffed like a rag doll in a cardboard box in our home as people gathered to mourn—perhaps my childish interpretation of what I saw but didn't understand. I've asked my mother about that particular memory and she says he was placed in a wooden coffin. I remember walking with my mother to the Catholic church for the burial Mass and then to the cemetery to bury him. After that, I had only a vague but disquieting sense of loss. It wasn't until my youngest daughter was four years old that I recalled that loss in full, and I mourned him then in a way I was never able to do as a child.

I am not sure exactly what happened to Papa Cata and that is one of the things that bothers me most about his sudden death. Perhaps as he was coming home that night, he suffered a stroke and collapsed on the road not far from our home. Perhaps he was assaulted, as bruises on his head suggested. At any rate, he was suddenly and inexplicably gone from my life.

Papa Cata was a gentle man and something of him has stayed with me.

I never knew my mother's mother, Flora Archuleta Cata. She was gone before I was born, disappeared or died—it's not clear which—so I know her only through my mother's stories, by the photograph of her with a short-cropped Pueblo hairstyle. I bear no physical resemblance to her that I can detect. She was a potter and sold her pottery to tourists to supplement Papa Cata's subsistence farming, often selling a tableful of pottery for $20, a significant sum back then, which bought such luxuries as butter. She had learned pottery-making from her mother and taught my mother, who also became a potter, exhibiting at Indian art shows. Povi in turn taught her daughters. Grandma Flora's descendants include an impressive number of artists, potters, and craftmakers.

My paternal grandfather, Andrés Zuni, was a small man, also gentle. We called him Gramps. He had light skin, hazel eyes, and white hair. I can see him sitting in a kitchen chair, his legs crossed, pointing with his finger as he talked. When I was little, he sat me on his lap and sang in Tiwa. He smelled of cigarette smoke and the outdoors. He was a hard worker, a farmer, working with livestock, strong in some ways, weak in others. Sometimes he drank too much. He had a yard full of farming implements, a wagon, a truck, and tractor, chickens and other birds, and at various times, pigs, sheep, and horses in a corral. He worked long and hard right up to his death at seventy-four years of age. He suffered a stroke when he was hauling bales and died soon after in the hospital. His wife, Evangelisita Zuni, was a strong, forceful woman, bearing the Tiwa name Narvessay which means "Aspen Headdress." People will tell you my grandmother was overbearing. And she could be authoritarian, the matriarch of her family and clan, strong and resourceful, but she could also be funny at times. I feel I missed out on really knowing who she was because she didn't speak English very well. And I didn't speak Tiwa so our communication was broken or translated through others.

Both Gramps and Nana Narvessay were orphans, and no one in my extended family can tell me anything of my great-grandparents. Gramps was born in the 1880s and Narvessay in 1900. As children, they lived with and worked for other families. Gramps had some schooling, attending St. Catherine's Indian School in Sante Fe until the sixth grade where he learned to speak English. My grandmother never went to school. In all probability, she was kept home to help the family she was living with. Unlike most of her peers, she had no introduction to white culture. For her entire life, she wore only traditional clothing (canvas shoes were a concession), the traditional hairstyle, and had minimal contact with the non-Indian world. It was late in her life before she acquired indoor plumbing, an electric stove, other modern conveniences. She often frustrated the family with her utter disregard for running life by a clock.

Nana was strong and healthy throughout her life, was eighty-seven years old when she died. She probably would have lived even longer, but she accidentally burned down her home when she left a pot of food cooking on the stove. She was outside hoeing weeds and had forgotten about the food. My grandmother could not stand to be idle even in her old age. She couldn't stand to have weeds in her yard, and as long as she could hoe them, she would do so despite scoldings by others. I think it was hard for her to lose her house and her independence and to live with her daughters. Not long after the fire, she fell and broke her hip and died within a short period.

Nana was fully traditional in her life and beliefs. I know she despaired that my life was different, that it had taken a turn she could never have imagined. As a young adult, I struggled to understand what she feared.

When I was eight, my family moved to the Southern Ute Agency in Ignacio, Colorado, where my father became the superintendent. I had no idea I was leaving behind one way of living for something entirely different. What I knew then was the village with its closely spaced adobe homes, dirt roads, the fields across the river, my grandparents' home, the Isleta Day School, the dances, the ceremonies, my relatives, the sound of Tiwa, a vague, disturbing sense of violence and alcoholism in the community. On the day we left, Nana cried and Gramps had us grandkids kneel while he prayed for us.

The move was exciting, especially the experience of snow, piled deep and lasting for days on end. My mouth dropped open at the government housing: white clapboard houses with pitched roofs and fenced lawns. The homes faced the Southern Ute Park, which included a recreation center, park benches, trees and grass, memorials to Ute chiefs, and a playground. The agency, a small community located on federal land a short distance from the small town of Ignacio, included a boarding school for Navajo students and consisted of an upper and lower campus.

For the first time, I became acutely aware of "Others" and that I could be perceived as different. At Isleta I had attended a Bureau of Indian Affairs tribal school with other Isleta children. In Ignacio, I was placed in a public school, which was attended by a variety of students: the Navajo students boarding at the agency, Indian children of BIA agency employees, Southern Ute children living within the district, and Mexican American and white students, though as I remember, the white students were in the minority. Like the Navajo students, I was coming straight from the reservation where lifestyles, customs, and speech patterns were taken for granted. In public school, other kids made fun of the braids I wore, my speech and its mix of English with Tiwa. That my braids could be an object of derision, especially since most Isleta girls wore them and since I connected them with Papa

Cata, bewildered me. It was my first encounter with the fact that things "Indian" could be a source of shame. In class I was far behind the other students. I had no idea what the multiplication table was what "x" signified, so I made up numbers to fill the blanks or tried to copy from students next to me. Phonics and dividing words into syllables were equally mystifying. I couldn't hear the proper pronunciation of my teacher's name, whether it was Mrs. Hope or Mrs. Pope, so I mumbled her name, hoping to get by.

I was quickly introduced to things I never experienced on the reservation—snow boots, sledding, ice skating, large homes with pitched roofs, yards with grass and trees, garages, a sense of "neighborhood," paved roads, hot lunch, other tribal cultures, notions of class and race—poor whites, dumb Mexicans, stupid Indians/savages. I learned class differences—children who wore clean pretty clothes and were well groomed, and those who weren't; those who had money for hot lunch and those who didn't. The groomed children were admired and popular; the others were not. Made conscious of the "Otherness" of Indians, my world began to divide into a world of Us and Them, us being brown-skinned people, them being whites. Learning these things did not come all at once nor was it acquired consciously.

A strategy I adopted to cope with this threatening situation was to do well in school. Once I memorized the multiplication table and began winning math bees, coming up with the answer so fast my opponent was left in the dust, I knew I was on to something. My team wanted me to win, the girls wanted me to win, my friends wanted me to win, Indians wanted me to win. And no one could make fun of me anymore. All I had to say in response to teasing was "So? At least I can multiply." They didn't have a response for that. Nor for the fact that I could spell, too. Looking back now, I can see how this was a serious undertaking—my goal was to prove Indians could beat whites at their own game. I was reacting not only against being made to feel bad about myself, but also against the message implicit in textbooks and the classrooms: Indians are inferior.

I was enriched with the wealth of culture within both the Mexican American and the Native communities. I learned about Indians of other tribes, in particular the Utes. The Ute people were friendly and generous, including me and my family and other agency families in their tribal dances and activities. I was never made to feel an outsider, unwelcome or resented. A number of Indian families also lived on the agency and I learned of other tribal cultures and lands in playing with these children. We were like an extended family, playing together, children of all ages, whites and Indians. We laughed, fought, shared secrets, plotted mischief, smoked pilfered cigarettes, told ghost stories, and sometimes separated, for moving around was part of the agency experience.

We lived at Ignacio for about five years, and when we moved to the Nevada Indian Agency at Stewart in 1966, I was entering adolescence with its accompanying angst and anxieties. Leaving close friends and a small school was difficult and not made any easier by moving from a rural, mostly nonwhite community to a larger town, predominantly white and middle class. The culture shock was jarring although fortunately the agency at Stewart was again a community separate from nearby Carson City, the state's capital.

Stewart was three miles south of Carson City and included the Stewart Indian School, both agency and boarding school being much larger than the Ute Agency. The campus was a green oasis in the midst of sagebrush with beautiful rock buildings, towering pines and oaks, and spacious lawns. Like all the other agency children, I did not attend the Stewart school but attended public school in Carson City. There I found adolescents my age trying to grow up too soon. In the midst of casinos operating full blast twenty-four hours a day, slot machines everywhere, even in grocery stores, these teens were much more sophisticated than teens I had known; they were West Coast–influenced, children of divorce, fashion-conscious, concerned with dating, going steady, making out, doing too much too soon. It was hard to know how to handle it and I found myself taking refuge in schoolwork. The school was much larger than the one I had attended in Ignacio and Native people were not a significant population in the town or the school. There were no reservations nearby, although an Indian colony of Washo families was situated on the outskirts of town. I saw a growing gap between Indian and white values and felt a helplessness at being caught between them. Personal appearance and attractiveness, family social position, money, and material possessions were measures of worth. Having any of these things gave you status in the public school. Being Indian or brown definitely did not.

For the most part, my school years in Carson City were marked by a distinct feeling of Otherness. (Perhaps the name of the capital is a clue: it was named after Kit Carson, the famed Indian killer and "frontier explorer.") Constantly being asked if I was Hawaiian, Polynesian, Oriental, Filipino, if I ate grasshoppers and bugs, if I lived in a tepee or a hogan, quickly became tiresome, at times, racist. True, it came from only a few, but it was enough harassment to make me wary even after it stopped. Native students were not expected to do well in school and most didn't. I became the anomaly, but once again it was out of spite, out of a struggle to hold my own that I worked to do well. But here, unlike in Ignacio, doing well was a solitary experience. I typically was the only Native student in my classes and did not receive the support of, nor could I give it to, other Native students. Outside of the classroom, I occasionally helped Native students by doing their homework, even taking tests for them so they could make it through another hoop in a system that had given up on them, that offered and asked nothing of them other than they not cause trouble in the classroom.

I attended junior high and high school during the years of the Civil Rights Movement, the Vietnam War, the counterculture movement with its accompanying political unrest and agitation and sexual revolution, and the burgeoning of the American Indian Movement. Like everyone else, I was impacted by these movements and my politics formed out of these various ideologies. I began to speak out in my classes and became the lone voice questioning America's treatment of Indian people. I know what I said made teachers and students uncomfortable—no one ever said anything when I broached the subject. Whether it was ignorance or indifference that kept them silent, I'm not sure. When I was a senior in high school and only one of a few Native students in the college prep classes, several white students indicated to me they had heard me all those previous years and respected me for speaking out; their words were unexpected but encouraging. It was largely the loneliness of this public school experience that made me stronger in my sense of Indianness. I was hundreds of miles from my own reservation, yet in the core of my being I knew who I was and I knew we were not an inferior people.

My only place of belonging became the Stewart campus, mixing with the agency children and students attending Stewart Indian

School. Lest I give the wrong impression, it was not that I did not have non-Indian friends, because I did. It was that with them, I seldom completely let down safeguards I had erected to protect myself.

At Stewart, the families were predominantly Indians of various tribal backgrounds—Lakota, Hopi, Paiute, Shoshone, Navajo, Cochiti, Eskimo, to name a few. Some full-bloods like me were a combination of tribal groups; mixed-bloods were few and far between. We agency children were a rambunctious group with a lot of room to move. The campus offered school facilities, a gym, student store, auditorium, and there were hills and a creek beyond the campus to explore, and down the road, a T-car racetrack, and the ominous minimum-security prison. Native students attending the Stewart school were an intertribal mix of Ute, Shoshone, Paiute, Hopi, Pima, Papago (Tohono O'odham), Washo, Apache, and other tribes from Arizona, Nevada, Utah, Idaho, and California. Whether an agency child or a boarding school student, we had one thing in common—displacement from our tribal homelands.

Even as kids, it was clear to us that Stewart Indian School was not providing its students with a good education. Their textbooks and classes were not on par with our public school experience. A number of Stewart students were unhappy and did not like being there, though for some, Stewart provided a stability and structure they lacked at home. Then there were those as well who enjoyed the extracurricular activities and the friends they made. The school was full of rules, almost like a military boot camp with runaways labeled AWOL and dormitory staff with demeanors of drill sergeants. But even with all its deficiencies and the growing awareness on our part of criticisms directed at the BIA (for whom our parents worked), Stewart was a source of pride for us. Stewart athletes were the best. They soundly trounced the white AA schools in basketball and were very competitive in football, track, baseball, and boxing, winning All-State titles. They gave us something to shout about.

Growing up with children of different tribal backgrounds, I developed a deep appreciation for the diversity of Indian people, for the uniqueness of tribal cultures, and for the values we have in common. Every summer when the Stewart students returned home, I was reminded, though, that an important part of being Indian is being a part of a specific tribal community. I never let go of the fact that home, Isleta, was the place to return to.

During my family's years at Stewart, our lives were comfortable. By this time, only three of us remained at home. I was aware of but not face-to-face with the economic and social ills on reservations, the very situations which brought many Stewart students to the boarding school and which existed in varying degrees at Isleta. Memories of the reservation of my childhood seemed so faint. Visits home to New Mexico were never enough to make up for years away. I realized that as a child I had no control over how I was raised—that it was not my fault I did not speak Tiwa and was not initiated in traditional ways, though some of my people scolded me about this, or scolded me about my parents.

The positive outcome of my years at Carson High School was that I obtained a solid college prep and I was accepted to Stanford University in the first years of its Native American program. Attending Stanford was a compounding of the struggle to maintain a Native identity, this time in a white elitist institution. Fortunately, I had the encouragement of other Native students and strong program support to make it through. My years in Carson City prepared me somewhat to withstand the disdain of some white Stanford students and alumni who saw minority students in general as lowering the quality of education and as mere affirmative action tokens who were otherwise unqualified to be there. To have such racial slurs said to our faces or to read them in print angered and insulted us. Experiences such as these did more to strengthen my politics of resistance than anything else.

I returned home to Isleta following graduation from college. This homecoming was fraught with conflict. Despite my solid identification with my Indianness, my sense of self was deeply challenged. I didn't meet the reservation standard of Indianness. I did not speak Tiwa, grow up in the traditions, or know the social rules I was expected to know. Ironically, I felt like an outsider among my own people. I had spent years among other Indian people who were not my own yet accepted me, and now I was made to feel marginal. Rejection is a painful experience that hits you at the core of your being. When it comes from others, from without, you can rationalize it, dismiss it, cope with it. When it comes from within, you're extremely vulnerable. I had to face the situation. Wasn't the intent behind removing Indian children from their homes and educating them in schools far from their reservation homes to hasten assimilation? To separate them from their people? I asked myself, Had it worked?

For a long time I was angry about the situation. However, I was forced to come to terms with who I am, what I can't change, and to accept both. I stepped out of myself and saw the effects of colonization and assimilation policies in my life and the personal and collective pain they can inflict. I saw the same effects at work on a tribal level, often leading Native people to reject one another. I understood my grandmother Narvessay's concerns for me, what happened to her as a child, orphaned and raised without a mother's love. I understood that nothing is as deep and abiding as a mother's love. I also understood how my father believed the American Dream was for Indians, too. After all, Indians, too, have fought for America, their homeland. I understood the choices and sacrifices he and my mother made, seeing their choices as part of a complex web of sociopolitical-economic factors at work in their lives. I accepted the fact that nothing is as simple as it seems. Our lives have significance not so much in their expression of individuality, but in their continuum. How we relate to one another in the here and now, how that's related to the lives of those before and those after us is what's important.

Just recently I learned from my father that before her death, Nana expressed a deep resentment, a bitterness even, at not getting an education. Other women her age had gone to school as children and learned to speak English, to read and write. Perhaps she felt cheated of what her peers experienced. Perhaps, after my dad's long government career and return home to farm, after seeing many of her grandchildren go to college, after seeing her two daughters also obtain college degrees, she felt she had been denied something of value. I wonder about her last sentiment. What does it mean to me?

When I first began to write I never wanted to include obvious autobiographical elements in my fiction, feeling that it was too self-conscious, too presumptuous, and I consciously avoided doing so. It is with great surprise in writing this essay that I see how much of my own life experience has come to unconsciously infuse by connecting and reconnecting my characters and fiction. And how so much healing has occurred for me. It's as if the words were always there on the tip of my tongue, ready to be voiced.

When it comes right down to it, I write as an act of resistance, to affirm myself as an Indian person in a tribal community as well as to affirm Indian people. I strive to use my education to help Indian people, especially Native students, realize empowerment through voice in big and small ways, individually and collectively.

I took a journey out of the pueblo long ago and it has been a long, hard journey back in. I'm home with the core of my being intact.

I am a daughter holding hands with other daughters in a long, unbroken line of daughters that stretches back through Time Immemorial. We flow together like a river, brown and sleek, a river full of bends and twists, quiet pools, sudden rapids, treacherous whirlpools. We carry all that preceded us upstream and we send downstream all that made us.

MOTION OF
FIRE AND FORM

Autobiographical Reflections

LOUIS OWENS

Louis Owens is of Choctaw, Cherokee, and Irish descent. Following several years as a wilderness ranger with the U.S. Forest Service, he returned to school to complete a PhD. Among his publications are two books on John Steinbeck, an annotated critical bibliography of American Indian novels (co-authored), a critical study called Other Destinies: Understanding the American Indian Novel *(1992), and, most recently,* Mixedblood Messages *(1998), a collection of essays on literature, film, identity, and environment. A prize-winning novelist, he has published* Wolfsong *(1990),* The Sharpest Sight *(1992),* Bone Game *(1994),* Nightland *(1996), and* Dark River *(1999). Owens is currently a professor of English language and literature at the University of New Mexico.*

I don't know how to write autobiography, and memory is the most un-
reliable narrator, so perhaps I should begin by at least trying to get a
few things straight: I was born in prison. I grew up in Mississippi and
California. I have lived a great deal in the outdoors. I am not a real Indian. I have eight brothers and sisters. My mother walked barefoot
across half of Texas. My father killed and ate another man's pig. The
world is dangerously literal. Autobiography contains too many "i" 's.
Were they to read what follows, and undoubtedly they will, my family
would surely remember our life differently. But since nothing has been
written down, I must put things together from the scraps of stories in
my memory and imagination beginning with Mississippi, where
everything begins.

How to evoke that feeling of a Mississippi mud road, late at night forty
years ago in the middle of nowhere on the way home from my granma
and grampa's house, which at one time had been a small church and
still had a steeple and cotton fields that came sneaking up from the
woods on all sides? The black bones of trees, what now after a college
education I call deciduous, on both sides of the road because it must
have been winter and probably there was ice in the ruts and in the
muddy stream beside the road and no moonlight at all that I can remember. The winter air frozen cold and thick as Karo syrup. A big car,
probably a forty-something Chevy or Ford, one of those cars that
make your parents say repeatedly, "Now don't you go to sleep back
there," because of carbon monoxide that would maybe kill you if you
went to sleep with any or all of your eight brothers and sisters piled on
top of each other. The same kind of car we'd drive back and forth to
California, across all that desert with canvas water bags hanging and
dripping from every sharp projection of mirror, hood ornament, and

door handle. Big and solid and perfectly crafted for pig-killing on a dark Mississippi night.

Dinner had been possum, I think, a greasy, strong-flavored, stringy meat my grandparents loved, and probably hominy, since there was always hominy at their house, and cornbread because there was always cornbread. There is the odor of wood smoke, kerosene, and rusty pump water, and in my memory a too-long farewell in the car out in the bare, hard-packed dirt yard, my grampa's two bony bluetick hounds lying in the lantern light of the porch. Then the sullen comfort of too many kids tangled and tired on the wide backseat—although we weren't nine yet, but only five. The Yazoo River, with its brown, impenetrable water, was off there in the dark, and perhaps I remember being six years old and sensing its presence not far away through the woods, maybe remember imagining that I heard the alligators barking the way I sometimes did at night in our plank-walled shotgun shack with its tar-paper sides and tin roof while our father was out there across the river hunting coons and, I now strongly suspect, poaching alligators. Our cabin stood a couple hundred yards from the river, facing the same mud road we were driving, with a big pecan tree across the road before the river jungle began, the tree underneath which I truly believe I saw one black woman cut another black woman with her straight razor one afternoon so that the cut one bled and died later, and even at five years old I knew or heard someone in the crowd of black people and Indians say it was "man trouble." Muscadines grew on vines in the thick woods by the river, and the river mud flaked in big cracks by the leaky rowboat I pushed us off in so we almost drowned trying to get to the other side, which was where they said Indians lived. Large, hidden things lived in the river—alligators, snapping turtles, water moccasins, catfish big enough to swallow a dog, needle-toothed gar—shadowy things just waiting for a foolish child. Across the river was a world I wondered about and dreamed about but never saw. Out of that world came the panther that followed my father back from hunting one night, crying, he said, like a woman in pain. On the roof of our cabin, the black cat walked furiously, screaming and terrifying us kids before it knocked the tin chimney off and leapt away into the night. Into that world my father disappeared when darkness came each evening.

Rainwater collected in a barrel on the front porch. At night there would be the acrid smell of my father's carbide hunting lamp, and by daylight there would be coonskins nailed to the shed wall and dark men and women coming to take away the bodies of naked flesh. In the fields I dragged a child-size cotton bag and the black cotton pickers laughed as they filled it for me and then carried me back to the shade of the trailers when I grew sleepy. All around me were relatives.

Born in prison because my father ran away from home when he was fifteen and lied to join the army during World War II and then went AWOL from the paratroops just before he was about to be shipped out for some invasion. His sharecropper parents were alone in Mississippi, and both got pneumonia at the same time and needed help to stay alive and get the cotton picked. When the army wouldn't give him emergency leave to help, he just left anyway and took care of them until they were better and then came back to turn himself in. So they threw him out of the paratroops and for punishment made him a policeman at the military prison in Lompoc, California, "the Valley of Flowers," where he was walking down the street one day and saw Ida Brown, dark-eyed and beautiful Oklahoman with long black hair, already at age twenty married and divorced twice and the mother of a boy and girl, waitressing in a café and said to his buddy, "Hey, that's an Indian girl," and claimed later that he also said, "and I'm going to marry her." So I was born in the military prison hospital to which my mother was brought because she had left what she and my grandmother Nora Bailey Brown—a more-than-half-Cherokee woman who bore my mother at age thirteen and was descended from a Cherokee mother who disappeared and left her to be raised by a grandmother named Storm and an absent mixed-blood father named John Bailey said in family myth to have been an "Indian scout" who guided wagon trains—called the "Nation" in Oklahoma and come out to California to work in the shipyards during the war and somehow drifted to Lompoc, where her sister married into an Italian family from near Pisa (the grandmother of which never did learn to speak English) and was working in a Chinese-owned American-style café when a cocky, nineteen-year-old fellow named Hoey Owens, whose mother was a Choctaw-Cajun woman from the Choctaw Strip in Catahoula Parish, Louisiana, and whose father was a dirt-poor Irish sharecropper across the river in Mississippi, came walking by and decided to marry her. "Indian scout" because, I suspect, he guided those "Sooner" land thieves into Indian Territory before reservations were allotted and legally thrown open to white settlement. A Judas scout, maybe.

Nobody saw the pig, but everybody heard it. In the headlights it was huge and dead with its throat cut by the time we kids were out looking and shivering in the cold night, the black blood spurting and pooling in front of the radiator. And then it was in the trunk of the car and we were home and a pit was dug beneath the big walnut tree behind the cabin and fire and neighbors from other cabins in the woods who today, more than forty years later, form a dancing, strutting tableau of mostly angular shadows around the corpse of the pig hanging over the fire from a big branch. Perhaps I remember staring through the rusty screen door of the kitchen at the gyrating, laughing, pig-eating men and women, and wandering through the mess of shadows made by fire and fired people. By morning the pig is gone, and today I know, somehow, that it belonged to the rich white man "up the road" and my father almost went to jail for it. And it's funny how a lot of years turn memories into that kind of thing, the way family stories when nothing is written down become the same kind of moonless dance and wild dream.

California, because that was where we settled more or less for good when I was about seven. In my immediate memory, I always leap to the belief that we moved first to the oak-and-pine coast range of the Santa Lucia Mountains miles up a dirt road behind the serious ranching town of Paso Robles. I remember that place with a feeling I can only define as love—remember the texture of the dry earth and rustle of prickly oak leaves, the heat of summer on wild oats and manzanita, the taste of a spring hillside when the world seemed startled with new grass. But it isn't true that we moved there first. We had already made at least one failed move to the state of my birth, initially to California's great Central Valley, where we lived in a small tent "city" on the outskirts of Delano while my father got work in the fields nearby. I recall now that our A-frame tent had a wooden floor and contained the chocolate cake of my fifth birthday. We lived there a few months (or weeks?) until my father was promoted and we moved into a little house on the "ranch" where he worked. It was there that he made slingshots for my brother and me, rock-hard oak forks with red rubber bands from old tire inner tubes. From that point on, we would always seek out the red "real" rubber from World War II as the best slingshot material, seldom finding it again. It was also there that I lurked just inside the kitchen door listening to my father explain to my mother that he had been called a "goddamn Indian" and fired by the field foreman, my very first concrete awareness that to be Indian was a bad thing. Only later, after we had returned to Mississippi in our shambles of a car, did I learn that somewhere before or after that exchange he had punched the foreman. Still an amazingly powerful man today, in his late sixties, my father has struck only two people in my lifetime, as far as I know: the foreman who cursed him and my mother's brother, bad Uncle Bob.

During that wandering time in California, we camped farther down the Central Valley, near the potato sheds at Shafter, where for a while we gleaned potatoes after the fields were harvested, and then we moved to Paso Robles, into the county "Housing Project" where our low-income apartment was surrounded by a paradise of mown grass and wild children. The project is still there today, seeming unchanged after so many years. Driving south from San Francisco on U.S. 101, I glance to my right and see the dull brown buildings and recall those months as a very happy time. It was in the project that a beautiful Border collie appeared magically during one of our baseball games and remained with us for the next nine years—Rex, the wonder dog. Still there between the freeway and the project are the train tracks, where my brother and I would lay wire in the path of the Southern Pacific so that the wire would be flattened to razor-sharp blades. With the un-flattened part wrapped around a stick, these were lethal weapons capable of beheading flowers, lizards, or anything with a low survival quotient in a kid's world.

And then we were abruptly gone from the project and living in Mississippi on a place still known in family stories as the "hog ranch," a time that has coalesced into a single image of a gray winter day and a mule with his head down against a muddy barn. I assume there were also hogs, but hogs do not populate my memories there. Then just as abruptly we were headed back to California, a trip that remains vivid because of a flash flood that swept like a mirage across the desert somewhere in New Mexico or Arizona, cutting the highway and leaving us stranded for some time—one day, two days?

Nine of us moved into a small house with flaking white paint set deep in the Santa Lucia Mountains west of Paso Robles, so remote that a bear came onto our porch one night and mountain lions left tracks in the yard. That was a secure and private world, where my older brother Gene looked up at me from deep in the cave we were digging and said, "Look at these Indian things," and we sat together in the sun to study two lovely arrow points and a tiny white stone doll dug from six feet down in the shaley earth. Who were those Indians, I wondered, finding it impossible to imagine real Indians amid all that light. Why had they set such things so carefully in the earth, and where were those people now? And then, just before my fifth-grade year, we moved ten miles away to the crumbling bank of the Salinas River, which was not a river at all but a lovely, wide sand-and-brush-and-cottonwood world filled with the rabbits and quail and doves and pigeons and deer we hunted.

California was a world as different from Mississippi as day from night, where a river was white sand rather than brown water and the hillsides were golden grain and shiny oaks rather than the black tangle of that Yazoo country. A world where my nine-year-old self had sat dreaming on a remote wild-oat ridge not far from the ocean and foolishly believed for a long time that everything was visible, nothing hidden. Where I followed after my brother as we learned from our father and Uncle Bob how to catch fish by putting crushed unripe black walnuts in a sack and dropping that sack into a pool so that the fish rose stunned and could be scooped out; how to turn a hollow log into a box trap for rabbits, possums, and, most often, pack rats; how to grapple with our hands for fish in stream and tide pool; and how to set deadfalls that never worked for small game. We graduated from slingshots to twenty-two, shotgun, and thirty-aught-six—hunting everything from squirrels to deer.

California was a world in which on a strange kind of absentminded automatic pilot I became the second after my brother (and today still only the second) in the history of our whole extended family to graduate from high school. And then, while my brother served three tours of duty in Vietnam, I drifted from high school to work in a can factory in Hayward, California, and then to a junior college and then, to my amazement and the astonishment of the few who paid attention, on to the University of California at Santa Barbara. So that now for almost twenty years I have lived in a world incalculably different from that of everyone else in my family. In troubled lives scattered across America, from Oregon to Arkansas, they see my name on books and shadows of themselves in the same books and they tell me with great tact how proud they are.

Not a real, essential Indian because I'm not enrolled and did not grow up on a reservation. Because growing up in different times I naively thought that Indian was something we were, not something we did or had or were required to prove on demand. Listening to my mother's stories about Oklahoma, about brutally hard lives and dreams that cut across the fabric of every experience, I thought that was Indian. We were "part Indian," she said, and my uncle Bob, out of jail temporarily and strutting in new hundred-dollar, un-paid-for cowboy boots, would be singing about "way down yonder on the Indian nation" and boasting that only a Cherokee could be as handsome as he. No one but a Choctaw, I thought, could be as beautiful as my father's mother, or as great a hunter as my father, and though in California I was embarrassed by our poverty and bad grammar, I was nonetheless comfortable with who we were. The only other Indian I knew in California was my best friend and hunting-and-fishing companion, an Osage with blond hair and light eyes. He was enrolled and somewhat smug about that fact, though it meant little to me then.

Now I know better, and in life's midpassage I have learned to inhabit a hybrid, unpapered Choctaw-Cherokee-Welsh-Irish-Cajun-mixed space in between. I conceive of myself today not as "Indian," but as a mixed-blood, a person of complex roots and histories. Along with my parents and grandparents, brothers and sisters, I am the product of liminal space, the result of union between desperate individuals on the edges of dispossessed cultures and the marginalized spawn of invaders. A liminal existence and a tension in the blood and heart must be the inevitable result of such crossing. How could it be otherwise? But tension can be a source of creative power—as such brilliant writers as Gerald Vizenor and Leslie Silko have taught me. This is an "other" territory that I, too, have claimed, like those early Choctaws who migrated westward across the Mississippi River, reversing the direction from which their ancestors had come carrying bones, to hunt and live and remain in Louisiana. I am descended from those people, *but I am not those people,* just as I bear the blood of the Trail of Tears and of an enormous Owens clan that reunites periodically somewhere in Kentucky or Tennessee, but I am not those people either. The descendant of mixed-blood sharecroppers and the dispossessed of two continents, I believe I am the rightful heir of Choctaw and Cherokee storytellers and of Shakespeare and Yeats and Cervantes. Finally, everything converges and the center holds in the margins. This, if we are to go on.

My paternal grandmother, Mahala Jobe Owens, whose name is not written down and no one in my family is certain of spelling correctly, is sixteen years old in a photograph. She is Choctaw and Cajun, my mother tells me, and her hair is thick and black and falls straight to the floor. Her white dress is buttoned at the neck and descends to her feet. She is extraordinarily beautiful, somber and dark-eyed, slim and proud-looking, or so I remember, for I haven't seen the photograph in at least fifteen years. Like so much in our family, it has been lost, is perhaps hidden and forgotten somewhere in a box or suitcase. The photo was taken in Louisiana, I think, probably in Catahoula Parish, where she was born, and probably just before she ran away with the gambler down the Mississippi River. And her father tracked them down in New Orleans with a gun and brought her back and forced her to marry the son of Welsh-Irish sharecroppers next door. Or so the family story goes. The story says my grandfather, my father's father, was her punishment as was a lifetime of sharecropping in Mississippi before my father borrowed money to move his parents to California, to live on a chicken ranch in a converted barn outside of Paso Robles, when I was in third grade. All of this is picture and story without text.

I believe that she never cut her hair. When I was young I'd watch her take it down at night and brush it, and just as in the photograph it touched the floor when she stood, but now it was silver instead of black. And almost as soon as they were in California, it seems in my memory, she was killed in an automobile accident and Grampa moved back to Mississippi.

I recall no photographs of my mother's mother, who finally drank herself to death when I was twenty. But I lived with her for a whole year once, and I remember her well. She was the one who was but thirteen and scarcely five feet tall when she bore my mother, the first of her three children. It was she who, already husbandless, gave her children away to a farmer who admired them at an Oklahoma country dance. After two years of beatings and worse abuse, my mother dreamed of little people who foretold the farmer's death. Three days after the dream, the man died from a snakebite and my grandmother returned to claim her children. My grandmother, who had been left by her own mother—through death or abandonment—shortly after birth and who had been raised by her grandmother in what she persisted in calling the "Nation" until her death. It was she who went through men by the score and whose postcards I discovered in my mother's papers after my mother died, each postcard from a different place in America—Boston, Albuquerque, Laramie, Seattle, San Diego, Tulsa, Little Rock, Las Vegas. What was she doing, that little half-Cherokee wild woman on the run in America? "Miss you. Wish you were here." Almost as though the Removal had buried a seed that drove her just as it would drive her only son, smooth-talking Uncle Bob, from state to state and in and out of prison all his short, hard-drinking life until he was finally murdered in a Texas oil field—but not before he totaled my thirty-six Chevy.

There are pieces of story, tantalizing fragments. Such as my mother's account of walking across half of Texas all of one long frozen winter, barefoot with her mother, little brother and sister, living in the woods or abandoned barns, eating roots, stealing food from gardens and chicken houses, living for two luxurious weeks in an empty rail car. They were going back to Oklahoma, I know, but I never found out why they were walking or where they were really headed. In retrospect, I believe I could see the marks of that journey in my mother's face all the years I knew her.

Not long ago my mother's sister, Aunt Betty, wrote to ask if I could find out who she was. The only surviving member of her family, my aunt—like my mother, uncle, and grandparents—has no birth certificate but only stories growing more distant each year. Born at home, in different homes, none of them had the luxury of a recorded birth. For fifty years she has lived in an Italian American world where her dark skin and hair fit perfectly, but now that she's old, she has begun to wonder, begun apparently to desire a record of her existence, unwilling to remain liminal and unwritten. She told me the names of her mother's father and mother, my great-grandparents, and I dutifully took the names to the National Archives. Sure enough he was there in the 1910 census for Oklahoma, in the Indian section, and there also on the Dawes Roll. John Bailey, a Cherokee mixed-blood. But her full-blood grandmother's name wasn't anywhere on paper and remains, therefore, unreal, without essence.

My sister's son, a father himself now and in the army, writes from Germany to tell her he wants to enroll his own infant son. He's thinking of college scholarships, an admirably farsighted young man. My good friend from childhood keeps a copy of his enrollment card taped to the wall above his computer, where he is active on an Indian Internet line. I imagine a vast new tribe of Internet Indians.

For seven years I worked seasonally for the U.S. Forest Service, building trails, being a wilderness ranger, fighting fires on a hotshot crew. I watched Rookie cut his big toe off with a double-bit ax and be packed out by mule, saw Mick laid out in an emergency room with his right hand severed at the wrist from a fire-line accident, and watched my friend Joe fell a tree the wrong way in a hard wind so that he turned and sprawled full-length on his running chainsaw. I climbed glaciated peaks to radio in reports of frozen lakes far below, and wandered the high country of the North Cascades when it was under ten feet of hard-packed snow, alone above timberline for days and weeks at a time in the most beautiful place in the world. I stumbled across a surly wolverine when there weren't supposed to be any in that country, and one morning I watched a mountain lion walk slowly across the zenith of a snowfield, outlined by the bluest sky I have ever seen. I fought fires in Washington, Arizona, and California, watching a project fire crown out in hundred-foot walls of flame that raced from ridge to ridge one night near Winslow, Arizona, and dodging flaming yucca balls at midnight in a steep canyon outside Tucson. I learned to drink great quantities of beer and climb granite faces as a sawyer on the Prescott Hotshots, which they told us was the only technical rock-climbing fire crew in America. I careened through burning mountains in helicopters driven mad by Vietnam vets, and I listened to a phone call telling me that two friends had been killed in such a helicopter after I'd quit to return to school.

Seven years of that, and then in the fall of 1990, as a newly appointed full professor at the University of California, Santa Cruz, I returned to the Northwest with my old journals, determined, twenty years after first seeing the Cascades, to retrace familiar routes with the vague idea of writing another book. The third day out, I found myself alone on the edge of a glacier and looking across a high route to the summit of Glacier Peak, a mountain called Dakobed by the Salishan people born there. The edge of the glacier was a steep ice field covered by a few inches of snow with a run-out ending thousands of feet down in a glacial river. On the other side of the first slope a series of crevasses began, their blue mouths opening to the black depths of the mountain. My ice ax firmly buried, I hesitated. The world was suddenly unfamiliar and very threatening, and I had decided to turn back and retrace my route down the rocks when I saw a shadow move on the ice. Looking up, I watched a golden eagle banking off an updraft close overhead. When I looked back at the glacier, I saw the tracks. A fresh, clear set of coyote prints began near where I stood and continued out onto the glacier. Hesitating no longer, I began to follow coyote, crossing the steep slope easily, remembering that it is fun to slide down a glacier. Where coyote leapt across the narrow end of a crevasse, I leapt, full pack and all. Where he strolled across an ice bridge, I did the same. Together our tracks emerged onto the rock crest on the other side of the glacier, and as I stood there in a tearing wind and looked out at what seemed a thousand miles of Cascade peaks, I imagined coyote doing the same. Why else would he be on a mountain of ice and rock except for the pure pleasure of it? As I cut across a snowfield to finish the high route, the eagle circled endlessly. Alone, as I would continue to be for the next ten days, thousands of miles from the Yazoo and Salinas rivers, I had never felt so at home in my life. Home had become a much bigger place, and the book I had imagined writing seemed unimportant.

Perhaps I began to write novels as a way of figuring things out for myself. I think my works are about the natural world and our relations with that world, with one another, and, most crucially, with ourselves. Though each of my works begins and ends with place itself, the mysteries of mixed identity and conflicted stories, both the stories we tell ourselves and the stories others tell about us and to us, are what haunt my fiction. In a novel called *Wolfsong,* I wrote of a young Indian coming home to a valley in the North Cascades, wondering who and where he is meant to be. In that novel, set in the Glacier Peak Wilderness, the omniscient narrator says, *"Sometimes at night, when he lay in bed and tried to figure it out, he felt as if he were descended from some madman's dream. Indians rode spotted horses over golden plains. . . . They lived in the light of the sun, where nothing was hidden and earth rose up to sky. . . . They sat horseback against the infinite horizon. . . . Those were the Indians they studied in school."*

In a second novel, called *The Sharpest Sight,* a work moving between Mississippi and California and drawing heavily upon my own family, I wrote of a young Choctaw-Cherokee-Irish mixed-blood who must learn who he is and how to balance a world that has led his brother to madness and destroyed him, a world of stories in deadly conflict. I used my father's name, Hoey, and my grandfather's name, Luther, in that novel, and I created an old Choctaw lady named Onatima whom I modeled upon what I remembered and imagined of my grandma. Onatima, too, ran away with a gambler on the great river. I also based a major character in that novel on my brother Gene, who had come back from three tours in Vietnam with such pain that he became one of the psychological casualties who disappeared into the Ozark Mountains of Arkansas. For me it had been as if he never came back from the war, and that is how I wrote the novel. Later, after emerging from long familial isolation, he would jokingly say to our sister, "Gee, first he put me in a mental hospital and then he killed me. What's he going to do to me next?" Because I wanted to explore mixed and relational identity—the liminal landscape of the mixed-blood—more fully, I also included in *The Sharpest Sight* a young mestizo named Mundo Morales who discovers in his own blood an inextricable web of inherited identities.

In a third novel, *Bone Game,* published in 1994, I reentered the life of Cole McCurtain from *The Sharpest Sight,* and the lives of his family, in order to examine imprints of evil left upon the American landscape by the European invaders' destructive violence. In that novel I delved further into my grandma's story—Onatima's story—imagining the feelings that must have driven her to flee with her gambler, and the pain of returning home to marriage. In this third novel Cole McCurtain, twenty years after going home to Mississippi in *The Sharpest Sight,* is still uncertain as to who he is. Maybe the message is that certainty is not a condition mixed-bloods can know.

My 1996 novel, *Nightland,* was written for my mother, who died five years ago and about whom I have never been able to write. She was a person of compassion so great it could have come only from long and difficult struggle. In 1999 I published *Dark River*, a novel that explores identity storytelling, and the four Owens novels preceding it.

Every work is a different gamble and exploration. Every work teaches me a great deal. As a university professor, I watch students bring me their stories, even their novels, and I marvel again and again at the force that drives us to so make and remake the world. I imagine a world crowded with stories that jostle one another and war for space, a world in which pigs are killed and eaten by dancing shadows and a young boy imagines that he watches and then carries that imagining with him for forty years. Stories that carry us from the muddy waters of the Yazoo River to a tent in California and a glacial world of sheerest blue and frozen light. What is this thing that so compels us to thus organize and articulate the world? It is all in the way family stories when nothing is written down become the same kind of moonless dance I recall from that Mississippi night so long ago, the motion of fire and form.

In the Garden

of the Gods

W. S. PENN

W. S. Penn is professor of English at Michigan State University,
where he teaches Comparative Multicultural Literature (the Oral
Tradition), Native American Literature, and Creative Writing
(fiction and narrative essay). His books include: The Absence of
Angels *(novel),* All My Sins Are Relatives *(narrative essays),*
The Telling of the World: Native American Stories and
Art *(edited), and* As We Are Now: Mixblood Essays on Race
and Identity *(edited). His new novel,* Killing Time with
Strangers, *is forthcoming from the University of Arizona Press,*
and his new collection of essays, Feathering Custer, *is forthcom-*
ing from the University of Nebraska Press. He is a winner of the
North American Indian Prose Award from the University of Ne-
braska Press and a Critics' Choice Award for the Most Acclaimed
Books of 1995–96.

I

28 April 1994: Chipeta Elementary, Colorado Springs. The second-graders sing patriotic songs.

And there is Scott, the child of my cousin (from the side of my family that, like Bartleby the Scrivener, I refuse), the eight-year-old kid who has sung Alan Sherman's "Harry Louis" instead of what I remember as "Glory Hallelujah," a song in which Harry Louis works for Ivan Roth and is cleaning out the warehouse where the drapes of Roth are stored—making Jews, Poconos vacationers, and anyone else who thinks Hal A. Lujah is more gory than glory, laugh to the core of their worldview and belief—sung it aloud to his second-grade class. Scott is Jewish, the son of a Jew and my cousin, his mother, who converted.

It's a bit difficult to determine whether it was Harry Louis or Scott's Jewish laughter that pissed off the capacious woman in floral blue who plays the piano and cues the little darlings in and out of the songs, but it did and so Scott is relegated to the chorus to play backup to the little redheaded kids who hold hands with ebony children whose parents have bought a house large enough to make them less black and more—if the new car lot out front of the school is any indication of identity—Honorary Members of the Order of Van-Americans, Non-conversion Chapter. Ward Cleaver must have driven a station wagon (I don't remember, at least in part because Father couldn't afford, and then refused to own a television, so watching Ward and the Beav depended on the confluence of time and place in, I would say now and given what I think of television, the wrong place and—as I always was—the wrong time, by which I mean not some nostalgic appeal to traditionalism that is being cast as the mother of all pearls by television, movies, and books, but a sense of personal responsibility and circularity that argued against the fragmented, dulled imaginations of my friends who lived in black and white and later became Persons of Interactive Color, eventually surrounded by sound as though the falsified emotions of *Chicago Hope* are more "authentic" in stereo). Ward Cleaver has come a long way, baby, and with a lot more baggage to haul around with him; he's gone from wagons to vans in a revelation of the monologic diversity among the middle class.

It is a monologue, from what I can tell, an "authentic" diversity that—from the way Scott slips back from the martialled line of second-grade singers, letting the line close on him so he becomes a head of serious hair behind the closed ranks of open mouths, barely visible to his mother, who is too short to overlook the kids in front of her boy—slips its hold on Cousin Scotty's person every time its grip tries to catch on the slick of his faith and the solid of his being. Scott knows—unlike his little sister, named Elizabeth after my dead Anglo mother—they ain't ever gonna quite be comfortable with Jews in this town, in which fundamental values act like condoms to keep them protected and not quite feeling the slip and slide of the truth that's all around them, values that tell them that Jews have money, and thus makes them a little less hated than Indians, who—as everyone knows—don't (even if they did they'd gamble it away in a peyote haze or under the influence of a most significant Anglo contribution to this continent—whiskey, scotch, or the variation, bourbon, distilled from indigenous corn by the great American heroes Jonathan "Jack" Daniels, his cousin James Beam, or, in a sign of their respect for elders, Old Grandad).

So I am there with my cousin and her husband and their daughter, but not because I would ever go hear a performance of "patriotic" songs, even under the influence of Old Grandad. Frankly, I'd rather marry Lorena Bobbitt except for the fact that Scott is family and I am a family man—when the family will have me (and Scotty's mother is the one from that side of the family who will). Just as I'd protest but go to hear my daughter or son sing songs, patriotic or otherwise (and knowing now that I'll teach them both Harry Louis, as well as "This Land Was My Land"), I have promised Scott that I'll come, a request he's made as though his somewhat removed cousin might protect him from the harpy who's waving her arms at the kids and nodding as though she has not merely made but invented these kids like god, and who hates Scotty.

The feeling is strange. My heart is estranged. I listen, trying to imagine who these tykes are, up on the risers with Scott, and worse, (I look around, overwhelmed by) who their gene pools are, these van-driving descendants of the very gene pools that invented Geronimo and Joseph, Seattle, and Sitting Bull and who are now watching their kids sing out "This land is my land, this land is your land," half of which strikes half of my urban mixblood heart as true. These happy parents and grandparents are completely unaware of the simple fact that their world is changing. Their children's world is already as changed as Old Joseph knew his was when he told Hinmot Tooyoolak-tekht, his son, that he saw a day when the whites would take the Wal-lowa Valley from the Nez Perce. All you have to do is look at these people to know what Old Joseph knew: that if they can't quite forget how and why they took the land, they'll make up patriotic songs as a veneer to the truth and sing them out with the passion of holy rollers over and over and over again until in the song, they believe. They will give themselves "splendid memories and star-spangled amnesia" (Kammen, 1991, 343). They will tell themselves what Robert Weeks DeForest told the huddled homogenizing masses at the opening of the Metropolitan Museum of Art in 1924: "We are honoring our fathers and mothers, our grandfathers and grandmothers, that their art may live long in the land which the Lord hath given us" (Kammen, 1991, 349). Or, "in an instance of manifest manners and the literature of dominance," they will write that the massacre of women, old men, and children—many of them babies—at Wounded Knee was the " 'last major battle of the Indian Wars' " (Vizenor, 1994, 50).

Strange how much I disbelieve these songs the children are singing. It surprises me how the words that would make their feelings static become metaphor in the drum of my hearing. It is like hearing or seeing an anticeremony in which the skin is flayed from the corpse of the van-driving world, in which the song and dance reveal the absolute fake to which Umberto Eco refers when he says that the American imagina-tion demands the real and, to attain it, invents the absolute fake. Here, in this song and dance of these human units, is the American Reality, and I am surprised not at the vision, but at the vision's virulence: as an urban mixblood writer, as a preserver and transmitter and not an ego (I hope, truly), I had thought I'd become sort of conservative (in the preserving sense) and staid (in the calm, habitual sense—the boring life of the writer who sits down every day and writes). But suddenly I want to shout out a sound that must be at least five generations old and take a stick to their coups of commerce, self-aware enough to know that were I to do that, I'd cause even more problems for my (Jewish) relatives, particularly Scotty, who is only a child. All I can do is lean over to my cousin and whisper and laugh—quietly—knowing that as an up-and-coming ethnomusicologist she believes no more in the message of these songs than in the baby Jesus, and that, as a Jew, she must have learned what I have always known in my dreaming heart: how quickly this generous fellow feeling behind these singers and songs can turn to murderous annihilation. First they see you as "an antithesis to themselves . . . [with] civilization and Indianness *as they defined them* . . . forever . . . opposites . . . as a threat to life and morals when alive," and then they regard you "with nostalgia upon . . . [your] demise—or when that threat is safely past" (Berkhofer, 1979, 29, my emphasis).

I try to smile with generosity and wisdom, with pity for these people whose most sexual experience is like Coyote behind the velutinous wheel of their *Caravans* and *Villagers* and "Grand" *Cherokees* and *Astros* (God! the names they pick, as though their vans could fly them like Carter Revard's songs up to the stars! It's too much; their vans—let alone their mechanical souls—are too heavy to do more than fart and die). I try to smile, and yet all I can hear is Jimmie Durham speaking—"I hate America. . . . I hate the culture of America. . . ."—and adding that he hates Indians, too, the writers and intellectuals who are money-grubbing opportunists and (sometimes hating myself, thus wondering if I am or Jimmie Durham is one of those latter and hoping to the stars that I'm not), I think, "That's it, isn't it? I hate America. I really do (at least when you aren't making me admit that I'm grateful for the life I do have) hate America."

I have always hated America, even from the time as a little lost kid I took up writing a journal as the only way I knew to speak the unspeakable (unspeakable, because my little friends, except maybe Bernie Schneider, would have laughed uproariously at me and turned it into another painful tease, enough of which already existed), and night after night I'd sit and pour out my hatred in words, English words, fast and unpunctuated but most always grammatical—having learned grammar's strengths and weaknesses better than my giggling peers—always feeling the anachronisms: women in curlers who would point the index of their fundamental values at me and sneer with distaste or men whose souls made them seem fat crows without feet or wings, blackened lumps of consumption: and always hiding the journals away, feeling as guilty as condoms about the total, almost physical hatred I felt, exacerbated by the hurt, the hurt, always the hurt because when they laughed at me, they laughed at Father and Grandfather.

The same guilt I feel now. My wife may hate this essay. A mixblood herself, though with no indigenous American blood in the mixture, she sometimes wonders what is happening here, with all this Indian stuff. She knows that over time I have gone from a voice that said I am a writer first, and a Native American writer second, to someone who now says, I am a Native American writer first, foremost, and only because unlike Jim Barnes, who says there is no such thing as Native American writing, only writing by Native Americans—a position which I honor and respect—because unless you say that "I am a Native American writer," it becomes all too easy for someone to say, "Forgive me for saying so, but Indians don't really make much difference these days."

So though my wife is proud and pleased and all those good things, she must sometimes wonder—as do I, as I sit here at Chipeta Elementary listening to the kids slide into a pressboard-and-glue composite of patriotism and conquest and possession and trivialization—What happened? My husband has gone from a mixblood Indian kid to a token man, a boy who once sang the patriotic songs (I am a citizen first, a Native American citizen second), to someone else. I, myself, fear becoming a someone who will have (as I will tonight, by the historical-autobiographical way) diarrhea whenever he hears the strains of patriotism and possession or a person who, in trying to debunk some of the myths and images and misconceptions, so enjoys the slurp of public approval for his debunking that I overstep and become a jerk-kneed monologue of political correctness.

I fear it partly because I'd like to drive a minivan.

In other words, I don't always hate America, just its commercialism and exploitation and hegemonic attitudes and the flames of its self-righteous Christianity. Because I love my wife, I hope that she can accept this manner of revelation in me with as much understanding and belief as she accepts my cousin's becoming a Jew. I fear it because I have children and they—as my grandfather allowed me—must come to their identities with pride and not with their hands out, and while I may guide, I have to let them be whatever they in their hearts know they are, and what if they decide they are not "Native American" but "Italian"—which is what I imagine my wife to be, given the way she can raise her voice and wave her arms about with passion and a certainty that vanishes when the argument's over?

I am determined to let them come to their identities like Scott, who asks, as we drive home, "Are you Jewish?"

We pass a country club formulated by one of the (is it vegetable or mineral?) Hunt family and propagated by the exclusive, patronizing (is it animal?) attitudes of the possessive rich (who would you trust if it was your brain? to which I answer, You trust teachers with the bumper sticker brains of your children every day). I like to imagine that it's in an attempt to bond with me when Scotty's dad comments on it being a place that wouldn't let them or me join, so Scotty completes the logical circle and asks the one question his fledgling identity knows how to ask, "Are you Jewish?"

"No." I laugh. "No. I'm Indian." I laugh, happy in the words, adding, so Scott doesn't think I am laughing at him, "But my grandfather used to say that hating Jews is just three letters away from hating Indians."

"So you can't join the club?" Scotty asks.

"No."

Scott looks distressed.

"But look at it this way. Who would want to? Would you want to join a club that wouldn't want you as a member?"

Scott considers.

II

The problem is that I don't really hate America.

What I hate is this feeling of being strange. I hate the fact that what I want America to do is like me, appreciate me, my presence, my act- and inactivity. I want America to have its own as well as to reward my own sense of fairness and self-responsibility by valuing my presence. But America can't. Besides the fact that capitalism admits of fairness only when it profits, America wants me to be dead. When the president's commissions count up Native Americans in this country, it refuses to count me because I grew up in the cities and not on a reservation and so I feel insecure. It's a mungy feeling that has in the past taken more deadly aspects (the usual yawn of drugs and alcohol in this chemical civilization) but, now that I have a family, remains in check—except that I get hurt and angry, sometimes, because of my insecurity. Nonetheless, I go on because, whether by dance or dream, singing or saying, I am compelled to try to make a place in the world for my children, as well as for the children, the same way D'Arcy McNickle tried to make a place for us children.

The way I choose to make this place—the way I chose from the very beginning, furiously writing writing writing, even as a lonely, discarded child, immature diatribes against what I saw as *America Around Me* and formalizing the process around twenty when Patricia, one of my two elder sisters, gave me a five-hundred-page bound blank book with a bright upholstered orange cover for my birthday—was through stories. I filled that book with stories and it was in my stories that I was strange and through stories that my strange became a comfort, acknowledged a place for myself, a place solitary though not foolish enough to reach solipsistic, a place silent yet wanting to be spoken.

Stories like "Dwarfheart"—do I need to list the puns, make sure you get them all the way my poet friends do?—in which the narrator is an illustrator for his best friend, Little Hamm, a black kid from the neighborhood who mimes beautiful mimes. As Hamm's mimes grow stranger, as the sad audience of daily livers ignore his silent telling more and more, the narrator becomes less imaginative, more linear, less illustrative and more documentary (with logical consequences and the cancers of editorial pens of indelible red) and tries to record as sadness the humorous tragic end of Hamm as he disrupts the logical timing of a new subway system and, painting sexual organs on the fronts of the two trains that will mate as violently as most Americans in front of some foreign dignitaries visiting the "city," jumps between the trains in a final mime of Hamm.

Stories like "Pandora's Chinese Box," in which the narrator is in the second person, the voice detached, a story that opens, "The only problem, then, is there is no problem." A story in which the people are movie extras on a beach where a chess match is being played and where a "boy" learns awfully that you do not ever reach out and risk disrupting the game. A story in which in response to the disintegration and random separations around them, people invent Nature's nature. A story that twenty years ago envisioned yuppy's puppies taking to the new and improved fakes of natural foods and painful exercise in an attempt to extend the veneer of their lives while forgetting about the substance.

Stories I still have, like "nocket," written in part as a response to those business cards born-agains handed out all over town with bleeding stigmata and the boldfaced lie, "Jesus Loves You So Much It Hurts," and in part as a response to my friend Steve Curry's mistress lamenting to me after Steve had returned to his wife and my goddaughters. Steve is Stanley in the story, and Stanley is a serious fellow, who gets confused in the narrator's mind with Jesus Christ. The first-person narrator opens:

"He's a too-serious fellow."

"But he loves me," Susan replied. "He used to say, 'I love you so much it hurts.'"

"So he said." I paused, thinking of the many permutations of what-could-be-said. "But loving crimps him. It does not make him smile The Smile."

Twisting her tactic, Susan convicted me of jealousy: I hadn't his ability of endless xerox, reproducing love upon love, joy after joy. I gazed defensively on Susan's luminescent portrait of Jesus over her mantel. He did rather spread it around. And he was still going. Did he have a higher quality control? Or was his advantage in management and long-range planning? "You have other pictures of him?"

"A few. In my scrapbook." Her hand stroked the tight tweed back to its ultimate hem. She searched the closet for the pix, as I considered. Were Susan and I speaking about the same person? We'd begun talking about her late lover, Stanley. Stanley was a fellow student—more a type than a real person, as all serfs are types. Only lately I'd been overwhelmed by the feeling that I was the fool's understudy in a well-rehearsed but very bad pantomime.

Every woman was an ordeal for me. Each one demanding a recreation of my past, confused by my attempts to sound interesting. I think women are taught well that nothing is more interesting to a man than talking about himself.

Stanley interests people. His fictions don't seem to lull listeners to sleep. And, like a master-sergeant, he can remake a tornado into inclement weather, commanding attention while taking the immediate threat out of the air. Yet listening to Stanley's tales, I find myself wanting to abdicate from potential significance like a poet whose lines have become arthritic or a saint whose grace has been cured in lies and preserved. What I desired was a woman who would allow.... What I'd gotten was something else, since I'd either boggle the moment's immediacy or panic and rave a while, then plunge like a cockroach for the nearest crack in the wall....

Susan showed me pictures of Stanley. Stanley writing. Stanley counselling. Stanley meditating. Stanley...

"Skiing?" I asked.

"Sure. He's always trying common experiences. Says they give him relevance."

"I can see he did not take sport lightly," I said. Was he frowning because he was an amateur? Everyone has noticed that amateur heroes don't often get caught laughing. Perhaps the concept of self-as-hero is a serious abstraction. But didn't Ulysses laugh without restraint, even among strangers? Can the novitiate be distinguished in this way? Do real heroes laugh at their hero-ness? "Does Stanley ever laugh uncued?"

"Stanley's a poet. His mind's above levity."

Falling upon the thorns of life and bleeding is no laughing matter. While I root around unthinking in my laughter-life, Stanley forges art in the smithy of his soul.

"Sorry. It just seems that Stanley talks himself up to laughter. Organizes spurs of the moment."

The narrator fails where Stanley succeeds:

Once I, too, had waxed well-schooled. Until broken by the insistent blows of Blue Notes.... To consider that at one time my mind was a volute of pressboard; my intuitions, the functions of root canals and logarithms. I, serious and certain like Stanley, until I whirled downward on extended fears—from Volute through Volvox and Vowel to Voyeur. Discouraged from playing, I became a not-disinterested spectator. . . . Stanley converted from portfolioed to paid, just before I was traded.

Yet he succeeds where Stanley fails. Intermingled and juxtaposed with the story of Susan and Stanley is the narrator's relations with Mimi:

"Slef, slef, slef." I tried to laugh it off.
"Boil, boil, toil and trouble, infiniteness comes from infinite bubble," Mimi said. She knew: Dancing is more fun than tetrasyllabic words and passive verbs. . . . Cowardice, Mimi has said, drives us from among the laughing into seriousness. We are heirs to 2000 years of expansions and accumulations of cowardice. . . . We perish in the quintessential fear of the idea, the sneaky suspicion that we are, indeed, at The Party, but have forgotten how to dance.

Together, Mimi and the narrator produce an "offspring" which speaks the single morpheme "nocket" from beneath its blankets. The story ends when the carriage inspector in the park demands they name their offspring officially since without a name, they are both guilty of falsity.

"We call her Nocket," Mimi smiled. "Little Nock, for short."
So, Little Nock. Created out of Mimi's collision with me, she isn't perfect. Her form is not polished, not tumbled grammatically. Yet she has content/inflection/tone. One says of her what one says of Rubinstein: She's alive, as if by magic, and she has a voice and can play out the piece. An unjust representation, perhaps.

Perhaps none of these stories is particularly good? Certainly, aspects of "nocket" seem immature. I have affection for them, however, and looking back at them now for the first time in decades, I fill with wonder at what I seem to have known then but forgot between "then" and "now"—"now" representing the last, oh, say six or seven years, and "then" embodying the potential that in my feeling strange while wanting to belong I might forget it all once more. I remember the years in Syracuse University's creative writing program; with the kindness and encouragement of my wonderful teacher and beloved friend, George P. Elliott, I tried to make my stories (and myself) more acceptable, more "realistic," more palatable (less strange), but I couldn't quite. Though the surface changed, became in some people's opinions more mature, below the surface of those stories is the same estranged voice:

The solitary narrator who does not judge but wonders at being judged in "Tarantulas." A postal worker who has taken cards and letters home and recopied them and made them his own, he sits in jail and writes down what he will tell the judge and jury, ending:

> There. Tonight I will correct this copy, and practice it for tomorrow. Tomorrow, I must go before them, let them look at me, ask me questions I cannot answer, decide my guilt. I wonder if they will understand that these were not someone else's letters. Perhaps not: perhaps the judge will want to ask why I did it, and I can read what I have written.
>
> I have begun to like it here. The routine is like any other, but I don't have to see anyone, except my attorney, and even he can be kept out.
>
> The oak stands against the winter, budless. It stands there like a dancer, arms arcing up, the fingers nearly touching high above the trunk. Its roots go far beneath the ground as if the earth has risen like dough around it and me, half sunk in the ground myself, and I can see the beginnings of a crack in the wall where the roots have tried to enter my cell. Yet, if I move my cot, the image of the tree against the white moon shifts, and if I rock my head, I can make the still dancer dance.
>
> As I look out the window and wonder how guilty I am, and of what, really, I can see against the far-away sky the dark lines which tell me that what they call my crime is delicate and dark and can only be judged—truly judged in detail—against a yellow New Mexico moon.

Or the narrator whose conclusions are all story-without-end as he sails away from his past in "Storm Watch":

> I have given up the hope for change. Sure, you can do little things within limits; but the kind of change we worked for, fought even each other for, seems, now, absurd. We live in a morning fog, unable to see beyond the rails. Perhaps I am wrong: you decide. For I have sailed around it, Kenny through it, and his cargo of anger and love has been dumped, like Beast's drooling head, in my lap.

I do not, even yet, know quite what to do with it except beg. But for what? for what?

I write to find out, to discover if things could have been different, but this is the conclusion I always come to.

Beast, in this case, is an oversized St. Bernard.

Too, there are the concerns with death, cycles of life, and place in the world of "Old Bird Young Bird" and in the dense, mythic imagery of "Red Rock Red Earth," in which the narrative voice finds his "other" in the reflection of the river:

It isn't possible to feel hatred for him anymore; the Gilas have taught me that, and a strange kind of love has grown up between us. Absurd, isn't it, to ramble on about love in a place such as this, with its high walls and red rock and the river, always the river, and yet sometimes I think that it began with my whispering to him, always at dusk, stirring up the flames of the sunset as though it were a threat, and hoping that he would desire to continue the amiable contention between us enough to be there the next morning. He never spoke back, never sighed even, but he is always there with the dawn. Oh yes, he changes, like the river, but then I change to and neither of us seems to outstrip the other in this, so we are happy, and I have given back all my stones to the river as a sign to him that he is free to go now, and yet he stays on to protect me from, from what? I don't know, for the Gilas have gone except for the husks of the ones I killed. One of them I keep near my shelter because it once looked like my brother, yet now I am not sure that I ever had a brother.

Soon I begin to sharpen a branch that is beached by the river. The ground is flat and red, the sun is hot, when I begin to make new marks in the sand. I no longer take stock the way I was used to doing, but I watch, and wait, for what I don't know; for death, perhaps, for my own floating, and I stay close to the river so that when the time comes it can carry me south. And I am grateful for it.

After my teacher George P. Elliott died and I buried his ashes in a ceremony on a hill outside Cazenovia, New York—a hill that over-looked the future from the silence of the past, the both of which George so loved—I subtitled this story "George's Elegy." Outside of the editor of *Black Ice* (who published it), George was the only one who ever liked that story, or who ever said, "I don't quite understand it, except for it's beautiful." So I gave it to him and will be honored if when we meet up again he'll have accepted the gift.

I did not learn much at Syracuse—but then I guess no one was supposed to, really. One thing I did learn was that my stories were inevitably different. When Michael something-or-other wrote a story in which the dying mother's heart was compared metaphorically to a dieseling internal combustion engine and the rest of the class approved, I realized that in some sense "their" stories had gone all confused and in the soft suck of emptiness any comparison may be made. It's not that to them machines seem almost alive—the way I have felt whenever one cheats me, stalls, or refuses to dish up what I have paid for. It's the reverse: to them, life is mechanical or at least life is confused with the mechanical or the objective—that which may be turned on and off, used up, exploited, and sold.

For a long time, I imagined that their stories were becoming so confused as to produce television until I realized that the most narrative and the most imaginative elements on television were often found in the commercials, not in the vacuous cans of laughter and tears produced by the jovial one-liners of sitcoms and PBS. Commercials are their stories and all the static images produced by PBS and the refuse of sitcoms are only filler to keep you coming back to the auction of commerce.

III

I feel close to D'Arcy McNickle, not because I imagine that I'll ever be as important or do as many good things as he, but because I imagine. As Gerald Vizenor has said, he values what it can do too much to let anyone restrict or limit his imagination. It is one of the true, great things about America: the freedom and the energy available to our imaginations and our ability to envision as well as try to shape the visions.

I feel close to D'Arcy McNickle because in picking up his posthumously collected and published short stories, *The Hawk Is Hungry,* I recognize an urban mixblood writer whose "Indianness" is not shown by the writer's speaking from the soapbox of content but by the way in which the writer says, speaks, tells his stories—of which, at

McNickle's best, there are none better. The way is a way that I have told stories; I, too, can see the possibility that I will have a collection that will not find book form until (and if then) after this life because while there are mix-blood Indian things in the how and way of the stories, there is little turquoise and fewer bright colors, only a question here and there and some Haida prints on the wall.

His novels are more apparently "Indian" in subject and event; his stories are American, and to recognize the "Indian" you have to pay attention to, for example, the way in which the point of his stories is neither plot—the end results of the events are often apparent from the first paragraph in combination at times with the title—nor message, but process, the how it is told and the sense, reinforced by the oral repetitions in, say, *Debt of Gratitude* or *Meat for God,* that it may be told again and again. There are the elements that get called "postmodern," even though many of those elements are and have been for Indians always available—the jump-cuts, the digression and embellishment and supplementation. There are the quiet understatement, the humor— always the humor (Smiley in *Debt* doesn't smile)—and the humane sympathies, especially for characters caught between two worlds (*Man's Work*), and the sense, around Henry Jim, of "history before there was history."

I don't want, here, to get too involved with the discussions about how there is no such thing as "Indian," only Osage, Choctaw, Nez Perce, Miwok, Chippewa, Blackfoot, and so on; no more than I want to say "European" and get into how there is no such thing, only Germans and French, Spaniards and Italians (or Geats or Celts or Moors), and so on. I do want to offer the idea that there may be a couple of ways "Indians" look similar enough to be grouped: one way that is important to me is storytelling and not only the respect most of us have for it, but also the ways in which we tend to do it.

For one thing, the stories of mine that were any good—and many were not—were told the only way they could be told. In a sense, they were from Grandfather and were told as they had always been told. When the other students criticized the lack of plot, the minimal "character development," the digressiveness, or the sense of conclusive inconclusion, I often did not know how to respond.

Plot to me was nothing: stories about Coyote or Snowbird or Bear are known, retold, and changed only in the details or fullness or language according to the age and experience of the participatory audience. Plot, a logically connected sequence of events, was then only a coat hanger on which to button and zip the clothes—which were the important parts—and now, given the falsity of logical sequence in a human and humane world, is a flat-out lie, a fake coat hanger on which only the emperor's clothes may be hung. The interest of life—and storytelling described life for me—was in the twists and turns, the digressions and jump-cuts, the strange and strangely connected apparent dislocations and disparities. They are what connect one human being to another.

As for the accusation that my characters did not develop, or only minimally, well, characters don't develop. Situations change, and the reader-listener gets to hear how the character responds to those changes. But Bartell D'Arcy, Kurtz, and Tayo don't change; they perhaps reveal the characters they began with and will end with, whether happily or not. The character named Merrill in *Early Age and Late Disorder* fears disorder:

> Order clung to Merrill like wet flannel. He had always feared disorder, and he had always tried to keep the flannel moist by controlling the dry winds that intruded upon his life. He had always been this way: never had he been late, even though the date on whom he attended like a royal palm might have been; he had had consistent and good grades in college (except in English in which the ambiguities caused a rash to break out around his neck); he had kept himself fit even into the meal-sack years of his forties; and when he had married, he had wedded a woman who wished above all to keep the top of the stove clean.

Merrill encounters the physical image of disorder in the shape of a woman—who reminds him of his mother—who sticks her tongue out at his commute bus. The reality of disorder seeds Merrill's character and we hope that he may manage to change in response to this discovery that beneath the surface of all his order is this chaos. It is then that he reveals his true character and he does what many but the strongest of humans does: he submits and complies to the appearances of order—as illicit as they are in the story—gives up his dreams (which were romantic and so authentic as to be fake), and ends the story falling asleep, "figuring up his dreams in columns." I remember that originally—because I was young and lacked immediate compassion for the difficulties of achieving and failures to achieve an ethical and responsible life—I wrote "little dreams in columns." But, besides the fact that "little" seemed to beat up on Merrill too much, they were not little. They were large, given the disorder he's discovered, and to figure up any dreams, hold on to any hopes for the future, seems to me coura-geous.

In terms of my stories, my favorite supplementary story—and the one I hope becomes a collection's title story—is "This Is the World." "This Is the World" begins the imaginative life of Albert (Alley) Hummingbird, my favorite mixblood character (although you'd not know he was mixblood except for the name), who later transforms into the narrator of my novel, *The Absence of Angels*. In the story, Albert is confused by the world and his humorous confusion is meant to de-bunk:

> There was a time when I was lighthearted. An idealist, I guess. At least people had called me that: "Idealist!" they'd say, as if they were saying "Sonuvabitch."
>
> And they were right. I was. I wasn't ashamed. What's wrong with having ideals? . . . Being an idealist most often means that you're poor. You're poor because you cannot see the joy of pushing memos around an office or the pleasure of strip-mining Pike's Peak. Being poor isn't as much fun as the politicians and the rich seem to think.
>
> Furthermore, being poor wastes a tremendous amount of time. You have to plan out your meals each week so you can afford to eat seven out of seven days. When you discover ground meat has gone up again, you have to stop and think about where you can trim your budget. You stand in drugstores to read magazines; you deliberate for days not just about whether you can afford a movie but also about which movie to see (see a bad one, and you can't afford the good one which will open as soon as you've spent the money on the bad one). You have to spend hours waiting in line to fill in forms that have been designed to cause mistakes, so you have to get back in line to get new forms—in order to apply for a job or to receive welfare. The worst thing about being poor is that, to listen to the politicians and their non-poor constituents, you don't exist.

The rich exist. You bet. If you don't believe me just ask any poor person. Ask any Vietnamese, or a Colombian, a Salvadorean. Or if you're a simple person, observe the meat counter at your local super. See the woman piling sirloin into the cart? She works for the rich. Or she is newly rich herself and has yet to learn how it's done.

With these things and more in mind, I decided to put off the cloak of poverty, to lay aside my ideals, and to join the legion of the rich.

I began with the barber. No, he was second. First came my father. I wrote him. "Guess what, Dad? I'm going to get a job." He wrote right back. He approved heartily. "Dear Son Albert," he wrote. "Now you can buy life insurance. You'll have retirement. You can pay taxes, buy a car, buy car insurance (be sure to get coverage for uninsured drivers), buy a house and get mortgage insurance, fire insurance, theft insurance, insurance against Acts of God and Congress, buy dental, medical and optometrical insurance. I'm proud of you, son. Love, Albert your dad."

Albert goes out and cuts his hair, gets a job with Syrachem Corporation, participates in the practical, capitalist world, and is happy deriving his opinions and ideas from *Reader's Digest* and sharing girlie magazines with one of his coworkers. The supplementation of the story occurs structurally halfway through when the story breaks, backs up, and starts again with "Let me tell you what I learned working for Syrachem." Known only as "The Kid," Albert makes the mistake of asking one of his line bosses what's inside the unmarked canisters leaving Syrachem's loading docks in unmarked trucks with secretive drivers. Re-covering much of the same territory as the first half in which he encounters unjust exclusion and racism when his coworkers learn his name is Hummingbird, the story moves forward to its end:

I was let go, of course. I wasn't fired, just laid off. Syrachem didn't want me to call attention to them.

I went home and took up my ideals again. My father was disappointed. My insurance lapsed. What can you do? Besides, I've figured out that I have more money now, without insurance; and so what if I go to my grave with cavities?

I thought about trying to stir up trouble over Syrachem's dumping poison near Syracuse. But while I was deciding that no one except some guy named Xuan would care, Syrachem packed up and vanished.

Poof! Gone. I wondered what became of Stuart, Andy, Henry, Frank? Were they poor now, too?

Cecil (Xuan) came by, wearing a chauffeur's uniform. He works for a rich man now, named Khuri, which according to Cecil is the Arab equivalent to our Smith. Cecil wanted to tell me that he had not been the one who left the note with my last name on Andy's cart.

"I know," I said.

"You believe me?"

"Yes," I said. "And may you never have Westmoreland's Revenge again." I smiled.

I still feel lighthearted in a way, but I feel older. I said that I felt as old as my grandfather. I feel older even, now—as ancient as my race itself.

Now I think: Mark Twain didn't have life insurance. I wonder if Dewey did?

They're dead, too, you know.

I gave a copy of "This Is the World" to an about-to-be-famous writer to read, and remember to this day what I sometimes ignore. His response was that he thought I had two stories here, not one; on top of that, he had crossed out many of the images and some of the repetitions. I realized then that not everyone would appreciate what I was doing but that I did know what I was doing, and I had to stick by it. "This Is the World" is a good story—so good as to make me wonder if the little "I" that I am actually wrote it, or if it was Grandfather, and I only the recorder of it.

Fighting against America's monologue can make you monologic. It can kill your sense of humor by separating you from what is vital, the same way many of my colleagues have separated themselves from storytelling and become critical. In the week following the pageant of patriotic songs at Chipeta Elementary, I took some Colorado College students up to see the Cliff Dwellings Museum (Manitou Springs) in the Garden of the Gods.

"Hey, look at this." I laughed. "The Anasazi used cement."

A young woman frowned. "You mean this isn't real?" she asked. She was plenty worried by the notion that the construction of an "authentic" imitation of Anasazi cliff dwellings had no warning signs, no direct indication that these were not "restored" dwellings but inventions.

"It's okay," I told her. "They're as real as any real thing. Even restored dwellings would be an invention." She didn't get it. But as we climbed through the "replica," I continued to point out the handrails of iron and the "logs" made of concrete and textured by machine.

In the gift shop—where we went to escape two schoolbus loads of kids who arrived to learn about "Indians" (but who were really just there to give their teachers a break from the day-to-day training of squirrels and monkeys)—were pots and feathered mirrors and paintings and key chains and an endless assortment of wooden figures and cheap silver plate and embedded turquoise. Every item had a sticker with the authenticating name of the "Indian" artist who had made that crap, and before we left the gift shop and the rather cynical little "museum" with dioramas of Anasazi life and the conclusions drawn by deaf anthropologists ("They must have . . . , They believed . . ."), the metaphor had made itself plain.

We sat outside on some benches and I asked my students who they considered worse, the man who appropriates cliff dwellings and builds a replica to make money in a location where the Anasazi never lived, or an artist who can prove quantums of blood and appropriates the image of himself that the anthropologists invented to make replicas, in clay or words?

Whether it's the veneer of patriotic songs or the priceless veneer of George Will's editorial call to "citizenship" (which means going along with his hegemonies) it is all static, fixed, and lost between the sleeping and the waking. It is the result of cowardice. Fear. That's why they make up Betsy Ross or appropriate the "pagan" Eastre. That's why they call Wounded Knee the last battle of the Indian Wars.

Here in the Garden of the Gods we are heirs to two thousand years of cowardice. Here we meet men and women driven from "among the laughing into seriousness." Here we meet up with ourselves, them as mostly non-Native in the fakery of Anasazi cliff dwellings, me as the re-membered Native in the fakery of "authentic" Indian art, all of us wanting a minivan.

But here, too, we can learn how to dance the dance of skepticism, the dance of laughter, and we can see the truth that everything connects to everything else. The world is metaphorical, not logical, circular, not linear.

Here, we can learn "how" and not the fake of "what," process and not plot, if we'll stop singing patriot songs and listen.

Just listen.

From a Place
Called Santa Rosa

GREG SARRIS

*Greg Sarris is the elected chief of the Federated Coast Miwok tribe
and professor of English at UCLA. He is the author of several
books, including* Grand Avenue, *which he adapted for the award-
winning HBO miniseries of the same title. His new novel,* Water-
melon Nights, *was published in September 1998 by Hyperion.*

One day in early spring I drove with Mabel McKay to the hills above Clear Lake in northern California. We parked on an old road well above the lake where there was a view of the water and steep, oak-dotted hills beyond. I was surprised when Mabel got out of the car. The weather was damp and cold and Mabel was getting on in years, over eighty. Grabbing my notebook and pen, I hurried out of the car and joined her in the drizzling rain. All afternoon I had been attempting to write down what she was telling me, stories that I had heard from her most of my life. People wanted to know about this renowned Cache Creek Pomo medicine woman and basket weaver, so I figured that if I was going to write and publish her stories, I better get them straight.

But Mabel wasn't saying anything just then.

I waited. Nothing. The heavy drizzle soaked my notebook, swelled the time and date on the page. Dew collected in Mabel's hair and covered her glasses. I wondered how she could see.

Then I found out.

She was facing east, toward Long Valley. I assumed that when she started talking it would be about Lolsel, the ancient village place there, and what her grandmother had told her. But it wasn't about that at all. She talked about Sulfur Bank, directly below us, near the water, about how her grandfather had danced with the people of that place after white settlers forced the Long Valley Cache Creek Pomo off their land. Mabel had gone to Sulfur Bank with her grandmother and participated in the old-time Bole Maru and Big Head ceremonies. She danced in the round house, holding on to her grandmother's skirt. Her grandmother was often sad, but when the old woman came to Sulfur Bank she was a different person, happy and light. Mabel could see the change in her grandmother's face as the horses pulled their wagon out of the eastern hills and into the village. There was a place on the road, a bend where you could hear the sounds of people singing before you could see the village. "And the clappers," Mabel said, taking the glasses from her face. "Them clappers," she repeated, her eyes bright, concentrated. "Them clappers sounding loud, echoing in these hills, echoing everywhere so the people would know."

Mabel would remember that place for as long as she lived, that bend in the road. She'd hear the voices, people singing, the clacking sound of split elderberry-wood clappers, announcing to everyone far and near that the people of Sulfur Bank were dancing. They were a generous people, sharing their songs and stories with the old Lolsel woman, Sarah Taylor, and her granddaughter, Mabel. Seventy-five years later or more, that place and its people and stories had become a part of Mabel's own story.

And mine.

I had never lived at Sulfur Bank, and before that morning, I had never stopped along the road to ponder what is now just another Pomo reservation with its typical small homes and open yards. I knew the Kashaya Pomo reservation at Stewart's Point on the coast well enough. But stories of this place had already figured in my life. I grew up in Santa Rosa, a town some forty miles west and south of Sulfur Bank and forty-five miles east and south of Stewart's Point. Santa Rosa is not only located between the two reservations, but close by to many other reservations and rancherias. No wonder it is the home place for so many local Indians. When I was growing up, in the sixties, most of us lived in South Park, a poor, ethnically diverse neighborhood behind the county fairgrounds. There I met and hung out with Indians from lots of different places—Stewart's Point, Tomales Bay, Hopland, Ukiah, Sulfur Bank. Mostly Pomo and Coast Miwok Indians. A lot of us were mixed—Mexican, Portuguese, Filipino. We told stories about one another. Stories about curses and Indian doctors, stories about who did what to whom, and who was really the father or sister or brother of somebody else. Elders upheld traditions. They spoke of, and maintained, unions and divisions between tribes and even within families. Parents talked about work, lost love. Us kids listened, talked now and then about our life on the streets, our fistfights and victories in the local pool hall. It was how we knew one another.

Anyway, one warm June day after my freshman year in high school, a family moved into the neighborhood from Sulfur Bank. A mother and her five or six children. Cramped into a beat-up, one-eyed tan Ford, their belongings stuffed into the trunk and tied over the top, they pulled up to an empty house on Grand Avenue. The ramshackle place looked even smaller than it was, dwarfed between two towering cypress trees.

We watched from the corner grocery as the family piled out of the car. First the mother, a broad dark Indian woman in a loose housedress, then the smaller kids, scruffy-looking little boys with tufts of straight black hair. Then the two girls. Not typical girls just off the reservation, quiet-acting and wary, but girls in loud colors, reds and yellows, clothes tight and short. Their hair was teased up, piled high on their heads, and from where we stood, we could see the pink-white color of their lipstick. One of the girls was quite tall, lighter-skinned than the other. She was actually the younger of the two, as we would find out later. It was the other one, the older one, who looked straight at us, bold as daylight. She stood and blew a huge pink bubble with her gum, snapped it, then went to her work unloading the car.

As it turned out, they were related to a family in the neighborhood. No surprise. And already the stories had started. About how they were from Sulfur Bank. How most of the kids had different fathers. How the mother's sister was in jail for shoplifting and, while reaching for a Filipino boxer in another cell, got trapped between the iron bars and had to be soldered loose. How Old Uncle, an Indian doctor on DeTurk Street, pulled bones from the mother's mother's eyes many years ago at Sulfur Bank. On and on.

But we paid little attention to those stories. It was the girls we thought about. Brassy girls, smelling of perfume and cigarettes, smelling of booze and pot, loud, laughing. It was the summer of love. Nineteen sixty-seven. Aretha Franklin singing "R-E-S-P-E-C-T," calling the shots. Free love. Drugs. The counterculture made its way into our neighborhood, took shape in the finger-popping and fast talk of these girls, who, like emissaries from another world, spread their message to every nook and cranny of our lives. We looked back and forth across the street, flirted. Before long, the invitations to the house—when the mother was up the street playing cards with her cousin. And then one thing after another, first in the dark and then in the light, alone just the two of you, then more, three, four, every which way. Stoned out of our minds. Lost in the dark, lost in the light, alone or together. Two or three months. Then it was all over. Back to school. Jobs. The older girl got pregnant sometime in the fall, had a baby. The father was black.

Seemed like the end of the story. Years passed, I graduated from high school, went to college. I never thought much about the girls. Then one day they came back to haunt me with no warning.

It was with Mabel. I was home from college and had paid her a visit, something I never failed to do when I was back in town. Over the years, I had lost contact with many of the Indians I had known as a kid, but never with Mabel. She was special, even before I knew how to appreciate her as a knowledgeable elder and model teacher. Since that first time I walked into her home, when I was about ten or eleven and had followed her adopted son Marshall home from school, she stopped me, made me think. I was a mixed-up kid, living here and there between families—white families and Indian families. I was hungry, I remember, and wanted something to eat. Without warning, Mabel turned around with a peanut butter and jelly sandwich and a glass of milk. "Here, sit down," she said. How did she know I was hungry? I hadn't asked for, or even mentioned, food. She stopped me. And she would do it again and again.

The night I was visiting her, when she brought up the girls from Sulfur Bank, was no different.

Actually, she brought up the mother. How the subject came up I don't recall exactly. It was late, and I would have left long ago if I wasn't still looking for a way to get information out of her for a professor of mine at the university. He wanted to know if Mabel used sacred crystals in her doctoring ceremonies, what herbs and plants she used. I must have looked silly asking her about such things. I had never paid much attention before. She chuckled in her inimitable way, never answering my questions, and kept on with whatever she was talking about. Suddenly, she paused and said, "Oh, yeah. About the laundry. Do you know ____?"

"Yes," I answered, remembering the two girls' mother. I told her I knew the woman's daughters in high school. Marshall knew them, too, though perhaps not as I did.

"Oh, yes?" Mabel took a sip of her coffee, then set her cup carefully on the table. "Hmmm," she said. "Well, I seen her for the first time today, first time since she was a girl. At the Laundromat I seen her. She said to me, 'Are you Mabel?' I said, 'Yes.' Then I seen who it was.

"It happened I seen her coming. I seen her in the car with those grandkids, the black ones. She was trying to hide them from me, even yet. Keeping them in the car when she was talking to me. Looking around to see if they jumped out. It was funny the way she did that.

"After while Marshall says, 'Who is that, Mama?' I say it's relatives, some kind. He says, 'Oh, do we have to claim them, too?' I start up laughing [chuckling]. Yeah, I said, we do.

"Well, not relatives that way, but her mother, ____, took in Grandma dancing up there by that place they call Rattlesnake Island [near Sulfur Bank]."

I tried to explain why Marshall might feel the way he did. I made a few derogatory remarks about the woman's loose daughters and about the woman's sister, the girls' aunt, who got stuck between the bars in the county jail.

Mabel looked up over her glasses, admonishing. "You don't know the whole story," she said. "What happened—"

I shrugged my shoulders. "What's there to know?" I asked, interrupting her.

"What happened, a man poisoned.

"See, them girls' grandmother, ____'s mother, she got fixed that way. How it happened, a man poisoned her.

"He wanted her, this man. She was beautiful, but she would do like this: doctor somebody, then get up and leave her equipment. If she liked a man she would do like that: get up and go out that way. Maybe not come back until the next day.

"Well, this man, he wanted her. But she was already married to another man. She said, 'I don't want you.' See, he was an old man and I guess she liked the younger men, I don't know [chuckling].

"He got mad then. He told her, don't be fooling around no more, no leaving your doctoring here and there.

"Then I don't know what it happened, but she got pregnant *again*. Some other man, not her husband, I understand.

"Then *he* got mad. He got *real* mad. Then he got sick, the old man. 'Send for ____,' he was saying: 'I'm dying and I need her to pray,' he was telling somebody.

"So she went there. And that's how it happened, they say. He tricked her, took something of hers while she was singing—I don't know what, maybe a pipe, cocoon, something, anyway—and fixed her with it. And that's how they found her in the morning. She was already dead with baby, frozen, they say. And he's the one cursed all them with that man-wild business. For generations, he was saying."

Mabel paused, sipped her coffee, then added, "And he was saying all peoples that fool with them could be fixed that way too. 'It could happen to them, too,' he was saying."

My mouth dropped open. Mabel looked at me. "Now what did you want to know about crystals?" she asked.

I didn't answer her. I didn't have to. I got her point. The herbs, her songs, all aspects of her doctoring ceremony were sacred, not just objects to be talked about, separate from Mabel's whole life. They were a part of her and, as a result, a part of me too. Like the girls from Sulfur Bank, and the story I just heard. They were not things separate from my own life. I was a part of them just as they were a part of me, and in ways I might not fully understand. I couldn't treat them any lighter or different from the way I treated my own life. They *were* my life. The story, the girls, Mabel. An occurrence at Sulfur Bank lived on, found itself on Grand Avenue in Santa Rosa, made itself anew in the place there, in the lives of all of us, whether we knew it or not. I knew it.

As was often the case after a conversation with Mabel, I found myself thinking for days on end. Needless to say, I didn't have the information my professor wanted. It was Christmas vacation, and I think I told him Mabel had gone away for the holidays. After I quit obsessing about whether or not I was cursed with sex-wildness of some sort, I began thinking about a multitude of other things. The story and my experience with it unexpectedly provided answers to a lot of questions and concerns I had regarding learning, particularly in terms of reading and writing. These answers would inevitably not only influence my teaching, critical work, and creative writing, but ultimately the book on Mabel McKay.

I was never a so-called model student. Not in grade school or high school, anyway. As mentioned, I was a mixed-up kid, troubled, on the streets. School never interested me. My complaint was not unlike the complaint of countless students: I can't relate. I only started studying in the eleventh grade, my junior year, and that was so I could go to college and get rich, the Horatio Alger story. I would pull myself up by my bootstraps. Along the way, I fell in love with literature. It reminded me of what I knew best: stories, gossip, Mabel and the other old folks talking. Faulkner and his rich, complicated stories about this person talking about that person talking about another person. A specific place in the South. Interrelated families. I knew of a place too. Santa Rosa with its interrelated Indian families in South Park. I heard the stories. But even so, even when I started to read all literature seriously, I found myself not drawing on my own experiences. I read the literature on the classroom's terms, as the professors wanted. It wasn't just that I had to chase this or that symbol, read the text this way or that. The reason for my detachment from the texts was more profound, and had to do with basic assumptions about reading or, for that matter, hearing stories in the classroom. My experience with Mabel and my experience in the classroom were fundamentally different, and operated from a different set of premises. Though I could not articulate all I began to think about after I experienced the story with Mabel, I had a good sense of what was at issue.

Basically, in school it was assumed that a story, written or otherwise, is separate from you, has a beginning and end, and is something you fix, frame, give meaning to. At home with Mabel the opposite was true: a story is not separate from you, has no beginning and end, and is not something you can fix or frame in any way. Rather, a story is something you establish a relationship with over time; it is something that lives with you forever, something that can be relevant in a multitude of ways and situations. As Mabel said to me: "Don't ask me what it means, the story. Life will teach you about it, the way it teaches you about life."

For me the problem with school in the past, in grade school and high school, wasn't just that the worlds of the texts (i.e., *Dick and Jane, The Great Gatsby*) were foreign to me, or that classroom modes of reading (and learning) required that I know (and give meaning) to the texts on the teacher's terms. I couldn't engage or talk back to the texts from my own knowledge base, my own experience. My experience could never touch the world of the text. The world of the text and the world of my life were seen as separate, independent of each other. Of course, the predicament I found myself in as a student was not unique. I would argue that most students find themselves in the same situation in the classroom. For those of us from marginal cultures, those of us farthest from the worlds of the classroom texts, the situation is just more pronounced, extreme. Those of us who succeed in these environments usually do so at the expense of our own experience and identity. We learn to put where we come from, who we are, on the back burner. We adapt to the world of the classroom, pushing our experience away, separate from the learning activity. The result is that we become effectively schizophrenic; a gap is formed between our home life and our school life. Or, if we don't become schizophrenic, we drop out, we leave, or slide through unengaged, barely there. Ultimately, the text and the institution are never challenged, informed by our particular experiences. In short, we are silenced.

This educational model characterizes what American Indian people have experienced from the beginning with the European invaders. Witness the missions, the boarding schools, the current tracking system that places so many Indians in remedial classes. Currently, 80 percent of Indian schoolchildren in California drop out of school by ninth grade. In other words, by the time our kids are fifteen years old, the majority of them are out of school. Their complaint: "I can't relate." Interestingly, American Indian students do as well as other students through third and fourth grades. In fifth grade, they begin to fall behind, or away.

Mabel provided me a model that could bridge the gap, heal. My experience with the story of the woman (and girls) from Sulfur Bank helped me not only to see the differences between modes of reading and learning with Mabel and with school, but also it illuminated pathways to empowerment and change for me in school. I began to see Faulkner in new ways, particularly with respect to his representation and understanding of nature and Indian. I was able to point out to one college professor that not all Indians passed a peace pipe in the Plains Indian tradition he was describing. My voice qualified, contextualized what I was being taught.

As a teacher I continue to look for ways to engage my students with what they are reading, always looking for exercises to bridge the chasm between their home life and school life. I begin my American Indian literature course at UCLA by telling a story told to me by my Kashaya Pomo and Coast Miwok elders. I then ask students, usually at the next class meeting, to repeat the story as they heard it. Invariably their stories tell them more about themselves than about the story or about the speaker and culture from which the story comes. Here students can see how they are approaching the story and begin to explore unexamined assumptions (based on who they are as students) by which they operate and which they use to frame the texts and experiences of members of another culture. This storytelling (about a story) engenders a reflexivity that pervades or establishes the groundwork for further study of American Indian texts. They learn as much about themselves as they do Indian texts.

In my written literary and social criticism, I interweave a myriad of voices with autobiography and theoretical discourse to create documents representing exchanges that open the world people share with each other. The objective of my critical work is not to have complete knowledge, say, of the text, not to frame it or tell its total story (which I maintain is impossible), but to establish and report as clearly as possible the dialogue where I inform, and am informed, by the text. As I say in *Keeping Slug Woman Alive,* "The report, or written criticism, then, becomes a kind of story, a representation of a dialogue that is extended to critics and other readers who in turn inform and are informed by the report."

In my fiction I create situations where stories always shape and influence characters. The characters must come to terms with their stories as they come to terms with their lives. In "Secret Letters," one of the stories in *Grand Avenue,* a man hears a story his father tells him and then must make sense of the predicament in which he finds himself.

There's a part of the story I didn't tell . . . I think of this days later. About how the old woman died, my great-grandmother. She was old, nearly a hundred, so her actual dying wasn't unexpected or unusual in any way. It was what happened afterward, after she passed on. The family never got her body home, back to our place on the coast.

As it turned out, she died here in Santa Rosa, while the family was on a trip. Within moments of her passing it began to rain, not just light showers but a downpour that lasted for days. There was lightning and thunder. Creeks swelled and overflowed their banks. The Russian river buried half of Healdsburg and all the towns below to the coast. People had never seen anything like it, not in the middle of September when even a sprinkle of rain is unusual. What's happening? The farmers wondered, seeing their fall crops, their grapes and prunes, ruined in the torrential rains.

The Indians knew, our family and the Indians from Santa Rosa. They knew what was happening. It was the last battle between my great-grandmother and old Juana Maria, the matriarch of the people from Santa Rosa Creek. Like my great-grandmother, Juana Maria was a bear person.

People knew their tribe's boundaries. They knew how far they could go in a grove of willows, which side of a creek to stay on. Everyone was careful not to cross these markers, not to trespass. Everyone except the bear people and a few others like them, the *Walepu* and other spooks. At night in their hides and cloaks of feathers, these people went anywhere. But when they crossed paths, one in another's territory, the fight was on. Great displays of strength, magic powers. Fifty-foot leaps into the air. Roars that caused rocks to roll down hillsides. Sharp whistles that pierced eardrums. Anything to intimidate their rivals or to kill them.

So it was between my great-grandmother and old Juana Maria. A year before she died, my great-grandmother told her daughter, my grandmother, that she had battled with Juana Maria for decades. When the family found themselves stopped by a washed-out bridge, when the wagon wheels sank in two feet of mud, they put two and two together. Old Juana Maria had another power, weather power, and she brought on the rains as a last offense. She wouldn't let my great-grandmother ever go home, back to her own territory. Only after the family buried the old woman in Santa Rosa did the rains stop.

"But that really wasn't the last offense," my father said when he told me this story. "There's more. The most important part for you and me." He looked out our reservation-home window to a large tan oak tree, then back at me. "You see, we knew something was up. A month later, after we finished in the crops and before we headed back up the coast, we went back for the old woman, our grandmother. She was in a pauper's plot in the town cemetery, and we went one night with picks and shovels to dig her up and take her home. But someone had already been there.

"The dirt had been turned up, spread around again, maybe just earlier that night, very recently. We dug down and found the coffin hacked apart, splintered wood everywhere. And our grandmother's body had been cut up too. Old Juana Maria had cut out her rib.

"There was no use but to cover her back up. Juana Maria and her people would always have Grandma. And this is what I'm getting at, Steven." He ran his hand over his face, looked out the window, then back at me. "A bear person can use that rib on her rival's family. She can teach her children to use it too. Even if there's no rib anymore, no signs. It's in the blood, the history. And that's what happened to you."

"So there's nothing I can do," I said to my father. I was seventeen years old and had gotten a girl pregnant. I wanted to do the right thing, for the girl and me, and had sought advice from my father. I hadn't expected this story. Now I was frightened. "No," my father said. "There *is* something you can do. You can say no. Don't marry the girl. Drop it. Forget it."

"Pauline's a nice girl," I protested. "You always said a man must take responsibility for what he does. Isn't marrying her the right thing to do?"

"You can't marry her, Steven." He looked at the floor and then continued talking without looking up. "Steven, they got me too. Zelda Toms, Juana Maria's granddaughter, got me. Zelda is Pauline's mother, right? Pauline's your sister, Steven."

I unbuttoned the top button of my shirt. I took a deep breath, several of them. I understood what my father was saying, the predicament I was in. Still I didn't agree with what he was telling me to do. "I've got to do something, Dad. I just can't leave her—"

"Look," he said, glaring at me. "She's your sister. Can't you see? This is the final embarrassment. They'll laugh at us forever. All our family will know. They got us in the end. There's nothing nice about any of those people. I know. And now you should know."

Mabel's book, *Mabel McKay: Weaving the Dream*, turned out to be a mixture of biography and autobiography, a bi-autobiography of sorts, a story that tells the story of my hearing her stories. Toward the end of the book, I write:

. . . Things came together. It wasn't just her story she had wanted me to know. While trying to help her, while trying to trace her story, I traced my own. I had pretty much sensed this. But it was more than that even. It was a blessing, a miracle. Here was a life that gave, a life only in the dream. I had never known her any other way. How else could I write her book? How else but from the dream, what I knew from her? Her story, the story, our story. Like the tiny basket in my shirt pocket, different threads, sedge and redbud, woven over one willow rod into a design that went round and round, endless.

With Mabel there was always a story. Lots of stories. About the woman from Sulfur Bank. About lots of people I knew in Santa Rosa. About me. The stories teach me many things, but most of all that they keep on, they live. They all started for me in Santa Rosa. Stories from other places—Sulfur Bank, Stewart's Point, Ukiah—came together there and lived on. And then they traveled with me from Santa Rosa, to the universities, to publishers, to towns and cities far and near.

As I sit writing this essay about what it means to be a Native American writer today, I live in Los Angeles, in the Hollywood Hills, a good five hundred miles from my home. I have a stupendous view of the city. Of course I think of Mabel. I think of the view she had that spring day above Clear Lake, all the things she saw that called up for me the story from Sulfur Bank. And Sulfur Bank was just one story that taught me important matters about stories and reading and writing. Certainly there were many others, endless others. But the story of Sulfur Bank is foremost in my mind now.

As I look down on the infinite city lights below me, many stories come to mind—stories of those lights. I think of my trip to the gym just hours ago, the bodies there, the invitations, the parties. I see the way sweat forms over a person's brow, I see the angles and curves of the body. Certainly, the lights are a siren call, loud, burning, a pathway away. It's easy. But I have an essay to write, I tell myself tonight. Yes, there's the story of that family from Sulfur Bank. I'll write about that. I know that story.

WIND CIRCLES

VICKIE SEARS

Vickie Sears (Cherokee) was born in 1941, and lived in the Pacific Northwest until she crossed over on May 27, 1999. She was the author of Simple Songs, *a collection of short stories (Firebrand Books). She published essays on feminist therapy and women in literature, while her poetry and short stories were anthologized in such collections as* Talking Leaves *(ed. Craig Lesley, 1991) and* A Gathering of Spirit *(1988). She completed a screenplay,* Grace, *which is currently in production by Native American Public Telecommunications.*

Writing is a wind. A movement in the ear that hears rattles beneath a tree and rests by a rock or in a field. It is the slow-water-rumble under winter ice. It is animal songs or people chatting in a café. It is listening on a park bench to those who will tell a story. And someone will always tell a story. Sometimes they can be written. Often they can only be stored for your own growing. Things are sometimes sparked that will allow you to write about something in yourself or one you've met. For me, everything I've written so far has pieces of my own life in it. In the only writing course I ever had, the teacher said, "Write about what you know." It was sage advice. Sometimes I want to recount a story shared by Elisi (grandmother) or about tribal history. All of these things are what bring the spirit—that fervor to write is a wind tunnel through which my mind weaves toward the exit via the pen. The writing may not always be an ecstasy, but it is a joy—a moving in a dreamdance. Under it all for me is a sense of land and my place in it—a believing that the words help continue that space. I knew I wanted to be a writer when I was five years old.

If I were to believe my mother, I am nothing more than an accident. Should I believe my father, I was born as a gift to the future. Therein has lain the conundrum of my life.

My father was a Cherokee who, during World War II, was stationed along the California/Mexican border riding a horse looking for spies. He met my mother, an English/Spanish woman, at a dance in San Diego. She bought the idea of "tall, dark and handsome," so I began. They eventually married and my brother arrived ten months after I was born.

We lived in a small trailer set in the desert wind. The wind became an abiding influence in my life. It was so much sound and vision—moving tumbleweed, flattening jackrabbit ears, the tortoise pulling in its head from flying sand. There was the clatter of pebbles against the tin that became an omnipresent, wrapping music. And the silences when it didn't blow was also a story, often a waiting—a knowing something would come—a rare water falling or twister. A something that would come as a difference.

My mother is a distant individual. She always wanted it to be clear that her Spanish heritage was of a Castilian nature rather than of the "wetback" variety. Mother believed in a large individualistic "I" that maintained an incredible distance between herself and everyone, including her children. My father was the nurturer who came home on the weekends to blow bubbles on our stomachs, ride us on his shoulders, and play his bugle. He was the one with brown friends, of whom mother disapproved, who would tell us the names of plants as we walked about, laughed or sang and always, in everyday conversations, told us stories. Some were Native people. Some were Mexican. What they held in common was a sense of "We" and family. Elisi came for visits. She brought the knowing of how strawberries came to be and rabbit trickster tales. She brought silent walks that were filled with peace. Mother's silences were a prelude during which we worried about what might come.

My mother's family was a fragmented unit that was small and seldom seen. One of the men in her family came and sexually abused me. Grandmother came for the yearly battle with Mom. Grandfather would arrive in an aura of woodcarving smells, house paint, and Fig Newton cookies, which were tucked into every pocket of his bib overalls. He was a steady adult, though seen infrequently.

By the time I was four, my father had been discharged to Washington State, where my mother was raised. Dad brought all of his family together: five sisters, a brother, and Elisi. We moved into a housing project. Dad's family moved into a four-block radius which my brother and I wandered almost at will, knowing it was all right to go to any relative's house. We felt safe. Where we did not feel safe was in our home, where the drinking increased and our parents' fighting grew more frequent. Dad complained about Mom going out more often on her own. Mom railed about Dad's "heathen" practices, how much time he spent with his family rather than with hers, the "negative" influence on us children and why didn't they speak only English in front of her? We became watchful children. By the time I was five, the squabbles became the arguments of divorce.

Court-appointed social workers interviewed my brother and myself, and we were taken from my parents. Father's relatives who offered my brother and me a home were deemed unworthy because "Indians have poor child-rearing skills." It is not an accident that I became a social worker. My brother and I went from Juvenile Receiving to Washington Children's Home Society and into many foster homes. As we left the courthouse, my Elisi said, *"A nv da di s di."* ("Remember.") My brother and I were positioned beside each other and I felt he became my responsibility. I began to tell him stories before he went to the boys dorm and I sang myself to sleep. I was keeping the language alive until it was finally beaten out of us.

I began to read. I found E. Pauline Johnson and Charles Eastman. Then I found Laura Ingalls Wilder. There was pride and internalized oppression converging. There was confusion. My head kept returning to Elisi's stories to remember what was warm, practical, and good. Without those tales I don't believe I would have been able to survive many of the things I was to see and experience.

In 1984, I published a poem about my Elisi, which ends with these lines:

Katydid keeps the tongue Cherokee hears our tales of then and now.
My memory
hears Grandmother's Aaay
and smiles.

It is a small return for the many gifts she gave me over the years.

When we were six and seven, my brother and I were sent to live in Walla Walla, to our first Native home. We had already been in several foster homes in which we were sexually or otherwise abused, so there was a lot of wariness going into the home. But it was a safe home. It was a place where the adults, Grace and Paul, listened and even cared about children. In "Grace" I wrote about a walk we took early one morning.

"We'll take a walk over to the alfalfa. I want to show you some colors."
We walked between the wheat and alfalfa, the air swollen up with
their sweetness. Grace
pulled down a piece of alfalfa and said, "Smell."

It was all sharp and tickled inside my nose, kinda like medicine . . .
Grace said, "See the different colors?"

After showing me the different colors, Grace promised she would
show me further nuances in the afternoon sun. She kept her word.

When Paul had a heart attack, my brother and I were returned to
the orphanage because they felt she was too old to raise small children.
It was an immense gift to my brother and me to have been there at all.
"Grace" is a chapter in the middle of a novel I am writing about my
brother's and my experience after going to the orphanage. A wish has
always been that Grace and Paul would read the story and recognize
what they gave.

When my brother and I returned from Walla Walla, he was sent to
live with my father's eldest sister. My father also lived with her as his
diabetes was critical. What was horrid about our separation was that no
one told me he was going to be gone or where he was going. With all
the power of a child, I had failed to honor my responsibility for his
care. For years, I carried the weight of my failure, but I began writing
by putting down stories I thought he should know or thoughts I
wanted to share. Once my writing was found by a staff person and
ridiculed before the other children, I began to memorize everything.
That painful experience was turned to a gift because I now try to see,
mentally photograph and use it all in writing.

Much of what I write is about healing, especially from abuses. For
twenty-six years, I have been a psychiatric/medical social worker who
is also a certified alcoholism/drug counselor. I have heard many stories, especially of Native people being taken from their families and
struggling to find and reclaim their identities. I do not think my tale is
all that unique. I do know that writing has always been an essential way
for me to heal.

The year before my father died, I got to live with him and his family. Elisi was next door and she reminded me of stories, histories,
beads, and the finger flash of her basketry. It was magic and it was pain.
I knew people and I did not. I was now the odd child with her "nose in
the book." I spent most of my time there just listening and relearning.

In a year, I returned to the orphanage and went to what I thought
was another Anglo foster home. I did not know the woman was my
mother, and I wanted to stay with my father. In "Keeping Sacred Se-

crets" I would write of my mother's initial reaction to the treasures of my father's home. "Everything was proudly displayed on the bed and dresser. Ginger looked at the bed and scowled. 'What is all this junk, Maryann?' Maryann's face went limp. 'Well this . . .' Ginger interrupted. 'I know what it is. It's the same voodoo crap that was around me the whole time I was with your father. It's not part of the real world and I won't have it in my house!'" Things were destroyed. I ended up burying everything. But there remained an omnipresent conflict between my mother and myself over what she considered Catholic and right versus what she considered "heathen."

At twelve, when my father died and my mother forbade me to travel crosstown to his family, I began to sneak off to the Indian Center in downtown Seattle. I became an intertribal person, learning from all the different tribal people who came there. I probably learned most of the Northwestern peoples, eventually becoming, as an adult, an adopted Quilieute. Many things were viewed differently from Father's beliefs, but there were enough comparable attitudes that allowed me not to feel so alone. I began to really lead the life of a breed—fighting internalized oppression and the overt racism of my mother and her community. My sense of place now came with the winds that swept down from the Olympic mountains, spun the waters of Puget Sound, and whipped the city valleys. My sense of strength became the sounds and smells of the Pacific Northwest.

San Francisco became home for my college years, but the only part of the geography that ever really claimed me was when the fog windrolled over the city to settle down to ground almost every day. Again it was the sound of wind—transitions. I became a radical anti-war civil rights activist writing angry polemics for a leftist magazine called *The Gaviota*. All the anger I felt as a child found form in politics. There was Vietnam, Martin Luther King, Bobby Kennedy, the taking of Alcatraz, and the activities of the Indian Center. There was also my war with diet pills and alcohol. The first was to make me "thin and right," while the latter was integral to the mystique of being a writer. But that transition of wind music again was telling me that being a Native writer meant more than Elisi's stories, beadwork, or making baskets. It meant really understanding the depths to which the government had sunk in committing genocide, both past and present. It meant understanding the racism of the family-court social workers by really assimilating the destruction of my family and looking at the obliteration of tribal/family integrity. It meant my having to face the racist practices inside my own family. My twenty-one-year-old self declared "no" to a specific set of political notions and continued working in several causes and drinking. It astounds me now that I even managed to complete college. As the drinking increased so did my sense that I would die as young as my father. In a story entitled "Connie," I wrote, "Out loud, Connie suddenly yelled, 'Shit! I've been drinking since I was seven and that ain't bound to stop now!" So I had to begin to look also at my alcoholism and the why of its being in my life. I read about alcohol. I wrote college papers about it. And I continued to drink, saying to myself, "I will be my father's child and die at age thirty-two."

It took eight years to complete my BA degree and leave the city to work on a tree farm. It went bankrupt and a new wind rose from the throats of the many turkeys who lived on the farms of southern Oregon. The silence of the nights would carry their chatter. It seemed to ask, Where is your pride? Do something besides clean houses—use yourself! I got lucky in going to work for the Office of Economic Opportunity and in finding a therapist. My best therapists, however, turned out to be the young people with whom I worked. Soon, I was writing grants to create drop-in centers for teens and an alcoholism/drug program for the many runaways of every ethnic group hitching along the I-5 corridor. I was writing and the Creator had blown me toward young people. I didn't want to teach anymore, I wanted to do something for all the children who felt like me as a young person. Quite suddenly I was more than an Anglo/Native. I was a woman with a cause come full circle to my history—a woman with a capacity to be of change and, hopefully, help. I was a mother, and a thirty-year-old sober individual grappling with a pain that is totally familiar—that of abused children. It is an issue of passion to which I have dedicated much of my life.

An oddity for me as a writer is that I have two writing careers. There is intentional teaching/mental health writing revolving around grant writing, program modifications, social work/mental health topics, and doing cross-cultural therapy. It is writing that mostly only mental health practitioners see. It has been an important bridging work, which, I like to believe, has led to increased cultural/ethnic awareness and greater sensitivity to the issues of young people. Life as a fiction writer/poet broadens my topics immensely, but I cannot help writing on the issues of child abuse. Like my father, I believe children are our future and deserve tender cultivation and care. In the story "Dancer" I was able to tell a true tale of a foster child whose self-esteem is increased by her learning to dance. "One night she speaks up at supper and says, right clear and loud, 'I'm an Assiniboin!' Clear as it can be, she says it again. Don't nobody have to say nothing to something that proud said."

Most of my work is about people growing—transforming themselves into more of who they want to be. To me that is a way of helping to create change. It is the wind circling around the trailer of my childhood, topping sand pebbles on the metal walks to remind me to say something—do something.

I don't always want to write about Native peoples but it just keeps coming up because there are so many wonderful simple stories of beauty and hope and the continuity of courage that have to be spoken. In no way would I think I could speak for my tribe or all Natives, but I can have the fortune to write about stories I see and it's always a gift to me. In 1985 I had a poem appear in *Ikon* about a couple I once knew on the Colville reservation.

MEM AND PEP

Old they were.
in their nineties.
living in the far back of the reservation
in a cabin so
ancient
no one could remember who or when built it.
A burnt grass ranch was their
breathing place.

They and the horses.
head throwing, mane whipping summersun sucking
beasts who more owned Mem and Pep than they them.

summerdry earthcrack
turned
winter broken hard
to
earthgreengrow year on year from

a childhood of growing together.

He pulled her into soft springgrain.
she rose indignant laughing ran.
things were full between them.

married they could not recall a time when
they were not together.

They went to the city only once
understanding
they had all they needed.

the city never fooled them.

Small changes came.
kerosene was good
a truck was fine but
essentials never came from the city.

Pep in wheelchair watched
a mellowed mingled Mem crawl to hide
in cornfield rows because soldiers were coming.

Mem jealous of Pep teased him for glaring
at all female ranch hands.

they enjoyed their game.

Such stories they could tell.

spirits wizards mile high trees

streamthick salmon caught in grasswoven nets.
cedar sage sweetgrass sacred tobacco
with meanings remembered
mostly
by Elders.

Mem built a livingroom middle fire
thinking herself in a long ago forest.

Pep never laughed.
he traveled with her.

They slept away hot afternoons.
preferred to do storyspinning nightwebs to
audiences of new generations.

One springwarm day Pep shook Mem
couldn't wake her
called from the cabin door.

Their son carried her away.
Pep's eyes silent loud.
On death's fourth day Pep sat in the window watching
mares with colts stomp springgreen grass.
finally spoke pointing
"You bring her here that woman with the spotted rump.
We'll ride to see Old Mem."

We did. He did. Died.

Knowing about that much of an ordinary loving song, I believe I could do nothing else but give it to the wind to circle.

I guess part of what I want to write about is that which is ordinary, yet so extraordinary in our daily lives. I recently worked on a screenplay in which the Native people were portrayed as ordinary individuals who were not "noble" or "savage." It was exciting to write. They are not trapped in a box canyon, as in *Dances with Wolves,* waiting for the Anglos to leave and save the village. They are just plain folks caught in life's vagaries. It may be too novel an idea for Hollywood, but we still need to give it a try.

Having been raised in so many foster homes and with a panoply of mixed-heritage adopted relatives from my mother and stepfather's relationship, I have intimate knowledge of some cultural behaviors that have shown up in some people. I think in particular of my stepfather's eldest sister, Aunt Teresa, about whom I wrote in "Pasta Saturday." She was a truly ordinary Italian Catholic woman who had an uncommon way of making pasta the first Saturday of every month. "Aunt Teresa took off her bathrobe and put on a half-apron. Mind you, she had on no other clothes. Only her glasses. She stood in the kitchen, hands on her hips, surveying the goods before making the sign of the cross and saying a brief prayer." Watching the dough and Aunt Teresa has always been one of my favorite experiences. Writing the story came out of someone asking me, "You remember Aunt Teresa's making pasta?"

It's that wind circling everywhere again. Such a nosy presence.

My sense of real belonging remains in the Pacific Northwest. I own my greatest sense of wholeness here. I feel I hear what the wind carries best as it weaves through pine and cedar. I have had to struggle with my internalized oppression along with an uncertainty of acceptance among both Natives and Anglos. I believe that is better as I accept myself with loving—as I accept my play in writing and storytelling as a way of healing as well. It's also better as we all take ourselves as tribal peoples catching stories, remolding them and tossing them back to the wind as a circle. If I am lucky, something I have written will help someone else as much as it did me to write it or give them as much play in as well crafted a way as possible, with the prayer that I'll keep growing and improving.

In the Past's
Familiar Tongue

JOHN E. SMELCER

John E. Smelcer, of Cherokee and Ahtna Athabaskan Indian ances-
try, was born in 1963. He is the executive director of the Ahtna In-
dian Heritage Foundation and on the faculty at Embry-Riddle
Aeronautical University. In 1998, he edited and published The
Ahtna Noun Dictionary. *His books on Alaska Native mythol-*
ogy include The Raven and the Totem, A Cycle of Myths,
and In the Shadows of Mountains. *His poetry books include*
Songs from an Outcast, Changing Seasons, The Snow Has
No Voice, *and* Koht'aene Kenaege', *a collection of poems writ-*
ten in his Indian language. In 1994, with D. L. Birchfield, he edited
Durable Breath: Contemporary Native American Poetry.
His poems have appeared in the Atlantic Monthly, The Kenyon
Review, *and elsewhere. He is poetry editor at* Rosebud.

NUNYAE SENK'AAZE

Da'atnae nii sii nunyae senk'aaze
ghayaaɬ tic'aa ikae daa.

Sii niic tah sii ciiɬ
yuuɬ deniigi
naan hwzaak'e
k'e deniigi nak'
yii dzaadze' tic'aa
ts'abaeli' eɬ k'ey—

sii nake'taen hnax gha tene
'eɬ 'aen sk'e
yii k'adiidi sesi.[1]

ANIMAL SPIRITS

Old men teach me animal spirits
wander the forests where they once lived.

I remember as a boy
chasing a moose
across a frozen field
until it vanished
in a tangled forest
of spruce and birch—

how I turned home on our trail
and found only my tracks
in the fresh crushed snow.

I was born in 1963 to a mother of Irish, German, and Cherokee descent. The Cherokee is on her mother's side. My father was born to a full-blood Ahtna Athabaskan Indian woman who had married a German immigrant fur trapper around 1934. Ahtna Indians are one of thirteen Athabaskan peoples living mostly in the vast interior of Alaska. There are some 1,000 Ahtna today, most living in small villages along the Copper River. Translated into English the name literally means "People of the Copper River." Its northernmost traditional range is Cantwell, a small community just a few miles south of Denali National Park. Its southernmost boundary is just north of Valdez in Prince William Sound, where the *Exxon Valdez* oil spill occurred.

My father, Charlie Smelcer, was born at Indian River in 1937 at a time when the territorial government (Alaska didn't become a state until 1959) still took children from parents and villages to place them in distant Bureau of Indian Affairs boarding schools where they were taught Western thought, religion, and language at the expense of their own culture's demise. Indeed, from about 1900 until the 1960s, Alaska Native languages were severely depressed. It wasn't until 1972 that the Alaska state legislature passed the Bilingual Education Bill, which allowed Native children to use and cultivate their traditional language in public schools.

When he was young, my father was sent to such a school in Valdez where Indian children were routinely punished, often physically, for speaking the language of their family. I have too often heard stories by elders of their mistreatment at such schools; most still bear some psychological scars from those years, others still bear the physical ones. Often, if Indian children were caught speaking their Native tongue at these schools, teachers beat them with sticks or forced them into hours of physical labor. Sometimes children were not allowed to eat if caught speaking non-English. It is no wonder that many Indians of my father's generation do not speak their Native language.

It has taken a lifetime for me to understand what happened to my father, but now, in my thirties, I am slowly beginning to make sense of a history of which he does not speak, a history that has reached through the decades to bruise my life as well, and I suspect that most Indian children born and raised by government-boarding-school-educated parents have been affected as well in one way or another. For my father, I have come to believe, the separation from family and tradition robbed him of his ability to genuinely love and trust others, and to forgive, especially to forgive me. We don't speak much although we both live in Alaska. We never did get along well. I recall very few times in my life when I felt that he was truly proud of me, and that longing for a closer father-and-son relationship, even in adulthood, occasionally shows itself in my poetry.

FATHER

My Irish friend, old enough to be my father,
follows close upon the narrow footpath
leading to Mendeltna Creek
beyond the muskeg and frost-sheathed pond
where tundra swans will sleep tonight.
So near October no grayling rise
to bend our lines taut into the icy current
flowing from Old Man Lake.

A raven shakes snow from its back
and huddles low against the slant wind
lifting a brittle leaf across the stream.

That stoic bird is you—
too hardened to complain,
as if it would somehow matter.
Fishing smooth water near your river cabin,
distant as this cold day to summer,
silence filled the void between us.

Father, that this were you beside me, the only sound
our footsteps upon the thin-layered snow.[2]

I wanted my father's love and respect so much that I followed in his footsteps. While a high school senior in Fairbanks attending the same school from which he had graduated twenty-five years earlier, I won an army ROTC scholarship that paid my full college tuition, living expenses, and monthly allowance at any university in America for the duration of my education. I attended the University of Alaska–Fairbanks, from which my father also graduated, and four years later I earned bachelor's degrees in anthropology and English. I later received an honorable discharge from the service after realizing that I had joined the military only to win my father's pride and respect.

I have spent most of my life in Alaska except for a few brief years when I lived in Bellevue, Washington; Sacramento, California; and a year in a small town in Sweden as a foreign exchange student. I grew up at Fort Greely and Fort Wainwright, two army posts in the deserted Alaskan interior. My father was an army officer, and because he is a half-blood Alaska Native, I think the military kept him close to home as an example to other Indians who might join the service as well. Either that or he just asked to be stationed there. I don't really know for certain.

Fort Wainwright is near Fairbanks, but Greely is a hundred miles from anywhere. The post is used mostly for cold-climate training and testing. They couldn't have picked a worse place. I remember winters so dark and long that I thought there was no other season, only winter. Fall is beautiful in Alaska, but short-lived. For a few brief and glorious weeks the colors rival those of Vermont in September, but very soon the leaves are buried under brittle snow with a northern wind driving the chill factor to sixty degrees below zero. I remember as a child temperatures sometimes falling to nearly eighty below and school being canceled. I also recall with fondness and a kind of homesick aching how safe it felt to be indoors looking out the thick frost-lined windows of my classroom at the roving snowdrifts slowly burying everything outside that didn't move or hide from the constant and deliberate onslaught of winter's greed.

Sometimes I spent weeks in the summer staying at my grandmother's house in the small town of Glennallen, just five miles north from where I have a cabin on the bluffs above the confluence of the Copper and Tazlina rivers. Grandma used to hand-sew moccasins and mukluks for me, made from moose hide and trimmed with seal, bear, caribou, beaver, and muskrat fur. I still have several pairs, which I have saved over the decades, the bottoms worn and brittle now, but I treasure them nonetheless. She still makes moccasins and necklaces for me and my daughter, but arthritis makes the work painfully difficult. On cold nights at her cabin she would pile ragged patchwork quilts and potlatch blankets on my small bed until I was warm in the heavy covers that pressed me into the thin mattress.

We had buffalo, too. They freely roamed Delta Junction and the army post. They had been transplanted a few years earlier because conditions were so much like their traditional range on the Great Plains. Some mornings I'd walk to school and find a herd standing between me and the school doors. I'd walk between them, unafraid. They became part of my daily routine, buffalo and moose in our front yard.

My mom's garden was always under siege during the long summer months when the sun never set and cabbages grew six feet across. My best friend since childhood, Andrew Stuart, lived next door. Both our fathers were captains or majors then, I think. Mine eventually retired a lieutenant colonel. Andy was afraid of the buffalo. Sometimes at night he couldn't sleep because he thought they were in his closet just beyond the dim crescent cast by the nightlight glowing in the narrow hallway.

I was raised on the same land as my father and his mother's ancestors before him for more than two thousand years. I learned to love nature, to listen to the wind, and to know the rise of a river by the way gray clouds move low overhead. From years of riverboating the Tanana River I learned to navigate the always-changing channels and shallow gravel bars of interior Alaskan glacial rivers.

When I was an undergraduate I read Mark Twain's *Life on the Mississippi* and I saw myself between those pages. I fell in love with literature then and I have been a writer since even though my education is almost entirely in comparative literature. I have attended a few graduate creative-writing courses as well as several writers' workshops or retreats. My recent poetry has been influenced by such contemporary poets as Tom Sexton, John Daniel, and John Haines, and others like Galway Kinnell, Wendell Berry, and Gary Snyder. My writing comes mostly from life and experience. Having read the world's master writers, I have drawn from what I learned in their work.

Like the cub riverboat pilot in *Life on the Mississippi*, I was raised at a place somewhat similar to that of Clemens's own childhood. In the vast frontier of Alaska I became a lover of rivers, accustomed to their habits and eccentricities.

Most of all, my childhood taught me to hunt and fish, things that are very much a part of my life and writing. Maurice Kenny, a Mohawk poet who grew up in New York State, was also raised by an Indian father who hunted and expected his son to follow in that ancient tradition, a tradition that views the animal as a gift to the hunter, to be treated with respect and honor. The death of the game brings life to the family and community. To disrespect the animal's gift is to dishonor the community. Every part of a moose, for instance, is used, its meat, sinew, skin, horn, nose, and hooves. We carry its spirit with us when we leave the forest and I have always been taught that that is the way it must be. Kenny once wrote that he is now more a hunter of words than a hunter of game. I am both, for the pursuit of either is both challenge and reward.

I recall one of my first hunting trips with my family in the fall of 1969, when I was six years old. My mother shot a moose near Denali while my father was off hunting in the bush. She emptied the Winchester into the animal, never hitting anything vital. It finally died before the box ran out of bullets. When my father returned he cut open the moose and placed me squarely in the middle of the rib cage, waist deep in warm blood with a red two-bladed pocketknife in my hand. He showed me how to cut out the organs and how to quarter the heavy haunches. I was happy. Since then I have been a hunter, and hard lessons have taught me to fear and respect the forces of nature. I could tell stories of bear maulings that have left testimony on my flesh, of wolves chasing me through thick snow in moonlight with nothing but a single-shot .22 rifle to defend myself; and sliding into a deep, blue-hued glacial crevasse where I pulled myself out six inches at a time with a hunting knife in each hand. Once, a large bull moose, easily weighing 1,500 pounds, dragged me inside my tent a hundred yards and into an icy river when I foolishly pitched camp on a well-worn animal trail.

Hunting is important to most Alaska Natives, who still rely heavily on game meat for survival. Because of this, subsistence rights are rigorously defended. For decades now Alaska Natives have fought political battles against the state and federal governments to preserve their rights to hunt and fish for survival as is their tradition. One of the most significant subsistence issues in Alaska today is led by my Ahtna relative Katie John, who is fighting the state in a landmark case to return fishing rights to Indians on the upper Copper River and its tributaries.

Twenty-seven years since I first joined my father in the field, I now hunt with my daughter, Zara. She went with me last fall when my wife shot a large bull caribou with beautiful antlers still in full brown velvet. Zara watched us quarter the animal and even helped a little. Mostly, though, she picked handfuls of ripe blueberries with her full-blood great-grandmother for pancakes and biscuits in the morning.

Whereas much of my poetry celebrates nature, sometimes it portrays scenes of hunting and fishing, taking just what I need to live, but leaving enough for the balance of nature that she may again provide for me and my family the next year. This, above all, may be the legacy my father leaves me, and I often feel his spirit joining me on the hunt.

RITUAL

The moose moves as silently as falling leaves.
Its muddy hooves blend limb and earth
like uprooted trees—tall saplings that dust the woods
and brush the forest with their passage. Fog
fills the sky like tribal smoke rising before me.

I sit, back turned to the wind and cold,
breathing out fire that stalks within me. My
breath conjures up my father who sat in this very spot
holding the ground in place,
cradling a rifle in his arms.

I hear branches snap in my chest, twigs that break
into green bones still alive with sap. Inside
my breast, a flame flickers against winter
licking at my numbness
as my father's hand curls around my finger.[3]

We have a fishwheel on the Copper River that is dark brown from its heavy load of glacial silt. These fish traps are secured along the river's edge where channels run deep and swift currents turn the wheel, their giant wire and birch baskets scooping handfuls of quicksilver salmon and dumping them into a wooden box the size of a pickup truck bed. This summer our wheel brought in two hundred red salmon in one day. It was so full that it was sinking and would surely have gone under if only another dozen fish had been caught. Much of the salmon is salted and hung to dry. Some is slowly smoked over alder after soaking in a sweet and salty brine. Some is canned. In the past few years my uncle Herb has been instructing me in the building, repair, and use of our family wheel. I wrote this poem after one hot August day at fish camp.

TAZLINA

The summer sky is clear save
Drum's cloud-tangled summit.

No shadows darken her
silt-smoothed stones
at the confluence where she is lost
in the salmon-choked Copper
where so many fishermen soon will
line the banks at Chitina,
their long nets lifting the braided water
where once only Indians hung
cranberry-red salmon
on diamond willow racks
to dry in the gentle breeze
that moved like a hungry wolf
along the water's edge to
taste the river's gift.[4]

When a strong run of fish comes through, Indian relatives from far away travel the shoulderless, permafrost-heaved highway to take home their share of the harvest. That is our way, and I always give part of my fish and game meat to elders, my full-blood great-aunt and grandmother usually taking the most.

One of our Indian villages, Copper Center, sits upon the southern shore of the Copper River only eighty miles from Valdez. In the early part of this century copper ore was heavily mined near the village and Chitina on what is now the Edgerton Highway. Today, however, there is little or no economy and most Copper River Indians live in substandard housing and exist below poverty levels. Influenced by another Alaskan poet, John Haines, I wrote this poem one evening after walking along the riverbank just beyond town, saddened by the decaying remains of a once-vibrant village community.

THE ROAD TO CHITINA

By the Edgerton highway, towards
Sanford, a tattered fishwheel,
its birch basket catching not even
the tired wind.

                Near the village,
when night fills tall shadows
like Raven's unfolding wings, a
truck rusts in an empty field.[5]

In the freezing winter of 1994, my full-blood great-uncle, Joe Sec-ondchief, died at the age of ninety-four. Born only fifteen years after Copper River Indians' first contact with whites in 1885, Joe was one of the few remaining speakers of our language. He spoke no English. His wife, Morrie, who is also full-blood Ahtna, still lives in the same small log cabin he built when they married in 1928. It is slowly sinking into the tundra and until last year she had only an old woodstove that creaked and moaned while it burned split spruce and birch. She still hauls water from a half-mile away. Morrie is now one of only about eighty surviving speakers of our language. Very little effort has been made to revive it, and almost all the remaining speakers are elders. The younger generations are not interested. A colleague in Fairbanks, linguist Michael Krauss, attributes this to radio and television, what he has called "cultural nerve gas."

I learned our language from my two grandmothers and from other elders. Now I am one of only a handful of Indian speakers, and I am the only tribal member able to write in our language. In 1998, I completed and published *The Ahtna Pronunciation Dictionary*, as well as two bilingual children's books and a language-poster series. About two years ago, I began to write poems in Ahtna and English. Since then, several poetry collections have been published written entirely in my grandmother's tongue, including this poem from *The Snow Has No Voice:*

TALT'AEZI BENE' XELTSE'E

Hwt'aedze xelts'e'de kolaexi Talt'aezi Bene'
saghani ggay ye ts' ezdaa
ts'abaeli det'en
luy'tniniltl'iits k'ay' giis kanghilyaan
tuu nelt' uuts'.

EVENING AT FIELDING LAKE

This evening at Fielding Lake
a raven sits in thick-branched spruce
while rain clouds
move below a full moon
turning the water black.[6]

Almost all Native American literature has been written in English. It's time for a canon in our grandmothers' tongues. Although the reading audience may be very small indeed, language is one of the key identifiers of cultural identity and differentiation. It's part of reclaiming our identity.

When my great-uncle Joe Secondchief died, the village held a potlatch in his honor. About two hundred Indians came from a dozen villages and a moose was killed for the event, as the government allows for such traditional cultural ceremonies. Porcupine, beaver, caribou, and bear were also served as were more contemporary dishes. I took time off from teaching at the university to attend with my two uncles. It was a cold weekend, one of remembrance, self-reflection, and sadness. We danced traditional dances all night, and my grandmother directed me as to who was to receive the many gifts of blankets, rifles, cash, and boxes of dry goods as she spoke to the participants in Ahtna and English. I will never forget the honor I felt in participating, nor the intense spirituality of the ceremony.

POTLATCH

All day they arrive at Copper Center
huddled along the frost-lined river
far from city lights
to mourn Great-Uncle's death.

From the sacred circle of our clan
skin drums echo
a feeble tremor in the frozen earth.
Elder voices lament through the Great House:

'Syuu' nac' eltsin yen
A potlatch is made for him.

Pulses quicken to the ancient rhythm.
Dancers stream like vibrations
across a wooden floor
heavy with rifles and colored blankets.

'Unggadi kanada'yaet yen ne'et dakozet
A potlatch song is sung for him in heaven.

My uncle and I fill the hollow in silence;
somber guests depart beyond a small church.

> A raven lights upon an Orthodox cross;
> our thoughts are soon filled like the grave.
>
> Tonight I have learned that there is an end
> to everything, to every light.
>
> In that end, even the yawning of brittle leaves
> breaks the solitude of night.[7]

Another loss that greatly affected my life and writing was the death of my younger brother, who killed himself in 1987 after a bout of depression caused by regret, legal troubles, and alcoholism. I've never drunk much or used drugs, but I've been depressed and had some troubles when I was in my late teens. After James's death my parents divorced and our lives went to hell for a while. It took me nearly five years before I could write about him, such was my own anger and remorse:

Changing Seasons

> Of course he still haunts me.
>
> I never expected him
> to jump into his grave that spring
> admitting it was over.
>
> On clear summer mornings
> I see our reflections upon the river
> as my fly breaks the smooth surface.
>
> And he walks with me in fall
> when I hunt grouse in thick alder,
> rifles strung heavy on bent shoulders.
>
> For many years I will find his footprints
> in fresh snow and hear him whistle
> from across the frozen river.
>
> He was always an impatient brother.[8]

An Indian cousin of mine, Kenny, killed himself with a rifle several years ago in Copper Center. Like my brother, depression and drink killed him. It wasn't so much his own drinking as it was everyone's around him. Their lives and deaths remind me of James Welch's *The*

Death of James Loney and D'Arcy McNickle's *The Surrounded*. In reading those novels I can't help but see my own relatives in their depictions of Indian life, especially the young men and boys, surrounded by the destructive influences of alcoholism, chronic unemployment, poverty, uprootedness, dissoluteness, and hopelessness. My novel, *A Cold Day to Die*, addresses these issues. I think Kenny was ambitious, wanting more out of his own life but trapped by the circumstances around him. He had a wife and child.

Suicide rates are high among Native Americans and highest of all among Alaska Native men between the ages of eighteen and twenty-nine. James and Kenny were in their mid-twenties when they, like many young Native men, fell into depression, the bottle, and eventually into their premature graves hacked out of the frozen northern soil.

Ralph Salisbury wrote in *I Tell You Now* about how much harassment and discrimination he suffered as a professor and how "the university is a battleground where the struggle for Native American survival must be won." I have certainly found this to be true. How fearful some colleagues are that Native American art, writing, and scholarship may not be second-rate as often stereotyped, but instead equal to and even surpassing their own! As a young Native American writer, teacher, and scholar, I have learned how effortlessly prejudice and discrimination deceive reason and human kindness.

Under state and federal laws, and by the Alaska Native Land Claims Settlement Act (ANSCA, Revised), I am legally recognized as Alaska Indian. I am a descendant of the Talcheena Clan of the Ahtna People. I am also Cherokee by blood. I have a BIA number and I was raised to know the traditions of my father's people. For the past three years, I have been the tribally appointed executive director of our Heritage Foundation. During my grade school years I participated in events supported by federal Native education programs designed for Indian students. I have never questioned my Native identity nor had anyone until I became a college professor and writer.

Just recently, I read an article in a newspaper about a seventeen-year-old from Mississippi who was raised by his mother after his parents divorced before he was one year old. Although his biological father was one-half Alaska Native, the teen never knew anything of that heritage. By his own admission he always considered himself just a "honky, white person" who knew absolutely nothing about American

Indian cultures or traditions. Finally, near adulthood, his grandparents (his biological father's parents) brought him to visit their village. It was then that he learned with great astonishment that he was Native American. The article continued, stating how he knew nothing about his father's heritage, and yet the teen and the article writer both concluded that he was truly Native and that this knowledge was very important to his life. I bring this up not from any spite (I am glad that the teen may choose to go on to learn about and eventually to participate in his newfound identity), but as a comparison to my situation and to that of others like me who have similar or less blood quantum but significantly more cultural involvement and knowledge.

My Indianness had not been disputed my entire life until my writings began to be published at a national level and I began to encroach on other writers' literary niches. Recently, several Indian writers have told me that my Ahtna and Cherokee ancestry and my status as an enrolled member in a federally recognized tribe does not support my Indian identity. One writer even wrote to me saying that people like me are never *really* Indian, and that no matter how fully my tribe accepts me as a member, other Indians are under no obligation to accept me at all. I agree in part with the latter portion of this statement, in that it is certainly not up to one tribe (Coeur d'Alene) to decide another tribe's (Apache) membership criteria. The letter concluded by telling me that I might find acceptance with others like me, those people with an "eye-dropper" full of Indian blood, but that the "true skins" will never accept me.

What bothers me so much about such attacks are the questions that arise from them. As described above, a teen near adulthood lives his entire life with absolutely no knowledge of his Native American identity nor any influence from Indian community or cultural tradition, yet because of such genetics alone he would be accepted as a Native American writing about the Native American condition by the above-mentioned Indian author should this teen pen a single poem. On the other hand, I have a similar blood quantum, have been raised by my Indian father and immersed in our traditional ways all my life, so much so that I participate in our traditional ceremonies and can speak and write in our near-extinct language.

I wonder that if a precise blood level is selected to define who is and who is not a Native American writer or artist, how many Native Americans would not be Indian at all, and what would happen to our children and grandchildren? Supporters of such "quantum logic" think too much of the present and of their niche in contemporary literature and art. But if "Indianness" is determined by a code that restricts too much only so that it limits new writers and artists from being accepted because of possible economic competition, what will happen to future descendants? Will our own children be alienated? Will reservation childhood friends be able to claim their Indian identity? If we say that an individual must be of a certain blood quantum to be a Native American writer, what will happen in twenty, thirty, or fifty years when, through natural deaths, suicides, intertribal marriages, and miscegenation, our own children will no longer be Indian under whatever blood-quantum standard is established today? Will the future destruction of Native American identity be at the hands of Native-imposed limits that do not preserve and cultivate tradition and culture, but instead alienate future members?

In my melancholy following these correspondences, when I too might have embraced the easy escape of my brother and cousin, I traveled instead to the sacred earth of my ancestors and there was lifted and given back my life and pride. I know who I am. No one will ever take that away from me.

RESURRECTION

A western wind has borne my lonely soul
to this sacred place,
its ancient village and rotting graves
set along the river's edge.

My lean shadow falls behind me,
disappearing in a dark forest of pine.
The river's song, rising on Eagle's slow wings,
echoes inside me.

In the past's familiar tongue
I reclaim myself.
The voice of ancestors lifts me
as I begin to heal.

The wind shifts, suddenly,
its breath filling my spirit like a sail.

> Resurrected, I leave at sunset
> knowing I will return to this sacred earth.

NOTES

1. This poem, written in the Ahtna Athabaskan language, is the first poem to be written entirely in the traditional dialect, which had no written form until recently.
2. From *Poetpourri*
3. From *The Beloit Poetry Journal*
4. From *Explorations*
5. From *The Kenyon Review*
6. From *Rosebud*
7. From *The Journal of Alaska Native Arts*
8. From *The Atlantic Monthly*

They Moved Over
the Mountain

Luci Tapahonso

A Diné (Navajo) from Shiprock, New Mexico, Luci Tapahonso is a widely published poet. She is the author of five books of poetry, the most recent of which is Blue Horses Rush In *from the University of Arizona (1997). She has published three children's books including* Songs of Shiprock Fair, *which celebrates the annual fall event in northwest New Mexico. She is a professor of American Indian studies and English at the University of Arizona in Tucson.*

I grew up in a large extended family, as is the Diné (Navajo) custom, on a large farm north of Shiprock, New Mexico, on the Diné Nation. We had a number of caretakers besides our parents; among these were older siblings, various relatives who lived with us off and on, as well as neighbors.

My earliest memories are of my mother singing as she performed various tasks: sitting at her sewing machine, cleaning house, or setting circles of flat dough in a hot skillet for fry bread or *naneezkadi,* tortillas. She was always busy, and no wonder; there were numerous children and various relatives. Sometimes in the afternoon, she would lie down for a while, and as if that were a signal, we would say to each other, "*Nihimí nésti!* Our mother's lying down!" We scrambled to lie beside her. She moved to the middle of the bed, and we arranged ourselves around her—dry elbows, knees, and dirty faces. "You babies, be still. I'm resting," she would say. We wanted to feel her skin, trace the designs on her dress, and listen to her hum until she fell asleep. What courage she had to nap with several kids crawling and wriggling right beside her.

Nihidá'í, one of our mother's brothers, lived west of our home, and he walked everywhere; he never owned a car. We often saw him approaching at a distance. Sometimes he would cut across the field, instead of taking the bottom road alongside the fields. When we saw him, we called out, "'*Aadi nihidá'í yaash yigaal!* Our mother's brother is coming!" We stopped everything and some children ran inside the house or the *chaha'oh,* the brush shadehouse during the summer, and began putting bread, coffee cups, and food on the table; others ran to meet him and walk back with him, holding his hands, or hanging on to his back belt loop. Still others darted frantically around the house looking in drawers and shelves, calling out, "*Tl'oolts'osi la, shimá!* My mother, I need some string now!" All the while, we called out over and over, " '*Aadi nihidá'í yaash!* Here comes our mother's brother!'" Our mother, or another adult, heated coffee and prepared to feed him. When he arrived at the house, we children would become very shy, but we stayed near him, fighting silently to sit on his lap, or we sat pressed against him. Still we were too bashful to speak. He would murmur to each of us, "My daughter, you've grown. Do you help your mother, my baby? Sit here, my little one." We'd smile while looking at the ground. Nihidá'í did not speak English, and he always seemed old to me because of his wise and gentle manner. While he drank coffee and talked with the adults, we'd stay nearby, sometimes sitting at his feet. After it was clear the "serious" conversation was over, one of us would hand two or three loops of cotton twine to Nihidá'í.

Nihidá'í was a master at telling and performing stories with string. As he talked, little characters or land formations appeared and moved flawlessly between his fingers as the story progressed. We were enthralled and amused each time. We were invariably consistent in this request, even in the summertime, though we knew clearly that string stories should not be told in the summer. He would say, "*Shuu shá'álchíní, shiigo eihane' igii doobda yajil tihdah.* Listen, my children, these stories cannot be told in the summer. Remember that, my little ones." So he sang to us, bouncing us one at a time on his knee. He sang humorous songs about goats, donkeys, lambs, and other animals. In many of the songs, animal sounds are imitated, and we all made the noises together and laughed until our stomachs ached. When he left, the whole process was repeated in reverse—the sudden shyness and quietness, the clingy possessiveness and our accompanying him until he told us to return home. Inevitably, one or two kids had fallen asleep during the stories, so there were fewer kids to see him off but the same number of puppies and dogs.

It was clear Nihidá'í loved us, though he never told us so. It was in his voice, his joy in seeing us, the way he endured our clinging hands, his pride in our presence. As we grew older, we often marveled at Nihidá'í's patience during his visits. As our mother's brother, he was the quintessential *adá'í* because he was responsible for our upbringing as much as our father was. In the Diné matrilineal culture, his role was to teach, guide, and discipline us. Thus we were careful not to do things that might be "reported" to Nihidá'í; we couldn't bear to disappoint him or make him sad. Sometimes when we were unruly, my mother would say, "I hope that I won't have to tell my brother about any of you." She'd say this quietly, almost under her breath, and we became frightened. Sometimes Nihidá'í watched us when my parents went on a trip, and we had such fun. He played with us, let us mess up the house, and essentially gave us all his attention. Much later, I learned that he was giving us "quality time." He had a family and children of his own, but when we were with him, we were "number one" to him. The same was true of our father's relationship with his nieces and nephews. Likewise, my mother had a number of relatives, and maybe friends, with whom she had close relationships. When she spoke of them, she often referred to them as her "sister" or "younger brother" as if they were her biological siblings. We knew who her "real" brothers and sisters were, but knew that to think of people in these terms was to show love and respect for them. Therefore, we did not use English terms such as "cousins" or "uncle" for anyone. Such titles seemed to connote a distance that didn't exist. We understood kinship roles such as this from early on, and it was hard to imagine being outside the security of such relationships.

Many years later, I wrote the following poem in tribute to Nihidá'í, who passed on in early 1985.

HILLS BROTHERS COFFEE

My uncle is a small man.
In Navajo, we call him, "shidá'í,"
   my mother's brother.

He doesn't know English,
   but his name in the white way is Tom Jim.
   He lives about a mile or so
   down the road from our house.

One morning he sat in the kitchen,
drinking coffee.
   I just came over, he said.
   The store is where I'm going to.

He tells me about how my mother seems to be gone
every time he comes over.
   Maybe she sees me coming
   then runs and jumps in her car

speeds away!
he says smiling.

We both laugh—just to think of my mother
jumping in her car and speeding.

I pour him more coffee
and he spoons in sugar and cream
until it looks almost like a chocolate shake.
Then he sees the coffee can.
 oh, that's that coffee with the man in a dress
 like a church man.
 Ah-h, that's the one that does it for me.
 Very good coffee.

I sit down again and he tells me,
 Some coffee has no kick.
 But this one is the one.
 It does it good for me.

I pour us both a cup
and while we wait for my mother,
his eyes crinkle with the smile and he says,
 Yes, ah yes. This is the very one
 (putting in more sugar and cream).

So I usually buy Hills Brothers coffee.
Once or sometimes twice a day,
I drink a hot coffee and

it sure does it for me.[1]

Sometimes on summer evenings, we cooked outside over an open fire and then ate sitting around the fire or at a picnic table. As we ate, my father or another adult would begin "talking." This type of talking was different in tone and subject from ordinary conversation. We learned early to remain quiet and still when they said, *"Ni zhe'e yalti,"* or *"Ah shi sinda heyda yalltii go."* "Your father is talking." "Sit quietly when someone begins to talk." They would tell stories about various ancestors or faraway relatives (whom we didn't see often), or they told about the stars and various astronomical bodies, or maybe they shared concerns or made plans. During these times, blankets were brought out for the little ones and we sat wrapped up, or leaned against the nearest adult while the youngest ones eventually fell asleep on someone's lap and were carried to bed. Such summer evenings were filled with quiet voices, dogs barking far away, the fire crackling, and often we could hear the faint drums and songs of a ceremony somewhere in the distance. There were no electric lights, and the night sky was so dark and black. When the adults talked about the stars, we'd lie on our backs wrapped in blankets and the stars seemed within reach. There were no highways nearby then, and many people didn't own cars. We could hear the horses snorting in nearby fields, frogs croaking, the tinkling of sheep bells, and the motor of an occasional passing car a few miles in the distance.

My childhood is intertwined with memories of various relatives "talking" to me and sharing by implication the value of silence, listening, and observation. We spoke Diné from birth, but because of our parents' negative experiences in school, they taught us basic English concepts like the alphabet, our American names (which we didn't use at home), our birth dates, and census numbers before we entered public school.

My father began school at a boarding school in the early 1900s. He was assigned his stepfather's name (Tohbaha tsoh) as his surname, rather than his given name, Ashkii Setah Begay ("the son of Hastiin Setah"). Traditional Diné did not have last names. He was given a teacher's first name, Eugene, and Tohbaha tsoh was Anglicized to Tapahonso.

He and other children were punished for speaking Diné, by both non-Indian and Indian school employees. He tells of little children who were forced to stand huddled in a group against a building in a snowstorm because they had spoken Navajo. Although he fared well academically, because of the memory of the various forms of punishment he and other children endured, he was determined that his children would not be mistreated because they knew only Diné.

My mother was the youngest in her family and began school because her parents felt that it would be in the family's best interests to have one educated child. The Diné were undergoing major cultural transitions in 1924, when she was taken to Shiprock Camp School. The family's livelihood—raising sheep and livestock and dry farming—was in imminent danger because of government-imposed sheep reduction programs, controlled grazing, and serious drought conditions. Her name, Honaazbah, became Lucille Descheene. She was allowed to keep her father's name, Descheene. She, too, tells of the harsh treatment of children, some as young as four years old. All were expected to answer questions in English, though they had just arrived at school. Their clothes and other personal items were thrown away and pronounced "filthy." They were then issued uniforms, identical gray dresses and sturdy patent shoes. My mother's eyes brim with tears as she tells of how she didn't understand why the school staff were so demanding and disrespectful to the children. "They didn't talk to us," she said, "they yelled and screamed at us like we couldn't hear. We couldn't understand English, but we weren't deaf. I hated English because I thought you had to yell if you talked English."

My father attended school through the fifth grade and loved reading. My mother stayed in school until she began high school, and loved athletics. My father served in the War in the Philippines and Japan, and then worked as an interpreter, among other jobs, for many years. My mother worked in the nearby Bureau of Indian Affairs boarding school dormitory caring for children whose experiences were similar to hers, albeit many decades later. She sympathized with the children, and took great care to be compassionate and to speak Diné to them. Besides, she often told us, many of the children were related to her, or to us (her children) through our father's clan. Thus her obligations extended beyond her job description. It may have been because of these experiences that they felt our success as adults depended upon formal education, as well as being knowledgeable about Diné family history and culture.

About fifty yards from our main house was an old storage shed, which was lined with bookshelves. My parents read to us in the dim coolness of the shed. We weren't allowed to take books from the shed because they might be lost or damaged. We learned to care for books so that everyone would have a chance to enjoy them. My parents subscribed to a number of magazines which were kept in the "old shed." My father is a great saver of things and all our school records and miscellaneous papers were stored there. So in addition to the usual stories and songs that were a part of ordinary Diné life, we were read to constantly.

In our early childhood, we children rarely left home, even though we lived only three miles outside of downtown Shiprock. Our contact with the "American" world was quite limited. Whatever was "out there" meant little to us. This was due, in part, to the fact that there was not yet electricity in the farm area of Shiprock—therefore we didn't watch TV. During the few times we encountered non-Navajos, we children didn't talk, but stayed near (or behind) the adults. We weren't afraid; it was that they seemed foreign to us—they talked loudly, gestured dramatically, and looked at us brazenly.

My first memory of speaking English in school consists of three words—"what," "yes," and "no." When a white adult spoke to me, I would say "What!" not as a question, but as a loud, emphatic answer. I repeated this until I understood what was being said. Since speaking Diné was forbidden, many of us did not talk at school or in the presence of whites. I also said "yes" and "no" in the same direct way, as if they might misunderstand that single word. It became clear that the two settings, school and home, were distinctly different places and incompatible. Yet because my parents had prepared us, and had read to us from storybooks, *Life* magazine, and *National Geographic,* I was intrigued by the surprises and mysteries the written word held, and learning to read and write came easily. Soon I was representing my class on "program nights," reading entire paragraphs from "Sally, Dick and Jane" books to a gym full of people.

Even though this was the case at school, daily life at home went on as usual. We had responsibilities of various types—chickens to bring in at dusk, wood and coal bins to replenish for the night, corn to pick and shuck, animals to feed, and a myriad of other activities we divided among ourselves. We had been taught that to "help out" was to be "of use"—a common characteristic in Diné culture. We turned many of the tasks into games: naming the furrows when we irrigated, and cheering for "our rows" as the water inched to the end of the fields. We learned to count in English and Diné when we planted corn. It was fun because there were so many of us and together, we were a creative and imaginative group. My parents would tell people casually that "our children really help out" so that they had time to devote to major tasks, such as weaving, preparing crops to store, construction, and farm work. We were aware that maintaining a farm, having a large family, and raising animals were hard work, and that our parents were seen in the community as industrious people. Our home life didn't change when we began school—we spoke a mixture of English and Diné, we were told stories and sung to, and various relatives visited or lived with us off and on.

This prose piece is about that period of my childhood:

It Was a Special Treat

Trips to Farmington were a special treat when we were children. Sometimes when we didn't get to go along, we cried so hard that we finally had to draw straws to decide fairly who could get to go. My oldest brother always went because he drove, my other brother went because he helped carry laundry, and my father went because he was the father, and my mother went because she had the money and knew where to go and what to buy. And only one or two kids were allowed to go because we got in the way and begged for things all the time.

We got up early on the Saturdays that we were going to town. We would get ready, sort laundry, and gather up pop bottles that we turned in for money. My father always checked the oil and tires on the pickup, and then he and my brothers would load the big laundry tubs, securing the canvas covers with heavy wooden blocks. We would drive out of the front yard, and the unfortunate ones who had to stay home waved good-bye sullenly. The dogs chased the truck down the road a ways before turning home.

In Farmington, we would go to the laundry first. It was always dark and clammy inside. We liked pulling the clothes out of the wringer even though my mother was nervous about letting us help. After that, we drove downtown and parked in the free lot north of Main Street. Sometimes my father got off at the library, and we picked him up after we finished shopping. Someone always had to "watch" the pickup, and usually the one who was naughty at the laundry had to sit in the pickup for two or three hours while everyone else got to "see things" around town. If my father didn't go to the library, the kids were off the hook, naughty or not, because he waited in the pickup and read the *Reader's Digest.*

When we stopped at Safeway, our last stop, it was early evening. My mother would buy some bologna or cooked chicken in plastic-wrapped trays and a loaf of bread. We would eat this on our way home. After the groceries were packed in securely under the canvas and wooden blocks, we talked about who we saw, what we should have bought instead of what we did buy (maybe we could exchange it next time), then the talking would slow down and by the time we reached the Blue Window gas station, everyone but my father was asleep.

He would start singing in Navajo in a clear, strong voice and once in a while, my mother would ask him about a certain song she heard once. "Do you know it? It was something like this . . . " and she would sing a bit, and he would catch it and finish the song. I would whisper to my sister, "He sounds like those men on Navajo Hour." "I know. It's so good," she'd answer, and we'd sleep until we reached home.[2]

In elementary school, I begged to attend Navajo Methodist Mission School in Farmington, thirty miles away. An older brother and sister had graduated from there, and the campus was beautiful, and there was a huge playground, which looked unused. I wanted to play there for hours and hours on end, and because I had heard that kids at boarding school had only one chore a day, rather than three or four chores as we did at home. Perhaps it was the "Sally, Dick and Jane" influence, but I knew that children elsewhere lived differently. Driven by my desire for one simple chore a day and nonstop play at a deserted playground, I was determined to be the best student in my grade. My parents finally agreed, in part because my teacher had said I had talent in music and art, and that the public school might not allow these "talents" to develop.

I was more proficient in English by then, and was not surprised to find that Diné was forbidden at the mission school. Students were undaunted by this restriction and simply waited for bedtime. After the dorm mother had gone into her room for the night, we jumped out of our little ruffled beds and gathered in moonlight beside a window or on one bed, and told stories in Diné. After school, we climbed the immense hills behind the school, and sat at the top overlooking Farmington, ate our after-school snack, our conversation mostly Diné.

My most difficult adjustment was to be separated from my siblings. I had never had my own bed, and for the first few nights, I slept on the hardwood floor rolled in a blanket, because I was afraid of rolling off the bed due to the smooth, tight sheets (we did not use bedsheets at home). The sheets seemed dangerously slick and cold. I always remember wearing polished cotton pajamas for the first time, and thinking that the combination of the two seemingly slippery fabrics was a perilous situation.

At Navajo Mission, I began reading books to fill spare time between school and meals as the fascination with the playground wore off after a month or two, and primarily because I couldn't understand the Christian religion. It seemed everyone but me was familiar with the concepts of Jesus, sin, and forgiveness. Although I grasped the fundamental idea of the world ending and "bad people burning forever," it seemed that there must be more, so a self-imposed project was to read the entire set of *Uncle Arthur's Bedtime Stories*—a series of Christian children's stories. I was mystified by the portrayals of God as all-knowing and ever-present, and that sin seemed to be unavoidable. I had discussions with the pastors, Mr. Bass and Mr. Cloyd, as well as various teachers.

When I came home, my parents explained that I was at boarding school for academic reasons, and they did not make disparaging remarks about the school or its teachings. Instead they and other adults emphasized I should remember that I am Diné and to remember everything I was taught at home. It was at Navajo Mission that I learned to love writing, reading, and acquired good study skills (probably against my wishes!). I was praised by teachers for creative skills— artwork, theater, leadership abilities, and writing.

Later, in public high school, I edited the school newspaper and yearbook, among other extracurricular activities. My English teacher at Shiprock High School, Norma Harvey, encouraged me constantly, and read everything I wrote beyond class assignments. She was excited about my writing, which I felt was ordinary adolescent expressions. I was writing only in English and it didn't occur to me that it was possible to also write in Diné, maybe because it appeared that it did not belong in academic learning. Thus I learned to associate the physical act of writing with English, and Diné occupied an entirely different sphere in my daily life. I began keeping a journal and another notebook for writing poetry. My family encouraged me indirectly by relying on me to write formal letters, draft "IOUs," or respond to or explain various documents. They said I was "good at that kind of stuff"—meaning written English.

Throughout the years following high school, when I had my eldest daughter, Lori, and worked at a number of jobs—waitress, telephone operator, and as a stringer for several local and national Indian newspapers—I continued to keep a journal, write poetry, and read avidly.

When I started college at the University of New Mexico, I began as a journalism major, then, in my sophomore year, enrolled in a short-story writing class Leslie Marmon Silko was teaching. This course turned out to be pivotal. I wrote my first short story, "The Snakeman,"[3] and later shared my poems for the first time. As a quiet, intense student, I was surprised and embarrassed by the enthusiastic response from classmates and Silko. The experience was one of exhilaration and, more important, of confirmation. I was genuinely surprised that ordinary Diné life and experiences could be considered "literature." The fact that Silko was Indian, twenty-eight years old, a mother, and a published writer had an equally enormous impact on me.

The experiences brought together the two seemingly disparate ways of thinking and speaking for me. The idea of remembering my distinct place within my family (biological, extended, clan, and tribal) sustained my family and me throughout college. Although I maintained strong ties with my community and continued to speak Diné, I did not learn to write or read it. My daughters' father, Earl Ortiz, is from Acoma Pueblo, and conversation in our home consisted primarily of English, Navajo, and Acoma phrases. Earl probably spoke more Navajo than Acoma. In Albuquerque, many of our friends, neighbors, as well as their teachers, spoke Spanish. Our daughters, Lori and Misty, were around four languages—Navajo, Acoma, English, and Spanish. Whereas my childhood stories are centered in one place, Lori and Misty have varied, myriad memories, including Shiprock, Acoma and Albuquerque, and finally, Lawrence, Kansas. Although I wasn't speaking Diné constantly, all emotional and primal occurrences were and are still expressed in my first language, regardless of other influences.

The writing process begins as thoughts or feelings in the Diné language, which are then translated. As I think of, or remember, incidents to write about, the initial idea or "telling" is in Diné, then it is literally translated in the physical act of writing or typing. The idea of writing means writing in English, but the Diné language is the language of basic emotions.

Over the last few years, I have begun to learn to write in Diné though I am not literate yet. I have also realized that there are many expressions and phrases that are best left in Diné—that the English translation falls short of conveying the true meaning. In those cases, I leave lines in Diné and allow the context of the poem or story to convey the connotative meaning. Because Diné seems to be a more sensual and emotional language, this does not appear to weaken the work.

It's important to allow the opportunity for my family, relatives, and other Diné people to hear in college auditoriums or hotel ballrooms (and wherever else I read) the kind of stories and humor in the language that defines us, our families and our very existence. If an audience is confused by the use of Diné, it is only a fraction of what my parents and other family members remember as their educational experiences. Unless our children (biological, extended, and clan) hear written literature as being relevant to their lives, they have little reason to write their own stories.

In 1990, we moved to Lawrence, Kansas, where my husband, Bob Martin, took the position of president of Haskell Indian Nations University, and I joined the faculty as assistant professor at the University of Kansas. I was not prepared for how much I would miss the mountains, the quality of light, and deep blue skies. I had not lived outside of the Southwest before. I dealt with homesickness by telling and retelling stories of my childhood and about our family and relatives in New Mexico. Bob and I had grown up differently, as he is Cherokee. As I remembered and told these stories daily for both him and my daughters, I wrote also. By talking and laughing, sometimes crying, about the part of our lives that would always be a part of the communities we come from, we were strengthened and reminded of the essence of storytelling.

Thus writing is a way to continue the practice of telling stories, of knowing our relatives, and of relaying our family and tribal history for our children and grandchildren, who live in a vastly different world than mine was. I tell the children and grandchildren stories about my siblings, my parents, their relatives, and about places at home, so that they will know the ways in which these stories have always been told. I write, too, to honor my elders: my parents, my relatives, clan, and tribal relatives. I want to share what they have given me as it defines my livelihood figuratively and metaphorically.

I will conclude with this story of my mother as a little girl—old stories such as this allow me to imagine *shimásáni,* my maternal grandmother, and *shicheii,* my maternal grandfather, both of whom died decades before I was born. This is a part of where my writing comes from—one of my mother's earliest memories, a window into my past almost eight decades ago. This is, for me, a "way of looking" both at the present and what is yet to come.

My mother was born at Rockpoint on the Arizona side of the Beautiful Mountain in the Carriso Mountain range. While very young, she and her family—her mother, sister, two brothers and stepfather—moved across the mountain to Niistáá, herding the sheep and horses ahead of them.

Tsinaabaas nakii bił jin naajiin. They had two horse-drawn wagons which they used in the move. When they left, some relatives asked them to leave one of the wagons, for they were highly prized and hard to come by. After much discussion, my mother's family left with both wagons. *Tsinaabąąs ei aheisii shimásáni bi inda, ako bi dashi la shido noo bini naa akoohotsa.* The wagons belonged to my grandmother, whose husband had bought them from a white man years before. But my grandmother's younger sister wanted one for herself, and for the use of the other relatives who would remain at Rockpoint. Since they were sisters, she could make this claim.

My grandmother thought ahead to the futures of her teenage sons and eleven-year-old daughter, and she refused her sister's request. Besides, they would also need the wagons to haul logs and water when they built their hogan and corrals at the new place. My own mother was still very small—maybe three years old.

So their departure was subdued and tinged with more sadness than usual because of this incident. Later on, her sister and others came to see them at Niistáá, and the sisters cried when they saw each other. They were happy to be together again.

T'ah ndi áníts'íísíigo ákodhodzaa, ákoh ayóó bénáshniih. Even though I was very little, I still remember this clearly, my mother said. On the way over the mountain, the weeds and plants were very high. My mother said, "I could barely see because it had grown higher than me in some places. I cried to walk, and they let me, but they had to keep an eye on me because I could easily get lost. I walked separating a path ahead of me with my arms. I remember that I was very little, and thought it was really something to walk alone in the tall plants."

NOTES

1. "Hills Brothers Coffee." *Saanii Dahataal: The Women Are Singing.* Tucson: University of Arizona Press, 1993. 27–28.

2. "It Was a Special Treat." *Saanii Dahataal.* Tucson: University of Arizona Press, 1993. 15–16.

3. "The Snakeman." *Saanii Dahataal.* Tucson: University of Arizona Press, 1993. 79–83.

RED ECHOES

CLIFFORD E. TRAFZER

Clifford E. Trafzer, of mixed Wyandot and German ancestry, was born in 1949. Among his many books are The Judge *(1975),* American Indian Identity *(1984), and* Renegade Tribe: The Palouse Indians and the Invasion of the Inland Pacific Northwest *(1986). He has written several children's books, edited the fiction anthologies* Earth Song, Sky Spirit *(1993), and* Blue Dawn, Red Earth *(1996), as well as a collection of traditional Native American stories from the Columbia Plateau. Vice chairman of the California Native American Heritage Commission, and professor of Native American Studies and History at the University of California, Riverside, Trafzer lives with his wife, Lee Ann, and his three children in Yucaipa, California.*

Along the northern banks of the Saint Lawrence River lived a group of Wyandot people, descendants of the Woman Who Fell From the Sky. Within the village lived a boy who was liked by his elders, particularly the very old. The boy was intelligent, articulate, well mannered, generous, and athletic. He deferred to elders and enjoyed listening to their stories, taking from the spoken words wisdoms of past generations. As he grew older, elders looked to him as a future leader, one who would work for the benefit of others rather than act in a selfish manner. The boy grew in the estimation of his elders, but his popularity among his peers diminished. The boys in the village became jealous of the boy, and some of them learned to hate him. They plotted against him, deciding to kill him in a plan that would exonerate all of them. The boys organized a hunting party, including the young man they despised.

In canoes they traveled to an island in the middle of the Great River, an island inhabited by a number of animals. When the boys paddled ashore, they agreed to hunt in different directions and return to the canoes just before dusk. All of them set out to hunt, including the young man the others wished dead. The young man carefully moved through the forest, searching for signs, but he found no skat or tracks. He found no animals at all, and before the sun traveled too far west, he returned to camp. He arrived as the sun was setting, only to find that the others had left. The young man was without a canoe in the middle of the raging river, far from shore. Nightfall quickly approached, so the young man determined to climb a tree and spend the night sleeping in the broad branches. Early in the morning, just before dawn, he was awakened by heavy breath down the back of his neck.

When the boy found enough courage, he looked up to see a Mountain Lion with his paw raised as if to strike. The young man closed his eyes and waited for the blow that would tear his head from his body. The blow never came. The young man looked again and saw the paw raised as if ready to strike. This time he saw a splinter lodged deeply in Mountain Lion's paw. In the young man's head, a voice told him to reach up and pull the splinter from the Mountain Lion's paw. When he pulled the splinter out, Mountain Lion thanked him and offered something in return. Mountain Lion gave the young man the gift of the hunter, saying that forevermore the young man would be a great hunter and provider for his friends and family. Mountain Lion told the young man that he knew the other boys had brought him to the island to kill him and that the boys had returned to the village to report his death. Mountain Lion assured him that the elders would not believe the tale, and they would return for the young man.

Mountain Lion told the boy to keep a pure heart, remembering always the good that he had given him and not the evil the boys had intended. This would be the young man's guiding principle, and he kept it with him throughout his life as a leader, provider, and warrior who worked for the good of others. He kept his story to himself until he grew old, and during his last days, he shared his story with others. They in turn shared the story, and through the oral tradition, it is still alive. Like other oral traditions, the story is part of Wyandot history and literature, offering ways of knowing that are as viable today as they were when people had closer relationships with the Animal and Plant people. These stories are a part of history ignored by most scholars, but not by Georges E. Sioui, a leader of the Wendat-Huron people and a professor at the American Indian Federated College, University of Regina. In his *Amerindian Autohistory*, Sioui writes that his father told him how to succeed in school and life.

> ... you must write down what you are told to be the truth; but don't believe that it is the truth. Our ancestors were good and generous, and they lived very happily here, on their land. Our people have suffered a great deal since the White people came here, though it's not the White people's fault. The Great Spirit wants them to be here, and He wants us to help them. One day you will write other books about history, and help people learn the truth. The day is coming when the Indians will be understood and cease to suffer. Time is the Father of Truth.

The use of oral history and oral literature are key elements in dealing with the Native American past. My works deal with diversity and similarities among Native groups, which is evidenced through oral traditions and histories given by tribal elders. This is the work set before me today, but as a child, I had no plans to write books or teach until I was in sixth grade. No one in my family—Indian or German—had much formal education. My grandparents on both sides of my family might have finished the sixth grade, but no more. My father and mother started ninth grade but quit because of World War II, although my mother completed high school through a correspondence course. Still, my elders valued learning, wisdom, and education. But as a child I had little use for school until my maternal grandfather changed my life. My grandfather was Earl Henry, a strong, quiet, and kind man, an Indian who had worked in factories in Ohio, particularly Cleveland, and owned some small businesses. When he was in his sixties, he became ill with liver problems and moved to Tucson, Arizona, but I did not know he was dying. The previous year, in 1960, my father had left Westinghouse over labor disputes and moved to Yuma, Arizona, to work as an upholsterer. My father had worked two jobs before the move, working in the factory eight hours before working at his upholstering shop. My grandpa Henry and Dad briefly owned a secondhand store, and Grandpa had encouraged my father to become an upholsterer to re-cover used furniture. My dad took a home-study course on the trade and learned his craft well.

During the summer of 1961, I visited my grandfather in Tucson. One day I watched a dark, summer storm build over the purple mountains to the west. Thunder crashed over the earth while zigzag lightning flashed across the sky. Rain pounded the desert floor in thunder bursts, creating a wonderful fragrance. My grandfather joined me after the rain had passed and asked if I wanted to take a ride with him. We traveled in a blue Ford Falcon up Speedway and onto the University of Arizona campus. We drove up a tree-lined street to a cul-de-sac where we parked in front of Old Main.

"When you grow up," Grandpa said, unexpectedly, "I want you to come to this college. I think you would make a good lawyer." That is all he said. I do not remember replying. I could hardly believe that anyone in my family thought that I should go to college, let alone law school. Colleges and universities had never been a part of our lives and the prospect of attending college had never occurred to me. But these words were important to me. They changed my life.

I have told young Native students that this was my Indian motivation day. My grandfather was one of the few people to encourage me to go to college, and I was profoundly and positively affected by my grandfather's words and the confidence he had in me. He died the next summer, but I never forgot his words. While completing high school, picking cantaloupes in the fields around Yuma, unloading cotton mote from metal freight cars in the summer heat, or spitting tacks with my father at his upholstery shop, I never forgot my grandfather's words.

I was only a fair student, but after my varied work experiences, I planned to attend college. At the end of my senior year, my father drove me to Flagstaff to enroll at Northern Arizona University. It was a memorable trip, eating sandwiches we had packed, a hamburger at a truck stop, and sleeping in the front of his Ford pickup under the shadows of the Mogollon Rim. That fall, my mother and father drove me to campus to begin a new journey. I majored in history because of my interest in the past, particularly our Native American past. My mother gave me her love of history and stories. She gave me a sense of direction and an attachment to souls that help guide our lives. My mother taught me about spirits and our link with the dead. She taught me of sacred things and places. I learned about ancient burials and recent cemeteries—like the Wyandot cemetery in Upper Sandusky where the people had worshiped at a Methodist mission before being forced into Kansas. My interest in preserving sacred places and protecting remains led to my appointment as a commissioner of the California Native American Heritage Commission. My interest in issues involving spiritual matters has informed my fiction and nonfiction writings.

Tobacco spoke with fire people, telling tales of woe and pain. Smoke rose high surrounding him, driving away cloud tails that had dogged The Wounded for so long. Wooden faces rubbed ash on his skin and hair, sang songs of planted seeds that found a home in his brain. Like the Mountain Masks before, they turned him about and set him into motion. Creation whirled around him so he could walk in all directions. Wooden masks from green trees, cut from living trunks, worked their magic in dream songs and masked poetry.

> Give it up to the clouds
> Death destroyed, Life begins

> Give it up to the clouds
> Let go of despair and hate
> Give it up to the clouds
> Send all the rage skyward
> Give it up to the clouds

Ancient masks dance about the room, casting shadows on the walls, reflecting brightly in the mirrors. Masks move about through smoke and mirrors, leaving silent songs and dream seeds planted deep into his mind. Masks wandered off in a concluding song, keeping low to the ground shaking Turtle Rattles. Tobacco songs danced in yellow and blue flames, shaking hands with fire people who silently watched the day pass into night and night into day.

My interest in the past led me to start a master's program in American history in 1970. That year the library hired me to help organize Special Collections. One summer I wrote a calendar of the Samuel Edward Day papers, a collection of original typed and handwritten letters, notes, business records, and reports. This was my first hands-on experience dealing with original documents, and my first publications were based on these sources. I used to study in Special Collections when they were located in the main library. I had a key, so Chancellor Damon and I would quietly do our work there. Chancellor is Diné, a Navajo from Window Rock, and he knew the Day family because today they are Navajo. He introduced me to Sam Day III, and I told him of my work with the Day papers. I honed my skills in oral history with Sam Day, his sister, and others in Chancellor's family who had known Naalt' Sos Nez Begay—"The Son of Tall Paper."

I found many gems within the collection and from oral histories that informed me about Navajo life and culture, including a story about the origin of the Naato Baca sandpainting. A boy was eager to go on his first hunt, but his father deemed him too young for the responsibility. Ignoring his elders, the boy set out one day to hunt without first doing a sweat, singing hunting songs, praying, or making other preparations in accordance with Hunting Way. The boy knew nothing of proper hunting procedures or the power of Hashch'éshzhíni, the Black God. The first day he hunted along the base of a mountain and found no signs of animals. He made a camp and that night saw a fire glowing at the top of the mountain. The next day he hunted up the mountainside to the top of the mountain where he believed he had seen the fire, but he found no evidence of the fire. For four nights he saw the fire and did not learn the mystery of it until the next day.

Once again he hunted up the mountainside to the top, where he saw a great snake monster named Clish Tso. The boy wanted to run away, but the small wind in his ear told him that if he was truly a hunter and a man, he would walk inside the great snake's mouth. And so he did, but the snake closed his mouth and the boy found himself in darkness, except for a ray of light deep inside the snake's body. The boy walked toward the light until he saw a snake man named Clish Tso. The face and body of the snake man was so powerful that the boy fainted. When he awoke, he no longer feared Clish Tso. The snake man sang over his body and used the power of a buckskin painting to cure him. The boy apprenticed with Clish Tso, learning the songs, procedures, and ceremony. When he was prepared to leave and take the medicine to his people, he asked Clish Tso for the buckskin painting. But the holy man refused to allow the boy to take it, saying that people would fight over the possession of such a powerful painting. Instead, Clish Tso taught the boy how to reproduce the painting on the ground using ground charcoal, rocks, pollen, and clay. In this way, the boy created the Naato Baca sandpainting and brought the power to the Diné.

I understood the importance of such tribal stories, but as an "academic," I had to reconcile the use of oral stories in historical writings. I looked to the works of Edward Castillo, Jack Forbes, Gerald Vizenor, Rupert Costo, Jeanette Henry Costo, and others for help in this matter. From elders, I knew that oral traditions were in fact history, literature, religion, and law, but few historians and "scholars" would have agreed. I determined that regardless of criticisms, I would weave the story of the Naato Baca sandpainting into my thesis and use oral accounts in my "scholarly" work every chance I had. Since 1971, I have included oral traditions in my scholarly work, in an attempt to accomplish the goals set forth so eloquently by Georges Albert Sioui. The use of oral traditions and ancient stories has been the source of great joy for me, but reviewers of my works often question the "validity" of oral accounts.

For example, when I was being reviewed for tenure at Washington State University, one white professor wrote that he "questioned the purity of my orientation toward history." On another occasion, a reviewer for the University of Oklahoma Press of *Renegade Tribe: The Palouse Indians and the Invasion of the Inland Pacific Northwest* insisted that I eliminate all of the oral history and traditions from the manuscript since we all knew that Native American oral stories were "fish tales that grow with the telling." I refused to delete the oral stories and histories or make other changes that would have made the book incorrect. I lost interest in the University of Oklahoma Press and the editors lost interest in the Palouse project. In 1986, Washington State University Press published the book, which won a juried award for the best book on Northwestern history. The book has been in print for over a decade in spite of the fact that it employs oral history and oral narratives—fish tales that grow with the telling.

My first formal writing dealt with the Day family and Navajo culture. Sam Day was the leader of a Navajo Yei dance team who participated in all of the major ceremonies. He was not Navajo and he was never a medicine man. But he was an unusual man who spoke Navajo, knew the importance of oral traditions, and wore all the masks representing the different Yeis in the ceremonies. He married Kate Roanhorse, and his children and their children are Diné who live on the reservation today. My association with Chancellor Damon, Sam Day, and other Navajos encouraged me to learn more about Navajo history, and when I began doctoral work at Oklahoma State University, I determined to write a history of the Navajo wars as a dissertation. My research was nearly completed when Myra Ellen Jenkins of the New Mexico State Archives told me that Frank McNitt had just published *The Navajo Wars* with the University of New Mexico Press. I was in Santa Fe at the time and drove to Albuquerque to buy a copy of the book. It was a tremendous history, but it ended in 1861 without addressing Kit Carson's campaign against the Navajos. I returned to Oklahoma to research another topic for my dissertation but determined one day to return to my Navajo work.

In 1973 I completed the PhD in history from Oklahoma State University, where I received an excellent education. Odie B. Faulk was a fine major professor, and he helped me overcome my fear of publishing. It was through his encouragement that the *New Mexico Historical Review* accepted my first scholarly publication. In the same year, I took a position as curator of a branch museum of the Arizona Historical

Society. During my three years as curator of Century House Museum, I researched and wrote *Yuma: Frontier Crossing of the Far Southwest.* I explored the importance of the lower Colorado River region as a geographical area significant to Quechan Indians, Spanish missionaries, settlers, soldiers, surveyors, and others. Since I had grown up in Yuma, I knew Lee Emerson, Rhoda Yuma, and Henry DeCorse. These elders helped me understand elements of Quechan culture, their views of the invasion of their lands, and the harm brought by disease, malnutrition, government policies, and agrobusiness. I also continued reading microfilm on Navajo history, and at a fiesta sponsored by the Yuma County Historical Society, C. L. Sonnichsen suggested I concentrate solely on Kit Carson's Navajo campaign. I started focusing my work on the last Navajo war and continued this work after moving to the Navajo Reservation.

In the spring of 1976, I visited Chancellor and Ella Damon at Window Rock, Arizona. Each night we built a fire outside their mobile home and shared stories and food. I met a number of people who told me traditional creation stories, Long Walk stories, and accounts of Sam Day and his family. One day Chancellor told me that I ought to move to the reservation and teach at Navajo Community College. We drove north through Fort Defiance, then to Navajo, Wheatfield Lake, and on to Tsaile, where we met with a few administrators at Navajo Community College. I interviewed for a job and was offered a position as an instructor in the Department of Navajo History and Culture. Teddy Draper, Michael Mitchell, and Willard Draper taught me a great deal about Navajo oral tradition, which helped me write *The Kit Carson Campaign: The Last Great Navajo War.*

Although I recorded a few oral histories, I found the work of Ruth Roessel entitled *Navajo Stories of the Long Walk Period* to be an invaluable source. While other historians may disagree, I believe the work to be an original source, just as valuable as anything left by soldiers or superintendents. So in crafting *The Kit Carson Campaign,* I used Ruth's work and other oral traditions people shared with me. I also took advantage of my residence at Tsaile to ride horseback and in my truck through the mountains, plateaus, and canyons where the events occurred. Willard Draper and members of his family accompanied me into the Canyon de Chelly, telling me stories told to them by parents, grandparents, and great-grandparents. I also used to walk into Canyon del Muerto from Tsaile Lake to learn more about Captain Albert H. Pfeiffer's trek through the northern branch of the canyon.

The real strength of *The Kit Carson Campaign* is the Navajo voice and the fact set forth by the people that they would have never surrendered if they had known of General James H. Carleton's demand to forcefully remove them to Hwééldi (imprisoned) at Fort Sumner. Moreover, the Diné argue that the New Mexican soldiers murdered civilians during the Long Walk. Both of these themes appear in nearly all of the oral traditions, but the written sources by Carson and the military escorts of the Navajos to the Bosque Redondo contradict these assertions. The Navajo oral traditions are on target, and the soldiers never admitted on paper to murdering men, women, and children who fell behind in their march to Hwééldi. While I was an instructor at Navajo Community College, I came to know Howard Gorman, Sr., who was on the board of regents for the college. Gorman was a man of great intelligence and integrity. His oral history about the Long Walk appears in Ruth Roessel's classic work, and it is poignant regarding the realities of the forced removals.

From Fort Defiance the Navajos started on their journey. That was in 1864. They headed for *Shash Bitoo'* (Fort Wingate) first, and from there they started on their Long Walk. Women and children traveled on foot. That's why we call it the Long Walk. It was inhuman because the Navajos, if they got tired and couldn't continue to walk further, were just shot down. Some of the wagons went along, but they were carrying army supplies, like clothes and food. *Jaanééz* (mules) pulled the wagons. So the Navajos were not cared for. They had to keep walking all the time, day after day. They kept that up for about 18 or 19 days from Fort Wingate to Fort Sumner, or *Hwééldi*.

On the journey the Navajos went through all kinds of hardships, like tiredness and having injuries. And, when those things happened, the people would hear gunshots in the rear. But they couldn't do anything about it. They just felt sorry for the ones being shot. Sometimes they would plead with the soldiers to let them go back and do something, but they were refused. This is how the story was told by my ancestors. It was said that those ancestors were on the Long Walk with their daughter, who was pregnant and about to give birth. Somewhere beyond *K'aalógii Dzil* (Butterfly Mountain) on this side of *Bilín*

(Belen) . . . the daughter got tired and weak because of her condition. So my ancestors asked the Army to hold up for a while and to let the woman give birth. But the soldiers wouldn't do it. They forced my people to move on, saying that they were getting behind the others. The soldiers told the parents that they had to leave their daughter behind. "Your daughter is not going to survive, anyway; sooner or later she is going to die," they said in their own language.

"Go ahead," the daughter said to her parents, "things might come out all right with me." But the poor thing was mistaken, my grandparents used to say. Not long after they had moved on, they heard a gunshot from where they had been a short time ago.

"Maybe we should go back and do something, or at least cover the body with dirt," one of them said.

By that time one of the soldiers came riding up from the direction of the sound. He must have shot her to death. That's the way the story goes.

Such oral histories not only enrich our sources, providing a Navajo voice in the historical drama, but they change historiography. Oral sources provide historians with new insight into historical processes, permitting outsiders an opportunity to enter selected realms of knowing that have been confined to particular Native communities for generations. Some historians refuse to use oral histories or try to understand elements of Native cultures. Some hide behind the claim that they are not American Indian historians but white historians studying white relations with Indians. They assume that as scholars they have no obligation to study Native Americans or their cultures. Often they are individuals who discount oral traditions or the importance of understanding traditional stories, culture, religion, and history in assessing historical events. In sum, they ignore Native American sources and only assess documents left by representatives of the United States government or non-Indian settlers, legislators, and correspondents.

In 1977, I moved from the deserts and mountains of Arizona to the Great Columbia Plateau of Washington. I took a professorship at Washington State University in Native American studies and history. Living in the heart of the Palouse country spurred my interest in Palouse Indian history. No one had published a scholarly book on the

Palouse, so I began collecting data that would result in *Renegade Tribe: The Palouse Indians and the Invasion of the Inland Pacific Northwest.* During my second year of work on the Palouse, Richard Scheuerman contacted me, offering to share all of the sources he had collected. He was knowledgeable about Palouse history, and we determined to work together on the Palouse book. More important, Scheuerman introduced me to Mary Jim, a Palouse elder born at the village of Tasawicks along Snake River. Mary, her daughter, Karie, and their relatives were the source of many conversations and oral histories that informed us about the relationship of Palouse people with mountains, rivers, plants, animals, and sacred places of the Columbia Plateau.

We were also aided in the Palouse project by Emily Peone of the Colville Reservation and Andrew George of the Nez Percé Reservation. Emily shared oral stories of her family, including those about Chief Kamiakin, one of the great leaders of the Yakima and Palouse people during the last century. She told the story of the Star Husbands and how her family was descended from the son of a Star Man. Years ago, after the first creation, when humans came to the land of the *Wahtee-tash,* or Animal People, two young girls named Tahpahlouh and Yaslumas went off to dig roots. One night while camping at the root grounds, Tahpahlouh pointed to Venus and said that she wanted her husband to be as beautiful as that star. Then Yaslumas pointed to Mars, saying that she wanted that star for her husband. The girls laughed and drifted off to sleep. They awoke in a strange world inhabited by two Star Men. The girls married these men and lived a wonderful life in a beautiful land, the girls unaware that they were in a Star World. During their first years in this new land, Tahpahlouh had a baby boy who would become the patriarch of the Weowict family (Kamiakin's grandfather was Chief Weowict). The men told the women to dig roots and gather berries while they hunted each day. The men instructed the women not to dig a certain root, but one day, their curiosity overtook them.

Tahpahlouh and Yaslumas dug the forbidden root, and when they pulled the long root from the ground, a wind rushed into the Star World. They peered down in the hole and could see earth below. Only then did they gain an awareness of their situation and realize that they were far from home. They replanted the root and determined to make a rope that would reach earth. When the men returned from hunting, they felt the new wind and asked their wives about it. The women pretended not to know about the wind and soon the men forgot about it. Each day the women braided a rope made from hazelnut bark. Now and then they tested it to see if it would reach to earth, and one day it touched earth. The women determined to descend the rope early the next morning, as soon as the men left the village. They executed their plan expertly, and they returned to their people to continue their adventures. Descendants of Tahpahlouh's and the Star Man's baby have not forgotten the origin of their leadership family, and today they live on many reservations in the Northwest.

Also important in the Palouse study was Andrew George, a spiritual leader of the Longhouse religion. I had heard of Andrew George long before meeting him at his daughter's home on the Yakama Reservation. When we met he did not hesitate in sharing many stories about the Palouse Indian history, drifting in and out of traditional stories that had been taught him by his elders. He had lived the "old life" as a child, residing in mat lodges and tepees along Snake River at the village of Palus. With his parents, Julie and Smith L. George, Andrew had moved across the plateau, gathering roots and berries, hunting and fishing. Shortly after the turn of the twentieth century, federal troops forced Andrew George and his family from their ancient village site, removing them by steamboat to Lewiston, Idaho. He walked from Lewiston to Lapwai, where the Palouse were enrolled on the Nez Percé Reservation. The personal story of Andrew George and his many traditional stories spoke volumes about the trials of the non-treaty and non-Christian Palouse people during and after the Nez Percé War of 1877. Andrew George was an inspiration as well as a source of power in completing the Palouse project. Portions of his story appear in *Renegade Tribe*.

Renegade Tribe is more than a tribal history of the Palouse Indians, since the major focus is on the significance of spiritual beliefs and family on the course of Native American history. The Palouse view the earth as a holy entity that gives life to all that lives. When the United States tried to force the Palouse and their neighbors to accept the Yakima Treaty of 1855 and remove them from all their villages to the Yakama Reservation, some Palouse joined forces with other tribal warriors to fight the army. Treaty and war are watersheds in Palouse Indian history, and these events are understood only in terms of Palouse spiritual beliefs, which tie the people to Snake River, Palouse Falls, and other geographic forms in their homeland, as well as the relationship of the people to plants and animals. Furthermore, family is an important factor in Northwestern Indian history—and all Native American history—because understanding families helps explain the events surrounding the Walla Walla Council of 1855 and the Plateau Indian War (1855–1858). Understanding familial makeup, marriages, leadership, jealousies, and conflicts also helps interpret the postwar period, as Palouses returned to their homeland or moved onto the Umatilla, Colville, Nez Percé, Yakama, and Warm Springs reservations.

While researching the Palouse book, my interest in Northwestern Indian history broadened. I composed other books and articles on the Plateau Indians, including an article, "Smohalla, the Washani, and Religion as a Factor in Northwestern Indian History," which appeared in the *American Indian Quarterly*. I also wrote *Chief Joseph's Allies*, which dealt with the Palouse participation in the Nez Percé War of 1877. I copied traditional stories from Northwestern Indians found in the papers of Lucullus Virgil McWhorter in Manuscripts, Archives, and Special Collections in Holland Library of Washington State University. McWhorter was an unusual man who preserved versions of several ancient stories. Since 1977, I have been collecting, editing, and interpreting these stories and has been published by Michigan State University Press as *Grandmother, Grandfather, and Old Wolf: Tamánwit Ku Sudat and Traditional Native American Stories from the Columbia Plateau*. The major focus of the book is the manner in which the traditional stories inform us about the spirit and the law of Chinookan-, Salishan-, and Sahaptin-speaking Indians from the region.

In 1981, I moved from Washington State University to San Diego State University, where I was a professor of Native American studies. Still, I continued my work on the Palouse Indians and began broadening my work on other Plateau Indian tribes. My work on the Palouse led me to the National Archives, Pacific Northwest Region, in Seattle, where I worked in the Yakama Agency Papers. After reading pages in several textbooks, I asked archivist Joyce Justice to see bills of sale, death certificates, birth registers, Indian police records, and the papers of the Indian court of justice. All of these documents suggested the need for a new methodology for me. I quantified the bills of sale, 1909 to 1912, and wrote an article entitled "Horses and Cattle, Buggies and

Hacks" based on the documents. The statistics suggest that women did most of the buying on the Yakama Reservation and they spent most of the money that was used to purchase horses, cattle, wagons, farm equipment, harnesses, and household goods.

Between 1909 and 1912, the people living on the Yakama Reservation (which includes fourteen tribes and bands) spent more money buying horses than any other item. Women bought more horses than did the men, and they bought more cattle, wagons, and household goods—which included flour, salt, nails, lumber, fencing, gloves, washing machines, etc. Men bought more harnesses and farm equipment than women, but the documents provided a Native voice that demonstrated that on the reservation, women continued their dominance in economic issues. Women had controlled the Plateau Indian economy during the pre-reservation era, and they continued to do so in the early twentieth century.

More important were the death certificates and birth registers. In 1987, I began collecting Yakama death certificates and birth registers. Originally, I copied only those documents from 1888 to 1930, but after coding and running this data, I decided that I must collect all of the available death certificates. The National Archives contained death certificates from 1888 to 1964, and I copied all of them with the intent of creating a database and interpreting my results. The documents were not flat pieces of paper to me. I saw them as another voice that had never been heard; I would bring this voice alive by analyzing the certificates of nearly four thousand men, women, and children. No one had studied death over time on an Indian reservation, and I wanted to use the death certificates to explain the major causes of death on the Yakama Reservation, the rates of death per one thousand in the population, and the infant mortality rate. In the book, I compare Yakama deaths with those of whites, nonwhites, people of Washington State, and African Americans. The result of this study is a book, *Death Stalks the Yakama: Epidemiological Transitions and Mortality on the Yakama Indian Reservation, 1888–1964,* which Michigan State University Press published in 1997. The study is analytical and interpretive, confirming high infant-mortality and death rates among Yakima in comparison to other populations resulting from tuberculosis, pneumonia, heart disease, and accidental deaths.

My work on death contains some traditional stories and oral histories, including one version of how Coyote lost immortality for all time. At the time of creation, the Creator determined that there would be a time for life on earth and in the Sky Above. People lived and died. Coyote had lost nearly all of his family, including his daughter, and he grew lonely for his dead loved ones. Coyote traveled west to the Spirit World and asked the Creator to allow him to return east with the souls of his loved ones. Reluctantly, the Creator allowed Coyote to take a buckskin bag full of souls back but warned him not to open the bag until Coyote crossed the fifth mountain to the east. Coyote agreed but after crossing the fourth mountain, he heard voices from inside the bag and he became so lonesome for his daughter and the others. He opened the bag and the souls returned to the Sky Above. This is the reason we experience life and death. This is the law.

Before Andrew George died, he told me that I was following a narrow path and that I could do more good for Native peoples by broadening my work. He suggested that I should expand my scholarly work to new areas. I had already started work on quantitative history and had long been interested in oral literature but had not developed my work in this area. While I was a professor at San Diego State University, Harold Jaffe, Larry McCaffrey, and Harry Pokenhorn encouraged me to submit an article or short story on some aspect of Native American literature to *Fiction International.* I gathered poetry, short stories, essays, and reviews from many Indian writers, and writings from a few non-Indians on Native literature. When I had sufficient material, I submitted all of it to the editors for their consideration. After sending the material out for review, the editors asked to use most of it as an issue on Native American literature. Several Native people appeared in this volume, and their work was well received. It was read by many people, including Nat Sobel, a literary agent in New York, who called me to ask if I would submit a proposal to him regarding an anthology of short fiction.

In the summer of 1992, Doubleday/Anchor accepted the proposal, and by the second week of September, I submitted *Earth Song, Sky Spirit* to the editors. It was an honor to work with thirty talented writers, particularly people who had not had a chance to publish a great deal. The writing of young Native writers is excellent, and more should have the chance to get their work out. Additional writers are included in the second anthology, *Blue Dawn, Red Earth,* which appeared in 1996. Whenever asked about these volumes, I say edited books always belong to the authors, not the editors. It is the authors who provide diverse thoughts, ideas, and details of the contemporary Native American experience through their fiction, fiction built on the foundation of the past given by elders through their stories and those of the authors themselves. In my introduction to *Blue Dawn, Red Earth,* I use a fictional elder to convey the relationship of younger people to elders and the idea of death and rebirth.

No sooner had the right foot of Agnes Yellowknee touched the earth than I heard her gasp and fall forward. I watched her fall, as if in slow motion. She crashed to the ground. At the same time, I moved in slow motion, tossing Cokes and potato chips in the air, my arms outstretched in a futile attempt to catch Agnes. I tried to break her fall, but she crashed to the ground before I reached her. But I was at her side in a moment, reaching out for her left shoulder and turning her over. Her head rested in my lap and I pushed her thick gray hair from her face. I ran my hands over her face, feeling the deep lines that crisscrossed her face. I gently caressed her worn face until I felt the change overcome her body. My fingers and mind felt the change and then my heart. She died in my arms, and I was unable to help her. Tears ran down my face, silent tears that came from deep within me. Warm tears mixed with cool air that turned to dark winds whirling around us. I bent over and kissed her cheek lightly as a small whirlwind danced around us taking her soul up to the sky. I rocked Agnes in my arms and cried, holding her body close.

One of the writers in all of the books of fiction I have edited is Darryl Wilson, who once shared some views about teaching the oral and written traditions. He told me that in the summer of 1994 he taught a writing class as part of the American Indian language institute at the University of Arizona. He told the Native students to take all their fears, inhibitions, and insecurities from their minds and place them on the table. After a few minutes, all of the students said that their problems were in front of them on the table. Wilson then told the students to push them aside and to leave them there throughout the course. Then he had them put imagination, creativity, and momentum in front of them and draw on them throughout the course. The product was a book entitled *Red Ink,* an anthology of mixed genre by young Native writers.

Wilson's efforts are similar to those of many Native writers who mentor young Native people in the art of writing, many through Wordcraft Circle of Native Writers & Storytellers. They are an inspiration to me, providing new visions for young people who have not had the chance to express themselves in the written word. The results of their work is already apparent, and the positive effect of the work will fundamentally change the way people view and deal with Native people. The heart and soul of American history, literature, environmental science, and many other aspects of this land are Native, and we know this through the words of elders, long past and recent past. It is through an understanding of Native American knowledge and ways of knowing that people will live in greater relationship with each other and the earth. Forests and plains, plateau and mountains, coasts and deserts, rivers and lakes resound with the ancient songs and stories of this land. They were put in motion at the beginning of time and echo still for those willing to listen.

THE BUFFALO ROAD

ANNA LEE WALTERS

Of Pawnee-Otoe descent, Anna Lee Walters currently lives in Arizona and teaches at Diné College in Tsaile. She is the author of many pieces of short fiction (e.g., The Sun Is Not Merciful, Firebrand Books, 1985), *and a novel,* Ghost Singer. *She has retold a traditional Otoe legend in a book for children called* Two-Legged Creature *(Northland Books), and also published* Talking Indian: Reflections on Survival and Writing *(Firebrand Books). Most recently, she has contributed a chapter on teaching* Native American Literature *to* Teaching and Using Multicultural Literature in Grades 9–12: Moving beyond the Canon *(edited by Arlette Willis, Christopher Gordon Publishers).*

> *Tihatura ru sik*
> The road has vanished
> *Taraha rahatura ru*
> The Buffalo Road[1]

So begins my third novel. So begins a reflection on the influences of "the buffalo road" upon my own work, expression, and creativity. So begins a particular orientation to aesthetics and unique expressive conventions found in tribal languages and the knowledge stored there. So begins an affirmation of the innate truth and integrity of preliterate traditions. So begins old stories and new.

> *Concentric rings. Motion. Sound.* Parí Pakuru.
> *Northeast. Southeast Southwest. Northwest.*
> *Above. Below.*
> *Voices. Music.* Parí Pakuru.[2]

Buffalo Road (a novel still in draft stage about the Pawnees in the last century), "Buffalo Wallow Woman,"[3] and other fiction I have produced over the years could never have been written in quite the way they were had they not been influenced by perceptions of aesthetics and "art" held by my family, and maternal and paternal tribal people. These notions are older than individuals in any single generation and *why* they are the core of our literature, ancient and modern (after five centuries of contact), ought to be an impetus for literary appreciation or study, rather than an afterthought. Ingrained in tribal language and literary conventions, they are inseparable from language environment, construct, use, and meaning. Stabilized long ago with language, tribal identity, and ways of life, these perceptions are always an aspect of tribal (and modern Native American) literature and its expressive forms. Use of even a single word in extant tribal vocabularies now, or a simple expression, is often enough to spring those core ideas and experiences forward into the light, where they will have particular significance for another of the same language background, and less meaning for others who do not share that background or experience. In this regard, tribal languages are like others in this country but they have not enjoyed the same appreciation or acceptance, sociopolitically speaking, in the last five hundred years. That they are whole, and are characterized by full development, has not always been accepted by non-Native people and non-speakers; therefore, what few assessments and studies that have been done on tribal languages often do not describe them in those glowing terms: as "whole," "full," and "rich in thought and expression," with a handful of exceptions, of course. A factor in this status undoubtedly is that so few studies have been done, and data is simply still insufficient and inconclusive at this time, five hundred years later. Then, perhaps other issues are involved as well. In any case, having had this kind of history for five centuries also says something significant in regard to the view of validity and integrity of tribal languages during this same time period. Clearly, when wholeness and full development of tribal languages are in question, so also are validity and integrity. Yet, only in tribal languages can be found the origins of separate tribal literatures and literary forms, and their artistic principles still at work today. Only in the wholeness of tribal languages and their conventions may be found a clear cohesive vision of the peoples' experiences, and meanings of those combined phenomena. Integrity is found here in this convergence and it is the basis of literary "art," "truth," and "aesthetics" among tribes today. This is where appreciation of modern "Native American literature" or "American Indian literature" begins.

For many centuries on the Plains, perhaps as far back as paleo times, the Pawnees (of Caddoan linguistic stock) and the Otoe-Missourias (of Siouan linguistic stock) followed the buffalo as a way of living purposefully with the workings of the sky and earth. The buffalo brought order, teachings, values, ethics, aesthetics, and life. The languages of these groups reflect long associations with the buffalo; literary forms and literature grew out of them. The peoples' experiences with the buffalo were holistic and visionary. They were expressed fully in integrated and complimentary preliterate forms which were always viewed as parts of a larger, whole, orderly vision that dignified the forms and the people. Evident in language and experience was the truth of their vision. In both groups, all of their expressive forms agree about that larger, whole, orderly vision. *The old ones were buffalo people. Buffalo. People.* "These were our ancestors," they say. *Ancestors.*

Both groups had Buffalo clans. Among the Otoes, this clan was originally called Buffalohead but later became simply Buffalo. There were certain rights and privileges that Waconda (the Creator) bestowed upon the Buffalo Clan in order for them to live with the workings of sky and earth. With these guiding principles disclosed fully only to them, the Buffalo Clan distinguished and marked themselves. But along with these privileges were responsibilities and weighty burdens to bear. For that is life's nature in the workings of the sky and earth; life must be treated just so, or it will not be valued or used wisely, and be gone too soon. That was what Waconda expressed to the ancestors, those Buffalo People, who were to guard, shield, and honor that mysterious force within themselves—but which came from without— where it lived and to which it always returned. That was what the Buffalo Clan had to do, *that was all they had to do.* It was so simple and it was so hard.

Socially, among the Otoes, for several generations, the tribe allowed themselves to be governed by the Buffalo Clan. Half the year was under Buffalo leadership, and during this time the clan made decisions about various events and tasks that were to occur during that time. Buffalo children were also promised in marriage to other clans because of ancient agreements made between the various clans to prevent clan hostilities among the tribe and to reunify the whole group every generation. In this tribe, the Buffalo Clan also regulated travel by individual tribal members and intertribal visitations. The other half of the year was regulated by another clan.

The Otoes, like the Pawnees and other buffalo-hunting Indians, made seasonal rounds on the buffalo road. Twice a year, after the horse became introduced to them, they had one major hunt, under the direction of the Buffalo Clan. Before that, hunts were more difficult. On each occasion, the chase was to supply all the food for everyone until the next chase occurred. Because of this cycle, the people prepared the meat supply in the most efficient and practical way to carry over until their stores were renewed again. They also made ingenious use of every part of the buffalo so that very little was left to be discarded or shared with predators, whom the groups regarded as necessary and even "good" in the workings of sky and earth.

Throughout time in the Pawnee way of life, the buffalo has figured in a very prominent way. It might also be said that the buffalo was always at the forefront of it. In their historical heydey, in what is now present-day Kansas and Nebraska, the people built large villages atop the bluffs that overlooked waterways and buffalo valleys. During this time, the buffalo held a principle place in everyday life, and in ritual village life and in Pawnee spirituality. Discoveries of large mud lodges, called *akar rarátau'* by the Pawnee, from this time period, sometimes sixty feet in diameter, with Pawnee altars still holding buffalo skulls, continue to be made by ranchers and farmers who are now in possession of the old Pawnee land. Some of these skulls undoubtedly were secured during buffalo hunts then, but others may have been passed down through clan and family lineages. The last buffalo hunt of the Otoes occurred while they were on the Nebraska reservation, probably about 1873 or 1874. For the Pawnees, it also happened in Nebraska in 1873, three years before the Pawnee exodus to Indian Territory.

Buffalo hunts had military precision; in fact, in some tribes, warrior organizations, societies, and subgroups had leadership of these. All who participated in a buffalo hunt had specific tasks and duties to perform, and the whole tribe was expected to be involved, with the exception of very young children, the elderly, and those who were ill. To make a successful hunt required coordination and collective, unified action; therefore, internal conflicts and squabbles were expected to be put aside for the well-being and life of the whole group. Individuals who violated this order were dealt with in a variety of ways, depending upon the tribe, and upon the nature of violation.

While the hunts were under the leadership of warrior groups in some tribes, the warriors were not able to call the buffalo to the people. That art required special abilities and knowledge of individual men or women, or subgroups of various societies or clans who knew what to do so that the buffalo would allow themselves to be killed, in order for the people to live. There had to be exchange and communication with the buffalo, through thinking, language, and behavior. Sometimes the whole tribe shared in this responsibility simply by following buffalo teachings as they were revealed by particular appointed groups or individuals. When the buffalo yielded to the people, life traveled out of the buffalo and into the people, leaving one form of being—empty and cold, and another, full and warm. Then the people had the responsibility of honoring the part of the buffalo that never died—the spirit. This wonderful undying essence in the unity of the sky and earth was what manifested itself again and again to the people, and they lived by these patterns. Life was always a gift, for themselves, for the buffalo, and all things in the workings of sky and earth. The cycles of life for the people and for the buffalo were "sacred" and "wonderful," they said. The concentricity of these cycles and interdependence were clearly evident in the people's thinking, language, and literature. Of the coordinated workings of the sky and earth—of all natural phenomena behaving as one unified thing, of which the people viewed themselves as a part—*"Waruksti,"* they said in Pawnee; *"Wah hoo nea tun,"*[4] they said in Otoe.

"Buffalo Wallow Woman" was written in the fall about six years ago; and *Buffalo Road* was also conceived in that season, although there were many previous winters in which the novel was working itself out. In a sense, "Buffalo Wallow Woman" gave birth to the novel, or in the movement of Buffalo Wallow Woman from beginning to end came forth a compelling and stirring vision of "the buffalo road" that has always lived in the thinking and language of the people. This is the beauty of "Buffalo Wallow Woman": that she lives here in this protected place of vision, experience, and truth. That her principles of life still apply in today's world. This is the truth of an old vision.

Prayer and song are a major part of tribal literary forms, and with them come peculiar thinking. Pawnee ceremonial structure and procedures were studied in the early part of this century, and there is a handful of material regarding these perceptions. However, even in this small library, it is quite evident that ideas about prayer, song, and ceremony are very complex. Very little is known about the Otoe-Missouria even now, and very little has been written about them. Despite this lack of written documentation, though, the people continue to pray and compose songs by ancient formulae and principles, still using tribal languages, thinking, and principles.

Prayer, of course, is the most formal, often with particular patterns to follow. In Otoe, prayer is called *Wah hoo geeh*. In both tribes, there are also particular orientations to note when prayer occurs and procedures to follow, depending upon the occasion. Oftentimes, songs too are considered prayers and they are expressed with the same formality. In both tribes, songs (made by individuals) are "owned" by particular families or groups, and others won't even sing them without mentioning the individuals or families who own them. They are in a sense considered "possessions." Sometimes, a family member is said to have "composed" a song, although everyone agrees that song composition is not like that. A song is believed to have life of its own; in both tribes songs come to individuals in times of stress, hardship, grief, love, and so forth. Songs are spoken of as having a "tail," being "caught," and so forth, as if they are living things that fly or dart about, and are in the form of an animal or bird. Both tribes view the owners of the songs as having certain "rights" to them, and others are careful not to infringe upon them. Although this may sound contradictory to the concept of the song having a "life" of its own, this is not so. It merely reminds the whole group that the song "went" to a particular family or person and this is reason enough to respect "ownership."

Songs sung by supernaturals, or animals, or other deities can be understood only in the context of stories or rituals that accompany them. In this wholeness, meaning is extended to all forms of expression and intensified. Pawnees have talked about some of their ceremonial songs having "steps," which relate to order, progression, sequence, development and action, following patterns, thinking, expressions, and the behavior of supernaturals or natural phenomena.

In Kansas and Nebraska the people followed many steps toward the buffalo road. Patterns. Movement. Directions. Language. Names. Songs. Stories. Prayers. Teachings. Observations of sky and earth. Unity. Order. Truth. Life. Patterns. Movement. Directions. Language. Names. Songs. Stories. Prayers. Teachings. Observations of sky and earth. These are but a few.

The steps began a long time ago, measured in thousands of suns, moons, and winters. *Patterns.* The place of the people in the universe was marked by the flow of key rivers and sounds from the heavens. *Movement.* Guardians surrounded them. *Directions.* The people thought and spoke their minds. *Pawnee language.* They thought about the suns, the moons, the winters, the rivers, the sounds in the heavens, the guardians, the directions, themselves and their speech, and knew what all these things were through their thinking and language. *Names.* They

raised their voices and thoughts and sent them out into the wind. *Songs.*
Endlessly, they marveled about these phenomena. *Stories.* They spoke *to*
these phenomena. *Prayers.* In this way, they survived. *Teachings.* They
watched above and below. *Observations of earth and sky.* These two were
inseparable in the people's thinking and language. *Unity.* All life be-
haved in a grand communication with each other. *Order.* The people
were a part of it. *Truth.* Sky and earth were father and mother to all. *Life.*

    The Buffalo Road is set in Kansas and Nebraska before there was En-
glish language. Therefore, old Pawnee thinking and language still pre-
vail in it. English began to be significantly adopted by the group after
their removal to Indian Territory, which is fairly recently. Back then,
present-day Kansas and Nebraska were known to them only through
their own language, which had a critical relationship to that land. Because historical conditions and circumstances led to a swift and invol-
untary departure from that place, their references to that place today
remain from that Pawnee language perspective only.

    Literally overnight, the people were gone. They left much behind.
That is clear, up there on those old windy bluffs where the people built
grand villages and gazed down from them at rivers and endless buffalo
country stretching out everywhere. Northeast. Southeast. Southwest.
Northwest. Above. Below. The wind blows hard up there, rolling
across the earth in a steamy wet breath. The wind is a voice they say in
all the literary forms—stories, songs, and prayers. Standing up there
on that ground where ancestors stood, old truths align themselves in
the four directions, in the sky and earth, and in the remains of wonderful grand old villages.

Taraha! Taraha!

Spirit radiates from that place and converges there. It is peculiar
golden light, spectacular colored moving stars, strange winds, neon
thunderbolts, white wolves, and mystical iridescent fog. Spirit is everywhere. This is what the people thought then and think now; all those
phenomena were layered into their thinking and their being. Language was a manifestation of all this interaction. The people spoke
truths to live by: *Sakuru* (the Sun), *Pa* (the Moon), *Pari su* (Hunter),
Taraha (Buffalo), and on and on. Parts of the whole. Parts of the whole
vision.

Buffalo. People. Ancestors. My grandmother and her father, on my mother's side, were members of the Buffalo Clan. On my father's side, there are also Buffalo Clan members in the extended family. Parts of the whole. Parts of the whole vision.

Buffalo stories. Modern and old. "Buffalo Wallow Woman." "Buffalo Dust"—my grandmother's real name. Buffalo lodge. Buffalo mud. Buffalo society. Buffalo man. Buffalo wool. Buffalo tail. Buffalo rattle. Buffalo dance. Buffalo country. Buffalo vision. Buffalo people. Buffalo. *Taraha!* Parts of the whole. Parts of the whole vision.

Some stories are both, modern and old. An example follows below. Some people would call it a modern story. Others would say that its very old. The story is "true." It happened around Pawnee, Oklahoma, very recently.

Just before dawn in late spring, a person went outside to watch the sunrise and to pray. He went to sit on the hills that overlook a small buffalo herd on the west side of Pawnee. It was still dark when the person arrived and chose a spot facing east. The small herd was down in the hill slopes. No one else was around at all. The person sat crossed-legged on the ground and began a small prayer. Suddenly, during the person's prayer, off in the distance, a baby cried. The person stopped praying and looked around, puzzled and concerned. But then the cry of the baby was gone and the morning was calm, the sky above had grown lighter. The buffalo herd had also moved up a little toward the person. When nothing else happened, the person resumed the prayer. Again, in front of the praying individual could be heard a baby cry. But the person did not stop what he was doing, and continued to pray with head down. Then another baby cry came from a different direction in front of the person. It happened several times, but the person did not look up and just kept on praying. Finally, when the prayer was completed and that person looked up in the direction of the herd, there were some yellow buffalo calves standing in the dewy morning. They sounded exactly like human children. The person was startled and amazed because nothing like that had ever happened to him before. Then, he remembered what the old folks had said long ago. They talked this way about the buffalo. "They're holy," they said.

I guess that songs, prayers, and stories are our old folks too. I mean they speak to us through their own voices and say the same thing, too. I guess it's up to us to listen and to learn.

The buffalo road—vision or metaphor?

The buffalo road preceded the people; they did not give birth to it or conceive it. It is its own manifestation in concert with the workings of the earth and sky. It has its own power, life, and voice separate from and yet linked to the people. It does not live through the people, but the people live through that vision. They receive blessings from it: language, expressive forms, ritual, food, aesthetics, order, and so forth. It is always there, visible or not, revealed in language, expressive forms and experience of the people. It is direct evidence of grand extensive order, equilibrium, and divinity. Explained fully in tribal languages, it is significant of the vast knowledge stored there.

There are many ways to live purposefully with the workings of sky and earth and to view these phenomena. This is evident in the numerous tribal languages which have existed on this continent over time. This divergent base of Native American literature, tribal languages, and peculiar expressive forms always enters into modern work, at least my own. Vision, standards, principles, and expressive forms of my tribal people are the core of aesthetics and art to which I yield first.

The Buffalo Road was written for several reasons. This was a way of life known by the Pawnee for the better part of their existence. Their language and experience is not well known, even now. The innate teachings of the buffalo road are wise and powerful, a body of knowledge still applicable in today's world, still meaningful. More than ever. More than ever.

It is that way in each generation and each time. Old teachings still have meaning, or they would not be true. In the vision of buffalo road is found knowledge, creativity, and expression. Only recently was that vision partly described (in English and Pawnee), at the turn of the century, and this may have been when the buffalo road became metaphor. But this was not what led me to write about the buffalo road, it was being in Kansas and Nebraska, with Pawnee people, and walking that old buffalo country in this modern time.

On one of these occasions, I was with my family, my brother and sisters at an old Pawnee battleground where many Pawnee men and women died over a century before. I asked my youngest sister, "What does it mean that our family—of all people—is standing right here, one hundred and twenty years later?" The sun was in her face and acres of sunflowers looked northeast. "On the exact spot, and to the day?" she agreed.

I believe this is the question that all literature tries to answer in its varied ways: "What does it mean that we are here today?" For myself, answers to this question and others lay in tribal languages. This is what our ancestors and elders expected us to know.

> *Tihatura ru sik*
> The road has vanished
> *Taraha rahatura ru*
> The Buffalo Road

NOTES

1. This is in the spelling used by James Murie, probably from the field-work of Gene Weltfish. This quote comes from a Pawnee song in *Ceremonies of the Pawnee,* by James Murie. It was published in 1981 (Volume 27 of the "Contributions to Anthropology" series) by the Smithsonian Institution.

2. Unpublished poetry by Anna Lee Walters. *Pari Pakuru* is Pawnee language.

3. This is a short story in *Talking Indian: Reflections on Writing and Survival,* by Anna Lee Walters. Ithaca, NY: Firebrand Books, 1992.

4. "It is holy."

THE CHILD
BEFORE MEMORY: RECOGNITION OF
THE "MAKER"

ELIZABETH WOODY

Elizabeth Woody, an enrolled member of the Confederated tribes of the reservation of Warm Springs, Oregon, was born in 1959. She has published three books: Hand into Stone *(poetry),* Luminaries of the Humble *(poetry), and* Seven Hands, Seven Hearts: Prose and Poetry. *Her work has appeared in numerous anthologies. She taught full-time in creative writing at the Institute of American Indian and Alaskan Native Arts, Santa Fe, New Mexico. Presently, she works as a program specialist for Ecotrust in Portland, Oregon.*

The land shapes us from within. The sensation is being entwined in its layering. The sequence is a spiral always swirling back toward itself. In the action of hand-weaving, this feeling is especially evident in twining. How regular and taut the textures of the fibers feel. The return marks itself as another season, another color. The food one takes in. The light one absorbs. Wind brushes past us in high desert junipers. The moon inside and its luminescence over mountains. The earth permeates the body with recognition from physical touch. Hemp. Cornhusk. Fiber. Shells. The volcanoes in our stories moved and lived. Before our human presence, they made way for the contour of skyline. The river shifted this way—left its mark. It made a way for us. Coyote walked here and made this so, in this time's beginning. Songs are sung through our lives and are part of how we follow the first teachings. There is a difference here. We dream. We know our bodies are made of all these elements. On this land we are all motion. We age. Society changes. New people arrive. Old people leave. Memory stays.

It is still possible for the poet, the storyteller, the singer, the maker, and the healer to revisit the inner location of occurrences or the innovation. The recognition of a person being a "maker" is important . . .

WEAVING

Weaving baskets you twine the strands into four parts.
Then, another four. The four directions many times.
Pairs of fibers spiral around smaller and smaller sets of threads.
Then one each time. Spirals hold all this design
airtight and pure. This is our house, over and over.
Our little sisters, Khouse, Sowitk, Piaxi, Wakamu,
the roots will rest inside.
We will be together in this basket.
We will be together in this life.

(from *Seven Hands, Seven Hearts*, Eighth Mountain Press, 1994)

Weaving, I learned of something significant. I learned that one does not worry while weaving. You recall things you have forgotten. There was a little cornhusk bag my grandmother, Elizabeth Thompson Pitt, gave to me. Sometimes I would open my music box on my bedstead bookcase and admire it. It had magic in its texture. It was made of cornhusks and yarn by my own grandmother. It was the first cornhusk bag she made when her grandmother taught her. It was possibly made from the husks of the corn in their garden my grandmother loved to reminisce about, as she thought of gardens often. This little cornhusk bag was among her things for a long time.

When I saw it for the first time, I was a small girl. I reached to touch it and asked who it belonged to. I expected my grandmother to say it once belonged to an ancestor. Like the beadwork of my grandfather's mother, for example. "It's mine," she told me, "I made it myself. My grandmother taught me." I held it. It fit in my hands perfectly and felt good. My grandmother took it back in her hands and admired it for a long time. In an unexpected gesture she gave it to me. There were times she would lend me a little beaded coin purse to take my lunch money to school in. I was careful to return it the same night. I never possessed anything so wonderful. Weaving, I thought of her little cornhusk bag. My hands felt good. My fingers felt strength. The movement became natural. I felt like a happy child.

My teacher, Margaret Jim-Pennah, started me out with fine linen yarn. She said later, when I had my root bag (*wapáas*) completed, I was a natural. She said weaving with such fine linen would either "make me or break me" as a weaver. She knew I was capable of pulling the fine threads together with my hands to make something I could be proud of. She didn't know I thought of my grandmother weaving. Later, I thought of my paternal grandmother, Annie Woody, weaving. My uncle Lewis described a spider making and remaking its web, marveling at its lightness and strength. I contemplated the stories of women who loved to weave. These particular baskets, *wapáas,* are the best storage system for a mobile people. It was part of trade. It was part of the betrothal exchange. Weaving has a long traditional history with us. We have always made these houses for our little sisters, the edible roots.

Sometimes the feelings of a moment are better expressed in the artistic motion or action of the creative individual. It is such, there are really no words to talk of this type of knowledge or moment growing within an individual. It becomes part of our language as a song, a symbol, or a family treasure. Once, my grandmother, late in her life, asked my aunt what she did for work. My aunt Lillian Pitt, a ceramicist, answered, "I make art." My grandmother asked after some thought, "What is art?" My aunt answered, "I make masks out of clay." My grandmother nodded her head, "Oh, then you are a maker. That's good."

In an interview with Larry Abbott for the new Santa Fe magazine *Indian Art*, I considered the difference between "white" and "Indian" art. I said, "In America I think there are many cultures combined, but if you are talking about white culture as something derived from Europe there probably is a difference. I don't think white culture and Native culture are separate in terms of making art. Bell Hooks was here in Santa Fe and gave a lecture in which she said, 'Art is the location of hope.' I don't think, if you take that as a definition, that hope is exclusively for one people or another. I do know that people have differing opinions about what makes art."

Then, in response to a question about the perception of a Native political ideology in my work,

For me the word "political" is inaccurate. What people see in my work as political has to do with being active. I see politics as reactive, people just reacting and responding to patterns of power in the society that we've made. For me to heal from the processes that I think are prevalent in our society, which can be best described as addiction, my own sense of direction and my own thoughts about correct action are derived from a spiritual sense, not from a political sense. Most of what I see as destructive, that is happening to people, the animals and the earth isn't based on politics; it's based on addiction. To heal from the effects of that kind of hard exchange—giving up life to make money—I had to look at a spiritual way of addressing that.

Western thought fragmented itself when spirituality was divided from science, whereas traditional Indian beliefs, expressed through differing people that I've encountered, don't talk about science as being separate. In fact, an aunt of mine—an extended family kind of aunt—said that in the Wasco language, the word for science also meant collaboration. So we're not individuals in that sense—making art all alone—but we are in collaboration with community, with the natural processes of the earth and we also are limited by the physical reality of what we can actually create. To think of the repercussions of what sound means and to think of the repercussions of what words mean and what light means when it hits something—that's spiritual to me. I don't know if I actually step into the political mode when I write poetry. It's just that those are the terms of the language I have to use for other people to understand what *I have witnessed*, because that's the common language—the political language—or if it's talking about environmental things, you have to talk about it in the form of language people can understand.

At times, art for an individual is to experience and make known through the filter of the art or the making of an object the opening of space for the viewer or the listener. This is the place that art truly makes its original imprint upon the maker and his sphere of influence. This is how I think of the work of my family and the work of my friends. As I told Abbott, "Art is a lifestyle, not separate from the human being who is actually the creator or the force of energy that's making these objects possible.... Art has to do with ethereal issues. We can't live without our physical bodies on the planet but we can continue to exist as spiritual beings or as essence of the earth."

The process of writing and making my art fills the spaces in my personal life, which is shaped by what I had previously thought of as breaks in legacy.

MEMORY DRAWN FROM ELIZABETH PITT,
SET IN PROPER PLACE BY NORA AND MARIE,
SITKA ALASKA, 1992

I.

As wayward fatigue wears into the body accustomed
to the position of invalid mannerisms, I am the inhabitant
inside the environment without song. The frazzled lineage
of dubbed-in memories of predestined salmon, designated
deer and elk tags. Bitter complaint and frailty
are the reprimand of asphalt, city night the cauldron
of bereavement. The traveled road of tourist into Basin
and Range is the corridor of fragrant skull-colored sage.

The juniper and evergreen designs of my Grandmother's
birthplace. The monochrome origins of acuity become
the glances' marked distance towards Wolf Point and Kah-
Nee-Ta's resting place. The medicinal in landscape
is my Grandmother, her forthright knowledge, the positive
of corporeality that I had thoughtlessly honored as a difficult
place. My conscience is a bundle calloused by the telling
five generations of Mother and Daughter, one step removal,
the rest the predicated heritage.

(from *Luminaries of the Humble* [excerpt, Section 1] University of
Arizona Press, 1994)

I had no understanding of legacy when it was first introduced to me.
This was through the subtle instruction of my maternal grandmother.
I looked at the precious heirlooms and listened to the stories attached
to them. I listened to my own attachment, a link to describe my place
within a family and a particular place. The words ring true, creates the
story that will make the work go well. Spinning stories back into existence intensified my desire to know more and examine those objects in
my mind after they were physically lost to us.

I believe this will is supported by the prayers of my mother's
mother for her grandchildren. I cherish the memory of her prayers, especially the song she said her great-grandmother Kah-nee-ta taught
her in preparation for the time my grandmother would be alone or sad.
The songs she sang most were *washat* ("worship") songs when the
music came over her.

As a little girl, I had outgrown a pink cloth wingdress made for my
aunt Lillian when she was small, so I didn't have a dress of my own to
fit me to dance in at a powwow in Warm Springs. I thought I needed to
have a dress to join the beautifully dressed dancers. When I asked if I
could dance without a dress, my grandmother said, touching my arm,
"You can dance if it is in your heart. Never feel ashamed of yourself
because of what you have to wear. Imagine this skin as your dress. Your
invisible dress." My skin was the dress given to me from my ancestors,
like the heirlooms that were bundled up in her room.

Many times my grandfather and grandmother shared anecdotes of
their early years at the dining table. While both had lost their parents
and siblings during childhood, my grandmother, a Tygh-Wyampum

woman, had a special upbringing. She was raised by her great-grandmother, Kah-nee-ta. My grandfather, Lewis Edwards Pitt, was part of a ranching Wasco-Wishram family. At age sixteen he and his brother lost their mother. She was preceded in death by her husband and this was a difficult era for a woman to be alone. My grandmother felt they were poor by comparison to my grandfather's memories of childhood. Kah-nee-ta had to resort to making her everyday clothing out of burlap sacking. After her chores, she would ride her horse with her dogs in the hills around the hot springs. This was her play time. She didn't have any toys. Grandfather, in an act of great tenderness, reached over me (as a child I sat between them most of the time) and said, "You must have been a beautiful little girl with long braids down your back on a beautiful horse."

THE INVISIBLE DRESS

It is tanned deerhide. Sometimes it is too large
because the Great Mothers made this two tail dress
for a powerful purpose. Constructed with water,
soaked in brains, scraped on tree posts with rib bone,
it was imbued during this process with thoughts
for protection and legacies.
They evoked the stars, the light with symbols,
patterned behavior with song. This was given in Dream.
The tones focused luminous depiction of story.
Neither flesh nor labor are empty of reflection.
Think of the deer. It is appropriate
to cover with the handiwork of survival.
The Great Fathers brought this passage about, safely
in their hands. Infinite in this dress, together,
brought back through hardship and inexplicable turmoil,
we emerge, again, wearing this dress, necessary
and radiantly fearless.

(from *Luminaries of the Humble,* University of Arizona Press, 1994)

The outward appearance of confidence that comes over me as I perform my work was given to me from the power of words. The development of writing poetry while plowing through adversity provided me with a hopeful attitude. I grew into a life of peace. My family supported this growth. Looking at my childhood in the sixties, I see this time period as being difficult for Indian people. I did not perceive my place or my gifts as part of lineage or concern myself with the nature of belief and practice. I did not understand that my grandparents had been through tremendous difficulties. For my parents and their siblings this is an era that is not often discussed. The changes, the desires, and fallacies of a contemporary American mainstream were not part of our sense of direction. We wanted the best, did well enough and worked hard. My grandparents deserved a rich old age. They were more concerned with generational continuity than material wealth.

My grandparents expected me to learn and do well in school. Many times they lectured about the necessity of going to college. I was told to save my money to pay for a good education. "You must never give up. College is like having savings." This is part of my heritage. I could have glimpsed the comprehensible parts of potential much sooner. I need to be more tolerant of weaknesses. My uncle once told me, and I marked in my journal, that "We have not yet begun to realize the potential of the human soul."

I belong to two strong, courageous groups of people, the Columbia River Plateau people and the Diné. These groups recognize and maintain connections to a source of vital landbase. In the Northwest we have laws given to the people by the Creator, through stories and gifts of oratory and language. I understand, as I meet more people from other places, that this integrity is honored in several ways, in distinctive languages. At times I did not see being a daughter of two landscapes and languages as a wonderful advantage. It has only been recently, within the last decade, that I have thought about my multiple citizenship in the Columbia River Plateau people and the Diné.

My immediate family, my grandparents Lewis Edwards Pitt, Elizabeth Thompson Pitt, my mother, Charlotte, my aunt Lillian, my uncle Lewis Pitt, have always spoken of my Diné heritage with great respect. I told my uncle Lewis I received a much needed letter from my father, Guy Woody, expressing his happiness that I was near him in Santa Fe, teaching at the Institute of American Indian Arts (IAIA). My uncle told me, "You have received your gift for writing from your father. He has always written wonderful letters." This is true. My love for language, the power of it, comes from the Southwest, as well. To paraphrase one of my thoughtful Diné students, Harrison Eskeets, "We have made language mundane." We are unaware of the "sacredness that emanates from our tongue." We have so much to learn from the older languages of the Americas. I have so much to learn and I am attentive to the way life unravels and reworks itself together again. I write of this in a poem that is included in my newest work, *Seven Hands, Seven Hearts.*

CHINLE SUMMER

Loneliness for me is being the daughter of two landscapes,
distant from the horizon circling me.
The red earth completely round.
The sky a deep bowl of turquoise overhead.
Mother and father. Loneliness
rising up like thunderheads. The rain pours over
the smooth rocks into the canyon that is familiar.

This is the road that leads to my father's home.
After twenty years I stand on the threshold of his mother's hogan.
Grandmother sits in the cool dark, out of the light
from the door and smoke hole. She talks softly
in the Diné language.

Talking to me as I grew in her warmth, my mother
lowered herself into this canyon, barefoot and unafraid.
She walked miles in high heels to church by this road
that runs alongside Canyon de Chelly.
She was a river woman walking in dust.
The Recumbent Woman whispers inside different languages.
I am one story. Beauty walked South then North again.
Beauty sparked physical creation.
A strong and wild will draws up the land into the body.
My journey circles back, unraveling, remaking itself
like the magnificent loomwork of my grandmother's center.
My grandfather once told me, "Lizzy, I was busy singing
over there ... you were here. So, I came home to see you."

In the beginning of my awareness of eminence in language, I realized its source in a complex belief system cannot be separated into segments. It remains in certain ways pure and necessary. It describes and bears the stamp of relationship to the land and collaboration among people of a specific place. We learn of new ways of describing our lives and the lives of other people brought to us from other places of the earth. I feel that we all have a base that is strong if we are attentive to the place where we live. The climate and geography describe and shape us. A friend once said, "Your voice has the lyric lilt of the Columbia River Plateau." He could also hear the "wind of the arid land of Arizona" in my tone. The land is part of our makeup. It has shaped my voice. When I went to school at the Institute of American Arts in the early eighties, each person I met had a story and a special way of being. They shared their place of origin. I heard the many dialects of English filtered through Native enunciation and slang. Of course many could tell I was from the Northwest by my accent and laughter.

Through my work with other artists and meeting with many people from separate areas of the country, collaboration had new meaning for me. In 1993 I was part of the nonprofit Americans for Indian Opportunity (AIO) Ambassadors Program for young Indian leaders. We met four times with one another and select leaders of many different regions and professions throughout the year. The first session began with personal oratory. We talked of our strengths. Some of the individual stories were essentially evocative of spiritual thought. Some people talked of what had shaped them in the form of surviving difficulties. We felt a powerful bond. We acknowledged the appreciation of our differences. We were from many regions of the country and sometimes individuals, like myself, were made up of many tribes and mixtures of people.

The final meetings were held in Cuernavaca, Mexico, and Mexico City. There we had audience with Nahuatl leaders, Otomi Indian leaders, and the populist party's presidential candidate. They impressed upon us the enduring Native peoples' desire for self-sufficiency and self-definition. As is often the case, this vocal leadership carries with it the threat of personal physical danger. The Nahuatl spiritual leader "Capitán" discussed with us the Aztec calendar, his view of its significance, and read it to us as a book. He told us that there were many books destroyed by the Spanish in purging Mexico of history. These books talked of the universe. If we could read these books, as they were intended to be read, the stars would be readable. We could see them as the eyes of night. We would know the meaning we possess as human beings and why we are on this earth. He described the "Worlds" to us, the history of humanity, the creation of all people, the ways we fouled our lives and earth. We were punished by the floods. We reemerged. He described the world we are now in as the "World of Consciousness" and that the next world will be the "World of Justice." This was a fresh way of describing history for me and predictions as part of the Aztec calendar, as it is more commonly known.

We must live as we have been instructed, or suffer in this world with those who live with no fear of punishment for their actions. Especially people who show a disregard for life. Capitán said that this calendar survived because it was a stone tablet and the Spanish in their plundering took it to the Vatican as spoil of their conquest. An astronomer recognized it as a calendar. A calendar that was far more accurate than the Gregorian calendar, which was off by three months. Capitán slapped his forehead, and with a grimace said, "And you know that really got to them, because 'time is money,' and all that time went to waste!"

He made us laugh with his physical sense of humor, even though he gave us a lecture of serious matters. The people who accompanied him were very kind to us. They prepared a meal of pre-Columbian indigenous food. It was such gentle food. We all felt wonderful afterward. We promised them we would not forget the people south of the political boundaries of our country. This experience made me recall the talk at the "Returning the Gift" conference, where writers from the South, some as exiles, spoke of the Eagle and Condor reuniting.

Throughout the year we talked of many things in the AIO program, and in my personal life, many new ideas came to light. We had fierce discussions about identity, sovereignty, and blood quantum. A topic like blood quantum is controversial and dramatically effects our lives. While we met in Washington, DC, I wrote a letter to my friend, Okanogan artist Joe Feddersen, about these experiences coupled with impressions of a recent trip "home." We used this letter in a 1994 collaborative installation of texts, and unusual book forms, at the Tula Foundation Gallery in Atlanta, Georgia. I feel that this letter, although suspended in my private thought, was shaped in part by the Ambassadors Program. Joe felt it described a sense of place and belonging, while knowing our differences even in the differing eras of a similar people.

In my journal of this project, when I began photographing the hands of the Ambassadors, I say about this part of the process,

I was thinking of what each person had said, more or less, about being an Indian, by looks, skin color and the psychic pain of identity and perception of themselves. That trust needs to be established to "reveal" oneself and also to see acceptance as a "given" or response to trust and honesty. What the A.I.O. "subjects" revealed to me was based on trust and honesty. Not a quality in terms of competitiveness or the dog-eat-dog world that is out there. I mean, the face itself can be used as a tool of deception whereas the hands can reveal character, by use, hard work or vanity. Hands are a tool and an aspect of ourselves that we take for granted. The genetic code of dexterity or strength, the fragility and the blemish are not covered up as easily or altered. Except by time and usage or care.

The letter I wrote to Joe from Washington, DC, demonstrates how the project caused a deeper examination into my own issues of identity and the sense of becoming mature:

May 13, 1994, Hyatt Hotels and Resorts

Well, Joe, am back east again. Saw Reyna tonight at the big reception. It's been a long trip, long week. My great-aunt Amelia passed away and we went over the mountains, took the car, my mother and sister, to Warm Springs. Although it was a somber event, people were saying good things and I really felt good I went over. Sometimes being there, just being home is the best medicine there is. My people are beautiful and as I was flying here, I shed a few tears, thinking how it is to be so far away. The more I travel, the more I understand how precious our country is. The truth and honesty that pours out of the folks at home. A portion of our family was not there, but Cyrus Katchia [and] his sister Caroline Tohet led out their family and people. As Cyrus passed, he waved his eagle feather at my mother and I to join the women. I was so touched to be remembered, but I couldn't speak.

As I twirled and moved my hand, my body began to feel sure and the world centered. I loved this woman and I hoped my thoughts helped. One cousin said, "Pray hard for everyone. If we get strong the world gets better." The salmon, deer meat, roots, fruit, corn, potatoes and the meal shared renewed my strength. It's odd to be thousands of miles away and thinking of telling you this. As Jolene and I walked outside, we strolled up the road, the air was rich with the exquisite smells of earth, sage, juniper. We were cupped in the liquid sense of sky, the mountain in the distance, the ground. Even some guys driving by hollered at us. They recognized Jolene. I even saw children who loved me when they were little. Now they are big. One girl asked for me, and I was so glad. She used to come over to my house to "play." She'd ask me to teach her things, play with Uppittee. Draw. She wants to be an artist. Both her parents went to I.A.I.A. It's so funny, because she always would ask to go to "Lizzy's" and one aunty thought I was a little girl and was surprised when she finally met me. Anyway, I wonder at times why I stay away so long. I guess because I would miss it, if I did visit more. Sometimes, the work, the work I do, doesn't seem to fit and then I know I'm gathering things, knowledge, ideas, meaningful images when I travel.

Anyway, just a short note before I begin the "big doings" here. I guess Alyce and Phillip have returned. Reyna filled me in on the wedding. Asked me questions about this and that. I forget not everyone does things the same. . . ."

(excerpt of letter used in "Archives" installation, Atlanta, Georgia, 1994)

Preceding this time period, for another collaboration with Joe Feddersen we were asked to create a broadside for the Seattle-based art magazine *Reflex*. In our discussions, which always began with the process of ideas being exchanged to intermix within our collaborations, I told Joe of an experience I had while washing dishes. I was listening to the old black-and-white television I had in my kitchen. A program came on the air about the inundation of Celilo Falls ("Wyam—Echo of Falling Water") by the Dalles Dam in 1957. It was a historical piece. As I turned to look, they were showing a commercial postcard of a non-Native man standing next to a pile of skulls and crossed bones, holding a pickax.

These bones were taken from the inundated burial islands of the mid-Columbia River. The bones were removed and shipped off to museum collections. I almost fainted, seeing the remains of my ancestors, and knowing that they were not reburied as I had always thought, but shipped off. As we talked, Joe brought up the many aspects to how "our inheritance is obscured by neglect." This was a title for a print he made partially in response to the destructive human impact upon the environment, especially the *Exxon Valdez* oil spill. We used images of Joe's black-and-white photographs of water, an empty reservoir landscape, and a commercial postcard found in the Oregon Historical Society photo archives similar to the one I saw on the television program. The poem was superimposed over the images.

Upon hearing of our project my friend and former schoolmate at IAIA, Phillip Minthorn, said these bones were also traded with other institutions besides the Smithsonian Institution. Another man while in Russia heard of some of these bones being housed in an institution there. When I gave a copy of the broadsides to my uncle Lewis, his son, Pita, asked very firmly, "Where are our ancestors' bones, and when are we going to get them back?" Fortunately, the tribes began the initial process of working for the return of our ancestral people's remains. A partial success was realized on December 20, 1994, when remains were returned from the Smithsonian Institution for reburial along the Chewana/Columbia River. It was a private ceremony comprised of Wasco people.

A storm blew in and passed, in a sense. We know that the University of California, University of Washington, and the Russian institution where the other people's remains are cached will need more pressure to complete the return of ancestral remains. When we can see the need to give without thought of personal gain, we become more humane and truly powerful.

My uncle Lewis relayed a story of Yakama elder Walter Spedis. As a young man he was asked to remove horses from a Wasco cemetery. He was a "cowboy." He tried with all his might, but he could not manage anything more than following the stampede in a circle. He said that when he gave up the idea that he was a cowboy, the horses flowed out of the cemetery like water. It seemed they were instructed in a way they could understand to do so, and it was done. He rode out behind them as a man freed from impatience and labels.

"Waterways Endeavor to Translate Silence from the Currents" is the poem from this series used on the *Reflex* broadside. It is part of the "Inheritance Obscured" section of *Luminaries of the Humble.*

> First of the voices are innocent from memory,
> desolate synthesis of weeping rain,
> into dry creek beds.
> Stone with roots, companion of guardians,
> bares itself toward the summit of crowns.
> The exchange of bones for sawdust, for silt, for worthless currency.
>
> The clouding springs hiss into veins of fissures,
> topsoil wears into desert, an illusion of prosperity,
> fringed by momentum of cutting down origin.
>
> The hiatus is the flourish of sword and degeneration.
> In our genesis, the beginning of words
> meant that we would not be without land or relationships.
> Vacuity, the lack of emotion etches into the destruction
> the scaffolds of abundance, rapids, falls, spawning beds,
> the echo of falling water. The nascent place of all
>
> the songs lingers amongst the multitude of ancestors,
> commonly wedged into bone hills, vandalized and catalogued.
> Dislocated from one another, we are now flooded,
> resting in place.
> We suffocate in the backwater of decadence
> and fractious contempt.
> Purity of the ancient is the language without tongues.
> The river elegantly marks its swirls on its surface,
> a spiral that tells of a place
> that remains undisturbed.

By the context of being part of a specific community, I could assume I possess inherent traits within the culture of the Columbia River Plateau. It is greater than experience. It is important to ensure we will have what we need, by maintenance of a mind-set to include the care of the land as part of care for ourselves. Witnessing how my community has thrived gives me a sense of security. I believe generosity is a characteristic of a group of people who are secure and competent. This is something I learned early on, in my grandparents' house, among my mother's relatives, as well as from personal experiences throughout my life. The telling and receiving of a story is a quality of generosity that I have taken for granted.

ROSETTE

Beading a story
is like a weaving,
a spiral, space making itself in the light
and colors pick up
what one loves on the needle
like a song.
over and over,
the repetition is solace.
A vibrant note in the thread
moves through this fabric.

(from *Luminaries of the Humble,* University of Arizona Press, 1994)

I had to investigate and accept all facets of the society that shaped me, the ancient, the relatively new presences, and the potential ways we have to self-destruct. I wrote a series of difficult poems in the section titled "The People" in *Luminaries of the Humble* that centers on addictive preoccupation and process in the nature of people, the horror of early death, the loss of children to adoption, the sense of futility, of victimization, and I close that chaotic sequence with a poem titled "Recovery." The persona in this poem is seen from afar.

In part, this poem came from listening to a Bill Moyer's program where he talked with Chief Oren Lyons of the Six Nations Iroquois Confederacy. Chief Lyons talked of the formation of the United States as a spiritual beginning from the perspective of the Iroquois people's sense of history. This was a pivotal point in history between people who held great potential. If we could see this event with the earth spinning in space, a new spiritual fire grew upon this continent at that time. I imaginatively begin to see my own recovery from alcoholism, chronic depression, and delayed stress syndrome as a small breath of a new life. It was my own life I worked to save with the support of my family and community, and from what seemed to be a serendipitous exposure to Native thought in a commercial venue.

RECOVERY

A match's spark is an element of premeditation,
contrived to stop this chill.
Hover near the flame.

The black sticks of strikes lie as ideograms.
The portrayals resemble emblems.
Act out. Strike back.
Pain is reckless.
itself a reaction, preserved in instinct,
of the restless. In the deep whisper of arriving naked,
we fill with the mother's sound in membrane.
The fine bones in the cavities quiver in assembly.

Without the reaction, pain is simple to endure.
The tissue in absolute hum
is bee's distance to winter,
moving as many to one obstinate dance.
We survive the blind disassociation from flesh,
the absence of sensation, absence of self.

Ice splitting the rock hasn't grown into itself.
We move fervently away from release into what is greater.
As we make this sound of matches striking in one breath,
the flame is so large.
A moment so fierce, it consumes
fear we have collected,
earmarked for the next arrangements.
Without our memories of one another,
frozen,
the flame is small, but spectacular, a luminaria.
in the expanse, a sky is fragile in the exhale,
a tendril swirl from the equator.
A new person is among the survivors.

In my first experiences of "contact," meaning when I had to hold
my own among strangers, was my entry into elementary school. I was
subjected to several types of prejudgment and the bias of the West. As
an adult I look back upon my school years with the two communities
of Madras and Warm Springs, Oregon, with fondness. I see the parts
that have worn thin with an idealization that there is a way to own

prosperity. The means are to be found in the American construct of freedom and democracy. This all seems to be without personal work to preserve history. When I first moved to Portland, Oregon, to attend Portland State University, I was surprised to notice how transitory the urban world was. I met people who had no homes. I met people who hadn't spoken to their family in years. I met with the heart of a dark mind. Some of the people I made friends with or made acquaintance with died. One person from Warm Springs was killed on her twenty-first birthday as she stepped between a shotgun of an unknown driver and her husband in an argument about traffic. Another woman whom I had great laughing sessions with was murdered by her boyfriend. Her friend who slept in the other room was killed, too. I compiled several of these stories in my poem in *Hand Into Stone* titled "Cold Blood." In a way, it is my process of coping with the sense of weakness engendered by the behaviors of addiction and violence.

Historical allusion in the passionate talk of patriotism caused me to look at the myths of "America." The reconstruction of history suits the ends and means of a system embroiled in materialism. To love our country, we need to "walk our talk," as it is said in the Alcoholics Anonymous fellowship. Through the unfairness of it all, the waste of human potential and lives, these sad memories have lost power to deplete my sense of purpose. I make poems and make objects. Through movement and creativity I work for health. I prepare to oppose any return or spiraling back into the inconsistencies of ignorance, to maintain a personal sense of well-being. I have spent a great deal of time looking at addiction. Especially since its patterns have imprinted themselves on my life so deeply. My mother sobered up in my early teens. My mother has stated many times it was thoughts of my sister and me that enabled her to continue living during times of chaos and duress. It took me ten years to write the poem "Perfidy." Her story is the framework of the poem. On the same night I watched the news flash of her escape from the University of Oregon Health and Science Center Hospital, the news brought to the world the first grisly terrors of the Manson murders. I did not know the escaped Indian woman was my mother. No one knew the meaning of the messages cut onto the chests of the murder victims. I went to sleep with a chill.

PERFIDY

A few sounds, over and again, grip me through this drunken mess.
I walk to the oblivious road, gone and done for.
A few beats of my pulse splinter through the plates of my skull.
The gun blast, I do not know where the bullet hit
or the depth of my wound.
My children, I regress.
I pray to Our Father, see Daddy
Mother does not condemn.

I have fruit so sweet with youth,
who are daughters, opposite
of self, like naïveté and craziness.

In the gentle possession of touch,
a hardened lullaby,
I see my daughters as magnets, together.
One large, one small.
I blow against the cyclone fence
and their unfailing grief and affection.

The television tells of my charm against calamity.
How the large Indian female,
shot in the head, late twenties, escapes
police guard and the university hospital.
The eldest daughter's skin shivers as she prays,
"If I die before I wake … "

The brain ferments itself out of pain.
I will not say who is the perpetrator.
I want to know the one face is free
to see the dead return.
The hair curls out white,
feathers over my angelic face.
I am an abrasive pendulum
swinging back and forth, hypnotic
as a knife.

My reprisal is only to live
and grow into my daughters.

(from *Luminaries of the Humble,* University of Arizona Press, 1994)

People die easily from lack of intervention. I have been shaped and influenced by my mother's recovery.

She sobered up in an era of political activism. She worked in the first free clinic in the skid row area of Portland, Oregon. She worked among the derelicts, the migrant workers, and the young socialists who would eventually become longtime friends. She was on the founding board of a now defunct Urban Indian Council, and was one of the first counselors at the Native American Rehabilitation Association of Portland, Oregon. She did many more things as a community activist.

It was during this proactive period of her life that my sister and I joined her. We marched in protests, brandished slogan signs for the Migrant Farm Workers of America, listened to impassioned speeches in a fairly radical, progressive environment of grassroots activities. We lived in the American Indian Movement house. As children, we watched the eagle appear over the crowds gathering in downtown Portland for one of the first Indian-organized spiritual walks, moving south from Seattle to Alcatraz, and its speeches and rally near the Bureau of Indian Affairs area office. We worked to collect food donations for the people in support of Wounded Knee. Most important, we were part of an active community, even though we were under scrutiny from the FBI. We felt strong in the presence of such bravery. My sister and I were the children of many people during this time.

My mother's boyfriend, Devere Eastman, was the first person who philosophically talked to us of Native religion. He talked of the Lakota ways. Outside of our life in Warm Springs, I had never met people who were practitioners of Native religion. In some ways, this was the first step of public resurgence of practicing the older ways. My mother joined the Washat and Washani/Feather religion of the Columbia River Plateau. Of those times, I barely remember what responsibilities she had. Now I know it takes years of devotion and participation. As a teenager, I began to feel that the "pan-Indian" political movement was losing relevance for me. Especially when the efforts at Wounded Knee seemed opposed by so many conservatives who had power over my life in school. I talked in class of the history of Wounded Knee with a red-faced science teacher, asking him if he knew that the people who were buried there were massacred. He could only sputter in rage, disclaiming the Indian militants as aligned with the communists to pull apart this country.

As an adult woman, I drove my mother to one of the Sun dances held in Mt. Hood National Forest. We brought my grandmother with us for the ride. As we sat in the car, my grandmother looked around, said, "EEEE, there's a lot of Indian people here. What's going on?" I said, "A Sun dance, Granma." She looked carefully at the people dressed in the Indian way, then asked, "Are they praying here?" I said, "Yes. It's the Lakota people's way." She bowed her head, "It is always good when people pray," and said a prayer in the Sahaptin language. I realized that my grandmother probably would pray for anyone and would have no problems with what I had thought of a "pan-Indian" approach, anywhere, anytime. I felt a little twinge of guilt. I had lost touch with the original thoughts that she had instilled in me about faith. People are necessary in the movement for a better life. *All people.* She was a tolerant woman.

Living in Madras, Oregon, we were regularly approached by the "Watch Tower" newsletter people who would come to our door. My grandfather would kindly turn them away. When my grandmother and I were alone and I saw them walking up to our house, I would run in to my grandmother: "People are here!" My grandmother would wipe her hands on her apron and answer the door with me holding on to her dress. I was shy of strangers. They would go into their talk, while we sat on the couch side by side. My grandmother would patiently listen to them. Then came the part about asking for a donation to continue God's work. My grandmother would get her purse and take out a dime, it was always a dime, and hand it to them. They would hold that dime, look at her, look at me, look at our house, thank her, and leave. I wonder what they thought of her. To my grandmother, a dime was a lot of money. She had no idea that the church people expected more from devout people. They probably wouldn't understand that my grandmother contributed daily to God's work through prayer at every meal and each night.

"Sovereign is only a sovereign if it acts as one" was stated by a fellow Ambassador, John Printup, who along with me and several other young Indian leaders of the Americans for Indian Opportunity Ambassadors Program discussed why and how we enact and reinforce tribal integrity in government and management of resources. In this statement, he was well grounded and educated in not only the American system of government, of which he was a part by being an employee on the state level, but also as a member of the Six Nations Iroquois Confederacy, the governmental foundations of which still continue from a model that could not be found in its entirety in the "Old World."

"Old World" is a title that we did not use much at Americans for Indian Opportunity meetings since much of our culture and most of our religion is as old as the earth. These religions have been practiced continuously. I learned more about this common thread between us during that year. I learned more about my own people as we worked on refining the AIO's Tribal Management System (TMS). The system's design is based upon consensual tribal governance, and is computer assisted. The democratic principles of the old government of my people were partly adopted by a tribal-originated constitution and bylaws ratified on February 14, 1938, in Warm Springs, Oregon. The beliefs and practices by the Warm Springs people, as we are collectively called, are based on ancient government. While this system of government is a means to enact some measure of self-governance during a time of looming federal presence, it is in principle how we align with our own time-honored and -honed models, described in the Declaration of Sovereignty of the tribes at Warm Springs, Oregon, of 1992.

It can culturally be spoken of, in terms of definition, that we had an egalitarian society, and its necessity for mobility, quick adjustment, and self-will was a consensual government of full participation. A society like this is comprised of strong individuals. And this strength is still necessary.

You can read of the good mind in archived narratives, especially evidenced in research through works by Native writers like Gloria Bird. In her book of poetry and prose, *Scattered Red Roots*, she collected people's narratives who were near Chief Joseph. He was a peace chief. He was responsible for the safety and well-being of the old people, women, children, and their livestock. Many of the poems sources are from research into people's narratives of that time. The collective tactical genius of the war chiefs as they attempted the exodus of the Nee Mee Poo/Nez Percé to Canada was incredible. Formerly called a war, this episode in Northwest history has been written about extensively. Still, the educational system's treatment of it is as a war, not as an attack by the U.S. military against an indigenous group of people comprised of mostly women and children.

In talking of the power of this work with my uncle Lewis, he said to me that as we were squeezed onto smaller and smaller tracts of land of our vast homeland, we had to become great strategists. He said the Natural Laws of the Creator, for example, said that women gathering food did so without men. As a demonstration of good faith concerning our neighbors, to maintain good thought, the men could not appear to be contentious. Still, they managed to have business, somewhere, near the women and children, in the mountains and meadows. He said, quite well, "We could not let our precious people be vulnerable. Yet we could not insult our neighbors by outright suspicion. We had to be tactically smart and respectful in order to live among so many different types of people."

Our subsistence lifestyle is maintenance of good thought. Our art, song, thankfulness, ceremony, and industry centered on the recognition of being aware of nourishment for our bodies is with life taken respectfully. We must give back, and not detrimentally impact the system of coexistence.

My grandfather would take us to the Deschutes River. We would park with the doors open for a breeze and wait to see the fish jump. He did this to please my grandmother. My grandmother would laugh and exclaim, "I saw a fish jump, another one, over there!" My grandfather would ask, "How did it go?" Grandma would arc her hand through the air and make an expressive plopping noise with her lips. He would laugh with such pleasure, watching her watch the fish. Trout, like the roots, berries, salmon, deer, elk, and many natural plants, are the lives we are in partnership with upon the land. My poem "Plateau Women" in *Luminaries of the Humble* describes the women's recognition of and participation with the elements of the land.

We are all capable of forgetting the stories of our past failures and loss, spoken of in original myths and stories of our communities. This may be a simplistic view; still, it is the manner in which I can best describe what I feel about my fears, which sometimes hinder my life's work.

This is how patterns effect me. I was told, as I left my home, that all

I have experienced in my small cloister of communities is a micro-cosm of the larger world. When I could begin to understand the ailments of the smaller, the complexity of the greater whole would become manageable. I could heal myself, work to restore peace in other ways, by example. I did not understand this direction given to me at the time, being young. Through serious reflection, I may only know the tip of the responsibility that I have as an artist, as a maker, as a poet.

As a child, before my memory had a name or function, I notice the light from my grandmother's room. Sitting on her sway-back bed, one hand holds a moccasin, the other pushes a needle in and pulls it through. She dips into an opened bundle. Her needle rises up with color. Her thread vibrates as she pulls the beads to the deer hide. This bundle is an old dress filled with mix-and-match beads, beeswax, old pieces of broken jewelry, buttons, and sequins. The pungent odor of smoked deer hide fills the room. I lean my belly on the edge of the bed. My hands move into the beads like they do into water. Remnants of older projects, the old mixed with new beads. I watch her pick up a color by some magical discernment onto her needle. The pattern is her own design. "I love the mountains," she says as she tacks down a stepped design border. She is quiet while beading. I ask if I can make something. She nods. We pick up beads together, making our own special choices. The beads become memories threaded into personal patterns. The strands circle my neck. Fragrant of smoked hide, these simple beads bring in the quiet of my grandmother to my heart. I thread extra needles for her. I love the smell of her beads.

Autobiography

OFELIA ZEPEDA

Ofelia Zepeda, Tohono O'odham (Papago), is a professor in the Department of Linguistics at the University of Arizona, where she also teaches in the American Indian Studies program. Her poems have been published in a number of journals and anthologies and her first volume, Ocean Power: Poems from the Desert, *came out in 1995. She is also the author of scholarly articles and* A Papago Grammar. *Since 1993 she has been the series editor of* Sun Tracks, *a Native American literary publication. In 1999 she was awarded a MacArthur Fellowship.*

I think that if I have to say something about my work I would point out at least three things that either influence or are reasons for my writing. The three will likely include people, the desert environment, and Native language literacy. These three overlap in many ways when I begin to talk about them. People certainly strongly influence me. Many of the ideas I get for poems come from other people, their experiences, their imaginations, and their dreams. Some of my work is certainly influenced by the people who are my immediate and extended family and the people who came before them. I am influenced by their stories and their lives. Many of the other people who influence my writing are ones I have met during my lifetime; again, their own stories and lives sometimes affect me greatly.

Perhaps the other thing that greatly influences my work, especially in the *Ocean Power* collection, is the landscape of the desert. It is not so much the land and the way it looks, but the events that take place in the desert, some of which are natural phenomena and others that are not. I am intrigued by the way people and the events in the desert respond to one another. Most significantly, like many O'odham, I am most intrigued by the events surrounding rain. The O'odham, like other Southwest tribes, have a considerable repertoire of oral tradition that treats the topic of rain. I am continually influenced by this rich oral tradition and that of the everyday talk of rain and related events. I like to think that the O'odham and the Pima Indians, our cousins, have some of the most beautiful oral text about rain and phenomena surrounding it. This is no surprise since one of the most important seasons in the desert is the rain season, which takes place in late July and August, and traditionally much ritual takes place so that this season might be a good one. For the O'odham much of this ritual is not only for rain, but is for what translates as "fixing the earth." O'odham claim they fix the earth each season for everyone; this is in essence what has been labeled by ethnographers as the beginning of the O'od-ham new year. So you can see why I would be so influenced by the act of rain in the desert. And memories from my childhood continue to be fresh in my mind when I think of the everyday events associated with rain in the desert.

And finally, another of the motivating factors of my work has to do with something purely pragmatic. I started writing in the O'odham language for my students in a university setting. This has extended to a larger audience. I like to think that writing and getting material published in my native language will serve to promote Native language literacy among O'odham speakers and students of the O'odham language, and also serve, on a global scale, to give an additional dimension to the language, the written form, thereby bringing it closer to the level of other so-called prestige languages of the world.

The O'odham language, like other American Indian languages, is in a precarious position as a spoken language. Although a large number of adults and young adults still speak O'odham as their first language, there is an ever-increasing number of children who are not learning the language in the home. In my efforts to promote learning O'odham as a second language, I find the written form of O'odham to be a new and exciting tool for young and adult learners. Using the written form of the language offers a new challenge to the speakers and students of this language. I like to think that writing creative text can inspire young writers and even adult writers to contribute to our growing literature of O'odham printed text. Such a genre would be of significance to mankind.

So, as the vehicle for talking about myself and my work I would like to take on these three things as influences for my work. As I discuss them I will include relevant samples of my writing.

Before I begin, though, I feel it is necessary to say something about the Tohono O'odham as further background for my work. I am Tohono O'odham, the tribe formerly known as Papago, of southern Arizona. This tribe, by and large, is not a very well-known tribe. It does not have the commercial appeal as compared with other tribes in Arizona, like the Navajo and the Apache and even the substantially smaller group, the Hopi. It is not clear why this is the case, but nonetheless this is our status. This status, of course, has its benefits; for instance, we are seldom interrupted by onslaughts of tourists or pilgrims in search of mystics in the depths of the Sonoran Desert. A result of the relative isolation and lack of notoriety of the O'odham is that it is one of the rare tribes that still maintain a large portion of their traditional territory as their contemporary reservation proper. The reservation, though, stops at the Mexico-U.S. border, while O'odham indigenous land, history, and families continue beyond the international boundary extending down to the ocean. It is beyond this border where some of my family stories begin. Both of my parents' families are from "the other side"; *ganhu 'aigojeḑ 'amjeḑ,* this is what one is called if her traditional homeland is in what is now Mexico. This adds further explanation to some of my writing, which will be made clearer later.

Although the O'odham in Arizona have an extensive reservation, second in size to the Navajo Nation, my family has never lived on the reservation. The explanation for this is because of their history as O'odham originally residing in Mexico and coming into the U.S. and Arizona only fairly recently. Like other Sonoran O'odham, as they are often called, once my family came into Arizona they lived in and worked the various border towns of the reservation including Ajo, Yuma, Casa Grande, Coolidge, Florence, and Stanfield. They lived and worked among other migrant workers, especially in the 1950s and 1960s, including Yaqui Indians, Mexicans, and blacks from the South. Even though many reservation O'odham worked harvesting cotton, a major commodity crop in southern Arizona, families like ours were a "marked" group of O'odham because we did not leave the cotton field areas after the season was over and return to the reservation, but instead lived there year-round. Reservation O'odham then labeled families such as ours as "in the cotton field O'odham," and even now as way of explanation I can explain my family's contemporary residence as, *toki 'oidag c-eḑ ki:* "living on cotton field farms." Presently, my extended family continues to live on the farms where cotton is still grown, although not to the extent that it once was. They continue to live in housing provided by the white ranchers they work for.

It was in these cotton field places that I spent my childhood. An anthropologist distinguished us as true rural Indians, since we did not live on the reservation nor were we urban; we were rural. However, even though we did live in this rural setting, our community organization replicated the traditional O'odham village community. We lived in neighborhood groups of relations. We all knew our relations, grew up playing together and burying our dead together. The home language was O'odham and it was very common for children to go to school speaking only O'odham; this was certainly the case for me and all my siblings. Briefly, regarding school, I believe it would be accurate to say the many "rural" O'odham children never experienced the devastation of attending boarding schools. Since we lived in these farming communities, there were small public schools in easy access. All of my siblings and I attended the local public school. And so even though we went to school only speaking O'odham, the trauma of being forced to learn English was not as great. The comfort level was built around the fact that there were so many of us in one small school that were related to one another, and we literally helped each other make the transition across languages. Now, as an adult, I have been the subject of some graduate students' studies involving bilingual adults. I am an anomaly, sometimes, since I did not have a traumatic language learning event in my childhood. I attribute this to the public schools I attended. It was simple then. English was for school and O'odham was for home, although on many occasions, especially social ones, O'odham was the language at school, again simply because of our sheer number at this particular school.

Finally, getting back to ritual and ceremony, even in the unlikely setting of cotton farms the traditional beliefs were held on to steadfastly. Many traditional practices were carried out in these communities, many of them small, private rituals involving only immediate family. For larger, important ones, ones carried out during special seasons, the families packed up and went home to Sonora, Mexico, back to the traditional villages, where the ceremonies were carried out uninterrupted by the demands of the manual labor of the farms and ranches. These trips to my maternal grandmother's village in Mexico are all a part of my childhood memory. The ceremonies and rituals, though, are a part of my parents' and older siblings' memories, and they have described them to me. Later, as an adult, I attended some of the ceremonies. The ceremonies, of course, have changed a little, they tell me, emphasizing what it used to be like when the previous generation was still alive. It is the memory of these people that influences me at so many junctures. I try to capture it in some of my work.

PULLING DOWN THE CLOUDS

Ñ-ku'ibadkaj 'ant 'an ols g cewagĭ
With my harvesting stick I will hook the clouds.
'Ant o i-wann'io k 'i-huḍiñ g cewagĭ.
With my harvesting stick I will pull down the clouds.
Ñ-ku 'ibaḍkaj 'ant o i-siho g cewagĭ.
With my harvesting stick I will stir the clouds.
With dreams of distant noise disturbing his sleep,
the smell of dirt, wet, for the first time in what seemed like months.
The change in the molecules is sudden,
they enter the nasal cavity.
He contemplates that smell.
What is that smell.
It is rain.
Rain somewhere out in the desert.
Comforted in this knowledge he turns over
and continues his sleep,
dreams of women with harvesting sticks
raised towards the sky.

(from *Ocean Power,* University of Arizona Press, 1995)

Part of this poem was inspired by an O'odham woman I met when I first came to attend the University of Arizona. She was a basketweaver and a singer in a traditional singing group that accompanied young O'odham traditional dancers. She, like many O'odham, lived for many years in Tucson, or as they say, "in town." And as a member of the O'odham in a town community, she involved herself with traditional activities of the tribe, but in an urban setting. She was well known for her traditional knowledge and her basketry and was in demand among the public schools in the city. She, along with the rest of the singing group and the dancers, performed regularly at social gatherings; gatherings organized either by the nearby reservation or by non-Indian groups. This was the first time I had seen traditional O'odham singing and dancing performed as an exhibition for audiences and where the performers were compensated for doing the exhibition. Even though it was an exhibition, my friend attempted to include as much of the traditional atmosphere that might accompany such a performance if done in the traditional context. She would do such things as yell words of encouragement to the dancers throughout their performance, telling them to dance faster, harder. I remember one time the dancers were performing outdoors on a basketball court and she commented on how their dances were wasted because there was supposed to be dancing on dirt. She said they needed the dirt under their feet so that when the dancers got going, the dust would rise into the air and mix with everything else and result in rain, the ultimate goal. In another piece I write about this, about making the dust rise and ultimately bring rain.

In this poem "Pulling Down the Clouds," my friend inspired the first part; the part describing the harvesting sticks for pulling down the clouds. She, like many O'odham women her age, still practiced the traditional harvesting of saguaro cactus fruit in the summer even though she lived in town. Every summer she went to her family camp in the desert and harvested. However, being an in-town resident, she told me of her dilemma associated with it. She and some of her friends found that they did not have a safe place to store their harvesting sticks the rest of the year. Harvesting sticks, for the uninitiated, are made from the ribs of dead saguaro cactus; oftentimes two or three are fastened together to make a very long stick. This is about the only stick that enables the harvester to reach the topmost fruit on the cactus. Typically, families just leave their sticks lying on the ground behind the house or in the tool area if they lived on the reservation, and no one bothers them. However, in the city, if one is renting an apartment or small house, there is usually not room even in a backyard for storing such a stick. My friend, though, came up with the solution. She tied her harvesting stick to the city electrical pole near her rented house. She thought it became camouflaged and no one bothered it at all for the entire year. She was proud of her solution, and that not even the city workers ever commented on her stick being tied there. I kept the telling of this incident for many years before I figured out how to tell it in a poem. And here in this piece it appears in repetitive lines in O'odham and in English.

Even though this piece, "Pulling Down the Clouds," is not a very long piece, another section of it is also a telling from another source. The part about the person being woken by lightning and the smell of rain is an incident my father told me about. Again it is a true incident and somewhat dreamlike. He said that he was not sure if he was awake

or just dreaming when all this occurred. My father is our family patriarch. In his mid-eighties, he lives with some of his adult children and
grandchildren, with the occasional adult male nephew. On one occasion when I was visiting him, he told me that when he was sleeping one
night he thought he saw flashes of light. At first he thought it was just
the rest of the family in the front room using the flash on a camera, but
he wasn't sure. He said he sort of lifted his head in half-sleep and
breathed in and that was when he smelled the wet dirt. It wasn't raining there, though, he knew that for sure, but it was raining somewhere
in the desert. All this lasted just a few seconds, and he said, "When I
comprehended all of what is going on outside, I just rolled over and
went back to sleep." He comments how something like the smell of
wet dirt woke him up. When he tells me this he questions whether he
was just dreaming or whether it was real. It was probably a little of
both.

These two incidents are small and for the most part insignificant;
they, however, affected me in a special way, a way that is difficult to explain. I held on to the telling of these two incidents for a few years before writing them in this piece.

In some of the first pieces I published, I write about the topic of
rain. Two of my pieces appear in the collection *Mat Hekid O Ju:/When
It Rains, Papago and Pima Poetry.* These two pieces are straightforward in
describing a facet of the O'odham (Papago), who wait for the rain. One
describes the activity around my family's household when it rains. At
the time this collection was published, I was also doing transcription of
O'odham and Pima songs, most of which were rain songs I found in
various collections at museums. I transcribed the song texts and then
eventually did interpretations and translation into English. This exercise was done for pedagogical purposes. Most of these short song texts
I used for my O'odham language classes at the university. I used them
as text for reading exercises because they were short and had poetic
language and were a departure from the cut-and-dry language dialogue texts.

Rain in the desert is a theme I continue in much of my writing. I
don't claim that I write about the land, the landscape of the desert, but
I know I am profoundly influenced by it. I like to think that I am more
influenced about the movements and the changes in the atmosphere of
the desert environment. Changes that occur most drastically when it

rains. I write about this topic in my introduction to the collection *Ocean Power: Poems from the Desert,* where I claim people living in the desert have an acute sense and appreciation for the changes rain causes. The people appreciate the benefits of rain, but also respect the uncontrollable power it has. And of course the O'odham have a great deal of oral tradition that speaks to the topic of rain. The oral tradition, whether it is in the form of song, oratory, speech, prayer, or story, can speak of the moisture and other minute instances of it in the most poetic way. There are O'odham and Pima songs of the moisture that is in the tiniest bead of dew on the wing of an insect, or emanating from the breath of a dove. Then there is moisture that takes grand shapes such as that of massive clouds, oceans, lightning, and powerful winds. And within the ceremonies that accompany the oral forms, rain is represented by the animals that serve as the effigies, including birds, ants, and frogs.

BLACK CLOUD

Black clouds lay off in the distance.
Like black buzzards, flying, far away.
Making noise, rumbling.
Black clouds,
drifting off in the distance.
Like black buzzards, flying, so far away.
Rumbling, thundering.
Suddenly they descend.

The preceding text is of a Pima cloud song that I transcribed and translated. The following in contrast, is a poem also about clouds.

CEWAGĬ

pi ṣa:muhim 'ab daha
'ab daha kc 'ab beihim g gewkdag
'ab beihim 'amjeḍ g s-ke:g hewel.
'I:da gewkdag mo na:nko ma:s.
'I:da gewkdag mo ḍ 'ep ge'e tatañ
'I:da tatañ mat 'ab 'amjeḍ o si 'i-hoi g jeweḍ.
'I:da tatañ mo we:s 'an i t-bijimdahim.

Summer clouds sit silently.
They sit, quietly gathering strength.
Gathering strength from the good wind.
This strength that becomes the thunder.
The thunder so loud it vibrates the earth.
The thunder that surrounds us.

(from *Ocean Power*, 1995)

After I had written this piece, I realized I essentially copied the format of the Pima song. Both pieces describe the evolution of an event, that of cloud formation and the final conclusion of rain. In the poem, though, I clearly include people in the event as opposed to the song. Donald Bahr, noted anthropologist, has commented to me that that was one of the distinguishing features of contemporary O'odham poetry and traditional songs. They almost never include direct references to people, with the use of pronouns or other grammatical markers, for instance, unlike the contemporary poems, where in so many instances the poems are of a personal nature and so do include references to people. So for me the events of rain in the desert almost always include the people.

Finally, one of the unique aspects of the topic of rain is the way the O'odham handle the language when they speak or sing of rain. I find the language richly poetic and imaginative. In regards to the oral tradition, the O'odham are people who I have described in other work as people who *oooh* and *aaah* about words and phrases, pay close attention to the creative manipulation of words by the speaker. O'odham people do have the most sincere appreciation for speakers who are thoughtful and creative with language. Many O'odham acknowledge in different ways the gift of a speaker. The speaker does not necessarily have to be a traditional orator. He or she may be doing something as routine as a Christian prayer, a eulogy, or opening remarks at some social or political function. The place and time of the speech does not matter, it is how the speaker performs that is important. And in many instances, the speech need not be serious; humor, and the creativity in performing it, is certainly as valid. Thus, today both traditional orators as well as individuals who simply speak well are held in high esteem; they are known by reputation. The same is true for singers and those who still dream the songs.

In my own way, I pay close attention to the speakers and their words, the singers and their songs. As a trained linguist, unlike other audiences of O'odham oral text, I have an additional perspective. I have learned, for instance, mostly from my graduate students, who measure and analyze O'odham song text with elaborate instruments and apply the most current theoretical framework, that O'odham songs have very complex metrical and rhythm systems. Singers must know these systems in order to make a good O'odham song. The singer has to be keenly aware of the length, stress, and syllable structure of O'odham words in order to make aesthetic-sounding songs. They are not only conscious of the word that is to be sung, but also of the syntax or structure of the sentence that is to be sung.

Song language, like spoken language, has its own grammatical structure. It is a grammatical structure that, of course, differs from the spoken form and so it is often the case that the meaning of O'odham songs is not easy to comprehend immediately. I personally find song text some of the most challenging to translate because of the difference in structure both at the word level and in the syntax. I have on many occasions listened to a song over and over again just to grasp the word that is being sung and then, oftentimes, the meaning comes much later or comes only when the whole content of the song becomes meaningful. I once thought that since I did not sing songs and was not close to anyone who sang, that was the reason I had so much difficulty in grasping the content of O'odham songs. I found later that even singers have the same problem with songs they were not familiar with; however, they were able to grasp words and meaning much more quickly than a nonsinger. So even though the linguistic dimension of my observation gives me some additional perspective, I like to believe that my sincere appreciation for the pure beauty of the words, the imagery, and the message the songs hold is still primary.

The following is an O'odham song where the theme is actually in the O'odham title I gave it, "Varied Colored Clouds." This is a sample of the manipulation of words using color terms that are not static, but constantly changing, in the same way that clouds behave. These varied-colored clouds are real and exist on different days, probably mostly likely in the summer. And only a singer could have captured it this way in a beautiful song.

NA:NKO MA:S CEWAGǏ

Ce:daghim 'o 'ab wu:ṣañhim
To:tahim 'o 'ab wu:ṣañhim
Cuckuhim 'o 'ab him
Wepeghim 'o 'abai him.

CLOUD SONG

Greenly they emerge.
In colors of blue they emerge.
Whitely they emerge.
In colors of black they are coming.
Reddening they are right here.

(from *Ocean Power,* 1995)

In this section I will address my third point about why I write. This deals with what I consider to be a more pragmatic reason: developing a literature in a Native language, which will then result in a desire for literacy in that language.

Briefly, O'odham, like other indigenous languages, is an oral language. Written O'odham is approximately twenty-five years old. Currently there are two competing writing systems. One system was developed jointly with an O'odham linguist and a non-O'odham linguist, the Alvarez/Hale system. The other was developed by linguists associated with the Summer Institute of Linguistics, an institute most widely known for its work in translating the New and Old Testaments into languages of the world. Although both writing systems are used for scholarly publications, in O'odham the tribe has endorsed the Alvarez/Hale system as the recognized system and stipulates in the tribal language policy that this system be used for teaching. Currently many O'odham who are literate are literate in both mostly due to the limited amount of material published in the two orthographies. Like many Native American languages, O'odham texts published in early collections were for scholarly purposes only and were done primarily for non-Indian people. The collections were by and large not user-friendly. One of my early objectives as an educator and linguist was to promote the use of written O'odham for speakers and students of the O'odham language.

This objective was brought to fruition in part within the past fifteen years, where I have been involved in co-coordinating and teaching in a summer program for teachers called the American Indian Language Development Institute, or AILDI. Here faculty come together each summer to offer courses on American Indian languages, linguistics, literature, and approaches for teaching with American Indian languages, in schools both on and off reservations. One of the primary reasons for creating the AILDI is the fact that nowhere at a university campus can speakers of Native American languages go to receive university-credited courses with content on their own language, whether it is in the area of linguistics, literature, or writing. And there is probably no college of education anywhere that directly attends to the needs of Native-language-speaking teachers who want to teach bilingually in their language. And so the AILDI was founded to try to meet some of these specific needs, needs that are most prevalent among Southwest languages.

As the AILDI became more established, other tribes from around the United States and Canada sent their teachers to the Southwest to attend AILDI. In the past fifteen years we have trained large numbers of Native American teachers in the field of Native language bilingual education, with skills in linguistic investigation on their own language, and course work on American Indian literature and creative writing in the Native language. In the early years of the AILDI we were concerned with meeting basic needs of Native-language communities and their schools. For many this was the development of practical writing systems. Since then the AILDI has assisted almost every language family in the Southwest in accomplishing this. We have also been instrumental in working with language families from as far away as Maine, Iowa, Oklahoma, and Canada.

Using the AILDI as a vehicle because of the type of participant it attracted, I began offering courses on creative writing in the Native language. For many participants who had been long entrenched in the rubric of American Indian educational policy and cannonical styles of bilingual education, their idea of Native-language literature for young readers was to translate standard children's stories from American culture. In the 1970s, when funding for bilingual programs was at its peak, almost every tribal language in the country had its translation of "The Three Little Pigs," "Little Red Riding Hood," "The Three Bears," and of course the popular song "Old McDonald Had a Farm."

For the educators who were doing these translations I would ask, "Why are you translating English text into your Native language when you have your own literature?" albeit at an oral level. Many of them said it was easier, others said that that is what they were instructed to do so as to be consistent with neighboring schools. As thinking about working with texts continued for these educators, they came to the realization that doing these text translations into the native language was actually a very difficult exercise. It was time-consuming, and oftentimes many concepts from the English version did not translate very well in the Native language. So with some reeducation these educators first began to work with transcribing their own community's stories. Many were tape-recorded so that the oral form was still available, but now there was the written form as well. The written form made the text more widely available to students and teachers. Writing made things convenient, accessible. In the classes at the AILDI, teachers were trained with skills to be their community's collector and transcriber and translator of their own stories. The teachers were also trained to pass on the skills to their students at various grades. Together they collected everything from personal histories, lullabies, songs, prayers, speeches, ethnobotanical descriptions, and recipes, among many other forms. These collections then started to become not only a part of the school's library, but the tribe's as well.

Finally, these same educators and new ones that continued to come to the AILDI began thinking about writing their own creative pieces. The style we chose was poetry. The form we chose as a model was Japanese haiku. The reason for this was largely in part influenced by a Japanese linguist and poet who works on American Indian languages and taught regularly in the AILDI. The poems then were short and succinct, although most writers did not meet the full criteria of haiku with syllable count. So the people wrote. They wrote mostly personal poetic pieces. Many wrote of children, grandparents, parents, dogs. And others wrote about their environment, the landscape, all in very beautiful, sensitive, and expressive ways. All the ones who participated in the first writing class in the Native language surprised themselves that this creative force was available to them. That a piece could be thought through in the language and then written down, and that there was no need to even consider the English language was a tremendous realization.

In the years the AILDI has been in operation we have been instrumental in publishing three books of creative works. The first was one that I edited, *Mat Hekid O Ju:/When It Rains: Papago and Pima Poetry* (University of Arizona Press). These are writings by Pima and O'odham (Papago) teachers who participated in one of our AILDI courses. Another is *Walk Strong,* a collection of Yuman language poems, edited by Lucille Watahomigie and Akira Yamamoto, published by Malki Press. The work in this collection included writing done in another AILDI course. And the Yuman anthology edited by Lucille Watahomigie and Leanne Hinton, *Wikame: Spirit Mountain* (University of Arizona Press), includes contemporary writing by Yuman language participants from the AILDI plus other Yuman-speaking community members. Other language groups, including Apache, Yaqui, and Navajo, that participated in AILDI writing courses have published some of their creative work in government-funded printing projects. These publications are typically printed in small quantities and are available only from the schools.

Through the AILDI, I, along with other faculty, have been successful in convincing Native speakers of some American Indian languages that it is possible to express creativity through writing just like one would in the English language. And finally, that it was possible to publish writing in the Native language so that their own versions and translations of their tribal stories and their poetry and songs could be available to large numbers of readers, including non-Indian ones.

This type of writing, writing in the Native language, especially contemporary writing, is only a small body of literature. But even with this small body it has some lasting effects. Young readers of O'odham, for instance, still use the collection *When It Rains* as a reading book for regular literature classes as well as for O'odham language classes. Teachers who contributed to this collection almost ten years ago still encourage Native language writing among their students and many of the teachers still write on occasion. This writing among the O'odham teachers has continued to the extent that we now have enough of a body of O'odham writing to compile a second volume of O'odham and Pima writing.

O'odham-language literacy is relatively low among the population. The ones who are literate are those who simply want to be. They have a desire. They are the ones who I look to as contributors to this slow-growing body of new texts. They are a small number and when they do write, they are held in high regard very much in the same way that good speakers are. What better reward?

In conclusion, I remain here a humble worker at my university. Here I am situated nicely, with my rural home only a short distance from Tucson, and the reservation of my tribe also a short drive from the city. And finally, with my family's traditional homelands in Sonora also a few hours from here. These places all surround me and of course influence me in what I do as a professional person here at this campus.

I find myself an interdisciplinary faculty member. I teach for the linguistics department, the American Indian Studies Program, and I'm devoted to the Native American language teachers affiliated with our College of Education. And like a well-trained educator, I continue to practice what I teach. I write my poetry when I can, which I find is usually in the summer. I continue to promote the beauty of language whether the language is spoken or written, or both.

Grateful acknowledgment is made to the following for permission to reprint previously published material:

THE BELOIT POETRY JOURNAL: "Ritual" by John E. Smelcer, published in *The Beloit Poetry Journal*, summer 1994, vol. 44, no. 4. Reprinted by permission.

CALIFORNIA POETS IN THE SCHOOLS: "Traveling to Town" by Duane BigEagle from *This Poem Knows You*, published by California Poets in the Schools, Statewide Anthology, 1984. Reprinted by permission.

THE CAROLINA QUARTERLY: "Red at Bacum" by Anita Endrezze, originally published in *The Carolina Quarterly*, vol. 50, fall 1997. Reprinted by permission.

THE COMSTOCK REVIEW: "Father" by John E. Smelcer, originally appeared in *Poetpourri*, published by *The Comstock Review* in 1995. Reprinted by permission.

DUANE BIGEAGLE: "Washashe Airlines" by Duane BigEagle, from *Returning the Gift*, edited by Joseph Burchac. Copyright © 1994 by the Arizona Board of Regents. Published by the University of Arizona Press. Reprinted by permission of the author.

THE EIGHTH MOUNTAIN PRESS: "Weaving" and "Chinle Summer" from *Seven Hands, Seven Hearts: Prose and Poetry* by Elizabeth Woody. Copyright © 1994 by Elizabeth Woody. Reprinted by permission of the author and the Eighth Mountain Press, Portland, Oregon.

FIREBRAND BOOKS: Excerpts from *Simple Songs* by Vickie Sears. Copyright © 1990 by Vickie Sears. Reprinted by permission of Firebrand Books, Ithaca, New York.

GRAYWOLF PRESS AND NORA DAUENHAUER: "My Aunt Jennie's Bed" by Nora Dauenhauer from *From the Island's Edge: A Sitka Reader* edited by Carloyn Servid. Reprinted by permission of Graywolf Press and the author.

GREENFIELD REVIEW PRESS: "My Grandfather was a Quantum Physicist" and "Birthplace" by Duane BigEagle, originally published in *Songs from this Earth on Turtle's Back*, Greenfield Review Press, 1983. Reprinted by permission.

INSIDE OSAGE: "Inside Osage" by Duane BigEagle, originally published in *Inside Osage* magazine, 1995. Reprinted by permission.

JOURNAL OF ALASKA NATIVE ARTS: "Potlatch" by John E. Smelcer, published in the spring 1994 issue of the *Journal of Alaska Native Arts*. Reprinted by permission.

THE KENYON REVIEW: "La Llorona" by Anita Endrezze originally published in *The Kenyon Review—New Series*, fall 1991, vol. XIII, no. 4. Reprinted by permission.

MAKING WAVES: "My Little Sister's Heart in My Hands" by Anita Endrezze, originally published in *Lost Rivers* (Guildford, England: Making Waves, 1997) and "Written in a Spring Storm" by Anita Endrezze, originally published in *The Humming of Stars and Bees* (Guildford, England: Making Waves, 1998). Reprinted by permission.

ONTHEBUS: "Two Heart Clan" by Duane BigEagle, originally published in *Onthebus*, vol. 1, no. 3, fall 1989. Reprinted by permission.

PLOUGHSHARES AND ANITA ENDREZZE: "Ponies Gathering in the Dark" by Anita Endrezze, originally published in *Ploughshares*, vol. 20, no. 1, spring 1994. Used by permission of the author and *Ploughshares*.

ROLLING STOCK: "Grandmother Eliza" by Nora Dauenhauer, published in *Rolling Stock*, no. 19/20, 1991. Reprinted by permission.

About the Editors

Arnold Krupat was educated at New York University and Columbia University. Among his books are *The Turn to the Native: Essays in Criticism and Culture* (1996), *Ethnocriticism: Ethnography, History, Literature* (1992), and *Woodsmen, or Thoreau and the Indians* (1994), a novel. He has edited *New Voices in Native American Literary Criticism* (1993) and *Native American Autobiography: An Anthology* (1994), and, with W. S. Penn, *Beyond Rites: An Anthology of Native American Drama* (forthcoming). He teaches literature at Sarah Lawrence College.

Brian Swann was educated at Queen's College, Cambridge, and Princeton University. He has published a number of collections of poetry and fiction, books for children, and translated volumes of poetry. He is also the author of *Song of the Sky: Versions of Native American Song-poems* (1993), *Wearing the Morning Star: Native American Song-poems* (1996), and has edited *Smoothing the Ground: Essays on Native American Oral Literature* (1993), *Essays on the Translation of Native American Literatures* (1991), *Coming to Light: Contemporary Translations of the Native Literatures of North America* (1995), and *Native American Songs and Poems* (1996). He teaches at the Cooper Union.

Krupat and Swann have co-edited *Recovering the Word: Essays on Native American Literature* (1987), and *I Tell You Now: Autobiographical Essays by Native American Writers* (1987).

A NOTE ON THE TYPE

The principal text of this Modern Library edition
was set in a digitized version of Janson,
a typeface that dates from about 1690 and was cut by Nicholas Kis,
a Hungarian working in Amsterdam. The original matrices have
survived and are held by the Stempel foundry in Germany.
Hermann Zapf redesigned some of the weights and sizes for Stempel,
basing his revisions on the original design.